LIBRARY OF NEW TESTAMENT STUDIES

437

Formerly the Journal for the Study of the New Testament Supplement series

Editor
Mark Goodacre

THE ABOMINATION OF DESOLATION IN MATTHEW 24.15

MICHAEL P. THEOPHILOS

t&t clark

Published by T&T Clark International
A Continuum Imprint
The Tower Building, 11 York Road, London SE1 7NX
80 Maiden Lane, Suite 704, New York, NY 10038

www.continuumbooks.com

© Michael P. Theophilos, 2012

Michael P. Theophilos has asserted his right under the Copyright, Designs and Patents
Act, 1988, to be identified as the Author of this work.

British Library Cataloguing-in-Publication Data
A catalogue record for this book is available from the British Library

ISBN: HB: 978-0-567-55468-0

Typeset by Free Range Book Design & Production
Printed and bound in Great Britain

CONTENTS

ACKNOWLEDGEMENTS

The completion of this volume has been a fascinating and enjoyable journey, which has spanned at least four continents. I owe a debt of gratitude to many more than I can mention in this brief note. I would particularly like to thank the guiding hand of my doctoral supervisor Professor Christopher Tuckett (Pembroke College, University of Oxford), both for his encouragement and his insightful comments on the research underlying this volume. Professor Christopher Rowland (Queen's College, University of Oxford) also deserves special thanks for the generous time he offered for discussion of several of the main arguments. My time at the Hebrew University, Jerusalem, helped shape the formulation of my research, especially those conclusions reached in chapter 4. To this end I wish to thank the Friends of the Hebrew University in London for their generous financial support, the Ecole Biblique for the use of the world-class library facilities, and the Kenyon Institute (Council for British Research in the Levant) for their kind (and practical) hospitality while residing in Jerusalem.

A personal note of gratitude goes to my family who showed continued support and confidence in both me and the project. *Tantus labor non sit cassus.*

Michael P. Theophilos

Introduction

Assumptions and Dating

1. Assumptions

For the purposes of clarity and argumentation there are certain assumptions that have been adopted in the writing of this volume. First, without necessarily implying the author's identity, for ease of reference and the sake of convenience the author of Βίβλος γενέσεως' Ἰησοῦ Χριστου ... is referred to as 'Matthew'.

Second, where the hypothetical 'Q' tradition is referred to, this does not necessarily assume Christian Hermann Weisse's 1838 two-source hypothesis (or related theories), but rather that the most plausible (or rather the least problematic) solution to the synoptic problem is Markan priority, with Matthew and Luke drawing on other written and oral traditions. As C. Tuckett has noted, this 'theory provides a reasonably comprehensive account of the development of the tradition on the basis of its main tenets of the dependence of Matthew and Luke on the Markan and Q traditions'.[1]

Third, debates concerning the use of rabbinic literature for historical research continue to be explored. On one side of the spectrum are those that uncritically employ every parallel from H. Strack and P. Billerbeck's encyclopedic *Kommentar zum Neuen Testament*,[2] in an attempt to reconstruct pre-70-AD Judaism. At the other extreme, primarily because of the problems of dating (but also partially in reaction to its former overuse), others have altogether abandoned their use of rabbinic material for New Testament research.[3] David Aus laments this latter situation by stating, 'Many NT scholars today employ the genuine problem of dating rabbinic

---

1   C. M. Tuckett, 'Luke', in *The Synoptic Gospels*, ed. J. Riches et al. (Sheffield: Sheffield Academic Press, 2001), pp. 252–342 (263).

2   H. L. Strack, and P. Billerbeck, *Kommentar zum New Testament* (6 vols; München: Beck, 1926–28).

3   See the following for the dangers of uncritical application of rabbinic texts for New Testament exegesis: J. Neusner, 'The Use of the Later Rabbinic Evidence for the Study of First-Century Pharisaism', in *Approaches to Ancient Judaism: Theory and Practice*, ed. W. S. Green (Brown Judaic Studies 1; Missoula: Scholars Press, 1978), pp. 215–25; S. Sandmel, 'Parallelomania', *JBL* 81 (1962), pp. 1–13; R. Bauckham, 'The Relevance of Extracanonical Jewish Texts to New Testament Study', in *Hearing the New Testament*, ed. J. B. Green (Grand Rapids: Eerdmans, 1995), pp. 90–108.

sources … as a cheap pretext for not even considering them … Yet a number of Jewish traditions from before 70 CE have been retained in the (patently later) rabbinic writings. Each individual tradition must be analyzed and evaluated on its own merits.'[4] In this manner, our current study will attempt to traverse a middle path which, while conscious of the problems of dating, will not shy away from drawing on a parallel for which there is sufficient evidence of a pre-70-AD date. This optimism partly stems from the prime importance of faithful transmission expressed in the Jewish tradition (*m.Erub.* 6.1-3a).[5] Additionally, there has recently arisen a loosely defined methodological consensus that affirms that at least some rabbinic material can be salvaged for pre-70 Judaism.[6] This study will accept the cautioning of the post-Neusnerian literature but also be of sympathetic disposition towards such scholars as Instone-Brewer who have attempted to date the rabbinic material more cautiously. This can be summarized as follows: The pre-70 origin of rabbinic material is considered more likely when (1) sayings are attributed to a pre-70-AD named individual;[7] (2) the anonymous tradition is assumed in a later tradition (i.e. logical precedence); (3) the use of parallel sources (Josephus, Philo, Qumran) indicate a similar ruling; (4) references to the temple are practically oriented rather than theoretically inclined; and (5) there is no unusually variegated structure within a tractate, in that later redactional additions are often appended to the ends of paragraphs rather than being integrated into the sense of each unit.[8] This will hopefully prevent what Samuel Sandmel's famous 1962 article called 'Parallelomania'.[9]

As the Isaiah Targum will be referred to on several occasions, the following should be noted. The Babylonian Talmud (*b.Meg* 3a) attributes the Targum to Jonathan ben Uzziel, a student of Hillel, and although it is conceded that the final form of the Targum is admittedly later, J. Draper notes that 'there is much to suggest that the original framework … derives from the Tannaitic period'.[10] Similarly, B. Chilton concludes that 'individual

---

4   R. D. Aus, *Caught in the Act, Walking on Sea and the Release of Barabbas Revisited* (Atlanta: Scholars Press, 2007), p. x.

5   D. Instone-Brewer, *Traditions of the Rabbis from the Era of the New Testament: Volume 1: Prayer and Agriculture* (Grand Rapids: Eerdmans, 2004), p. 28.

6   Z. W. Falk, *Introduction to Jewish Law of the Second Commonwealth* (vol. 1; Leiden: Brill, 1972), p. 3; J. Nuesner, *A History of the Mishnaic Law of Purities* (Leiden: Brill, 1977), p. 23; E. P. Sanders, *Judaism: Practice and Belief, 63 BCE–66 CE* (London: SCM Press, 1992), p. 6; H. L. Strack and G. Stemberger, *Introduction to Talmud and Midrash*, trans. Markus Bockmuehl (Minneapolis: Fortress, 1996), pp. 57, 133.

7   Instone-Brewer, *Traditions*, p. 31 notes that 'the attribution of a saying to a named rabbi cannot be assumed to be correct, but extensive historico-critical work has suggested that such attributions are generally correct'.

8   For an example of an obvious later addition discernible from the structure of the unit see *m.Ter* 1.1–3.2, cited in Instone-Brewer, *Traditions*, p. 38.

9   Sandmel, 'Parallelomania', pp. 1–13.

10   J. Draper, 'The Development of "the Sign of the Son of Man" in the Jesus Tradition', *NTS* 39 (1993), pp. 1–21 (5).

passages, in their coherence with Rabbinica, intertestamental literature and the New Testament, and in their allusions to historical circumstances, may be datable to a considerable extent'.[11]

Fourth, we are interested in the Matthean text in its extant form. As B. Childs has mentioned in a different context, 'the determination of its present function is exegetically far more important than recovering an earlier oral stage'.[12] As such, reference will be made to Mark for redaction-critical concerns; however, detailed discussion of source criticism and of redactional layers will not overtly be pursued. Our concern is what the text *in its current form* has to say about the 'Abomination of Desolation'. This general approach has traditionally been understood as 'composition criticism', a term believed to be derived from E. Haenchen.[13] Bauer and Powell describe 'compositional criticism' as emphasis on 'the total editorial achievement of the evangelist ... rather than the minute "process" according to which the evangelist brought about changes, omissions, and additions to his *Vorlage*'.[14] Similarly, B. Charette states that:

> Composition criticism is the product of a recent trend in redaction criticism which, admitting the limitations of earlier forms of the method, recognizes that the concerns of an Evangelist are to be found not merely in the study of the changes he has made to his sources but also in the study of the completed work he has produced.[15]

In this regard R. E. Brown states that 'we cannot afford to lose sight of Matthew's highly effective narrative because of attention to comparative details'.[16] This approach then is closely aligned with 'narrative criticism', and despite the conclusions of Moore,[17] are effectively interchangeable when applied to our methodology.

---

11   B. Chilton, *The Isaiah Targum* (New York: Glazier, 1987), p. xxv.

12   B. Childs, *Isaiah* (London: Westminster John Knox Press, 2001), p. 16.

13   E. Haenchen, *Der Weg Jesu: Eine Erklärung des Markus-Evangeliums und der kanonischen Parallelen* (Berlin: Walter de Gruyter, 1968). See discussion in S. D. Moore, *Literary Criticism and the Gospels* (New Haven: Yale, 1989), p. 4; B. Charette, *The Theme of Recompense in Matthew's Gospel* (Sheffield: Sheffield Academic Press, 1992), pp. 16–17.

14   D. R. Bauer and M. A. Powell, *Treasures New and Old* (Atlanta: Scholars Press, 1996), p. 3.

15   Charette, *Recompense*, pp. 18–19.

16   R. E. Brown, *An Introduction to the New Testament* (New York: Doubleday, 1997), p. 172.

17   Moore, *Criticism*, p. 4 argues that compositional criticism is 'a method aligned with *narrative criticism* but in the last analysis clearly distinguishable from it' (italics his). He also argues that 'Whereas compositional criticism extends the tradition of redaction criticism by reason in an overriding interest in the evangelists' theologies, narrative criticism represents a break with the tradition in the sense that the focus is no longer primarily on theology' (p. 7). It is not evident that such a nuance is adhered to by those who claim to be operating within either realm.

Fifth, while citations of the Hebrew Bible in the New Testament are fairly apparent,[18] it is notoriously difficult to define what is and what is not an allusion. Furthermore, in the assessment of a proposed allusion, the method is not mechanical, but rather requires the recipient's appropriate conceptual understanding of the intended aesthetic parallel. Often the modern reader, attempting to straddle the hermeneutical chasm, errs either in identifying allusions where they are not or missing allusions where they are. Amid this maze, there are several features which, when taken together, help to identify a parallel as intended.[19] They include (1) key words or phrases (including order, metre and patterns); (2) similar circumstances; (3) similar narrative structure; (4) that the proposed source is congruent with the theological trajectory of the document; (5) that the author uses a similar or related allusion elsewhere in their work; (6) that there is a similar application of the Old Testament source in other documents outside the one considered; and (7) that there is appropriate rationale for the allusion or typological association. This process will be referred to as 'intertextuality'.[20]

Sixth, it is important to note that any proposed use of the Old Testament in Matthew is cumulative, not resting on the strength of any one argument but rather on the entire narrative's literary impression. Thus we proceed with caution, cognizant that texts have the potential to be 'deliberatively interactive and full of allusive reciprocal discourse'.[21]

18   D. S. New, *Old Testament Quotations in the Synoptic Gospels, and the Two Documentary Hypothesis* (Atlanta: Scholars Press, 1993), p. 14 suggests that 'a quotation will normally have an introductory formula … Should this formula be lacking, evidence that it is the intention of the author will suffice. This evidence could take the form of several words identical to an OT text.' H. B. Swete, *The Gospel according to St. Mark* (London: Macmillan, 1902), p. 24 concludes, 'by passages formally cited we understand 1) an introductory formula or 2) those which, not announced by a formula, appear from the context to be intended as quotations or agree verbatim with some context in the O.T'.

19   For several of the following points I am indebted to D. C. Allison, *The New Moses: A Matthean Typology* (Minneapolis: Fortress Press, 1993), p. 16; R. E. Watts, *Isaiah's New Exodus in Mark* (Grand Rapids: Baker, 1997), p. 8; R. Hays, *Echoes of Scripture in the Letters of Paul* (New Haven: Yale University Press, 1989), pp. 1–33; S. E. Porter, 'The Use of the Old Testament in the New Testament: A Brief Comment on Method and Terminology', in *Early Christian Interpretation of the Scriptures of Israel: Investigations and Proposals*, ed. C. A. Evans and J. A. Sanders (Sheffield: Sheffield Academic Press, 1997), pp. 79–96.

20   We here refer not to Saussurean poststructuralist literary theories (J. Kristeva, *Desire in Language: A Semiotic Approach to Literature and Art* [New York: Columbia University Press, 1980], p. 69 'every text is from the outset under the jurisdiction of other discourses which impose a universe on it'; cf. J. Culler, *The Pursuit of Signs: Semiotics, Literature, Deconstruction* [London: Routledge, 1981], p. 105; R. Coward and J. Ellis, *Language and Materialism: Developments in Semiology and the Theory of the Subject* [London: Routledge, 1977], p. 52) but rather to the general echo or recollection of a previous event, story or vocabulary shared between two texts.

21   Allison, *Typology*, p. 16.

2. Issues in Dating

We now turn our attention to the most plausible date of composition for the Gospel of Matthew. In an attempt to answer this question we will, by necessity, mention patristic testimony, early citations and allusions, and internal evidence.

Scholarly debate regarding Matthew's Gospel has placed the date of its authorship as early as 40 AD and as late as 110 AD.[22] The majority opinion is that the Gospel was composed in the last quarter of the first century AD.[23] There are a number of interrelated questions which influence any dating hypothesis, including, but not limited to (1) patristic testimony and early citations or allusions, (2) the solution to the synoptic problem, and (3) internal evidence. We will proceed by investigating each of these in turn.

Although controversial, the earliest apparent reference to Matthew's Gospel has generally been taken as Papias' words recorded by Eusebius in *H.E.* 3.39: Ματθαῖος μὲν οὖν Ἑβραΐδι διαλέκτῳ τὰ λόγια συνετάχατο, ἡρμήνευσεν δ' αὐτὰ ὡς ἦν δυνατὸς ἕκαστος ('Now Matthew made an ordered arrangement of the oracles in the Hebrew dialect and each one translated as he was able'). R. H. Gundry has argued that if indeed Papias is to be understood as referring to our Matthew, then this places composition not later than some time at the end of the first century, as Papias was well known in the time of Ignatius (died c. 107 AD) and Polycarp (c. 70–155).[24] Furthermore, Davies and Allison note that Eusebius records the words of Papias '*before* turning to the persecution in Trajan's day (98–117)'.[25] Thus several commentators conclude that the *terminus ad quem* for Matthew would be c. 100 AD.[26] Davies and Allison are typical when they state 'Polycarp (d. c. 156 AD), the Epistle of Barnabas (c. 135 AD) and Justin

---

22 H. Grotius argued for 40–50 AD, M. Meinertz and J. A. T. Robinson argued for 50–60 AD; B. Reicke argued for 50–64 AD; G. Maier argued for c. 60 AD; R. H. Gundry argued pre-63 AD; F. Godet and W. Michaelis argued for 60–70 AD; W. C. Allen argued 65–75 AD; C. F. D. Moule and E. E. Ellis argued for pre-70 AD; K. Stendahl, A. Wikenhauser, and P. S. Minear argued for 70–110 AD; A. von Harnack argued for 70–75 AD; J. Weiss, W. Sanday, and W. R. Farmer argued for 70–80 AD; A. Plummer argued before 75 AD; D. Hare argued c. 80 AD; E. Renan, T. Zahn, B. W. Bacon et al. argued for 80–100 AD; P. Bonnard, W. Grundmann, J. P. Meier, and U. Luz argued for 80–90 AD; B. H. Streeter argued for c. 85 AD; J. C. Fenton argued for 85–105 AD; E. Lohse argued for c. 90 AD; E. von Dobschütz and G. D. Kilpatrick argued for 90–100 AD; G. Strecker argued for 90–95 AD; M. S. Enslin and F. W. Beare argued for c. 100 AD; and F. C. Baur, O. Pfleiderer, H. J. Holtzmann et al. argued for a date after 100 AD. Cited in W. D. Davies and D. C. Allison, *The Gospel according to Matthew* (vol. 1; Edinburgh: T&T Clark, 1988), pp. 127–28.

23 However, as will be discussed further below, there are a growing number of modern scholars who argue for a pre-70-AD dating.

24 R. H. Gundry, *Matthew: A Commentary on His Literary and Theological Art* (Grand Rapids: Eerdmans, 1982), pp. 610–11.

25 Davies and Allison, *Matthew 1*, p. 128.

26 *Pace* U. H. Körtner, *Papias von Hierapolis* (Göttingen, 1983).

Martyr (100–65 AD) all knew and used Matthew, which must accordingly have been in circulation by the year 100.'[27] Further support is found in the letters of Ignatius of which Streeter states 'even in his [Ignatius'] seven short letters there are ... fifteen passages which look like reminiscences of Matthew';[28] of these sayings, two are 'unanimously attributed to the editor of Matthew rather than to his sources'. The first of these are the parallel from Mt. 3.15 in Ig. *Smyrn* i.1, 'Being baptised by John that all righteousness might be fulfilled in him'. The second, 'bear all men as the Lord does thee ... bear the sickness of all' (Polyc. i.2-3 cf. Mt. 8.17). These examples show that Ignatius was familiar with not only general Gospel traditions, but specifically with material which Matthew redacted. These examples have typically been taken as providing reasonable evidence that the *terminus ad quem* of Matthew's Gospel is c. 100 AD.

The *terminus a quo* of Matthew's Gospel is fixed by the latest dateable event recorded in the writing, i.e. Jesus' death in 30 or 33 AD. Beyond this there is little agreement on the way in which the internal evidence leans in regard to date. For the purposes of our investigation, however, we have assumed the inherent plausibility of the two-source hypothesis regarding the Synoptic Problem: that is, Markan priority, with Matthew and Luke drawing on other written and oral traditions. The predominant scholarly opinion regarding the date of Mark has typically been understood as mid to late 60s or very shortly after the fall of Jerusalem.[29] If then Matthew were dependent on Mark, this clearly places Matthew chronologically after Mark.[30] Thus, whereas external evidence suggested a date for Matthew not later than 100 AD, current research on the Synoptic Problem would suggest a date not earlier than 70 AD, and although this is not definitive, we are left with a period of 70–100 AD as a possible date of composition. We now turn to internal evidence to see if it might shed further light on the dating of Matthew.

There are three lines of internal evidence that have bearing on our discussion. First, the redactional insertion of Mt. 22.7, second the seemingly developed theology of 28.16-20 and third, possible elements of Jewish background (in particular the use of *rabbi* and the *birkat ha-minim*). First, Mt. 22.1-10 narrates the parable of the wedding banquet, wherein it is noted (22.7) that 'The king was enraged. He sent his troops, destroyed

27   W. D. Davies and D. C. Allison, *Matthew: A Shorter Commentary* (London: T&T Clark International, 2004), p. xii.

28   B. H. Streeter, *The Four Gospels* (London: Macmillan, 1925), p. 505.

29   W. G. Kümmel, *Promise and Fulfillment* (London: SCM Press, 1957), p. 98; R. Pesch, *Das Markusevangelium* (2 vols; Freiburg im Breisgau: Herder, 1976), p. 14; M. Hengel, *Studies in the Gospel of Mark* (London: SCM Press, 1985), p. 30.

30   It is, however, open to question how close to 70 AD Mark was actually composed (either before or after), and how long one should reasonably allow for Mark's Gospel to come into circulation and availability to Matthew. These questions are inherently difficult to resolve.

those murderers, and burned their city.' Most commentators have without further thought ascribed this redactional insertion as an *ex eventu* reference to the burning of Jerusalem by Titus in 70 AD.[31] Some commentators have felt uncomfortable about the possible referent of ὁ βασιλεὺς as Caesar, an identification which Davies and Allison suggest makes 'nonsense of the rest of the parable'.[32] It might be the case that the burning of a city fell within the general domain of literary *typos* when describing the condemnation of a city under God's wrath (Isa. 5.24-25). Nonetheless, one could argue that despite the possibility of this theme functioning as a literary *typos*, what would draw Matthew to such a text in the first place? Could one not argue that it was indeed the destruction of Jerusalem? It seems apparent that although 22.7 does not demand a post-70-AD date, it may lean in that direction.

Second, commentators have frequently noted elements in Matthew's Gospel which seem to indicate a developed sense of theological matters: in particular, ecclesiology in Matthew; Christology of the birth narrative; and antipathy towards Judaism. Commentators suggest that a dating toward the end of the first century is to be preferred, which would provide the appropriate time frame for such ideas to develop. However, as Davies and Allison have noted, 'such arguments are much less compelling than widely assumed'.[33] The developed sense of ecclesiology could perhaps be accounted for through Matthew's hypothetical community audience, and hence the author would be more inclined to include material related to these concerns.[34] Furthermore, one could argue that the high Christology in the Matthean birth narrative (cf. προσκυνήσω in Mt. 2.2, 8, 11), is no more advanced than that which can be reconstructed from the authentic Pauline literature (Phil. 2.6-11). Matthew's polemic against Jewish leaders could be attributed to the difficulties believers in Jesus suffered at the hands of non-Christian Jews before 70 AD (Acts 4.1-4; 8.1-3; 9.1-2, 13-14, 21; 22.4-5, 19-20). One element however, is particularly outstanding, the Trinitarian formulae in 28.19, 'Go therefore and make disciples of all nations, baptizing them in the name of the Father and of the Son and of the Holy Spirit.' Davies and Allison state that this 'involves a step towards later Trinitarian thought not taken in any other NT writing',[35] and hence are 'disinclined to place the document ... too many years before the beginning of the second century AD'.[36] This conclusion however, should be tempered slightly in view of other

---

31 U. Luz, *Matthew 1–7: A Commentary*, trans. W. C. Linss (Edinburgh: T&T Clark, 1989), p. 58.

32 Davies and Allison, *Matthew 1*, p. 131.

33 Davies and Allison, *Matthew 1*, p. 132.

34 That is, if it is accurate to speak of a Matthean community which is being addressed.

35 Davies and Allison, *Matthew 1*, p. 133.

36 Davies and Allison, *Matthew 1*, p. 133. See also the detailed analysis of J. Schaberg, *The Father, the Son and the Holy Spirit* (Chico: Scholars, 1982); L. Abramowski, 'Die Entstehung der dreigliedrigen Taufformel – ein Versuch', *ZTK* 81 (1984), pp. 417–46.

Matthean material that potentially does set the trajectory for early Trinitarian development. At this point in the narrative Jesus has already spoken (1) of God as Father (Mt. 11.27; 24.26); (2) of himself as the Son (11.27; 24.36; and 16.27); and (3) blasphemy against God's work in himself as blasphemy against the Holy Spirit (Mt. 12.22-28). In light of this Mounce states 'That Jesus should gather together into summary form his own references ... in his final charge to his disciples seems quite natural.'[37] In view of this and other New Testament material,[38] it seems difficult to argue purely on the basis of Mt. 28.19 that the Trinitarian formula requires a date towards the end of the first century when, admittedly non-exact, but nonetheless comparable language is used in earlier New Testament documents.

The third stream of evidence typically brought into discussions regarding the date of Matthew is that of late-first-century Jewish background, namely (1) the use of *rabbi* and (2) the *birkat ha-minim*. The complicating factor in these discussions, of course, is whether the hypothetical 'Council of Jamnia (Jabneh)' ever actually occurred. The theory was first proposed by Heinrich Graetz in 1871,[39] and supported by F. Buhl, H. E. Ryle, Robert Pfeiffer, O. Eissfeldt, and others. They all affirmed the basic premise (based on *m.Yad.* 3.5) that the Hebrew Scriptural canon was closed 'by the specific religious authority of 72 elders when R. Eleazar ben Azariah became head of the Academy at Yavneh about A.D. 90'.[40] This prevailing scholarly consensus was challenged at various levels by J. P. Lewis and S. Z. Leiman on the basis of the absence of significant support in ancient Jewish, Christian, or classical texts.[41] Perhaps then, all that can be assumed, is that 'Jamnia' refers to the general period of the later first century somewhere in the vicinity of 85–90 AD during which Jewish developments were significant. Nonetheless, it is typical of commentators to suggest that up until 70 AD the term *rabbi* functioned as a mark of courtesy or respect, much as 'Sir' might function in the modern world. However, after the period of Jamnia, it became a 'title for ordained scholars authorized to teach'.[42] Goldin summarizes: '[the title Rabbi] ... was apparently part of a large, new program of Talmud Torah. Every one must study Torah, and henceforth the man of authority is the rabbi, the sage who goes through the discipline of a student of the sages and becomes a master at Torah.'[43] The Jerusalem Talmud, *Sanhedrin* i.2, reads 'At first each one would appoint (ordained) his own students, as Rabban

---

37   R. H. Mounce, *Matthew* (San Francisco: Harper and Row, 1985), p. 277.

38   1 Cor. 12.4-6; 2 Cor. 13.13; Tit. 3.4-6; 1 Pet. 1.2; Jude 20–21.

39   H. Graetz, *Kohelet oder des Somonische Prediger* (Leipzig, 1871), pp. 155–56.

40   J. P. Lewis, 'Jamnia (Jabneh), Council of', in *Anchor Bible Dictionary*, ed. D. N. Freedman (vol. 3; New York: Doubleday, 1992), pp. 634–37 (634).

41   J. P. Lewis, 'What Do We Mean by Jabneh?', *JBR* 32 (1964), pp. 125–32; S. Z. Leiman, *The Canonization of the Hebrew Scriptures* (Hamden: Archon Books, 1976).

42   Davies and Allison, *Matthew 1*, p. 135.

43   J. Goldin, 'The Three Pillars of Simeon the Righteous', *PAAJR* 27 (1957), pp. 43–58 (55).

Johannan ben Zakkai ordained Rabbi Eliezer, Rabbi Joshua, and Rabbi Joshua appointed Rabbi Akiba, and Rabbi Akiba, Rabbis Meir and Simeon.' As such, during Jamnia, the sages were 'legitimised as guarantors of the tradition [and] given an official status with a title'.[44] In light of this, several commentators, of which Davies and Allison are typical, state the following, 'It is tempting to see a side-glance at Jamnia in Mt. 23:5-10 "... but you must not be called rabbi", ... The Jamnian usage is revealed in 23:8, where "rabbi" is understood as "teacher".'[45]

Further to our discussion is the controversial *birkat ha-minim* (the curse on the heretics), which has often been used as evidence that Matthew was composed after the Jamnian period. The *birkat ha-minim* is attested in the twelfth of eighteen benedictions which have traditionally been ascribed to Rabban Gamaliel II, collated sometime after 80 AD.[46] Benediction 12 states:

> For apostates let there be no hope, and the dominion of arrogance [Rome] do Thou speedily root out in our days; and let the Nazarenes [Christians] perish as in a moment, let them be blotted out of the book of the living and let them not be written with the righteous. Blessed are Thou O Lord who humblest the arrogant.[47]

Approaching the matter in two distinct fashions are Hummel and Kilpatrick. On the one hand, Hummel argues that the relationship between the church and synagogue in Matthew is still very close, and that the Jewish leaders 'are not yet the object of polemical Jamnian legislation'.[48] On the other hand, Kilpatrick interprets the elements of persecution as not merely sporadic mistreatments but as more thoroughgoing official measures reflecting the *birkat ha-minim*. The issue is complicated further by the possibility of similar types of excommunication recorded in the book of Acts, which predate the Jamnian period. If people were accustomed to the types of behaviour recorded in Acts 7 (the stoning of Stephen) then it is possible that the events Matthew relates are not unique to the Jamnian period.[49] Furthermore, R. Kimelman argues that the attested date for the eighteen benedictions, and in particular the *birkat ha-minim*, was not a decisive decision or event, but rather the

---

44   W. D. Davies, *The Setting of the Sermon on the Mount* (Cambridge: Cambridge University Press, 1964), p. 272.

45   Davies and Allison, *Matthew 1*, p. 135.

46   *Berakoth* 4.3, 'R. Gamaliel says, "Each day a man should pray the Eighteen [Benedictions]." R. Joshua says, "[Each day one should pray] an abstract of the Eighteen." R. Aqiba says, "If one's prayer is fluent he prays the [full] Eighteen [Benedictions]." "But if not [he should pray] an abstract of the Eighteen."'

47   Cited in E. Fergurson, *Backgrounds of Early Christianity* (Grand Rapids: Eerdmans, 1987), pp. 460–61.

48   Davies and Allison, *Matthew 1*, p. 136.

49   Acts 13.50; 14.19; and 21.30 lend additional support to this hypothesis of early tensions.

cumulative process of previous conflict and sentiment.[50] He notes that the *birkat ha-minim* does not reflect a moment 'in the history of the relationship between Jews and Christians ... the separation was the result of a long process dependent upon local situations and ultimately upon the political power of the church', and that the separation of church and synagogue was 'not decisive ... but it gave solemn liturgical expression to a separation effected in the second half of the first century'.[51] Within this paradigm of slow development of Christians and Jews (including occasional conflict in their growth apart), it is entirely conceivable that there could be such tensions at an earlier stage in the parting of the two ways.

What conclusions can we thus make regarding the date of composition for Matthew? On the whole, as it may be evident, the question of dating is exceedingly difficult. Nonetheless, as was noted in our discussion of external evidence, the *terminus ad quem* for Matthew would be c. 100 AD, and, realistically, the *terminus a quo* would be somewhere around 69–70 AD. Although it is problematic to reach any sort of more specific certainty, perhaps all that can be said, given the prominence of certain terminology (*rabbi, teacher,* etc.) and the similarity between the issues of the mid-seventh and early eighth decades of the first century AD, is that Matthew was possibly composed somewhere in the Jamnian period,[52] i.e. 80–85 AD. This is, however, by no means definitive.[53]

50   R. Kimelman, '*Birkat Ha-Minim* and the Lack of Evidence for an Anti-Christian Jewish Prayer in Late Antiquity', in *Jewish and Christian Self Definition*, ed. E. P. Sanders, A. J. Baumgarten, and Alan Mendelson (Philadelphia: Fortress Press, 1989), pp. 226–44.

51   Kimelman, '*Birkat*', p. 226.

52   Davies and Allison, *Matthew 1*, p. 136.

53   For arguments regarding an earlier dating see J. Nolland, *The Gospel of Matthew* (Grand Rapids: Eerdmans, 2005), pp. 14–16. It is important to note that our later use of J. Kloppenborg, 'Evocatio Deorum and the Date of Mark', *JBL* 124 (2005), pp. 419–50, in regard to Mt. 24.1 is for the purpose of contributions to the Roman practice of the *evocatio deorum*, rather than conclusions regarding the later dating of Mark.

Chapter 1

Scholarship on the τὸ βδέλυγμα τῆς ἐρημώσεως

1.1. Introduction

This chapter surveys modern scholarship on the enigmatic phrase βδέλυγμα τῆς ἐρημώσεως in biblical studies, with primary reference to the synoptic tradition. Although our later focus will be on Matthew's usage, commentators and readers alike have often assumed that the findings of a discussion of the Markan phrase can be directly applied to the Matthean context. We find this approach untenable, and for the purposes of understanding how the Matthean phrase has been implicitly understood it is necessary for the full spectrum of synoptic interpretations to be assessed. Significant in this regard is the relative paucity of specific Matthean studies on the βδέλυγμα τῆς ἐρημώσεως. The discussion is also complicated by the pluriformity of approaches to what has now become known as the 'eschatological discourse' of the synoptics. In this regard, D. Ford comments that Mark 13 (and parallels) have 'provoked more scholarly controversy than ... any other [passage]'.[1] Similarly, J. van Dodewaard has noted that the evangelists' record of 'woorden van Jesus hebben ten allen tijde de menschen gefascineerd'.[2] Specifically in regard to the identity of the βδέλυγμα τῆς ἐρημώσεως, D. E. Nineham contends that this 'presents the exegete with difficulties as great as any in the Gospel'.[3] B. Rigaux echoes this sentiment in stating that it is 'Une crux interpretation célèbre'.[4] Thus we proceed with caution in navigating through the rather complex history of exegetical tradition.

---

1   D. Ford, *The Abomination of Desolation in Biblical Eschatology* (New York: University Press of America, 1979), p. vii.

2   J. van Dodewaard, 'De gruwel der verwoesting (Mt. 24:15=Mk 13:14)', *St. Cath* 20 (1944), pp. 125–35 (125). English trans.: 'Jesus' words have fascinated all people at all times'.

3   D. E. Nineham, *The Gospel of St. Mark* (London: Penguin Books, 1963), p. 351.

4   B. Rigaux, '"βδέλυγμα τῆς ἐρημώσεως" Mk 13:14; Mt. 24:15', *Biblica* 40 (1959), pp. 675–83 (675). Compare V. Taylor, 'The Apocalyptic Discourse of Mark XIII', *ExpTim* 60 (1949), pp. 94–98 (94), 'one of the unsolved problems of New Testament exegesis'. A. Feuillet, 'Le discours de Jésus sur la ruine du temple d'après Marc XIII et Luc XXI, 5–36', *RB* 55 (1948), pp. 481–502 (481), 'Dans les Èvangiles, il n'est sans doute pas de passage plus obscur que le discours de Jésus sur la ruine du temple rapporté par les trois synoptiques.' English trans.: 'There is undoubtedly no passage in the gospels which is more obscure than the speech of Jesus, recorded by the three synoptics, concerning the destruction of the temple.'

1.2. Survey

1.2.a. Intentional opaqueness and ambiguity

In H. W. Weiffenbach's 1873 monograph entitled *Der Wieder-kunftsgedanke Jesu*, he puts forward the simple hypothesis that the enigmatic phrase βδέλυγμα τῆς ἐρημώσεως was employed with deliberate ambiguity.[5] Several decades later J. Weiss argued that a hearer/reader in the first century would have had just as much difficulty interpreting the phrase as modern commentators. He states that the Gospel writer 'does not interpret it … he only says that a horrible desecration of the temple must take place before the end can come'.[6] More recent studies have also acknowledged the possibility of the hidden nature of the phrase. W. Barclay admits that 'no one quite knows what the desolating abomination is'.[7] A. I. Wilson comments that 'the significance of the phrase is not transparent, quite probably intentionally so'.[8] V. Taylor expresses a similar approach in noting 'the general atmosphere of reserve which marks the passage'.[9]

However, it seems apparent that an affirmation of the ambiguity of the phrase to secondary readers and/or listeners (ancient or modern) need not imply that within its original literary context it did not have a more definite meaning. Indeed, it seems highly dubious that an evangelist would include something in their gospel if they did not have something quite specific in mind. What then would be the motivation for including it?

1.2.b. Temporal heathen desecration which awaits a future restoration

Although this is less prominent in current scholarship, the βδέλυγμα τῆς ἐρημώσεως' was interpreted by several nineteenth-century German scholars as a temporal heathen desecration which awaited future restoration. One of the earliest in this regard was C. H. Weizsäcker's 1864 work entitled *Untersuchungen über die evangelische Geschichte*.[10] This later found support in K. T. Keim's

---

5   H. W. Weiffenbach, *Der Wiederkunftsgedanke Jesu* (Leipzig: Druck und Verlag von Breitkopf und Härtel, 1873), p. 126.

6   J. Weiss, *Das älteste Evangelium: ein Beitrag zum Verständnis des Markus-Evangeliums und der ältesten evangelischen Uberlieferung* (Göttingen: Vandenhoeck & Ruprecht, 1903), p. 78.

7   W. Barclay, *Matthew* (2 vols; Daily Study Bible; Edinburgh: St Andrew's, 1958), p. 2.338.

8   A. I. Wilson, *When Will These Things Happen? A Study of Jesus as Judge in Matthew 21–25* (Nottingham: Paternoster Press, 2004), p. 142.

9   V. Taylor, *The Gospel according to St. Mark* (London: Macmillan, 1952), p. 511.

10   C. H. Weizsäcker, *Untersuchungen über die evangelische Geschichte* (Gotha: Besser, 1864), p. 125.

Geschichte Jesu von Nazara; he stated that the author of the apocalyptic discourse 'feared only a heathen desecration of the temple ...
and counseled Jews and Christians, in face of this horror, to migrate
from Jerusalem and Judaea, and to wait upon the hills the speedy
redemption of the immediately returning Messiah'.[11] Writing in the
early twentieth century, J. Wellhausen suggested that the phrase in
Mk 13.14 (and parallels) 'does not end in annihilation ... [but] after
the grievous tribulation and desecration, Jerusalem and the temple will
finally be rescued and the Diaspora led back [to it]'.[12] In this way, the
coming of the Messiah was envisioned as the deliverer of the temple
(cf. 2 Bar. 6.8).

This interpretation, however, sits rather uneasily with the introductory verses of the eschatological discourse (Mk 13.1-2; Mt. 24.1-2),
which seem to indicate that the temple *is* destroyed and *stays* destroyed.
There is not even a muted suggestion that the temple will be rebuilt or
restored to its former glory.[13] Mark 13.2 states 'Then Jesus asked him,
"Do you see these great buildings? Not one stone will be left here upon
another; all will be thrown down."' Noting this, E. Lohmeyer concludes
that 'this event [Mk 13.14; Mt. 24.15] changes the sanctuary, which
hitherto was the sole and true place of God and his worship, into the
place of devilish triumph and of the final destruction'.[14]

1.2.c. A pagan idol of some description

The most common modern interpretation of the βδέλυγμα τῆς
ἐρημώσεως has been its identification with a pagan idol of some
description. R. H. Gundry is typical when he states that it is an 'idol
or pagan altar that causes worshippers of the true God to stay away
from the place of sacrifice'.[15] There have been three main proposals in
terms of defining this concept more specifically.

1.2.c.i. A statue erected by Hadrian

Taking his lead from Jerome, F.C. Baur[16] suggested that the βδέλυγμα
τῆς ἐρημώσεως referred to an equestrian statue of the Capitoline
Jupiter, erected by Hadrian on the site of the demolished temple.[17]

---

11   K. T. Keim, *Geschichte Jesu von Nazara* (Zurich, 1872), p. 238; cited in G. R.
Beasley-Murray, *A Commentary on Mark 13* (London: Macmillan, 1957), p. 60.

12   J. Wellhausen, *Das Evangelium Marci* (Berlin: G. Reimer, 1909), p. 103; trans.
Beasley-Murray, *Commentary*, p. 60.

13   See chapter 3 for further discussion.

14   E. Lohmeyer, *Das Evangelium des Markus* (Göttingen: Vandenhoeck & Ruprecht,
1967), p. 184.

15   Gundry, *Matthew*, p. 481.

16   F. C. Baur, *Kritische Untersuchungen über die kanonischen Evangelien* (Tübingen,
1847), p. 606.

17   Cf. Jerome *Comm. in Ev. Matt.* 24.15.

In support of this, A. Schlatter argued that this was a common view amongst the Jews of the period.[18] *m.*Taan. 4.6 states

> Five events took place for our fathers on the seventeenth of Tammuz, and five on the ninth of Ab. On the seventeenth of Tammuz (1) the tablets [of the Torah] were broken, (2) the daily whole offering was cancelled, (3) the city wall was breached, (4) Apostemos burned the Torah, and (5) he set up an idol in the Temple. On the ninth of Ab (1) the decree was made against our forefathers that they should not enter the land, (2) the first Temple and (3) the second [Temple] were destroyed, (4) Betar was taken, and (5) the city was ploughed up.

However, as Ginzberg has noted, 'Apostomos' was a nickname for Antiochus Epiphanes,[19] and as such, there seems no reason to associate the reference in *m.*Taan. 4.6 with any subsequent event in the first century CE. In this light, Ford concludes that the Hadrian hypothesis is historical speculation 'based on hazy recollection'.[20]

1.2.c.ii. An image introduced by Titus

One of the strongest exegetical traditions of the βδέλυγμα τῆς ἐρημώσεως phrase in the Patristic period was its association with the statue of Titus built on the site of the desolated temple. Chrysostom (along with Theophylact, Euthymius Zigabena et al.) advocated this interpretive approach. Chrysostom on *Matthew* 24.1ff. comments,

> For He brought in also a prophecy, to confirm their desolation, saying, 'But when you shall see the abomination of desolation, spoken of by Daniel the prophet, standing in the holy place, let him, the reader understand'. He referred them to Daniel. And by 'abomination' He means the statue of him who then took the city, which he who desolated the city and the temple placed within the temple, wherefore Christ called it, 'of desolation'. Moreover, in order that they might learn that these things will be while some of them are alive, therefore He said, 'When ye see the abomination of desolation'.

However, again it may be said that it is highly questionable whether it is plausible on historical grounds to affirm that such an event ever occurred. Indeed, W. D. Davies and D. C. Allison conclude that there is 'no real evidence for such a statue'.[21] Beasley-Murray concurs and proposes that the tradition arose from the recollection of Titus' plant-

---

18   A. Schlatter, *Der Evangelist Matthäus* (Stuttgart: Calwer Verlag, 1963), p. 172.

19   Cited in I. Singer and C. Adler, *The Jewish Encyclopedia: A Descriptive Record of the History, Religion, Literature, and Customs of the Jewish People from the Earliest Times to the Present Day* (12 vols; New York: Funk and Wagnalls, 1925), p. 2.21.

20   Ford, *Abomination*, p. 159.

21   W. D. Davies and D. C. Allison, *The Gospel according to Matthew* (vol. 3; Edinburgh: T&T Clark, 1997), p. 345 n.116.

ing standards bearing Caesar's images in the temple area (see discussion below).[22]

1.2.c.iii. The attempted profanation of Caligula

In 1868 O. Pfleiderer, on the assumption that Daniel refers to an idol being introduced into the temple, suggested that the βδέλυγμα τῆς ἐρημώσεως referred to Caligula's attempt to set up his own statue in the temple.[23] Several more recent commentators have also found this interpretation convincing, arguing that in Mark's pre-synoptic tradition (*Vorlage*), Caligula was understood as the referent.[24] In support of this, reference is made to Josephus' *Ant.* 18.261, where it is stated that, upon Caligula ordering Petronius to set up a statue of himself in the temple of God, 'they [the Jews] besought him ... not to pollute the city by setting up a statue'.[25]

This interpretation has suffered critique mainly from contemporary studies in Old Testament scholarship wherein there is a shift away from seeing the βδέλυγμα τῆς ἐρημώσεως of Daniel as an idol per se. J. Lust has convincingly argued that the phrase, based on its attested semantic domain, 'is nowhere associated with an idol'.[26] Lust also notes that there is no source before the late third-century Porphyry, which refers to a statue in connection with the βδέλυγμα (abomination). Furthermore, Petronius did not eventually carry out Caligula's command[27] and hence technically the abomination never

---

22　Beasley-Murray, *Commentary*, p. 63.

23　O. Pfleiderer, 'Über die Komposition der eschatologischen Rede, Mt. 24:4ff', *Jahrbücher für deutsche Theologie* 13 (1868), pp. 134–49 (135), 'the Jewish country folks in the villages ... in [Mk] vv. 14ff are commanded to fly to the mountains, with allusion to the terrifying spectre that at that time was perpetually agitating Jewish fantasy, the prospect of a fresh desecration of the temple after the fashion of the earlier occurrences and intentions of Antiochus Epiphanes and of Gaius Caesar'. English translation from Beasley-Murray, *Commentary*, pp. 63–64.

24　C. C. Torrey, *Documents of the Primitive Church* (London: Harper and Brothers, 1941), pp. 31–33; T. W. Manson, *The Sayings of Jesus* (London: SCM Press, 1957), pp. 329–30; L. Gaston, 'The Messiah of Israel as the Teacher of Gentiles', *Int.* 29 (1970), pp. 24–40 (23–29); L. J. Kreitzer, 'The Horror! The Whore! The Abomination of Desolation and Conrad's *Heart of Darkness*', in *Apocalyptic in History and Tradition*, ed. C. Rowland and J. Barton (Sheffield: Sheffield Academic Press, 2002), pp. 284–318 (288–90); D. A. Hagner, *Matthew 1–13* (Dallas: Word Book Publisher, 1993), pp. 699–700; N. H. Taylor, 'Palestinian Christianity and the Caligula Crisis. Part 1. Social and Historical Reconstruction', *JSNT* 61 (1996), pp. 101–24; N. H. Taylor, 'Part II. The Markan Eschatological Discourse', *JSNT* 62 (1999), pp. 13–41.

25　See also *Ant.* 18.271.

26　J. Lust, 'Cult and Sacrifice in Daniel. The Tamid and the Abomination of Desolation', in *Ritual and Sacrifice in the Ancient Near East: Proceedings of the International Conference Organized by the Katholieke Universiteit Leuven from the 17th to the 20th of April 1991*, ed. J. Quaegebeur (Leuven: Uitgeverij Peeters en Departement Orientalistiek, 1993), pp. 283–99 (289–90).

27　Caligula died shortly after writing a letter to Petronius regarding his punishment for not carrying out this task.

occurred. It seems odd that an evangelist would include a detail that was unfulfilled. That was, unless it had a future referent, which would mean it did not refer to Caligula's attempted profanation.

1.2.d. The Roman coin

K. D. Dyer's recent study on Mark 13 entitled *The Prophesy on the Mount*[28] discusses the βδέλυγμα τῆς ἐρημώσεως at considerable length. Taking his cue from the enigmatic editorial phrase 'βδέλυγμα τῆς ἐρημώσεως' (let the reader understand), Dyer asks 'What do people in oral cultures read?'[29] He responds by noting that, in first-century Mediterranean village life, the circulation of coins operated as one of the most efficient and concrete forms of 'text' used to 'differentiate news from rumour'.[30] In this light, Dyer suggests that Mk 13.14 (and parallels) should be understood as a reference to the graven image of Vespasian on coins in the Eastern part of the Empire from 69 AD onwards. As Vespasian went from Judaea to Egypt and then to Rome to be enthroned, Dyer argues that the coins would have appeared before he was emperor. Consequently, this would have 'enabled a pause in the Jewish War of some six months, and provided the last chance for Judaeans to flee before Titus was sent back overland from Egypt to complete the siege of Jerusalem by mid 70 CE'.[31] Thus anyone who could 'read' the coins would have advance warning of the fate of the Jewish revolt and could flee to safety.

Although Dyer's attempt displays appropriate attention to the concept of reading in a predominantly oral culture, there are some hurdles to be overcome before one could accept his hypothesis. A question arises as to whether the language of 'standing' (ἑστός in Mt. 24.15; ἑστηκότα in Mk 13.14) is appropriate, given that the referent is a coin. Furthermore, should this interpretation be applied to the Matthean tradition, one would also need to explain the congruence of ἐν τόπῳ ἁγίῳ (in the holy place) for a coin.

1.2.e. The Roman army

There are two related proposals which argue that that it was the actual presence of a Roman army which was the 'abomination' (βδέλυγμα). The first proposal (1.2.e.i) involves Pontius Pilate, Prefect of Judaea, who infamously attempted to have his soldiers march into Jerusalem

---

28   K. D. Dyer, *The Prophecy on the Mount: Mark 13 and the Gathering of the New Community* (Bern: Peter Lang, 1998), pp. 221–32; see also K. D. Dyer, '"But Concerning that Day ..." (Mark 13:32). "Prophetic" and "Apocalyptic" Eschatology in Mark 13', in *Society of Biblical Literature 1999 Seminar Papers* (Atlanta: Society of Biblical Literature, 1999), pp. 104–22.

29   Dyer, *Concerning*, p. 112.

30   Dyer, *Concerning*, p. 112.

31   Dyer, *Concerning*, p. 112.

with their standards bearing a bust of Tiberius Caesar.[32] Pilate, however, did not eventually carry this out due to the threat of Jewish uprising. This would seem to question the validity of this interpretation, as has already been noted for 1.2.c.iii above. It seems unlikely that the evangelists would refer to an event which anticipates the temple's imminent destruction, yet which is neither fulfilled nor causes the desolation of the temple. Furthermore, Pilate's unfulfilled proposed 'abomination' occurred decades before the temple's final destruction, and thus is at odds with the closely related exhortation to 'φευγέτωσαν εἰς τὰ ὄρη' (flee to the mountains).

The second proposal (1.2.e.ii) of Roman 'abomination' (βδέλυγμα) involves Titus entering the sanctuary of the temple. Several authors have suggested that Josephus' account in *War* 6.260 provides the background for this event:[33] 'And now, since Caesar was no way able to restrain the enthusiastic fury of the soldiers, and the fire proceeded on more and more, he went into the holy place (τοῦ ναοῦ τὸ ἅγιον) of the temple with his commanders, and saw all that it contained.'[34]

Whereas the first hypothesis (1.2.e.i) erred by proposing Pilate's actions too early in the chronology of the Jewish War adequately to explain the flight oracle, the second (1.2.e.i) proposes actions which would be too late. When Titus was standing in the sanctuary there was hardly any realistic opportunity for Judaeans to flee to the mountains. Furthermore, the temple was in flames and the Jewish sacrifices had ceased long ago. Balabanski also argues that 'the perfect participle [εστηκότα/εστὸς] indicates the beginning of a *process which is bound to a specific person*. Titus' acclamation as victor would be ... understood as a single event.'[35]

---

32   *War* 2.169-174; *Ant.* 18.55-59.

33   Pesch, *Markusevangelium*, p. 2.291; D. Lührmann, *Das Markusevangelium* (Tübingen: Mohr, 1987), pp. 221–22. See also J. A. Bengel, *New Testament Commentary* (repr.; Grand Rapids: Kregel, 1742), p. 270.

34   Furthermore, in *War* 6.6.1 the Romans 'carried their standards into the temple court and, setting them up opposite the eastern gate, there sacrificed to them, and with rousing acclamations hailed Titus as imperator'. For use of weapons in Roman religious worship see I. Haynes, 'Religion in the Roman Army: Unifying Aspects and Regional Trends', in *Römische Reichsreligion und Provinzialreligion*, ed. H. Cancik and J. Rüpke (Tübingen: Mohr Siebeck, 1997), pp. 113–26.

35   V. Balabanski, *Eschatology in the Making* (Cambridge: Cambridge University Press, 1997), p. 123. Compare O. T. Owen, 'One Hundred and Fifty Three Fishes', *ExpTim* 100 (1988), pp. 52–54, who attempts, unsuccessfully in this author's view, to establish Titus as the subject of Abomination through the similar Gematria of שִׁקּוּץ מְשֹׁמֵם and Τίτος. The arbitrariness of this approach and the undefined nature in which it is employed brings Owen's conclusions into serious question. For another variation see Günther 1973 (cited in Kreitzer, 'Horror', pp. 288–90), who argues that it was the appearance of Titus' army under the command of Cestius Gallus, on Mount Skopus during November 66 CE.

1.2.f. The Anti-Christ

Another prominent interpretation of the βδέλυγμα τῆς ἐρημώσεως phrase in Patristic exegesis was that of the 'Anti-Christ'. Although Jerome argued for a historical reference to the statue erected by Hadrian (see 1.2.c.i above), he also notes an additional eschatological aspect. In regard to Dan. 11.36 he says:

> From this place on the Jews think that Antichrist is spoken of ... a king shall arise who shall do according to his own will, and lift himself up against all that is called God, and speak great things against the God of the gods, so that he shall sit in the temple of God and make himself god, and his will be performed, until the wrath of God be fulfilled: for in him shall the end be. Which we too understand as Antichrist.[36]

Of particular interest in the works of Hippolytus[37] is the claimed parallel setting of Mark 13 and Matthew 24 with 2 Thessalonians 2. Similarly, Irenaeus[38] has Jesus speak nearly the exact words recorded in Paul's discourse in 2 Thess. 2.4-6 rather than the traditional material in Matthew 24 and Mark 13. Developing his predecessors' suggestions, Victorinus also connects Mk 13.14 with the Johannine apocalypse (Rev. 13.14).[39]

This interpretation has found widespread acceptance.[40] Advocates typically argue along the following lines. First, Mark uses the masculine participle ἑστηκότα as opposed to Matthew's neuter ἑστός, which suggests that in Mark's case a person was in view. Second, the close verbal similarities to 2 Thess. 2.6-7 suggest some sort of parallel is intended.[41] And third, some considered the Danielic passages to have a future fulfilment that would thus fit well with the 'Anti-Christ' interpretation.

In response, with reference to the first point, it should be noted that a masculine participle, although lending itself to a more personal meaning than the neuter construction, does not exclusively refer to a person. C. S. Evans is on comparably sound exegetical ground in claiming that Mark's masculine participle could equally refer to 'a statue or an image of a

---

36   Cited in Ford, *Abomination*, p. 161.
37   Hippolytus *Antichristi* 62.
38   Irenaeus *Adv. Haer.* 5.25.5
39   Beasley-Murray, *Commentary*, p. 66.
40   A. Loisy, *Les Évangiles synoptiques* (2 vols; Paris: Cerf, 1907–1908), p. 2.420; A. H. McNeile, *The Gospel according to Matthew* (London: Macmillan, 1915), p. 348; B. H. Branscomb, *The Gospel of Mark* (London, 1937), p. 237; E. Klosterman, *Das Markusevangelium* (Tübingen: Paul Siebeck, 1950), p. 191; J. Schniewind, *Das Evangelium nach Markus* (Göttingen: Vandenhoeck & Ruprecht, 1952), p. 171; W. Foerster, 'βδελύσσομαι...', in *TDNT*, ed. G. Kittel and G. Friedrich (Grand Rapids: Eerdmans, 1964), pp. 1.598–600; Lohmeyer, *Markus*, 276.
41   For parallels but with different conclusions between the two sections, see D. Wenham, *Rediscovery of Jesus' Eschatological Discourse* (Sheffield: JSOT Press, 1985), pp. 175–80.

pagan deity'.[42] Second, as D. Wenham[43] has argued, the close verbal parallels between 2 Thessalonians 2 and the synoptic eschatological discourse can be accounted for by a pre-synoptic tradition from which both writers drew their theological material and shaped it accordingly. In this regard Beasley-Murray concludes that 2 Thess. 2.4 'extends the idea of Mk 13.14 and fills it out from Dan 11'.[44] Third, it is not clear that an expectation of a future fulfilment of Daniel would exclude the previously surveyed interpretations in favour of an Anti-Christ figure, for in some sense all interpretations of the βδέλυγμα τῆς ἐρημώσεως appeal to Daniel as prior historical antecedent, and as such a literary allusion.[45]

1.2.g. The deeds of the Zealots during the siege of Jerusalem

The main modern proponent of the view that the βδέλυγμα τῆς ἐρημώσεως phrase refers to the deeds of the Zealots during the siege of Jerusalem is V. Balabanski who, in her 1997 work entitled *Eschatology in the Making*, argued this at length.[46] Following on from other commentators who have suggested a similar interpretation based on the use of שִׁקּוּץ for Israel's covenantal infidelity,[47] Balabanski finds an initial clue in passages from Josephus where the temple is polluted, not by Gentiles but by those from *within* Israel (*War* 4.388).[48] Furthermore, Balabanski notes that Dan. 8.11-14; 9.27; and 11.32 are all related to cultic transgression. Seen in the light of *War* 4.387 ('the Zealots caused the prophecies against their country to be fulfilled') and Josephus' common description of the Zealots as 'cultic transgressors',[49] Balabanski

---

42   C. S. Evans, *Mark 8:27–16:20* (Nashville: Nelson, 2001), pp. 319–20.

43   Wenham, *Rediscovery*, pp. 175–80.

44   Beasley-Murray, *Commentary*, p. 68.

45   One must be careful to note that several commentators see a double fulfilment of Mark 13, Matthew 24, and thus an author can affirm a future eschatological interpretation (i.e. Anti-Christ) as well as a more historically grounded initial interpretation. In this regard Hagner contends that Matthew writes concerning the events of Jerusalem's destruction in 70 AD; this, however, does not prevent 'the elastic symbol from also being applied to something lying in the future. But that possibility is not in the evangelist's mind', D. A. Hagner, *Matthew 14–28* (Dallas: Word, 1995), p. 701.

46   For a detailed discussion on the controversial nature of the 'Zealots' see R. A. Horsley, *Jesus and the Spiral of Violence: Popular Jewish Resistance in Roman Palestine* (Minneapolis: Fortress Press, 1993); R. A. Horsley and J. S. Hanson, *Bandits, Prophets, and Messiahs: Popular Movements in the Time of Jesus* (San Francisco: Harper and Row, 1998). A similar viewpoint, yet more specific, is offered by J. Marcus, 'The Jewish War and the *Sitz im Leben* of Mark', *JBL* 111 (1992), pp. 441–62 (454–55) who suggests the revolutionary leader Eleazer ben Simon as the likely candidate.

47   1 Kgs 11.5; 2 Kgs 23.13; Ezek. 5.11. Pfleiderer, 'Komposition', p. 135.

48   Balabanski, *Eschatology*, pp. 124–25.

49   See μιαίνω (to stain) in *War* 4–6; τὸ μίασμα (pollution/sacrilege) in *War* 6.110; ἡ ὕβρις (insolence/contempt) in *War* 4.150; ὑβρίζω (to behave arrogantly) in *War* 4.190; ἀνόσιος (unholy/wicked) in *War* 7.379; ἀσέβεια (ungodliness); ἀσεβέω in *War* 6.95, 127; τὸ ἀσέβημα (ungodly act); ἀσεβής (impious). References cited in Balabanski, *Eschatology*, pp. 124–25 n.41.

argues that the background to the βδέλυγμα τῆς ἐρημώσεως in the synoptic tradition is specifically related to Jewish Zealot activity. In this sense it was the impious actions of the Zealots, rather than any pagan Roman influence, that rendered their activity in the temple an 'abomination'. S. Sowers' former research supports Balabanski's thesis that the one 'standing where he ought not/in the holy place' is more specifically Phanias installed as High Priest in 67–68 CE (*War* 4.147-57).[50] Josephus considers this outrageous because (a) he was not qualified to operate as High Priest in the Holy of Holies and (b) he had strong connections with the Zealot party. Balabanski et al. suggest that, when the 'readers' of Mark or Matthew saw this event, they would know it was now time to flee.

In response, Evans contends that Balabanski's conclusions must be tempered with the acknowledgement that Josephus' depiction of Phanias may well be a reflection of his biases (a) for the Zadokite priestly aristocracy and (b) against the Zealots.[51] It is also apparent that several Jews and Christians would not have seen Phanias' appointment as negative. Indeed, *War* 4.160 tells of the priestly aristocracy 'bitterly reproach[ing] the people for their sloth' and relates that Jesus the son of Gamala, and Ananus the son of Ananus attempted to 'excite them [the Jewish people] against the Zealots'. It is in this regard that Davies and Allison conclude by stating that 'there is no real evidence of ... the Zealots' occupation of the holy place ... [nor] ... the Zealots' choice of a new high priest'.[52]

1.3. Context of Proposed Question

The primary research question that will be undertaken in this study concerns the meaning of the βδέλυγμα τῆς ἐρημώσεως in Mt. 24.15. The significance of the study is to propose a revised model for understanding the enigmatic Matthean phrase through a contextual exegetical approach which gives due weight to Old Testament intertextual prophetic echoes. Of the exegetical conclusions surveyed above, we propose that the last option comes closest to the original intent of the saying, in that it was a Jewish group who were the abomination (cf. *War* 4.147-57, 387, 388; 5.394-95), yet with a significant difference. We intend to demonstrate that the phrase was employed as a prophetic oracle of doom against Israel for her apostasy. This seems to be reflected in several aspects of Matthew's arrangement of material. Significantly, Mt. 23 (the preceding chapter) consists of the seven 'woes' to the Scribes and Pharisees, is the culmination of a growing resistance to Jesus' words

---

50   S. Sowers, 'The Circumstances and Recollection of the Pella Flight', *Theologische Zeitschrift* 26 (1970), pp. 305–20; Balabanski, *Eschatology*, pp. 129–34.

51   Evans, *Mark 8*, p. 319.

52   Davies and Allison, *Matthew 1*, p. 346 n.116.

and deeds, and concludes with the phrase 'your house is left to you desolate' (Mt. 23.38). This prepares the context for Jesus' response to the disciples' admiration of the temple buildings (Mt. 24.1-2). The working hypothesis of this volume is that the phrase βδέλυγμα τῆς ἐρημώσεως, given its background primarily in Daniel, but also taking into serious consideration its intertextual echoes in the prophetic literature of the Hebrew Bible (especially Jeremiah and Ezekiel), refers to Israel as the abomination and the destruction of the temple as the desolation (i.e. an ironic reversal of perceived recipients of divine wrath). In this way Matthew presents Jesus as thoroughly Jewish and standing in the long line of Israel's prophets, uttering a divine oracle of judgement against Israel. Although there was common expectation that the 'pagan' nations would experience Yahweh's judgement, Matthew presents Jesus as the mouthpiece announcing divine retribution (destruction of the temple) which is to fall upon Israel for her idolatrous disregard of covenant obligations.

Chapter 2

STRUCTURE AND SIGNIFICANCE

2.1. Introduction

This chapter will argue for the possibility that the first Gospel has potentially been influenced by the Deuteronomistic blessings and curses (Deuteronomy 27–30). In this sense within Matthew's Gospel, chs 5–7 function as blessings, and ch. 23 functions as the respective curses. Furthermore, Matthew's presentation of Jesus' lament over Jerusalem (23.39) seeks to emphasize Israel's culpability in rejecting her Messianic King. This then provides the framework for understanding the Matthean apocalypse (ch. 24), which then primarily refers to the destruction of Jerusalem through the advent of the Son of Man. We will conclude by demonstrating that the idea that Jerusalem's destruction was engendered by Israel's infidelity is a common motif in post-70-AD pseudepigraphical material.

2.2. A Structural Overview of Matthew

In regard to the structure of Matthew's Gospel, much scholarly endeavour has been undertaken in attempting to discern a structural arrangement of material. One of the earliest and most influential structural hypotheses was B. W. Bacon's Pentateuchal theory,[1] in which he proposed that Matthew's Gospel was composed of five main sections, alternating between narrative and discourse material. This structure was employed, Bacon proposed, to present Matthew's Gospel as a counterpart to the five-part Torah. The main divisions of Bacon's proposal were as follows: Preamble (1.1–2.23); Book 1 (3.1–7.29); Book 2 (8.1–11.1); Book 3 (11.2–13.53); Book 4 (13.54–19.1a); Book 5 (19.1b–26.2); and Epilogue (26.3–28.20). The strength of this hypothesis resides in the fivefold refrain that concludes each main section of discourse.

Mt. 7.28   Καὶ ἐγένετο ὅτε ἐτέλεσεν ὁ Ἰησοῦς τοὺς λόγους τούτους

---

1   B. W. Bacon, *Studies in Matthew* (London: Henry Holt, 1930), pp. 187–89.

Mt. 11.1   Καὶ ἐγένετο ὅτε ἐτέλεσεν ὁ Ἰησοῦς διατάσσων
τοῖς δώδεκα μαθηταῖς αὐτοῦ
Mt. 13.53 Καὶ ἐγένετο ὅτε ἐτέλεσεν ὁ Ἰησοῦς τὰς
παραβολὰς ταύτας
Mt. 19.1   Καὶ ἐγένετο ὅτε ἐτέλεσεν ὁ Ἰησοῦς τοὺς
λόγους τούτους
Mt. 26.1   Καὶ ἐγένετο ὅτε ἐτέλεσεν ὁ Ἰησοῦς πάντας
τοὺς λόγους τούτους

In each summary statement the first six words are identical. The second half then refers to Jesus' teaching: words in 7.28; 19.1; 26.1; instruction to the twelve in 11.1; parables in 13.53; they are thus linked by their summary of Jesus' spoken activity. Bacon finds additional support for this in an early second-century Greek fragment first published in 1917, which consists of 'six iambic verses apparently designed as a prologue to Matthew'.[2] The first two lines read as follows: Ματθαῖος εἴργει τῶν Ἰουδαίων θράσος. Ὥσπερ χαλινοῖς πέντε φιμώσας λόγιας ('Matthew curbs the audacity of the Jews. Checking them in five books as it were with bridles').[3] This ancient tradition lends support to an early interpretation which envisioned Matthew's Gospel as a fivefold counterpart to the Pentateuch. The strength of this structural analysis is the fivefold structural marker, which commends itself *a fortiori* beyond the tripartite division proposed by Kingsbury et al. on the basis of the repeated phrase Ἀπὸ τότε ἤρξατο ὁ Ἰησοῦς in 4.17 and 16.21.[4]

Although he does not develop an alternative, Davies argues against Bacon's structural analysis and questions the validity of re-occurring words as a significant connecting formula. He sceptically concludes, 'can they bear the structural strain imposed upon them by Bacon?' To which his answer is a definitive no![5] His reasoning for adopting such a position is based on the earlier research carried out by Hawkins in his work entitled *Horae Synopticae*,[6] in which Hawkins identified other ancient literature bearing a fivefold division. Examples offered are (1) the Psalter (Pss 1–41; 42–72; 73–89; 90–106; 107–50) in which the books conclude with a similar formula (Pss 41.13; 72.18-19; 89.52; 106.48; 150);[7] (2) the five

2   Bacon, *Studies*, p. xvi n.8.
3   Greek text from Bacon, *Studies*, p. xvi n.8; trans. Davies, *Setting*, p. 18.
4   J. D. Kingsbury, *Matthew: Structure, Christology, Kingdom* (Philadelphia: Fortress, 1975), pp. 2–7. It stands to reason that if Kingsbury finds significance in the replication of a phrase as determinative for structure which is both shorter and less frequently attested (i.e. three vs five), then it is difficult to argue that a fivefold hypothesis is less convincing. Other structural hypotheses have been proposed including Stonehouse's theological/biographical division and Goulder's lectionary hypothesis. See Hagner, *Matthew 1–13*, pp. 1–2.
5   Davies, *Setting*, p. 17.
6   J. C. Hawkins, *Horae Synopticae: Contributions to the Study of the Synoptic Problem* (Oxford: Clarendon Press, 1899), pp. 132–33; cited in Davies, *Setting*, p. 15.
7   Davies, *Setting*, p. 15.

Megilloth;[8] (3) the five divisions of Ecclesiasticus; (4) the five divisions of Proverbs (Prov. 1–9; 10–24; 25–29; 30; 31); and (5) the five sections of Enoch (*1 En.* 1–36; 37–71; 72–82; 83–90; 91–108). As such, Davies argues that the fivefold division was merely a common literary convention, employed out of convenience in arranging material.

What is one to make of these other works that display a fivefold division? Upon first reading this seems to tell strongly against a Pentateuchal schema for Matthew's fivefold division. However, upon closer inspection, rather than telling against Pentateuchal recollection, the fivefold schema significantly contributes to such a reading. Such is the case with the Psalter, which in Jewish tradition typologically portrays David as a Mosaic figure precisely on the basis of the fivefold division of the Mosaic Torah.[9] Furthermore, Philo designates the psalmists as τῶν Μωυσέως γνωρίμων τις (disciples of Moses) in *Conf. Ling.* 39, which again suggests a link between the speaker/writer of the Psalms and Moses. In this way, Hawkins' original objection (followed by Davies') to the Mosaic fivefold division of Matthew, based upon a similar division in the Psalms, does not negate Pentateuchal typology, but rather opens up the possibility for allusion and recollection.

With regard to the Megilloth, Ecclesiasticus, Proverbs, and Enoch, the conspicuous absence of any transitional formula and the, at times, somewhat arbitrary division, especially in regard to Proverbs, concerning which there is significant disagreement,[10] caution must be exercised against hastily attributing the fivefold division to a common literary motif devoid of Pentateuchal significance.

---

8   Esther, Ruth, Song of Songs, Lamentations, Ecclesiastes.

9   Midrash Ps. 1.1 states 'The foremost among the prophets – he is Moses ... [and] foremost among the kings – he is David. You find that whatever Moses did, David did. As Moses led Israel out of Egypt, so David led Israel out of servitude to Goliath. As Moses fought the battles of the Lord against Sihon and Og, so David fought the battles of the Lord in all the regions around him ... As Moses became king in Israel and in Judah ... so David became king in Israel and in Judah. As Moses divided the Red Sea for Israel, so David divided the rivers of Aram for Israel, as it is said "David ... divided the rivers of Aram" (Ps. 60:1, 2). As Moses built an altar, so David built an altar. As the one brought offerings, so the other brought offerings. As Moses gave five books of Law to Israel, so David gave five books of Psalms to Israel ... Finally, as Moses blessed Israel with the words "Blessed art you, O Israel" (Deut. 33:29), so David blessed Israel with the words "Blessed is the man."' This reinforces the idea that the five books of the Torah were given by God through Moses and reciprocally the five books of the Psalms came from David. David as a new Moses figure has been proposed by various commentators; however, the most recent substantial investigation is that of Allison, *Typology*, pp. 35–45.

10   Various proposals for the structure of Proverbs have been suggested. R. E. Murphy, *Proverbs* (Nashville: Thomas Nelson Publishers, 1998) proposes a tenfold division based on the speakers of the proverbs. W. McKane, *Proverbs* (London: SCM Press, 1970), alternatively proposes an eightfold division which can be grouped in three larger sections of (1) instruction genre, (2) sentence literature and (3) poems and numerical sayings.

Davies nonetheless attempts to expunge any residual Pentateuchal typology suggested by the fivefold division of Matthew's Gospel on the basis of his supposition that the transitional formulas were present in one of Matthew's sources, a document which he calls 'proto-Matthew'.[11] Davies, following Godet, suggests that the similarity of Lk. 7.1 with Mt. 7.28, both of which are located after the extended sermon discourse, supports a common origin for both, and as such nothing can be uniquely attributed to Matthew in the implementation of this phrase. He concludes that '[this] division, if it be derivative, cannot be of dominant significance in deciphering the intention of the evangelist'.[12]

However, in this regard, three things may be said. First, Davies' argument seems to be weakened by the simple fact that a hypothetical source 'proto-Matthew' is not known to exist. Second, this single similarity may be somewhat stretched. Apart from different Greek constructions used for introduction (Mt. 7.28 Καὶ ἐγένετο ὅτε ἐτέλεσεν; Lk. 7.1 Ἐπειδὴ ἐπλήρωσεν), Jesus' speech is variously described as τοὺς λόγους τούτους (Matthew) and τὰ ῥήματα αὐτοῦ (Luke), which again cautions against too close an association. It is in this sense that Kurt Aland designated the parallel to a small font text in his *Synopsis Quattuor Evangeliorum*, indicating that the association is possible but not substantially persuasive.[13] Similarly, Luz concludes, 'How far Matthew followed Q can hardly be recognized, since Luke 7:1a is completely Lukan.'[14] Third, in addition to there being no direct evidence for a 'proto-Matthew' document, what documents do remain, namely canonical and other Gospels, indicate that the other four insertions of the transitional formula into Matthew's Gospel are unique to Matthew.

A fascinating additional phenomenon commends investigation as the possible impetus for Matthew's textual marker. As noted above, the repetitive transitional formulae are common in ancient Jewish literary works.[15] Allison notes that the book of Deuteronomy has a most striking formula which appears three times (31.1, 24; 32.45), in which the first half is more stable than the second.[16]

---

11   Davies, *Setting*, p. 18.
12   Davies, *Setting*, p. 19.
13   K. Aland, *Synopsis Quattuor Evangeliorum* (10th edn; Stuttgart: Biblia-Druck, 1970), p. 73.
14   Luz, *Matthew 1–7*, p. 455.
15   To the above examples given by Davies in the Psalter can be added Judg. 2.11; 3.7, 12; 4.1; 6.1; 10.6; 13.1 'the Israelites (again) did what was evil in the sight of the Lord', Allison, *Typology*, p. 192.
16   Allison, *Typology*, p. 193.

Deut. 31.1   Καὶ συνετέλεσεν Μωυσῆς λαλῶν πάντας τοὺς
                λόγους τούτους
Deut. 31.24   Ἡνίκα δὲ συνετέλεσεν Μωυσῆς γράφων
                πάντας τοὺς λόγους...τούτου
Deut. 32.45   καὶ συνετέλεσεν Μωυσῆς λαλῶν παντὶ Ισραηλ

Several commentators have suggested that Matthew's formula was written with the Deuteronomistic texts on the horizon.[17] Support for this is seen in the phrase τοὺς λόγους τούτους/τούτου occurring twice in the Deuteronomistic formulae (Deut. 31.1, 24) and thrice in the Matthean formulae (Mt. 7.28; 19.1; 26.1).[18] Furthermore, in only one other instance (Num. 16.31) does καὶ introduce [συν]τελέω attached to a subject (either Ιησους or Μωυσῆς) functioning as a description of the type of authoritative speech delivered.[19]

In this regard Luz asks 'Is he [Matthew] influenced by Old Testament formulations? ... Does he want to recall Deuteronomy deliberately?' To which he concludes that due to the lack of specific literary connections, when they 'could have been formed easily',[20] a direct parallel is not in view. It seems unavoidable to concur with Luz on this point due to vocabulary dissimilarities such as τελέω cf. συντελέω.[21] These verbal considerations, in addition to the expanded five (cf. three) references in Matthew, tell against a *direct* relationship with the transitional formula quotations in Deuteronomy. Nonetheless, it is possible that Matthew worked with a general recollection of this Deuteronomistic phrase and that it provided the impetus for his modification and integration of the expanded fivefold form into the textual fabric of his own work.

In this regard, Matthew's Gospel displays significant features which favour Bacon's original fivefold division. Bacon, however, went on to argue that each one of these five sections directly corresponds to its Pentateuchal counterpart.[22] However, as Wright et al. have noted,[23] too

17   H. Frankemölle, *Jahwe-Bund und Kirche Christi* (Münster: Aschendorff, 1984), pp. 334, 370; J. Gnilka, *Matthäusevangelium* (2 vols; Freiburg: Herder, 1988), pp. 1.283–84; H. M. Teeple, *The Mosaic Eschatological Prophet* (Philadelphia: Society of Biblical Literature, 1957), p. 82.

18   Allison, *Typology*, p. 193.

19   Allison, *Typology*, p. 193.

20   Luz, *Matthew 1–7*, p. 455.

21   Matthew uses τελέω seven times (7.28; 10.23; 11.1; 13.53; 17.24; 19.1; 26.1). Although Matthew does not use συντελέω, other NT writers employ the term (Mk 13.4; Lk. 4.2, 13; Acts 21.27; Rom. 9:28; Heb. 8:8).

22   Bacon proposed that Book 1 (Mt. 3.1–7.29) parallels themes in Genesis; Book 2 (Mt. 8.1–11.1) parallels themes in Exodus; Book 3 (11.2–13.53) parallels themes in Leviticus; Book 4 (Mt. 13.54–19.1a) parallels themes in Numbers; and Book 5 (19.1b–26.2) parallels themes in Deuteronomy.

23   N. T. Wright, *The New Testament and the People of God* (London: SPCK, 1993), p. 387; Davies and Allison, *Matthew 1*, pp. 61–62.

much is claimed for this parallel; it is somewhat strained and distorted, various elements being found in the 'wrong' corresponding book.[24] The most serious weakness of this kind is the description of the baptism and temptation narratives in recollection of the Exodus, appearing in Bacon's proposed 'first book', which he designates as corresponding to Genesis.[25]

Wright,[26] however, alternatively develops Bacon's proposal more plausibly by integrating Lohr's chiastic analysis[27] which focuses attention on the climactic thirteenth chapter of the Kingdom parables. Lohr's chiastic analysis can be summarized as shown in Fig. 2.1.[28]

24 Another suggestion includes the five-part division based on the law code in Deuteronomy 12–26 falling into five parts (12.2-8; 12.29-17.13; 17.14–18.22; 19.1–25.19; 26.1-15). See S. D. McBride, 'Polity of the Covenant People: The Book of Deuteronomy', *Int.* 41 (1987), pp. 229–44.

25 Allison, *Typology*, p. 195 points to Jesus' baptism as recalling Israel at the Red Sea. It is also significant to note in this regard that Paul (1 Cor. 10.1-5) likens baptism to Israel's passage through the Red Sea. In regard to the temptation, Matthew seems to have overlaid or combined the existing Israel typology (Jesus answers Satan from texts which all come from passages concerning the testing of Israel in the wilderness [Deut. 8.3; 6.16; 6.13]; the nature of temptation is echoed in Israel's forty-year [cf. Mt. 4.2] wilderness wandering; Israel was tempted by hunger [Exod. 16.2-8], tempted to put God to the test [Exod. 17.1-3 and tempted to idolatry [Exodus 32]) with specific Mosaic/ Exodus elements. The redactional activity which most clearly illustrates this phenomenon is the unique Matthean phrase καὶ νύκτας τεσσεραέκοντα (and forty nights) in Mt. 4.2 not found in Lk. 4.1-13 or Mk. 1.12-13. Most commentators have suggested either the figures of Moses or Elijah as antecedents for the addition, as they are the only two figures in the Old Testament who fast 'for forty days and forty nights' (Exod. 24.18; 1 Kgs 19.8). However, given that various other aspects of Elijah's life are presented as imitative of Moses' life, it is plausible to suggest that there is a similar typology at work here also. The Matthean phrase seems to recall the figure of Moses, as was the inference of many early commentators on Matthew 4 (Irenaeus *Adv. Haer.* 5.21.2; Eusebius *Dem. ev.* 3.2; Chrysostom *Hom. on Matt.* 13.2; Augustine *Serm.* 252.11; *Ep.* 55.28). The 'forty day and forty night fast' of Moses was also a celebrated achievement (Philo *De som.* 1.36; *Ant.* 3.99; *Siphre Deut.* §131b). Other parallels which support Mosaic typology in Matthew 4 noted by Teeple, *Mosaic*, pp. 76–77, are the redactional ἀνήχθη (Mt. 4.1) and the ὄρος ὑψηλὸν λίαν (Mt. 4.8) which were drawn from the Mt. Nebo tradition (cf. LXX Deut. 34.1 καὶ ἀνέβη Μωυσῆ ... ἐπι τὸ ὄρος ... καὶ ἔδειξεν αὐτῷ). Allison, *Typology*, pp. 170–72 also argues that Mt. 4.8, 'Again the devil took him to a very high mountain, and showed him all the kingdoms of the world and the glory of them', echoes Moses' position at the top of Pisgah looking into the promised land (Num. 27.12-14; Deut. 3.27; 32.48-52; 34.1-4). His conclusions are based on a similar narrative pattern where a supernatural figure shows a hero the entirety of a realm which they will not inherit.

26 Wright, *People*, p. 387.

27 C. H. Lohr, 'Oral Techniques in the Gospel of Matthew', *CBQ* 23 (1961), pp. 403–35.

28 Lohr, 'Oral,' p. 427; cf. Davies and Allison, *Matthew 1*, p. 60.

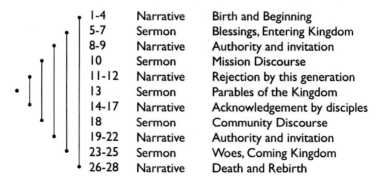

1-4	Narrative	Birth and Beginning
5-7	Sermon	Blessings, Entering Kingdom
8-9	Narrative	Authority and invitation
10	Sermon	Mission Discourse
11-12	Narrative	Rejection by this generation
13	Sermon	Parables of the Kingdom
14-17	Narrative	Acknowledgement by disciples
18	Sermon	Community Discourse
19-22	Narrative	Authority and invitation
23-25	Sermon	Woes, Coming Kingdom
26-28	Narrative	Death and Rebirth

Fig. 2.1 Lohr's chiastic analysis

Wright proposes that the first and last blocks of teaching (5–7 [111 verses], 23–25 [136 verses]), each of which is substantially longer than the three intervening teaching blocks (10.1-42; 13.1-52; 18.1-35), contribute to this chiastic schema.[29] Both blocks focus on a repeated phrase in each section.

Blessed are the poor in spirit, for theirs is the kingdom of heaven.
Blessed are those who mourn, for they will be comforted.
Blessed are the meek, for they will inherit the earth.
Blessed are those who hunger and thirst for righteousness, for they will be filled.
Blessed are the merciful, for they will receive mercy.
Blessed are the pure in heart, for they will see God.
Blessed are the peacemakers, for they will be called children of God.
Blessed are those who are persecuted for righteousness' sake, for theirs is the kingdom of heaven.
Blessed are you when people revile you and persecute you ... your reward is great in heaven

Woe to you, scribes and Pharisees, hypocrites! For you lock people out of the kingdom of heaven.
Woe to you, scribes and Pharisees, hypocrites! For you ... make the convert... twice the child of hell
Woe to you, blind guides, who say, 'Whoever swears by the sanctuary is bound by nothing
Woe to you, scribes and Pharisees, hypocrites! For you tithe ... [but] have neglected ... the law
Woe to you, scribes and Pharisees, hypocrites! For you clean the outside of the cup and of the plate
Woe to you, scribes and Pharisees, hypocrites! For you are like whitewashed tombs
Woe to you, scribes and Pharisees, hypocrites! For you build the tombs of the prophets

Fig. 2.2 Repeated phrases in Matthew 5–7; 23

29   Wright, *People*, pp. 387–88.

The ninefold blessings and sevenfold woes prepare the reader, not for *direct* Pentateuchal correspondence (*pace* Bacon et al.), but for the more generalized pattern of blessings and curses in the renewal of the covenant summarized in Deuteronomy 27–30. These chapters form part of Moses' speech addressing Israel as they gather on the east of the Jordan, before going in to possess the land. There, the covenant is set out in terms of curses and blessings corresponding to fidelity to Yahweh. Wright notes that the sixteen curses in Deut. 27.15-26 and 28.16-19, and amplified in Deut. 28.20-68, conclude with the threat of exile should the Israelites not keep the covenant. The four blessings which are set out in Deut. 28.3-6 and amplified in 28.1-2, 7-14 (summarized again in Deuteronomy 29) demonstrate that Israel will be her own judge in this matter, bringing blessing or cursing on herself dependent on her response to Yahweh. This is specifically referred to in Moses' departing speech, 'I have set before you life and death, blessings and curses. Choose life so that you and your descendants may live, loving the LORD your God, obeying him … so that you may live in the land that the LORD swore to give to your ancestors, to Abraham, to Isaac, and to Jacob' (Deut. 30.19-20). In this light, Matthean structure may be represented as shown in Fig. 2.3.

Some have criticized this fivefold analysis on the basis that it marginalizes the birth narrative to (just) an introduction, and the crucifixion and resurrection as (mere) epilogue. While this remains somewhat problematic, perhaps a more helpful way of understanding the so-called 'epilogue' would be as 'climax', and in this way, the proposed fivefold chiastic structural arrangement does not merely reduce the important events of crucifixion and resurrection to 'epilogue' but concentrically builds towards them throughout the entire Gospel.[30] Furthermore, in a work which claims on so many levels to fulfil the Scripture (explicit citation, paradigmatically, thematically, and use of vocabulary), this sequence of five can hardly be ignored. In this sense, perhaps Matthew's structure can be understood as typologically expounding his theological programme. The fivefold division lends itself to a 'Pentateuchal' reading in which the Deuteronomistic blessings and cursings are dependent on Israel's response to the protagonist.

There are, however, further clues that a relationship exists between chapters 5–7 and 23 of Matthew.[31] Michael D. Goulder has argued for the Matthean origin of chapter 23, in which Mk 12.38-40 is expanded on the

---

30   Perhaps similar to the various movements of an orchestral piece introduced by an overture and concluded by a finale. Additionally, one could argue that the criticism is misdirected since it fails to note that the five blocks concern Jesus' teaching, none of which occur during his infancy or crucifixion.

31   In addition to those discussed below, there are also connections between the larger units of the first and last blocks of teaching. The parable of the houses on rock and sand in 7.24-27 seems to foreshadow the parables of judgement in 25.1-12, 14-30, 31-46. Wright notes that the language of the 'great house which is to fall' (Wright, *People*, p. 387) prepares the reader for ch. 24.

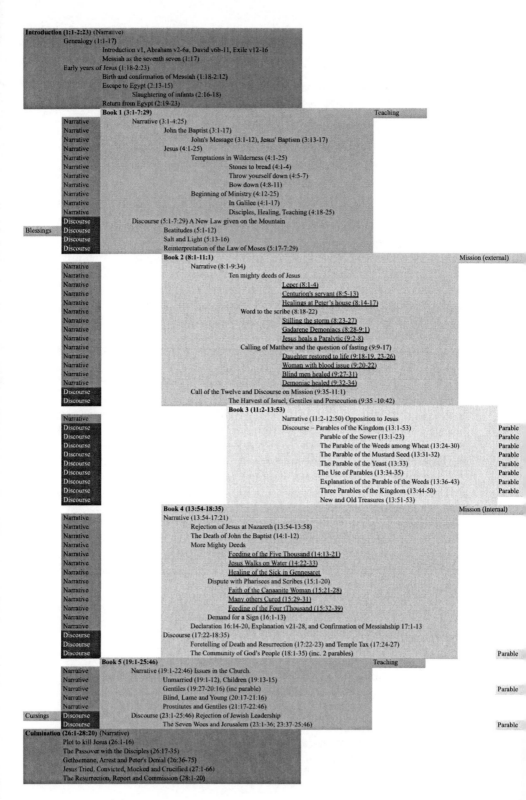

Fig. 2.3 The structure of Matthew

basis of the Old Testament.[32] Although this particular approach has failed to convince the majority of scholars,[33] his analysis of vocabulary in Matthew as a whole has some important implications for our discussion. In Newport's analysis of Goulder he notes that several words appear predominantly and sometimes uniquely in Matthew 5–7 and 23.[34] First, θυσιαστήριον occurs six times in Matthew, exclusively located in either 5–7 or 23 (5.23-24; 23.18-20, 35). Likewise, ἁγιάζω occurs solely within the chiastic bookends of chapters 5–7 and 23 (6.9; 23.17, 19). Second, there is also vocabulary which, although not unique to 5–7 and 23, is unique to 5–7 and 23–25, that is, the larger section of the final discourse section of which Matthew 23 is a part.[35] In this regard, μωρός occurs twice in 5–7 (5.22; 7.26), once in 23 (23.17) and thrice in 25 (25.2-3, 8; wise and foolish virgins). Third, there is some vocabulary which is predominantly in 5–7 and 23 but attested in one or two other locations in Matthew. These include, ὄμνυμι (5.34, 36; 23.16, 18, 20-22; 26.74), γέεννα (5.22, 29-30; 10.28; 18.9; 23.15, 33), πρὸς τὸ + infinitive (5.28; 6.1; 13.30; 23.5; 26.12), ὁ πατὴρ ὁ οὐρανιος (5.48; 6.14, 26, 32; 15.13; 18.35; 23.9), θεάομαι (6.1; 11.7; 22.11; 23.5), and φονεύω (5.21; 19.18; 23.31, 35). If, as has been argued above, chapters 5–7 and 23 are deliberately stylized, then the frequency of similar vocabulary is readily explicable.[36] Newport concludes, 'it would appear, therefore, that several of those words which Goulder is ready to count as Matthean are characteristic not of the gospel as a whole, but rather of ch. 23 and the Sermon on the mount'.[37]

Strengthening the parallel between these units are two literary idioms: hyperbole and doubling. Hyperbole is used exclusively in the plank of 7.4 and the camel of 23.24;[38] and verbal duplication is employed for the vocative or particle in 5.37; 7.21; and 23.37. There is also a similar positive attitude towards the synagogue and the Torah. Within Matthew 5–7; 23 references to συναγωγή are consistently referred to as 'the synagogue'.[39] This avoids the

32   M. D. Goulder, *Midrash and Lection in Matthew* (London: SPCK, 1974).

33   D. Catchpole, 'Review of *Midrash and Lection in Matthew*, by M.D. Goulder', *EvQ* 47 (1975), pp. 239–40; C. L. Mitton, 'Review of *Midrash and Lection in Matthew*, by M. D. Goulder', *ExpTim* 86 (1975), pp. 97–99; A. H. Harvey, 'Review of *Midrash and Lection in Matthew*, by M.D. Goulder', *JTS* 27 (1975), pp. 188–95; K. G. C. Newport, *The Sources and Sitz im Leben of Matthew 23* (Sheffield: Sheffield Academic Press, 1995), pp. 19–55.

34   Newport, *Sources*, pp. 24–56.

35   See below for discussion of ch. 23's inclusion within the final discourse unit of Matthew.

36   Newport, *Sources*, p. 23.

37   Newport, *Sources*, p. 32.

38   Matthew 21.21 can be explained as a reference to the destruction of Mt. Zion and as such not hyperbolic at all. See N. T. Wright, *Jesus and the Victory of God* (Minneapolis: Fortress Press, 1996), pp. 334–35.

39   Matthew 6.2, 5; 23.6. The only exception is 23.34 which could be explained in terms of the context being one of intense polemic.

separatist language of 'their synagogue(s)' (4.23; 9.35; 10.17; 12.9; 13.54) and as such, operates within a more amenable context. This is also apparent in the presentation of the Mosaic office in 23.2-7 and the Mosaic Torah in 5.17-19.[40]

The only place in Matthew where both the disciples (ασμαθητὰς) and the crowds (ὄχλους) are mentioned together as Jesus' audience is at 5–7 and 23. Upon first encounter, 5.1 could be interpreted as Jesus escaping from the crowds to offer instruction to his disciples ('When Jesus saw the crowds, he went up the mountain; and after he sat down, his disciples came to him'). However, in light of the concluding verses in 7.28–8.1 this is not plausible: 'Now when Jesus had finished saying these things, the crowds were astounded at his teaching, for he taught them as one having authority, and not as their scribes. When Jesus had come down from the mountain, great crowds followed him.'

Matthew 23 and 5–7 are also complementary in that they condemn unnecessary ostentation. In the lead-up to the pronouncement of the first woe, Mt. 23.5-7 denounces the show of religious clothing (v. 5), places of honour in social and religious gatherings (v. 6), and honorific titles (vv. 7-10). In like manner, 6.1-18 exhorts people to perform their religious acts of alms, prayer, and fasting out of the public eye.[41]

As was indicated in our above discussion of vocabulary, the motif of oath taking (ὀμνύω) appears in Matthew 5–7 and 23; both 23.16-22 and 5.33-37 caution the reader against the abuses of this practice. It is quite clear that 5.34-37 condemns the practice altogether: 'Do not swear at all ... Let your word be "Yes, Yes" or "No, No"; anything more than this comes from the evil one.' Matthew 23.16-22, however, is somewhat more ambiguous on first reading, as it is not entirely clear whether the text is advocating a complete ban on oath taking, or the appropriate caution in oath taking. F. W. Beare suggests that there is real tension:

> The third woe ... is related to [the] injunction against swearing which is the theme of the fourth Antithesis (5.33-37) ... These verses [Mt. 23.21-22] do not deal with further distinctions of detail, but seem to express the thought that whatever form of words is used, the one who swears is really swearing by God, and his oath is equally as binding in whatever form. In the Antithesis on the other hand, we have a flat prohibition of swearing.[42]

---

40   For detailed discussion of Mt. 23.2-3a see below.

41   There is a note of tension in 5.16: 'In the same way, let your light shine before others, so that they may see your good works and give glory to your Father in heaven.' However, this may be resolved by attention to the underlying essence of the warnings that people should not seek after human recognition. Newport, *Sources*, p. 163: 'the truly righteous person will be recognized as such wherever he goes; he does not need to seek recognition, for his piety will be apparent to all'.

42   F. W. Beare, *The Gospel according to Matthew* (Oxford: Blackwell, 1981), p. 454.

This juxtaposition need not be overemphasized. It is quite clear that ch. 23 addresses 'outsiders' whereas chs 5–7 refer to 'insiders'.[43] In this regard, Mt. 23.16-22 seems to utilize a rhetorical device known as *reductio ad absurdum*. The opponents' position is adopted for the sake of argument ('Woe to you … who say', v. 16) and then taken to its logical conclusion (vv. 21-22). When the opponents' argument is found to be inconsistent, the interlocutor implicitly advocates the abandonment of the initial premise, in this case, making oaths. Understood in this sense, there are significant parallels between the two pericopes.

The theme of religious devotion disproportionately directed towards less important matters of orthopraxis finds attestation in both 5–7 and 23. The parable in 7.1-5 exhorts the one who would seek to remove the splinter of wood from his neighbour's eye to first remove the plank in his own. Similarly, in 23.23-24, Jesus' hearers are denounced for tithing mint, dill, and cumin while neglecting justice and mercy and faith. This motif aids in the broad parallelism between 5–7 and 23–25.

The theme of persecution in Mt. 23.34-35 also finds a parallel with 5.10-12.[44] Many commentators have seen 5.11-12 as a 'Matthean formulation',[45] primarily on the basis of the shift from the general in vv. 3-10 to the specific in v. 11ff., and the shift from present participles (vv. 4, 6, 7) to perfect participles.[46] This may provide a clue that Matthew sought to strengthen the thematic parallels between 5–7 and 23.[47]

In S. E. Porter's comments on method and terminology in discussion of the use of the Old Testament in the New Testament, he provocatively asks 'if one is writing to an uninformed audience who does not know the source text, does that mean that the echoes are no longer present? If they are clear to another audience, does that mean that the text itself is now different, or

43   There is no real disparity between the point made here and our earlier linking of 5–7 and 23 based on 'crowds and disciples', as within both groups there are both positive and negative persons. For a comprehensive discussion of crowds in Matthew see J. R. C Cousland, *The Crowds in the Gospel of Matthew* (Leiden: Brill, 2002), who argues that the crowds are ambivalent, sometimes positive (4.25; 7.28; 9.8; 12.23; 21.9) and sometimes negative (26.47, 55; 27.24). It is important to note that their final status remains open.

44   Contra Newport, *Sources*, pp. 172–73, who sees radical discontinuity between Mt. 23.2-31 and vv. 32-39, and hence hesitates to affirm any kind of parallel with Matthew 5–7.

45   R. Bultmann, *The History of the Synoptic Tradition* (trans. J. Marsh; Oxford: Blackwell, 1963), p. 110.

46   Beare, *Matthew*, pp. 135–36; H. B. Green, *The Gospel according to Matthew* (London: Oxford University Press, 1975), pp. 78–79; McNeile, *Matthew*, pp. 53–54; Bultmann, *History*, p. 110; Luz, *Matthew 1–7*, pp. 228–29, 241–43; Davies and Allison, *Matthew 1*, pp. 459–66.

47   Other references to persecution include, Mt. 5.44; 7.6; 13.21; 22.6; 24.9; and 25.34. See D. R. A. Hare, *The Theme of Jewish Persecutions of Christians in the Gospel According to St. Matthew* (Cambridge: Cambridge University Press, 1982), p. 121.

only the audience?'[48] In noting that a citation or allusion is not dependent on the recipient, Porter highlights the importance of the author's identity in the process of interpretation. Indeed, one could imagine an author alluding to an Old Testament text with which his recipients were unfamiliar; however, it strains credibility to suggest that an uninformed author wrote to informed recipients.[49] The same question could be raised regarding the audience's awareness of structural patterns or other literary features. How likely would it be that Matthew's readers would have recognized the connections between the blessings of ch. 5 and the woes of ch. 23? Are there any indications which might suggest that Matthew expected or aided his readers in such understanding?

One such indication may be apparent in the use of the bracketing technique over a larger scale within Matthew's Gospel. Several commentators have noted a variety of paralleled themes at the macro-level.[50] For example, the divine presence which features in 1.23, 'Emmanuel, which means, "God is with us (μεθ᾽ ἡμῶν)"', is also prominent in 28.20: 'I am with you (μεθ᾽ ἡμῶν) always, to the end of the age.' Second, both (1) the Gentile women in Matthew's genealogy (1.3, 5, 6) and (2) the Magi in 2.1-11, seem to parallel the prominent place given to Gentiles in 28.19. Even closer verbal parallels are apparent in the vocabulary of the Magi pericope. In 2.11, 'they saw (εἶδον) the child with his mother Mary, and they bowed down and worshiped (προσεκύνησαν) him' (cf. 2.2, 8) is comparable to 28.17: 'When they saw (ἰδόντες) him, they worshiped him (προσεκύνησαν).' Third, angelic appearances are particularly significant in 1.20, 24; 2.13, 19; and 28.5, and fourth, there are parallel themes of kingship and authority in 1–2 and 28.18.

Examples such as these serve two purposes. First, they demonstrate that if there was a commonly occurring Matthean technique of separating paralleled material over the large scale structure of his Gospel, then perhaps readers would be more perceptive of possible connections between chapters 5–7 and 23. Second, although a reader might be more disposed to notice themes at the beginning and the end of a work (i.e. material paralleled in Matthew 1–2 and 28), that chs 5–7 and 23–25 form the first and last teaching blocks within the Gospel is perhaps modestly comparative.

Although the 'woes' of Matthew 23 are not precisely the self-proclaimed curses of Deuteronomy, in contemporaneous literature οὐαί does form the natural antithesis to μακάριος. Examples of such are attested in LXX wisdom literature, LXX prophetic literature, Pseudepigraphal material, and the Apocryphal Gospels. Ecclesiastes 10.16-17 arranges the terms in parallel, οὐαί σοί Ϙοε το ψοὺ,πόλις, ἧς ὁ βασιλεύς σου νεώτερος καὶ οἱ ἄρχοντές

---

49   The perceived recipients (and their perceived ability to recognize the reference and broader context) could of course influence the author's motive for including material.
50   H. J. B. Combrink, 'The Structure of the Gospel of Matthew as Narrative', *TynB* 34 (1983), pp. 61–90 (71); J. C. Fenton, 'Inclusio and Chiasmus in "Matthew"', *Studia Evangelica* 1 (1959), pp. 174–79.

σου ἐν πρωίᾳ ἐσθίουσιν· μακαρία σύ (Blessed are you), γῆ, ἧς ὁ βασιλεύς σου υἱὸς ἐλευθέρων καὶ οἱ ἄρχοντές σου πρὸς καιρὸν φάγονται ἐν δυνάμει καὶ οὐκ αἰσχυνθήσονται. The terms occur in similar paralleled fashion in the introductory and concluding verses of Isaiah 31, which explicates the folly of Judah's dependence upon Egypt for protection against the Assyrian forces (31.1-3). Rather than foreign dependence, the prophet advocates complete trust in Yahweh, who will fight and defend Jerusalem (31.4-9). In this presentation, Isaiah 31 is bracketed with reference to οὐαι/μακάριος at the beginning and end of the pericope (cf. Isa. 30.1 .οὐαι; 30.18 μακάριοι).

C. Tuckett has noted that in Luke (contra Mt. 5.1-12) 'the beatitudes are matched by a parallel series of woes ... so that the blessing is matched by a corresponding woe'.[51] Although there is some debate as to whether Q 6.20-26 included the antithetical 'woes', Kloppenborg's *Excavating Q*, lists 6.24-26 as 'probable'.[52] Similarly, I. H. Marshall notes that 'it is generally agreed that a common core lies behind Mt. and Lk. at this point'.[53] If this is so, then perhaps there is further support for reading Matthew 5–7 in connection with chapter 23. Certainly a listener/reader who had some exposure to the material tradition which lies behind Matthew or Luke might be more perceptive of the implicit connections between Matthew 5 and 23. Indeed, L. T. Johnson suggests that 'Luke has Jesus contrasting sets of blessing and woe, the contrast reminds the reader of the "blessings and curses" of Deuteronomy.'[54] It is our suggestion that Matthew has undertaken a similar parallelism in aid of his chiastic structure.

Although this is not a totally obvious literary structure, there are some points in its favour: (1) the discourse units 5–7 and 23–25 stand as the header and footer of teaching material in Matthew; (2) they are substantially longer (5–7 [111 verses], 23–25 [136 verses]) than the three intervening teaching blocks (10.1-42; 13.1-52; 18.1-35); (3) the repeated phrase of blessing (x9) and woe (x7) occurs uniquely in Matthew 5–7 and 23–25; (4) audience; (5) vocabulary; (6) thematic parallels; (7) idiomatic expressions; and (8) it does not lie outside reasonable possibility that attested parallels between the opening and closing chapters would have alerted the readers to other such devices. On this basis we tentatively suggest that Matthew may have intentionally stylized 5–7 and 23 to form some kind of parallel bookends.

It has been suggested in our discussion so far that one plausible way of understanding the influence of this schema are the Deuteronomistic blessings and curses summarized in the renewal of the covenant at Mt. Ebal (Deuteronomy 27–30). In regard to the Jewish background of Matthew and Luke's material on blessing and woes, Nolland states that 'a remote parallel is provided by the lists of blessings and cursings in ... Deut. 27.15-26;

---

51 Tuckett, *Luke*, p. 296.

52 J. S. Kloppenborg, *Excavating Q: The History and Setting of the Sayings Gospel* (Minneapolis: Fortress, 2000), p. 100.

53 I. H. Marshall, *The Gospel of Luke* (Grand Rapids: Eerdmans, 1978), p. 246.

54 L. T. Johnson, *The Gospel of Luke* (Collegeville: Liturgical Press, 1992), p. 111.

28.1-6, 15-19'.[55] Should one not find this connection convincing, one could perhaps say that Matthew 5–7/23 does parallel Deuteronomy 27–30 as (1) a summary of the law and (2) the promise of reward and punishment. However, in addition to this one may wish also to consider that (1) in both Deuteronomy and Matthew, Israel's fate is determined by her response to Yahweh; should she flaunt her covenantal status then she is in danger of bringing curses upon herself (cf. Matthew 23–24), and (2) the geographical locations, although not exclusively unique, are similar (Deut. 27.12 τὸν λαὸν ἐν ὄρει, Mt. 5.1 εἰς τὸ ὄρος).[56]

Furthermore, additional support for the possibility of Deuteronomy's influence on Matthew is found in the significant number of quotations and allusions noted by commentators. M. J. J. Menken lists fifteen quotations and over forty allusions (based on Dittmar's 1903 study).[57] Menken notes that 'Deuteronomy has been one of the main quarries from which Matthew drew Old Testament quotations ... Among the five books of the Torah, Deuteronomy scores highest ... '.[58] Furthermore, presuming the two-source solution to the synoptic problem, the largest majority (47 per cent) of quotations from Deuteronomy are from Matthew's *Sundergut* (Mt. 5.21, 27, 31, 33, 38, 43; 18.16) – seven in total.[59] This pervasive influence offers some support for seeing Deuteronomy's influence in Matthew 5–7 and 23.[60]

2.3. Lament over Jerusalem (Mt. 23.37-39)

Matthew's presentation of chapter 23 concludes with Jesus' lament over Jerusalem. Matthew 23.37 emphasizes the extent to which Yahweh, through Jesus, has attempted to reconcile Israel's idolatrous covenantal state, 'How often have I desired to gather your children together as a hen gathers her brood under her wings, but you were not willing.'[61] Israel's

55   J. Nolland, *Luke 1:1–9:20* (Dallas: Word Books, 1989), p. 279.

56   Wright, *People*, pp. 387–88.

57   M. J. J. Menken, 'Deuteronomy in Matthew's Gospel', in *Deuteronomy in the New Testament*, ed. S. Moyise and J. J. Menken (New York: T&T Clark, 2007), pp. 42–62 (42–43).

58   Menken, 'Deuteronomy', p. 43. Menken goes on to note that 'even if one takes into account that quotations from the Decalogue may come from either Exodus or Deuteronomy, Deuteronomy is still the winner'.

59   Five were derived from Mark (Mt. 15.4 [Mk 7.10]; Mt. 19.7 [Mk 10.3]; Mt. 19.18-19 [Mk 10.19]; Mt. 22.24 [Mk 12.19]; Mt. 22.37 [Mk 12.30]), three were derived from Q (Mt. 4.4 [Lk. 4.4]; Mt. 4.7 [Lk. 4.12]; Mt. 4.10 [Lk. 4.8]).

60   For the prominence of the book of Deuteronomy in the Second Temple Period see T. H. Lim, 'Deuteronomy in the Judaism of the Second Temple Period', in *Deuteronomy in the New Testament*, ed. S. Moyise and J. J. Menken (New York: T&T Clark, 2007), pp. 6–26.

61   A striking literary parallel to the imagery of the hen and the chicks is *5 Ezra* (2 Esdras) 1.30-40, however *5 Ezra* has typically been seen as a second-century Christian addition to the Jewish work of *4 Ezra* (3–14). Both Evans and Stanton argue that the influence seems to be from the canonical tradition to *5 Ezra* rather than vice versa (C. A. Evans,

sustained refusal to accept Jesus is highlighted in the parables after his entry into Jerusalem. The (enacted) parable of the fig tree (21.18-22), the two sons (21.28-32), and the wicked tenants (21.33-41) all condemn Israel for her stubborn rebellion. Some commentators have suggested that the reference to the hen and chicks refers to a farmyard fire, wherein the hen has been scorched and the chickens protected under her wings.[62] This image of fire displays a particular resonance with the following verse which refers to Jerusalem's ultimate fate, 'Behold, your house is left to you desolate.'[63] The description of Yahweh's departure from the temple, and its consequent destruction, echoes elements of Jeremiah's words against Jerusalem 'But if you will not heed these words, I swear by myself, says the LORD, that this house shall become a desolation ... I have forsaken my house, I have abandoned my heritage; I have given the beloved of my heart into the hands of her enemies.'[64] Josephus may allude to a similar idea when he states 'Moreover, the eastern gate of the inner [court of the] temple ... was seen to be opened of its own accord ... this signal foreshowed the desolation that was coming upon them. Moreover ... they heard a sound as of a great multitude, saying, "Let us remove hence."'[65] The abandonment of the temple by Yahweh and its consequent destruction by Roman fire is alluded to in Tacitus' *Histories* 5.13:

There came forth prodigies, which this race, addicted to superstition, though against religiosities, does not have a law to propitiate either by sacrifices or by vows. There were seen in heaven forces rushing together, a reddening of arms, and the temple lit up by a fire coming down from the clouds. The doors of the shrine were suddenly opened, and a voice, greater than that of a human, was heard to say that the gods were departing. Simultaneously there was the unnatural movement of a departure.

Noncanonical Writings and New Testament Interpretation [Peabody: Hendrickson, 1992], pp. 10–11; G. Stanton, '5 Ezra and Matthean Christianity in the Second Century', in *A Gospel for a New People*, ed. G. N. Stanton [Edinburgh: T&T Clark, 1992], pp. 256–77); although the general concept is echoed in a pre-first-century-CE text, *Sir.* 51.12, 'give thanks to him who gathers the dispersed of Israel, for his mercy endures forever'.

62 Wright, *Jesus*, pp. 570–71. Being shielded under wings is a common Old Testament motif; Deut. 32.11; Ruth 2.12; Ps. 17.8; 36.7; 57.1; 63.7; 91.4; Isa. 31.5; 2 *Bar.* 41.4; 2 *Esd.* 1.30. For Old Testament imagery of Israel's gathering see Deut. 30.4; Ps. 106.47; 147.2; Isa. 56.8.

63 Some manuscripts exclude ἔρημος; for further discussion see below, 2.4.

64 Jeremiah 22.5; 12.7, cf. Ezek. 10.18-19; 11.22-23. For the theme of Yahweh abandoning the temple and its consequent destruction see D. I. Block, *The Book of Ezekiel: Chapters 1–24* (Grand Rapids: Eerdmans, 1997), p. 360; L. J. Hoppe, *Holy City: Jerusalem in the Theology of the Old Testament* (Collegeville: Liturgical Press, 2000), pp. 93–94. Jesus' lament over Jerusalem also seems to allude to 2 Chronicles 24 where the murder of Zechariah and Joash's defeat are connected via the language of abandonment, which finds ultimate expression in the fall of Jerusalem and the destruction of Solomon's temple (2 Chron. 36.15-21).

65 *War* 6.293–300.

In this sense the prophetic lament over Jerusalem (v. 37) is tied in with the oracle of Yahweh's departure from the temple and city and its subsequent destruction (v. 38). To this issue we will return in chapter 3 when we discuss J. S. Kloppenborg's recent suggestion of the influence of the Roman practice of the *evocatio deorum*.[66]

2.4. *The Problem of Textual Variation in Mt. 23.38*

In the Nestle-Aland (twenty-fifth edition), Westcott Hort and Weiss' critical edition of the New Testament, ἔρημος was omitted in 23.38 so that the text read ἰδοὺ ἀφίεται ὑμῖν ὁ οἶκος ὑμῶν (lit. 'Behold, left to you, the house of you'). However, in the twenty-seventh edition of the Nestle-Aland (NA[27]) and the fourth edition of the United Bible Society's reconstructed Greek text (UBS[4]), the editors opted for the inclusion of ἔρημος so that 23.38 read ἰδοὺ ἀφίεται ὑμῖν ὁ οἶκος ὑμῶν ἔρημος ('Behold, your house is left to you desolate'). In the NA[27] the textual unit is marked with a †, which denotes that the textual variation represents an 'immer um schwierige Textentscheidung'.[67]

The noun ἔρημος is included in the majority of manuscripts,[68] with the notable omission in B.[69] Of a contentious nature is the reading represented in 𝔓[77] (P.Oxy 2683 + 4405) for which there is a part lacuna for 23.38. The NA[27] cites this verse in support of the longer reading. However, it is referred to in the apparatus as 𝔓[77vid] which indicates that the editors could not determine the reading with 'absolute certainty ... [although it] always indicates a high degree of probability',[70] and 'when an inference is drawn from the extent of a lacuna, it is carefully verified that the manuscript cannot be cited equally well for other readings in the tradition'.[71] There has, however, been considerable debate surrounding this decision.

---

66   Kloppenborg, 'Evocatio Deorum and the Date of Mark', *JBL* 124 (2005), pp. 419–50 (434–41).

67   E. Nestle, K. Aland, and B. Aland, *Novum Testamentum Graece* (27th edn; Stuttgart: Deutsche Bibelgesellschaft, 1991) (NA[27]), 'Einführung', p. 15; 'always a very difficult textual decision'. In the NA[26] it was used to indicate a change from NA[25].

68   ℵ C D E F G H K S U W X Y Δ Θ Π Ω 0102 0138 *f*[1, 13] 2 28 33 157 565 579 700 892 1009 1010 1071 1079 1195 1216 1230 1241 1242 1253 1344 1365 1424 1546 1646 2148 2174 2358 𝔐 lat sy[p. h] mae[1] bo[pt] Cl Eus Bas. Further external support for the inclusion of ἔρημος in 23.38, not referred to in any current critical editions of the NT, can be found in the writings of Basil of Caesaraea (*terminus ad quem* 379 AD). On two different occasions, Basil cites 23.38, and on both occasions he includes the longer reading (*Mor* 30.2; 70.35). J. F. Racine, *The Text of Matthew in the Writings of Basil of Caesarea* (Atlanta: The Society of Biblical Literature, 2004), p. 200.

69   Also ommited in L ff[2] sy[s] sa bo[pt] mae[2].

70   Nestle, *Novum*, p. 55.

71   Nestle, *Novum*, p. 55.

The importance of $\mathfrak{P}^{77}$ is highlighted by the fact that it is the oldest extant witness (late second/early third century) to this section of Matthew's Gospel and as such would provide further external evidence for either its inclusion or omission. $\mathfrak{P}^{77}$ reads as follows for → 28-30,[72] i.e. vv. 37a-39a:

 τας πτερυγας ου[κ ηθελησατ]ε ϊδο[υ
αφειεται ϋμιν ο [*c.*8] λε
[γω γ]αρ ϋ[μιν] ου μη [με ιδητε απ

After ϋμιν ο, problems arise since there is a lacuna of approximately eight letters which would favour ὁ [οἶκος ὑμῶν] λέγω, as there does not seem to be enough space for ὁ [οἶκος ὑμῶν ἔρημος] λέγω. However, it should be noted that J. D. Thomas's estimation of eight letters[73] is on the conservative side. Parsons, in the *editio princeps* of P.Oxy 2683, allowed for up to fourteen letters. However, with the subsequent discovery of 4405, a fragment from the same codex leaf, it would seem to limit the lacuna to a maximum of eleven characters assuming there was an even left margin. Part of the problem in determining the line length and hence lacuna is that the line above has twenty-seven characters and the line below has twenty-three. Furthermore, both Thomas and Parsons respectively claim that the letter before λε on line 29 'is much easier to reconcile with a sigma than with nu'[74] and 'is much more like c than ν'.[75] Thomas resolves this by suggesting that $\mathfrak{P}^{77}$ (P.Oxy 2683 + 4405) 'did indeed include ἔρημος but that there was some error in the lacuna'.[76] The examples he suggests are that either οἶκος or ὑμῶν may have been omitted. The nature of the trace before λε in line 29, however, has recently been challenged by P. Head, who argues as follows:

> Close examination of the papyrus casts doubt on whether the extant ink is really part of a sigma at all (as to read it as a sigma creates another problem that requires a unique variant to be postulated in the intervening space). It seems more likely that $\mathfrak{P}^{77}$ should be read as a witness for the shorter reading here ... [although] not itself decisive.[77]

---

72   The symbol → refers to the direction of fibres on the papyrus. The numbers following are the line numbers starting at 1 on ↓.

73   D. J. Thomas, 'Matthew xxiii 30-34; 35-39', in *The Oxyrhynchus Papyri Vol. LXIV*, ed. E. W. Handley et al. (London: Egypt Exploration Society, 1997), pp. 10–12 (10).

74   Thomas, 'Matthew', p. 11.

75   P. Parsons, 'Matthew xxiii 30-34; 35-39', in *The Oxyrhynchus Papyri Vol. XXXIV*, ed. L. Ingrams et al. (London: Egypt Exploration Society, 1968), pp. 1–4 (4).

76   Thomas, 'Matthew', p. 11.

77   P. Head, 'Some Recently Published NT Papyri from Oxyrhynchus: An Overview and Preliminary Assessment', *TynBul* 51 (2000), pp. 1–16 (7–8). K. S. Min, *Die früheste Überlieferung des Matthausevangeliums* (Münster: Walter de Gruyter, 2004), pp. 196–200 argues similarly, noting, however, that in principle it is also possible that ὑμῶν was excluded in place of ἔρημος.

In terms of the ink preceding λε on 𝔓⁷⁷, there is only the faintest trace, which could either be the top right corner of a lunate sigma or the right vertical of a nu. However, Head makes two other comments which would tend to support the inclusion of ἔρημος in 𝔓⁷⁷. First, Head profiles 𝔓⁷⁷as closely allied to Sinaiticus, by stating that 'in text the manuscript is close to Sinaiticus, and therefore to our modern critical editions'.[78] As noted in our discussion above, Sinaiticus includes the variant and as such supports the longer reading of Mt. 23.38 in 𝔓⁷⁷. Second, Head notes that the variations in the text of 𝔓⁷⁷ 'reflect idiosyncratic spellings (e.g. in v. 37: αποκτιννουσα, ηθεληκα and/or the influence of the parallel passage in Luke 13:34), evident in επεισυν[χ]αι and ορνιξ, both in 23.37'.[79] This would support the possibility that the scribe of 𝔓⁷⁷ was harmonizing Matthew to Luke. Although harmonization usually proceeded in the opposite direction (Lk to Mt), there are other converging lines of evidence that would suggest that this may be a possibility in Mt. 23.28.[80] Notwithstanding, the reading of 𝔓⁷⁷ evades definitive conclusion and as such one must acknowledge the difficulty of appealing to the fragmentary 𝔓⁷⁷ in support of either the shorter or the longer reading.

Nonetheless, the external evidence for the inclusion of ἔρημος is both early and geographically widespread. It seems that the problem of external attestation would instantly vanish, in favour of its inclusion, if Vaticanus (B 03) had the longer reading. Various scholars regard ἔρημος in Matthew as a scribal gloss.[81] Those who argue for the shorter reading often point to Jer. 22.5 as a text to which scribes may have attempted to conform their text: ἐὰν δὲ μὴ ποιήσητε τοὺς λόγους τούτους, κατ᾽ ἐμαυτοῦ ὤμοσα, λέγει κύριος, ὅτι εἰς ἐρήμωσιν ἔσται ὁ οἶκος οὗτος ('But if you will not heed these words, I swear by myself, says the Lord, that this house shall become a desert'). However, there is at least one significant problem with this view. If the scribe was attempting to adapt his source to include an allusion to Jer. 22.5, why has he used ἔρημος in place of the smoother εἰς ἐρήμωσιν?[82] Others have argued that scribes may have added ἔρημος to the Matthean text as an explanation of ἀφίεται ὑμῖν ὁ οἶκος ὑμῶν. But, problematic for this view is that the parallel passage in Lk. 13.35 is not amplified. Even though ℵ W f¹ include ἔρημος in Mt. 23.38, they omit it in Lk. 13.35. What accounts for

78   Head, 'Papyri', p. 7.
79   Head, 'Papyri', p. 7.
80   See below for further discussion.
81   See D. E. Garland, *The Intention of Matthew 23* (Leiden: Brill, 1979), p. 200 n.120; P. Gaecher, *Das Matthäus Evangelium* (Innsbruck: Tyrolia-Verlag, 1963), p. 755; P. Hoffmann, *Studien zur Theologie der Logienquelle* (Münster: Verlag Aschendorff, 1972), p. 172.
82   According to A. Huck and H. Greeven, *Synopses der drei ersten Evangelien* (Mohr: Tübingen, 1981); K. Elliott and I. Moir, *Manuscripts and the Text of the New Testament* (New York: Continuum, 1995), p. 33, a reading which makes a parallel dissimilar is more likely to be original.

the inconsistency in this apparent desire to explicate the shorter reading?[83] Perhaps the most plausible explanation is that ἔρημος is foreign to Lk. 13.35 but original to Mt. 23.38.

There are three other lines of evidence that further support the longer reading, which when taken together may tip the balance in favour of the inclusion of 'ἔρημος'. First, although Plummer[84] argued for the shorter reading on the basis that non-Matthean ἔρημος weakens the '*dative incommodi*', his argument could also be used to support the alternative, in that it would indicate that the longer reading is the *lectio difficilior* and as such the *lectio potior*. Further in this regard, Garland refers to the longer phrase as 'not particularly good Greek'.[85] This is most apparent in a literal translation of the phrases. The shorter phrase displays a symmetry which is unbalanced by the presence of ἔρημος. This would then provide motivation for scribal omission.

(a) ἰδοὺ ἀφίεται ὑμῖν ὁ οἶκος ὑμῶν: Behold, left to you, the house of you.

(b) ἰδοὺ ἀφίεται ὑμῖν ὁ οἶκος ὑμῶν ἔρημος: Behold, left to you, the house of you – desolate.

Second, somewhat related to our first consideration, scribes could have been tempted to omit ἔρημος as superfluous.[86] This suggestion has often been made on the basis of the idea that the *Shekinah* (God's presence) departing from the temple results in its destruction.[87] The strength of this proposal lies in the well-attested tradition that when God's presence withdrew from the temple, its destruction was near. Ezekiel 8.6 states 'do you see what they are doing, the great abominations that the house of Israel are committing here, to

---

83   It is generally accepted that ἔρημος is not original in Lk. 13.35 as it is omitted in P[45vid75] ℵ A B K L R S V W G D P *f*[1] it vul syr[s] sa, and included in Lk. 13.35 D E G H M U X Θ *f*[13] 33. The external evidence favours its exclusion from Luke. For similar conclusions see J. Fitzmeyer, *The Gospel according to Luke X–XXIV* (New York: Doubleday, 1985), p. 1036.

84   A. Plummer, *An Exegetical Commentary on the Gospel according to St. Matthew* (London, 1910), p. 325.

85   Garland, *Intention*, p. 200 n.120.

86   This was the main consideration in Metzger's analysis of the authenticity of the longer reading. B. Metzger, *A Textual Commentary on the Greek New Testament* (Stuttgart: Deutsche Bibelgesellschaft, 1994), p. 51.

87   E. Haenchen, 'Matthäus 23', *ZTK* 48 (1951), pp. 38–63 (55–56); W. Trilling, *Das Wahre Israel* (Munich: Kösel-Verlag, 1964), p. 86; Garland, *Intention*, p. 202 n.121. See discussion on 24.1 in chapter 3 for related discussion of the connection between the deity's departure and the temple's destruction in Graeco-Roman literature. One such example is recorded by Strabo in *Geography* 17.41.7–8 in his description of Alexander's siege of Tyre: 'There were other strange happenings too ... someone reported, on the Tyrian side, that he had seen a vision in which Apollo told him that he would leave the city. ... the Tyrians were so credulous that they tied the image of Apollo to its base with golden cords, preventing, as they thought, the god from leaving the city.'

drive me far from my sanctuary?'[88] Similarly, 2 Bar. 8.1b-2 notes 'a voice was heard from the interior of the temple after the wall had fallen saying: "Enter enemies, and come adversaries; for he who kept the house has forsaken it."' Among the portents recorded by Josephus, the following is instructive:

> at that feast which is called Pentecost, as the priests were going by night into the inner court of the temple ... [they] reported that they were conscious, first of a commotion and a din, and after that of a voice as of a host, 'We are departing hence' (μεταβαίνομεν ἐντεῦθεν).[89]

A further interesting parallel which ties the wider tradition to our discussion in Matthew are the types of deed recorded which cause the removal of God's presence from the temple.[90] Ezekiel 11 associates the shedding of blood (v.6, 'You have killed many in this city, and have filled its streets with the slain') (cf. Mt. 23.29-36) with the departure of God's glory (vv. 22-23, 'Then the cherubim lifted up their wings, with the wheels beside them; and the glory of the God of Israel was above them. And the glory of the LORD ascended from the middle of the city, and stopped on the mountain east of the city').

Also, at various points in the Targum of Isaiah, the absence of the *Shekinah* is equated with the corruption of the leaders, the shedding of innocent blood, and the consequent destruction of the temple. Targum of Isaiah 4.4-5:

> When the Lord shall have taken away the filth of the daughters of Zion and banished those who shed innocent blood who are in Jerusalem from its midst ... And then the Lord will create over the whole sanctuary of the Mount of Zion and over the place of the house of the *Shekinah* a cloud of glory.

The implication is that the *Shekinah* presence was absent while the 'filth of the daughters of Zion' was in Jerusalem. Similarly, 5.5 associates the absence of the *Shekinah* with the destruction of the city, 'And now I will tell you what I am about to do to my people. I will take up my *Shekinah* from them, and they shall be for plundering; I will break down the place of their sanctuaries, and they will be for trampling.' The threat is also reiterated in 8.17 when the prophet declares 'For this reason I prayed before the Lord, who threatened to take up his *Shekinah* from those of the house of Jacob ... .' Two passages which link the shedding of inno-cent blood and judgement are 26.21: 'For behold, the Lord is revealed from the place of his *Shekinah* to visit the sin of the inhabitant of the earth upon him, and the earth will disclose the innocent blood which is

---

88   Cf. *T.Levi* 15.1: 'Because of these things the temple, which the Lord shall choose, will be desolate in uncleanness, and you will be captives to all the nations.'

89   *War* 6.299-300.

90   The analysis here predominantly follows Garland, *Intention*, p. 202 n.121.

shed on her and will no longer cover her slain.'[91] The polemic against the corrupt leadership is evident in 1.15: 'And when the priests spread forth their hands to pray for you, I take up the face of my *Shekinah* from you ... there is no pleasure for me to accept your prayers, because your hands are full of innocent blood.'

Garland[92] also notes T. *Yom* 1.12 which narrates the story of the incident of the two priests: while running up the ramp of the altar, the slower one pushed the other in order to arrive at the altar first. The one who was pushed retaliated and used the sacrificial knife to stab the other. The story continues by stating that since the victim was still alive, the knife was ritually clean and sacrifices could continue, and concludes that 'this teaches that the uncleanness of the knife was of greater importance than the shedding of blood'. It then refers to Manasseh and his shedding of blood (2 Kgs 21.17) and maintains that 'it is because of the guilt of bloodshed that the *Shekinah* has withdrawn and the sanctuary is polluted'.[93]

Similar conspicuous themes are evident in Matthew 23. Within the immediate context, it is a portion of the corrupt Jewish authorities (23.4-28)[94] and the shedding of innocent blood (23.29-35) that has resulted in the temple being abandoned (23.38) and awaiting destruction (24.1ff.). That is, the departure of the *Shekinah* functions as a convention for speaking generally about coming judgement and specifically concerning the destruction of the temple,[95] and as such, scribes may be tempted to omit the ἔρημος as superfluous in Mt. 23.38.[96]

---

91   For the image of judgement see 29.2: 'Yet I will distress the city where the altar is, and it will be desolate and evacuated, and it will be encircled before me with the blood of the slain as the encircling of the altar with the blood of holy sacrifices all around on the feast day.' Cf. also 5.6-9 'They will be cast out and forsaken ... They multiply sins ... The prophet said, this was decreed before the Lord of hosts when I was hearing with my ears: "Surely many houses shall be desolate, large and beautiful houses, without inhabitant."' 32.14-15a, 'For the sanctuary is desolate, the multitude of the cities which were its service are devastated; our stronghold and our hiding place has been searched, now it is desolate and devastated for a time; a place that was a house of joy, a pleasure for kings, now has become a plundering of armies. All this until a spirit comes for us from him whose *Shekinah* is in the heavens of height ... '

92   Garland, *Intention*, p. 202 n.121.

93   Cf. also *Isa. Targ.* 28.1, 4 where the *Shekinah*'s departure was a punishment of 'the wicked one of the sanctuary house'.

94   The problematic text of 23.2-3 in which Jesus advocates adherence to the scribal and Pharisaic teaching will be discussed below.

95   The departure of the *Shekinah* has been noted by Goldberg as a Rabbinic convention in referring to the destruction of the temple in 587 BC. See A. M. Goldberg, *Untersuchungen über die Vorstellung von der Schekinah* (Berlin: de Gruyter, 1969).

96   Although there is not scope for developing this theme in the current work, it is not insignificant to note the high Christological claim implicit in 24.1 of Jesus who then departs from the temple and foretells its destruction. One could argue that Jesus is presented as embodying the presence of God. For further discussion see chapter 4 and comments on Mt. 24.1.

Third, there is some possibility that the Matthean scribes are assimilating their text to Luke. The main external witness in this regard is Vaticanus (B). However, three problems immediately arise if B is harmonizing Matthew to Luke: (1) B is not prone to harmonization in general; (2) B would be harmonizing Matthew to Luke rather than the normal direction of Luke to Matthew; and (3) B would be harmonizing by omission.

Although harmonization by omission is not normally a very strong argument, there are cases where Vaticanus (and other manuscripts) do harmonize Matthew to Luke. Exactly this phenomenon seems to have occurred at (1) Mt. 8.9 in ℵ B a b c g¹ h k q, with the addition of τασσομενος in harmonization to Lk. 7.8. Other cases could also include (2) the addition of επετιμησεν in B* D e (cf. *txt* ℵ B2 C L W Θ *f*1.13) in Mt. 16.20 as a harmonization to Lk. 9.21; (3) the addition of τρηματος in ℵ* B in Mt. 19.24 as a harmonization to Lk. 18.25; (4) the addition of πολλαπλασιονα in B L 579 in Mt. 19.29 as a harmonization to Lk. 18.30.[97]

An objection, however, is that these examples are additions rather than omissions, as is the case in Mt. 23.38. There is, however, an example where Vaticanus' (B) text of Matthew does harmonize by omission to Luke. In Mt. 7.9, B omits εστιν in harmonization to Lk. 11.11. Furthermore, Vaticanus' tendency to omit or shorten texts is evident in 109 textual variation units in Matthew where B has a shorter reading than the NA²⁷ text.[98] In support of this general conclusion, yet in regard to a different textual discussion, D. A. Black notes B. Metzger's comment that the Alexandrian texts, of which Vaticanus is a major witness, have a particular 'penchant for pruning unnecessary words'.[99] This seems to account for the shorter reading in B at Mt. 23.38.

Amid the finely balanced nature of the evidence, it may seem that the most plausible reading is ambiguous at best.[100] Of particular difficulty is the frequently noted element of circularity in text-critical study, in that a

97   Further examples of harmonization to Luke. in other synoptic gospels include the addition of αυτον χριστον ειναι to Mk 1.34 in B L W Θ *f*1 28 in harmonization to Lk. 4.41. An example of Matthew being assimilated with other texts includes the addition of φωνης to Mt. 24.31 as perhaps a harmonization to the common usage in the LXX (Exod. 19.16, 19; 20.18; Lev. 25.9; Josh. 6.20; 2 Sam. 6.15; Ps. 97.6; Song 8.1; Amos 2.2; Isa. 18.3; 58.1; Jer. 4.19, 21; 6.17; 49.14; Ezek. 33.4; Dan. 3.5, 7, 10).

98   1.25; 3.2, 7, 14, 16 (x4); 4.1, 24; 5.1, 16, 18; 6.1, 21; 7.9, 24; 8.7, 13, 21, 23; 9.14, 17, 27, 32; 10.7, 14, 23 (x2), 33, 37; 11.8, 19; 12.15, 18, 38, 47, 48; 13.16, 17, 28, 35, 44, 45; 14.2, 3, 10, 29, 30, 36; 15.2, 14, 15, 27, 32; 16.2, 17 (x2), 21, 22, 24; 17.21; 18.11, 15, 27, 28, 34; 19.3, 9, 10, 11, 17; 20.5, 10, 15, 18, 21 (x2), 23, 26, 32; 21.43; 22.21, 37 (x2), 39 (x2); 23.1, 13, 14, 24, 37, 38; 24.39; 25.6, 22, 40, 41, 42; 26.3, 4, 42, 45; 27.16, 17, 40, 64; 28.14, 15.

99   D. A. Black, 'The Text of John 3:13', *GTJ* 6 (1985), pp. 49–66 (54), cited in B. Metzger, *The Text of the New Testament* (Oxford: Oxford University Press, 1968), p. 546.

100   Regardless of which reading is adopted, both are ancient and go back to an early form of the textual tradition. If ερημος is not original it may suggest something regarding early scribal interpretations of Matthew's narrative.

text-critical decision cannot be solved in isolation from other exegetical issues. Joël Delobel explores this idea by suggesting that textual criticism and exegesis are 'Siamese Twins'.[101] In this light, the common model that text critics do the initial work to establish the text, and that subsequently the exegete does his/her work, is a radical over-simplification. As Tuckett has noted:

> one cannot separate the domain of working of text criticism from the rest of the discipline of NT study entirely. Unless a text-critic is to follow a principle based solely on external attestation of readings, some kind of overlap between textual criticism and exegesis is inevitable. If internal considerations ... are to play any role, then one is immediately engaged in an interplay between textual and exegetical considerations.[102]

Although several of the arguments discussed above may be reversible for the shorter reading, an appeal to the cumulative strength of the following may tip the balance slightly in favour of the longer reading. In this regard, the following are significant regarding the longer reading: (1) significantly stronger external support; (2) *lectio difficilior*; (3) the suggestion that the longer reading can be explained by a scribe assimilating to Jer. 22.5 begs the question as to why ἔρημος was used in place of the LXX's smoother εἰς ἐρήμωσιν; (4) the omission which resulted in the shorter reading can be accounted for by its superfluous nature given the context and in comparison to other similar literature; and (5) there are occasions of B's omission in Matthew harmonizing to Luke; as such, we tentatively hold that a reasonable case can be made for the longer reading at Mt. 23.38.[103]

2.5. The Relationship of Chapter 23 to the Surrounding Material

There does however remain the question of the relationship of Matthew 23 to the surrounding material. Contra J. Dupont,[104] Davies and Allison see Matthew 23 as the conclusion of controversies in chapters 21–22 and not as 'the beginning of a new discourse

---

101 J. Delobel, 'Textual Criticism and Exegesis: Siamese Twins?', in *New Testament Textual Criticism, Exegesis and Church History*, ed. B. Aland and J. Delobel (Netherlands: Pharos, 1994), pp. 98–117 (98).

102 C. Tuckett, 'The Minor Agreements and Textual Criticism', in *Minor Agreements*, ed. G. Strecker (Göttingen: Vandenhoeck & Ruprecht, 1993), pp. 119–42 (136).

103 This is certainly the opinion of U. Luz, *Das Evangelium nach Matthäus 3 Teilband Mt. 18–25* (Düsseldorf: Benziger Verlag, 1997), p. 377, who states that ἔρημος 'ist textkritisch sicher ursprünglich'.

104 J. Dupont, *Les trois apocalypses synoptiques: Marc 13; Matthieu 24–25; Luc 21* (Paris: Cerf, 1985), pp. 467–68.

which extends through 25'.[105] This view is supported by J. P. Meier who argues that '23.37-9 seem intended to form a climax. The leaving of the temple (24.1), the narrowing down of the audience to disciples (24.3) and the change in subject matter and style do not recommend joining chaps. 24–5 to chap. 23.'[106] Nonetheless, it is evident that there are several considerations which, at the very least, establish Matthew 23 as the linking chapter, functioning both as conclusion (to Matthew 21–22) and introduction (to 24–25). As such, the viewpoints of Dupont and Meier are not to be seen as mutually exclusive, but rather as complementary. K. Syreeni concludes that 'Matthew could have it both ways.'[107] However, in terms of Matthew's blocks of material, chapters 23–25 should perhaps be seen as a unit, as Mk 12.41-44 (the story of the widow's mite) is not included after the parallel reference in Matthew, in order to make the connection of Mt. 23.39 and 24.1 clearer. D.A. Hagner suggests that this aids in 'connecting the discourse more closely with the woes of chap. 23'.[108]

Further to the connection of Matthew 23 with material following, rather than preceding it, are the following considerations. First, in a unique redaction, Matthew includes a reference to the description of the fate of the unfaithful slave in 24.51 which is different from the counterpart in the Lukan tradition. Rather than describe 'that slave' (ὁ δοῦλος ἐκεῖνος, Lk. 12.45) as being placed with the ἀπίστων (unfaithful, Lk. 12.46), Matthew's parable casts the wicked slave (ὁ κακὸς δοῦλος) as suffering the same fate as the 'hypocrites' (ὑποκριται), who, given their prominence in the previous chapter, are undoubtedly the Scribes and Pharisees.[109] Matthew 24.51 states that καὶ διχοτομήσει αὐτὸν καὶ τὸ μέρος αὐτοῦ μετὰ τῶν ὑποκριτῶν θήσει· ἐκεῖ ἔσται ὁ κλαυθμὸς καὶ ὁ βρυγμὸς τῶν ὀδόντων ('He will cut him in pieces and put him with the hypocrites, where there will be weeping and gnashing of teeth'). In this regard K. Clark argues that:

> the faithful slave of 24.45 represents the gentile Christian who stands ready for the imminent coming of his Lord; while the wicked slave, unimpressed by the imminence of his Lord's return, represents recalcitrant Judaism condemned in wailing and gnashing of teeth to the lot of the 'hypocrites' (24.51). This word is peculiar to Matthew, and surely reflects ch. 23.[110]

Second, in connection with this, although not a unique feature in the synoptic tradition, Matthew incorporates a 'woe saying' at 24.19: 'Woe to those who are pregnant and to those who are nursing infants in those

---

105　Davies and Allison, *Matthew 3*, p. 258 n.2

106　J. P. Meier, *Matthew* (Dublin: Veritas Publications, 1980), p. 261.

107　Cited by Garland, *Intention*, p. 234.

108　Hagner, *Matthew 14–28*, p. 686.

109　Οὐαὶ ὑμῖν, γραμματεῖς καὶ Φαρισαῖοι ὑποκριταί, Mt. 23.13, 15, 23, 25, 27, 29. The phrase is identical except for v. 13 which has the post-positive δὲ.

110　K. Clark, 'The Gentile Bias in Matthew', *JBL* 66 (1947), pp. 165–72 (167).

days!' This element contributes to the thematic parallel of the woes in ch. 23 (vv. 13, 15, 16, 23, 25, 27, 29).

Third, whereas Luke omits any explicit reference to the βδέλυγμα[111] Mark notes that it ἑστηκότα ὅπου οὐ δεῖ (stands where he ought not, Mk 13.14). Matthew refers to the entity occupying ἐν τόπῳ ἁγίῳ (the holy place, Mt. 24.15). In our hypothesis, this Matthean description coheres well with the location of the High Priest in the temple as representative of the people. The temple as τόπος ἅγιος (holy place) is celebrated in the Psalter at various points including Ps. 23.3 'Who shall go up to the mountain of the Lord, and who shall stand in his holy place?' The concept of priestly service and the τόπος ἅγιος are closely related in the LXX as attested in Lev. 6.19 (Mt. 6.26): 'The priest that offers it shall eat it: in a holy place (ἐν τόπῳ ἁγίῳ) it shall be eaten, in the court of the tabernacle of witness.'[112] Thus Matthew enhances the continuity between chs 23 and 24 by including a specific reference to the activity of Israel's representative leaders.

Fourth, in his description of the Scribes and Pharisees, Matthew has Jesus accusing them of being ὁδηγοὶ τυφλοί (blind guides, cf. Mt. 23.19, 24, and 26). There may be some connection with 24.11, where the false prophets (πλανήσουσιν πολλούς) (will lead many) astray. The parallel is not exact but deserves some consideration.

Fifth, a parallel with considerably more weight is that of Mt. 23.34 and 24.9, which tells of the coming persecution because of allegiance to Jesus. Matthew 23.34 notes, 'Therefore I send you prophets, sages, and scribes, some of whom you will kill (ἀποκτενεῖτε) and crucify (σταυρώσετε), and some you will flog (μαστιγώσετε) in your synagogues and pursue (διώξετε) from town to town';[113] Mt. 24.9 similarly notes, 'Then they will hand you over (παραδώσουσιν) to be tortured (θλῖψιν) and will put you to death (ἀποκτενοῦσιν), and you will be hated (μισούμενοι) by all nations because of my name.' Also of relevance is Mt. 24.49, which, in regard to the parable of the wise and foolish servants, states, 'and he begins to beat (τύπτειν) his fellow slaves, and eats and drinks with drunkards'. In all these circumstances, the fate of God's people is persecution and death. Matthew seems to highlight this as a natural consequence of Israel's disbelief and refusal to accept Jesus' legitimate kingship.

Finally, the time frame of coming consequences is paralleled. Although we will return to this issue in our subsequent discussion, it is sufficient for the time being to note the following. Both Mt. 23.36 and 24.34 describe

---

111 Luke 21.20, Ὅταν δὲ ἴδητε κυκλουμένην ὑπὸ στρατοπέδων Ἰερουσαλήμ, τότε γνῶτε ὅτι ἤγγικεν ἡ ἐρήμωσις αὐτῆς. See discussion below.

112 Also see Exod. 29.31; Lev. 6.16, 26-27, 36; 8.31; 10.13-14 in reference to the tabernacle.

113 In a general sense, this also recalls the period of Antiochus Epiphanes recorded in 1 Macc. 1.51-53 which naturally strengthens the association with the βδέλυγμα τῆς ἐρημώσεως (cf. 1 Macc. 1.54).

the discourse as occurring in γενεὰν ταύτην /γενεὰ αὕτη (this generation). Matthew 23.36 states 'Truly I tell you, all this will come upon this generation.' Similarly, Mt. 24.34 records, 'Truly I tell you, this generation will not pass away until all these things have taken place.' This overall conclusion, however, raises the issue of how Mt. 23.39 is to be understood given the strong theological overtones usually associated with it. It to this issue we now turn.

2.6. *The Problem of Mt. 23.39*

Matthew presents Jesus quoting Ps. 118.26: 'For I tell you, you will not see me again until you say, "Blessed is the one who comes in the name of the Lord."' This is the verbatim phrase that the crowds cry out during Jesus' entry into Jerusalem (21.9). The referent is obviously set in a future context (for Matthew's Jesus); however, it most plausibly refers to the historical circumstances of 70 AD rather than to 'the future day of his second coming', as per Chrysostom.[114] Davies and Allison suggest that this 'makes for continuity with the following chapter'.[115] The problem of this verse is that many commentators have seen in it a positive element of redemption amid a chapter of unmitigated critique. This issue will be discussed below.

Matthew introduces Jesus' speech with λέγω γὰρ ὑμῖν (Mt. 23.39), whereas Luke begins with λέγω δὲ ὑμῖν (Lk. 13.35). Although the difference is only one word, Matthew's γὰρ, in place of Luke's δὲ,[116] seems to make the connection clearer with the surrounding material. In this sense the γὰρ operates as a causal explanation[117] for the pronouncements of Matthew 23 and, as such, makes the connection clearer to Israel's theological culpability for Jerusalem's destruction (cf. Mt. 23.38, 24.1ff.).

With specific reference to the quotation from Ps. 118.26 (117.26 LXX), commentators have typically seen it as either an offer of hope for Israel's

---

114 Cited in Davies and Allison, *Matthew 3*, p. 323. See discussion of Apocalyptic below.

115 Cited in Davies and Allison, *Matthew 3*, p. 323.

116 This is, of course, assuming that the conjunction in Luke is original. It is omitted in 𝔓⁴⁵ ℵ* L. Its inclusion in 𝔓⁷⁵ ℵ² A B D R W Θ Ψ *f* ¹ ⁺ ¹³ suggests its originality. However, its absence would further strengthen this point.

117 H. G. Liddell and R. Scott, *Greek–English Lexicon* (9th edn; Oxford: Clarendon Press, 1996), §11,283 lists three uses of the conjunction γὰρ; (1) argumentative; (2) epexegetic; (3) strengthening. The use in Mt. 23.39 corresponds with the first of these, in that it introduces the reason for the statement.

salvation[118] or a declaration of unqualified judgement.[119] Those who point to a positive interpretation often note that the vocabulary of εὐλογημένος does not typically refer to the negative concepts such as fear and trembling. However, it is important to note that the words in 23.39 describe the content of the words spoken, not the state of those who give them utterance. As various other contemporary sources indicate, it is quite common for condemned sinners to bless God in an attempt to alter their fate.[120] Furthermore, commentators are nearly unanimous that 'it would be jarring indeed for a straightforward promise of salvation to follow the declaration of judgement in v38'.[121]

Davies and Allison have argued for an intermediate position which sees the verse referring to Israel's eschatological redemption. In this sense, the words 'until you say' are determinative,[122] in that 'when the people bless him, the Messiah will come' not 'when the Messiah comes, people will bless him ... Israel's redemption ... [is] a firm hope, its date [however] is contingent upon Israel's acceptance of Jesus'.[123] Davies and Allison offer four arguments for their interpretation: (1) the contingency of final redemption is well attested in Jewish sources; (2) ἕως is understood as a conditional sentence 'in which the realization of the apodosis is dependent on the realization of the protasis';[124] (3) there are similar types of argument in Rabbinic sources of eschatological redemption; and (4) Genesis 1–12 and T.Levi 16 have a similar pattern of sin, judgement, and hope.[125]

Davies and Allison's approach is to be commended for taking into consideration the undeniably strong context of judgement; however, it ultimately fails to convince. The interpretation fundamentally understands the quotation as a positive element of hope, even if it is somewhat delayed by a divinely executed retributive process. Although it is possible that Matthew intended to recall some sort of echo with the Jewish literary

118 R. H. Fuller, 'Matthew', in *Harper's Bible Commentary*, ed. J. L. Mays (San Francisco: Harper & Row, 1988), pp. 951–82 (976); M. D. Goulder, *Luke* (Sheffield: Sheffield Press, 1989), pp. 429–30; Gundry, *Matthew*, p. 474; Marshall, *Luke*, p. 577; D. Patte, *The Gospel according to Matthew* (Philadelphia: Fortress Press, 1987), pp. 329–30.

119 F. C. Fenton, *The Gospel of St. Matthew* (Philadelphia: Westminster, 1977), p. 377; Gnilka, *Matthäusevangelium*, p. 2.305; Manson, *Sayings*, p. 128; J. P. Meier, *Matthew* (Dublin: Veritas Publications, 1980), p. 275.

120 2 Macc. 1.27; 2.18; *1 En.* 57.1; 62.6, 9-10; 63.1-12; 90.34; *Pss Sol.* 8.28; 11.2-6; 17.26, 28, 31, 34-36, 43-44; *2 Bar.* 77–78; *4 Ezra* 13.39; *T. Ash.* 7; Philo, *Praem. Poen.* 117; *Exsecr.* 165; *b. Meg.* 29a; *b. Pesah.* 117a. See Davies and Allison, *Matthew 3*, p. 323 and P. Volz, *Die Eschatologie der jüdischen Gemeinde im neutestamentlichen Zeitalter* (Tübingen: Mohr, 1934), pp. 344–50.

121 Davies and Allison, *Matthew 3*, p. 323.

122 Davies and Allison, *Matthew 3*, p. 324. Also argued by H. van der Kwaak, 'Die Klage über Jerusalem', *NovT* 8 (1966), pp. 156–70.

123 Davies and Allison, *Matthew 3*, p. 324.

124 Davies and Allison, *Matthew 3*, p. 324.

125 Davies and Allison, *Matthew 3*, p. 324.

sources listed by Davies and Allison (cf. #1, 3–4 above), there is no indication that he intended to do so. Furthermore, ἕως can also mean 'when you [have said]', so that the verse would read, 'You will see me and you will say … ' This links the seeing, saying and coming in the same context and, as such, does not require temporal antecedents (contra Davies and Allison). Liddell and Scott define the semantic range of ἕως as 'a relative particle, expressing the point of time up to which an action goes, with reference to the end of the action, *until, till*; or to its continuance, *while*'.[126]

But the question still remains as to how this should be understood. The clue seems to lie in the use of the Old Testament quotation from Ps. 118.26. In Luke the quotation is placed earlier in the narrative (Lk. 13.34-35), so that Jesus' entry into Jerusalem is presented as its fulfilment (Lk. 19.38). However, in Matthew it occurs after Jesus' entry into Jerusalem (Mt. 21.1-11) and points forward to a future event. We will argue that this final coming refers to the Son of Man destroying Jerusalem.

The phrase quoted in Mt. 23.39 'εὐλογημένος ὁ ἐρχόμενος ἐν ὀνόματι κυρίου' is the verbatim phrase found on the lips of the crowds in Matthew's description of Jesus' entry into Jerusalem (21.9), 'The crowds that went ahead of him and that followed were shouting "Hosanna to the Son of David! Blessed is the one who comes in the name of the Lord. Hosanna in the highest heaven."' As many have suggested, Jesus' entry into Jerusalem is laden with motifs and metaphors which proclaim him as the Kingly Son of David (cf. vv. 5, 9).[127] Although 21.1-9 largely follows Mk 11.1-10, Matthew uniquely adds a note on the Jerusalem inhabitants' response in 21.10, 'When he entered Jerusalem, the whole city was in turmoil, asking, "Who is this?"' The question asked, no doubt, has a condescending tone: 'who is this that dares enter Jerusalem with such pomp and circumstance?' N. Lohfink has noted that 'a welcoming confession corresponding to the cry of the multitudes at the gates remains conspicuously absent'.[128] Jerusalem's response is reminiscent of the fear that gripped Herod and the city at the announcement of Jesus' birth (2.3). The reaction of the city's inhabitants is so unimpressive that it is doubtful whether 21.1-11 can be referred to as any kind of triumphal entry;[129] it is remarkably anti-climactic.[130] If there is any uncertainty regarding the unwelcome response,

---

126 Liddell and Scott, *Lexicon*, p. 751.

127 Hagner, *Matthew 14–28*, p. 68; P. van Bergen, 'L'Entrée de Jésus à Jérusalem', *QLP* 38 (1957), pp. 9–24; W. Telford, *The Barren Temple and the Withered Tree* (Sheffield: JSOT Press, 1980), pp. 251–69; D. Catchpole, 'The "Triumphal" Entry', in *Jesus and the Politics of His Day*, ed E. Bammel and C. F. D. Moule (Cambridge: Cambridge University Press, 1984), pp. 319–34.

128 Cited by D. J. Verseput, 'Jesus' Pilgrimage to Jerusalem and Encounter in the Temple: A Geographical motif in Matthew's Gospel', *NovT* 36 (1994), pp. 105–21 (116).

129 This title has dominated in description of the synoptic triplet.

130 C. Meyers, *Binding the Strong Man* (New York: Orbis, 1988), p. 294, 'The episode, resembling carefully choreographed street theater, is designed to give intentionally conflicting messianic signals.'

Matthew banishes all doubt in the subsequent narration of events: (1) temple action (21.12-17); (2) the cursing of the fig tree as a figurative of the temple mount (21.18-22); (3) the disputations with the rulers (21.23-27 [priests and elders]; 22.23-33 [Sadducees], 22.41-45 [Pharisees]); (4) the parable of the sons and wicked tenants (21.28-45); (5) and the parable of the wedding banquet (22.1-22). All these condemn the composite groups of Israel for her covenantal infidelity. It is in this context that Matthew 23, and indeed 23.39, should be understood.

Determinative in this regard is Paul Duff's article arguing that Jesus' entry into Jerusalem is a combination of Zechariah's Divine Warrior and Graeco-Roman entry processions.[131] Our concern is primarily with the entry processions that illuminate the reading of 23.39.[132] Significant in this regard is Josephus' account of Alexander the Great's entry into Jerusalem:

> Then all the Jews together ... greeted Alexander with one voice and surrounded ... [then] he gave the high priest his right hand, the priests ran along by him, and he came into the city; and when he went up into the temple, he offered sacrifice to God, according to the high priest's direction.[133]

Although Duff et al. have noted that this is most probably fictitious,[134] it is derived from Greek epiphany processions. Dionysius' procession at Athenian festivals was typical of this:

> When Antony made his entrance into Ephesus, women arrayed like Baccanals, and men and boys like satyrs and Pans, led the way before him, and the city was full of ivy and thyrus-wands and harps and pipes and flutes, the people hailing him as Dionysius Giver of Joy and Beneficent. For he was such undoubtedly, to some.[135]

This idea of divine visitation was then applied to Royal Hellenistic entry processions. The King of Attalus of Pergamum is presented as entering Athens in the following manner:

> For he was met, not only by all the magistrates and the knights, but by all the citizens with their children and wives. And when the two processions met, the warmth of the welcome given by the populace ... to Attalus, could not have

---

131 P. B. Duff, 'The March of the Divine Warrior and the Advent of the Greco-Roman King: Mark's Account of Jesus' Entry into Jerusalem', *JBL* 111 (1992), pp. 55–71.

132 For the following discussion I am indebted to Duff, 'Warrior'; he does not however use the material in the same way as is argued below.

133 *Ant.* 2.332–336

134 Duff, '*Warrior*', pp. 58–59; W. W. Tarn, 'Alexander: The Conquest of Persia', in *Cambridge Ancient History*, ed. D.M. Lewis (6 vols; Cambridge: Cambridge University Press, 1927), pp. 6.352–86; U. Wilken, *Alexander the Great* (New York: Dial Press, 1932).

135 The entry of Antony into Ephesus recorded by Plutarch *Ant.* 24.3–4.

been exceeded. At his entrance into the city by the gate Dipylum the priests and priestesses lined the street on both sides: all the temples were then thrown open; victims were placed ready at all the altars; and the king was requested to offer sacrifice. Finally they voted him such high honours as they had never without great hesitation voted to any of their former benefactors.[136]

Duff offers a third example of Demetrius Poliorcetes who enters Athens in 307 BC; after liberating the city from the control of Cassander, he was championed as benefactor and saviour (Plutarch *Demetr.* 9.1). Every time Demetrius subsequently came to the city he would receive an appropriate welcome (13.1) with incense, garlands, libations, and choruses.[137] Among other similar stories,[138] D. Catchpole has identified what he calls 'a family of stories detailing the celebratory entry to a city of a hero figure'.[139] He goes on to argue that the 'ultimate precedents are to be found in Israelite kingship ritual'.[140] The prototypical example offered is 1 Kgs 1.32-40, which includes acclamation (v. 34), ceremonial entry (v. 35), the figure riding on a royal animal (v. 38), and the crowd 'playing on pipes and rejoicing with great joy' (v. 40).

Subsequent stories of this nature are well attested in the Maccabaean literature. On two occasions, after military victory, Judas Maccabaeus returns to the land of Judah in procession.[141] After his victory over Gorgias and subsequent return, Judas receives praise which echoes the language of the Psalter: 'they sung hymns and praises to heaven, for he is good and his mercy endures forever' (1 Macc. 4.24, cf. Pss 100.5; 106.1; 107.1; 118.1-4, 29; 136.1ff.). Furthermore, after Judas's victory over Ephron and procession back to Mt. Zion, it is recorded in 1 Macc. 5.45-54 that he participated in offering sacrifices, 'because they had returned in safety; not one of them had fallen'.

Similarly, upon entering Gaza (1 Macc. 13.43-48), Simon Maccabaeus cast away the idolatrous inhabitants (vv. 47b, 48), cleansed idolatrous houses (v. 47b), and entered the city 'with hymns and praise (ὑμνῶν καὶ εὐλογῶν)'. In the subsequent narrative (1 Macc. 13.49-51), Simon enters Jerusalem expelling those who pollute the city (v. 50b). He is welcomed by the faithful with songs in the following manner: 'they entered with praise and palm branches, and with harps and cymbals and stringed instruments and with hymns and songs' (v. 51).

---

136 Polybius 16.25.5-8.
137 Duff, 'Warrior', 60.
138 See also *Ant.* 11.342–45 of Alexander's entry into Shechem; *War* 1.73; *Ant.* 13.304–306 of Antiogonus' returning from a campaign with soldiers; *Ant.* 16.12–15 of Marcus Agrippa's welcomed entry into Jerusalem with acclamations, before he went to sacrifice; *Ant.* 17.194–239 of Archelaus' processional entry into Jerusalem and subsequent participation in sacrifice at the temple.
139 Catchpole, 'Triumphal', p. 319.
140 Catchpole, 'Triumphal', p. 319.
141 1 Macc. 4.19-25, cf. *Ant.* 12.312; 1 Macc. 5.45-54; *Ant.* 12.348–49.

Acclamation is also seen in Jonathan Maccabaeus' entry into Askalon (1 Macc. 10.86, cf. 11.60). The people of that city express their acceptance of his authority by meeting him ἐν δόξῃ μεγάλῃ (in great glory). Similarly, Apollonius son of Menestheus is welcomed into Jerusalem with δᾳδουχίας καὶ βοῶν (a blaze of torches and with shouts [2 Macc. 4.22]). The author describes this welcome as μεγαλομερῶς (magnificent).

It can be seen from these examples that there are predominantly two significant motifs in entry processions: (1) hymnic acclamation by those welcoming the ruler into the city; and (2) the right to perform the rite of sacrifice as an 'act of appropriation'[142] over the city. Furthermore, similar themes are found in Roman triumph processions, where the victorious general and his entourage would ride into their own city on chariots,[143] with soldiers singing 'Io triumphe' (Hurrah, Victory!) to their leader.[144] The procession would then be concluded with a feast at the temple. Significantly, these are the two elements that Jesus is denied by those resident in Jerusalem, namely, hymnic praise (Mt. 21.10-11) and appropriate temple practices (Mt. 21.12-17).

One particularly instructive element in this regard (which ties into our discussion of 21.1-11 and 23.39) is Alexander the Great's entry into Phoenician Tyre (332 BC). After Alexander's victory at Issus, many of the Phoenician towns willingly submitted to him and opened their gates in surrender, including Aradas, Marathus, Sigon, Mariamme, Biblos, and Sidon.[145] In the account given by Flavius Arrianus, as Alexander approached Tyre he was met by ambassadors who immediately offered him submission. Upon being sent by the city, their rulers had resolved to comply with any stipulation demanded by Alexander. However, after Alexander requested that he sacrifice to their patron deity as a symbol of his legitimization as ruler, the people refused, saying that they would grant any other request except sacrifice in the temple.[146] In response, Alexander undertook an immense seven-and-a-half-month siege against the city.[147]

Thus, because the Tyrians had displayed an inappropriate welcome to Alexander, the city was destroyed, 8,000 people were slaughtered, and 30,000 sold into slavery. It is our contention that a similar motif is present in Matthew's presentation of Jesus' entry into Jerusalem (21.1-9), his rejection (21.10–22.46), and Jerusalem's consequent cursing

---

142 Duff, 'Warrior', p. 60.

143 Plut. *Aem.* 32.4–9; *War* 7.149–52; App. *Mith.* 116–17; Dion. Hal *Ant. Rom.* 2.34.1.

144 Plut. *Aem.* 34.7; App. *Pun.* 66; Dion. Hal. *Ant. Rom.* 2.34.2. See Duff, 'Warrior', pp. 62–63.

145 Arrian II.13.7–8; 15.6–7; Quintus Curtius IV.1.15–16.

146 The Tyrians rejected him in Arrian II.16.7–8.

147 The length of time was largely due to the 150-foot walls and well-fortified harbour.

(23.1-39) and destruction (24.1-51). Israel's sin is the rejection of her rightful king. The clue to this is in the quotation of Ps. 118.26 in 21.9 and 23.39. Because Israel had offered an inappropriate welcome to Jesus (21.10), he will return to Jerusalem, as Alexander did to Troy, to besiege the city and destroy it. Thus the reference to 'you will not see me' (v. 39), is not a conditional promise of salvation, but a reference to the advent of the Son of Man coming to destroy Jerusalem, an event which was enacted through the armies of Titus Flavius Sabinus Vespasianus in 70 AD.[148]

Some may question the legitimacy of associating the Alexandrian event and the story of Jesus, given that approximately three centuries separate the figures. First, it is significant to note that Tyre was one of the main city-states of the Phoenicians. Second, Tyre had previously interacted with Israel commercially and religiously.[149] Second Samuel 5.11 records that Tyre's King, Himran, sent the cedar trees of Lebanon as construction material for the building of David's palace. Himran continued supplying goods (both cedar and gold) for Solomon's construction of the temple (1 Kings 5). Furthermore, a different Himran was sent to help in various aspects of building the temple (1 Kgs 7.13-51). Solomon joined Himran in merchant ventures of exotic goods (1 Kgs 10.22, cf. 22.48). Furthermore, at the time of the building of the second temple, the Tyrians exchanged the cedars of Lebanon for food, drink, and oil (Ezra 3.7). Important to note is the recurring theme of emphasis of Tyre's participation in temple-related events.

A negative appraisal of the Tyrians is amply attested in the Old Testament. The most significant and well-remembered interaction between Phoenicia and Israel was that of Jezebel daughter of Ethbaal, King of Tyre, and wife of Ahaz, a negative opinion of which is strongly expressed in the narratives of Elijah and Elisha (1 Kgs 16.29–2 Kgs 10.35). Furthermore, in addition to the many other oracles against Tyre in the prophetic literature,[150] Neh. 13.16 records that the merchants of Tyre violate the Sabbath by selling their goods to those in Judah and in Jerusalem on the Sabbath, as a consequence of which Nehemiah says the following: 'Did not your ancestors act in this way, and did not our God bring all this disaster on us and on this city? Yet you bring more wrath on Israel by profaning the Sabbath' (Neh. 13.18). In the context of the New Testament, Jesus is

---

148 The use of pagan nations to inflict punishment on Israel is a common theme in the Old Testament. See Deut. 28.62-68; Isa. 9.18-21; Amos 2.12-16; 5.3. This issue will be addressed in a subsequent chapter, specifically in terms of forms of representation.

149 The potential allusion to Tyre is made all the more likely when the city's prominence is taken into consideration. Tyre (Τυριος, Τυρος) is mentioned foty-nine times in the LXX; Josh. 19.29, 35; 2 Sam. 5.11; 24.7; 1 Kgs 5.15; 7.1-2; 9.11-12; 1 Chron. 14.1; 22.4; 2 Chron. 2.2, 10, 13; 1 Esd. 5.53; Jdt. 2.28; 1 Macc. 5.15; 11.59; 2 Macc. 4.18, 32, 44, 49; Ps. 44.13; 82.8; 86.4; Job 10.10; Sir. 46.18; Amos 1.9-10; 3.11; Mic. 7.12; Joel 4.4; Zech. 9.2-3; Isa. 23.1, 5, 8, 15, 17; Jer. 29.4; 32.22; 34.3; Ezek. 28.2, 12; 29.18, 20.

150 See Isa. 23; Jer. 25.22; 27.3-7; 47.4; Ezek. 26.1–28.19 (esp. 28.2, 9, where the prince of Tyre asserts that he is God); Joel 3.4-8; Amos 1.9-10; 3.11; Zech. 9.2-4.

recorded as visiting the region of Tyre (Mt. 15.21-28; Mk 7.24-31), and people from Tyre were among the crowds that heard him speak (Mk 3.8; Lk. 6.17). In Luke's account of Paul's missionary journey in Acts 21.3-7, Paul stopped in Tyre on his way to Jerusalem.

In regard to the records concerning Alexander's siege of Tyre, should one suppose they had fallen out of popularity by the first century AD, one needs only to consider the Roman author Quintus Curtius Rufus, who describes the siege of Tyre at length. Common scholarly consensus holds that Quintus composed his *History of Alexander* some time between 31 and 41.[151] Because this was the decade of tyrannical rule from Tiberius to Caligula, some commentators have suggested that Alexander's portrayal as one who evolved from conqueror to paranoid tyrant was intended to parallel the tyranny of Tiberius and Caligula. Others have noted that Curtius Rufus' record of the trial of Philotas (a Macedonian cavalry officer executed by Alexander in 330) could be based on an incident that took place during the reign of Tiberius.[152] If these suggestions are accurate, then it certainly lends support to the idea that Alexander's siege of Tyre may find typological portrayal in a first-century document such as the Gospel of Matthew. The importance of Quintus' description of the siege of Tyre in the *History of Alexander* 4.4.10–17 deserves particular attention. Also of consequence is the record of Alexander's dream of Tyre falling as recorded in Plutarch 24.2–5. Significant for our own discussion is the report that many of the Tyrians dreaMt. that Apollo was going over to Alexander, not necessarily because of Alexander's superior military powers, but because Apollo was 'displeased at what was going on in the city' (Plut. 24.4). That is, inappropriate behaviour on behalf of the inhabitants of the city which elicited the wrath of not only Alexander, but also of Tyre's tutelary deity.

In Matthew's conception, therefore, just as Tyre participated in the building (and reconstruction) of Israel's first and second temples, it will now be used as an image of destruction by foreign force – process that is initiated in Matthew because of Jerusalem's inappropriate welcome of her rightful king. In this sense, the quotation from the Psalter in 23.39

151 Qunitus Curtius Rufus' work originally consisted of ten books but books 1 and 2 are now lost. The main source for his composition was a work by the similar title (*History of Alexander*) by Cleitarchus (a contemporary of Alexander) whose source is believed to be Alexander's court historian Callisthenes of Olynthus. Other sources could have included the memoirs of Onesicritus of Astypalaea and Nearchus, Alexander's helmsman and his fleet commander.

152 D. Harden, *The Phoenicians* (London: Penguin Books, 1963), pp. 421, 51, 114–21; W. Rutz, 'Zur Erzählungskunst des Q. Curtius Rufus', *Hermes* 93 (1965), pp. 370–82; S. Moscati, *The World of the Phoenicians* (London: Phoenix, 1970), pp. 26, 126; A. B. Bosworth, 'History and Rhetoric in Curtius Rufus', *ChP* 78 (1983), pp. 150–61; J. E. Atkinson, 'Q. Curtius Rufus' "Historiae Alexandri Magni"', *ANRW* II.34.4 (1997), pp. 3447–83; E. Baynham, *Alexander the Great: The Unique History of Quintus Curtius* (Ann Arbor: University of Michigan Press, 1998), p. 90; J. R. Ashley, *The Macedonian Empire* (North Carolina: McFarland and Company, 2004), pp. 238, 243.

looks back to Jesus' inappropriate welcome (21.1-11) and forward to the destruction that will soon occur (24.1-51). It seems no accident that the content of Hallel Ps. 118 includes references to military victory (vv. 10-18), entering gates (vv. 19-20), a rejected cornerstone (v. 22; cf. Mt. 21.42), and the day of the Lord (v. 24). In an all too abbreviated note, George Cox concludes that Israel 'will recognize their Messiah only when it is too late'.[153] This naturally raises the thorny question as to how the language of Matthew 24 should be understood. The details of this issue will be addressed in a subsequent chapter.

2.7. *The Problem of 'Doing, Keeping and the "Seat of Moses"' in Mt. 23.2-3*

If, as we have been arguing thus far, the content of Matthew 23 is to be understood as the Deuteronomistic curses in response to Israel's failure to maintain her covenantal obligations, what is one to make of vv. 2-3a? 'The scribes and the Pharisees sit on Moses' seat; therefore, do whatever they teach you and follow it.' To say that these strike the reader as out of place is certainly an understatement given the context of denouncement which follows. Indeed, M. A. Powell notes that many scholars have seen these verses as a 'vagrant pericope that simply cannot be reconciled with the theology of the overall work'.[154] One such commentator, J. D. Kingsbury, confesses that, 'to date, no scholarly proposal for resolving these apparent contradictions has proved entirely satisfactory'.[155] The difficulty of assimilating these verses, both into their immediate context (Matthew 23), and the broader trajectory of Matthew's Gospel is highlighted by the way in which vv. 2-3a have traditionally been understood. S. H. Brooks begins his monograph discussion of material unique to Matthew in the following manner: 'In Matthew's text, Jesus affirms the right and authority of the officials of Judaism to interpret Torah. He warns both the crowds and the disciples,

---

153 G. E. P. Cox, *The Gospel According to Matthew* (London: SCM Press, 1952), p. 143. In regard to 23.39, Newport states that it is 'clearly an end time event' which 'more likely ... expresses the conviction that Jews will one day recognize Jesus for who he is. That day will be the Judgement, when Jesus will return as the eschatological Son of Man to judge the earth,' Newport, *Sources*, p. 176. As we have argued above, the context would suggest otherwise. Cf. P. Bonnard, *L'Evangile selon Saint Matthieu* (Neuchâtel: Delachaux & Niestlé, 1972), p. 344; P. Benoit, *L'Evangile selon Matthieu* (Paris: Cerf, 1961), p. 144.

154 M. A. Powell, 'Do and Keep What Moses Says (Matthew 23:2-7)', *JBL* 114 (1995), pp. 419–35 (419).

155 J. D. Kingsbury, *Matthew as Story* (Philadelphia: Fortress, 1986), p. 67. Similar sentiment expressed by E. P. Blair, *Jesus in the Gospel of Matthew* (Nashville: Abingdon, 1960), p. 114; Haenchen, 'Matthäus 23', 38–40; S. van Tilborg, *The Jewish Leaders in Matthew* (Leiden: Brill, 1972), pp. 134–37.

however, not to practice the example of these leaders.' He goes on to say: 'In Mt. 23.1-3, Jesus affirms both the right of the Jewish leaders to interpret Torah and the accuracy of their interpretation; then in Mt. 23.16-22, he explicitly denies their interpretation.'[156] This echoes G. Bornkamm's traditional summary which states 'Mt. 23.2 grants to the scribes and Pharisees that they sit on the *kathedra* of Moses: their teaching is not attacked but declared to be binding (23.3). What is attacked is the discrepancy between what they teach and what they do, their hypocrisy.'[157] This however, assumes that the flaw of the scribes and Pharisees was their inability to follow their own (correct) teaching.[158] However one understands 'the seat of Moses' (see discussion below), there is still the problem of having Jesus grant legitimacy to the teaching of the scribes and Pharisees where in the rest of Matthew's narrative there is only intense rivalry between Jesus' and the Pharisees' interpretations of the Torah.[159] The problem is not with the scribes' and Pharisees' adherence to their teaching, but with the teaching itself. Such is made evident in the Sabbath controversy in 12.1-14; the dispute of ritual hand washing in 15.1-2, 10-20; the condemnation of those who inappropriately participate in temple offerings while neglecting their familial duties in 15.3-9; and the denunciation of Pharisaic teaching on divorce practices in 19.3-9. Additionally, there are several instances of Jesus warning *against* the teachings of the scribes and Pharisees. Matthew 16.12 states: 'Then they understood that he had not told them to beware of the yeast of bread, but of the teaching of the Pharisees ... '[160]

The severity of the disjunction between the exhortation in vv. 2-3a and (1) the following discourse and (2) the larger narrative themes on controversy over interpretation has caused more than one commentator to assign vv. 2-3a to a pre-Matthean source.[161] D. E. Garland notes that 'Certainly all are agreed that vv.2-3, 5b-7a, 8-10 comprise pre-Matthean Jewish-Christian material.'[162] However, as Powell has noted, 'the

---

156 S. H. Brooks, *Matthew's Community: The Evidence of his Special Sayings Material* (Sheffield: JSOT Press, 1987), p. 11.

157 G. Bornkamm, 'End-Expectation and Church in Matthew', in *Tradition and Interpretation in Matthew*, ed. G. Bornkamm, G. Barth, and H. J. Held (London: SCM Press, 1967), pp. 15–51 (24).

158 Garland, *Intention*, p. 46 suggests that this is 'the only place in Matthew where it is possible to construe the Jewish leaders in a positive light'.

159 Powell, 'Do and Keep', p. 421.

160 Cf. Mt. 15.14; 23.15.

161 Matthew 23.2-3 is unique to Matthew, and therefore on our assumed two-source hypothesis (for assumptions see discussion in preliminary pages) Matthew uniquely contributed these verses.

162 Garland, *Intention*, p. 19 n.29. For similar approaches see E. Klosterman, *Das Matthäusevangelium* (Tübingen: Paul Siebeck, 1927), p. 182; G. D. Kilpatrick, *The Origins of the Gospel according to Saint Matthew* (Oxford: Clarendon Press, 1946), p. 30; Bultmann, *History*, p. 113; H. C. Waetjen, *The Origin and Destiny of Humanness: An*

question then becomes not, Why did Matthew write this? But, why did he incorporate into his Gospel material that contradicts the perspective he apparently wants to convey elsewhere?'[163] Gundry similarly questions the dismissal of this *crux interpretum* by appeal to a pre-Matthean source by stating:

> Matthew was neither a dim-witted tailor who, contrary to Deut. 22.11, sewed together a literary garment of wool and linen without knowing the difference between his materials, nor a modern churchman who saw contradictions in the tradition that came to him but deliberately included everything so that ecumenicity might swallow up theology, lumps and all.[164]

There has been no lack of responses attempting to solve the conundrum of the content and context of vv. 2-3a. No fewer than twelve interpretations have been proposed.[165] Much ink has been spilt as to whether the 'seat of Moses' is actual, metaphorical, or both.[166] However, for the purposes of our discussion, this point is somewhat neutral; what is of importance is the sense in which the injunction to ποιήσατε καὶ τηρεῖτε whatever the scribes and Pharisees εἴπωσιν ὑμῖν should be taken.

Although some commentators argue that the verses are devoid of any real meaning and that the words are 'no more than a foil for a charge that they do not themselves practice what they preach',[167] there is also the suggestion that Matthew refers here to Christian Pharisees with whom he predominantly agreed,[168] or that Matthew acknowledges Pharisaic halakhah to remain partially intact with the synagogue.[169] However, given their later condemnation as 'blind guides' (23.16, 17, 19, 24, 26)

Interpretation of the Gospel According to St. Matthew (California: Crystal Press, 1976), p. 232 n.2.

163 Powell, 'Do and Keep', pp. 421–22.

164 Gundry, *Matthew*, pp. 454–55.

165 Powell, 'Do and Keep', pp. 419–35; Davies and Allison, *Matthew 3*, pp. 269–70; Nolland, *Matthew*, p. 922.

166 For the reference as figurative, see Grundmann who concludes that the 'Kathedra des Moses ist Bild für seine Auturität', W. Grundmann, *Das Evangelium nach Matthäus* (Berlin: Evangelische Verlagsanstalt, 1975), p. 483. Hill, however, says the reference is 'not simply a metaphor' but there was an 'actual stone seat in front of the synagogue, where the authoritative teacher (usually a Scribe) sat' (D. Hill, *The Gospel of Matthew* [London: Marshall, Morgan & Scott, 1972], p. 310). Hill predominantly bases his analysis on S. Sowers, 'The Circumstances and Recollection of the Pella Flight', *Theologische Zeitschrift* 26 (1970), pp. 305–20, for whom there is considerable support including Benoit, *Matthieu*, p. 139; K. Stendahl, *The School of St. Matthew and Its Use of the Old Testament* (Philadelphia: Fortress, 1968), p. 792; Gundry, *Matthew*, pp. 435–54.

167 Beare, *Matthew*, p. 448.

168 Noted in Davies and Allison, *Matthew 3*, p. 270.

169 R. Hummel, *Die Auseinandersetzung zwishcen Kirche und Judentum im Matthäus-evangelium* (Munich: Chr. Kaiser Verlag, 1966), pp. 31–32.

this, to say the least, strains credibility.[170] Some commentators have gone so far as to suggest that an emendation be accepted on the basis of sy^c and that in place of ποιήσατε καὶ τηρεῖτε (do and keep), ἀκούετε should be read so that the meaning would be 'Hear what they tell you but do not do as they do.'[171] However, as is evident from the external evidence, there is no trace of Syrus Curetonianus' reading in any other manuscript tradition and this would be a very difficult case to argue, especially given the interpretive difficulty of the phrase and the potential motivation for scribal change. Others have suggested that the imperatives (having identical morphological form) should be replaced by indicatives, i.e. 'whatever they say to you, you (as a matter of fact) do and observe'.[172] Others have suggested that the key to understanding vv. 2-3a is the use of the aorist ἐκάθισαν to refer to an earlier period. In this regard, Allen says 'the editor writes from his own standpoint, and looks back at a time when the scribes and the Pharisees were in power'.[173] However, the following two imperatives suggest a present aspect. If the aorist is understood as a gnomic, i.e. a timeless, action, the difficulty resolves,[174] that is, except for the residual problem of why one should nonetheless 'do and keep' what they say. Another solution which hinges on ἐκάθισαν is reflected in the NASV's translation: 'scribes and Pharisees have seated themselves in the chair of Moses'.[175] Lenski argues that this position has been usurped without divine commissioning,

> With ἐκάθισαν Jesus states merely the fact, which does not in any way admit the right of these men to Moses' seat. They were not called to this seat as Moses had been. He assumed the seat reluctantly, but these false followers of his assumed his seat of their own accord and were determined to have and

170 The suggestion by J. Jeremias, *New Testament Theology* (London: SCM Press, 1971), p. 210 and D. A. Carson, *The Sermon on the Mount* (Grand Rapids, MI: Eerdmans, 1978), pp. 472–74 that we are here dealing with irony, or hyperbole, has neither received widespread support nor has it been developed beyond cursory citation.

171 A. Merx, *Die vier kanonischen Evangelien nach ihrem ältesten bekannten Texte: Das Evangelium Matthaeus* (Berlin: Georg Reimer, 1902), pp. 319–22.

172 See Davies and Allison, *Matthew 3*, p. 270. Klosterman, *Matthäusevangelium*, p. 233 also understands the phrase as concessive, 'although you …'.

173 W. C. Allen, *A Critical and Exegetical Commentary on the Gospel According to St. Matthew* (Edinburgh: T&T Clark, 1912), pp. 243–44; cf. F. Hahn, *The Titles of Jesus in Christology: Their History in Early Christianity* (trans. H. Knight and G. Ogg; New York: World, 1969), p. 402 n.1; Garland, *Intention*, p. 47 n.41.

174 See examples of the gnomic aorist in W. W. Goodwin, *A Greek Grammar* (London: Macmillan, 1916), §1292; N. Turner, *A Grammar of New Testament Greek: IV Style* (Edinburgh: T&T Clark, 1976), p. 33.

175 W. Beilner, *Christus und die Pharisäer: Exegetische Untersuchung über Grund und Verlauf der Auseinandersetzungen* (Vienna: Herder, 1959), p. 20 n.13; J. H. Moulton and W. F. Howard, *A Grammar of New Testament Greek: Accidence and Word Formation* (Edinburgh: Clark, 1929), p. 458; T. Zahn, *Das Evangelium des Matthäus* (Leipzig: Deichert, 1903), p. 641.

hold it. They were self-appointed usurpers and acted as though their dicta were as binding as the revelations God made to Moses, 15.3-9.[176]

As ingenious as this suggestion is, there is little other corroborating support.[177] A more promising hypothesis is that proposed by Gnilka who suggests that vv. 2-3a should be understood in a restricted or qualified sense, in that people were encouraged to 'keep and do' only when Moses was truly taught.[178] Gundry says 'so long as sitting in Moses' seat qualifies the speaking of the scribes and Pharisees, "all things whatever" does not include their interpretive traditions, but emphasizes the totality of the law'. [179] Allen similarly states, 'we must suppose that a limitation is to be inferred from "sit in Moses' seat." Do all things that they teach, insofar as in harmony with the spirit of the Mosaic law'.[180] A significant modification of this, which ultimately seems to resolve the tension of vv. 2-3a, is Powell's reading, which proposes a model based on the scribes and Pharisees' 'social position as people who controlled accessibility to Torah'. Because no copy of the Torah was available, it was necessary for them to learn Torah from the synagogue. In this sense they should 'do and keep' what the scribes and Pharisees εἴπωσιν (speak, i.e. Torah recitation), but not follow their interpretation.[181] As Powell notes, support for this comes from an interchange between Jesus and his disciples after the transfiguration. In 17.10 the disciples refer to Mal. 3.22 [LXX; 3.23 MT; 4.5 Eng.] though not asking 'why do the scriptures say ...?' but 'why do the scribes say that Elijah must come first?'[182] Powell concludes: 'apparently their only knowledge of scripture is what they have heard from the scribes'.[183] This approach

176 R. C. H. Lenski, *The Interpretation of St. Matthew's Gospel* (Ohio: Wartburg Press, 1943), pp. 893–94.

177 A further view is that the injunction to 'do and keep' was binding only during the pre-resurrection period. Waetjen, *Origin*, pp. 216–19; J. P. Meier, *Law and History in Matthew's Gospel* (Rome: Biblical Institute, 1976), pp. 25–40; J. P. Meier, *The Vision of Matthew: Christ, Church and Morality in the First Gospel* (New York: Paulist Press, 1979), pp. 26–39; and J. Marcus, 'The Gates of Hades and the Keys of the Kingdom (Matt. 16:18–19)', *CBQ* 50 (1988), pp. 453–54 note that just as every detail of the law was to be kept (5.19) and that the mission was to be exclusively directed towards Israel (10.5), so too were there other temporal aspects which needed qualification. Powell, however, finds this unconvincing and points to Mt. 18.17 as evidence that 'Matthew blurs the distinction between the two epochs' of initial presentation and later church (Powell, 'Do and Keep', p. 426).

178 Gnilka, *Matthäusevangelium*, p. 2.274.

179 Gundry, *Matthew*, p. 455. This view is also represented in the church fathers: Chrysostom *Hom. On Mt.* 72.1; Calvin *Inst.* 4.10.26. Cf. Haenchen, 'Matthäus 23', pp. 135–36.

180 Allen, *Matthew*, p. 244. Also see Bonnard, *L'Evangile*, p. 334; Gundry, *Matthew*, p. 454–55; Plummer, *Matthew*, p. 314.

181 Powell, 'Do and Keep', pp. 419–35.

182 Powell, 'Do and Keep', p. 434.

183 Powell, 'Do and Keep', p. 434.

seems most plausibly to account for the injunction to 'do and keep' all that the scribes and Pharisees say. The residual issue of the seat of Moses can also be understood as a reference either to their necessary position as keepers of the Torah, or to affirming the office without necessarily affirming those who occupy it.

Verses 2-3a state that 'The scribes and the Pharisees sit on Moses' seat; therefore, do whatever they teach you and follow it.' Rather than undermining our conclusion that ch. 23 functions as the Deuteronomistic woes of covenantal infidelity, these verses highlight the leaders' position of authority and responsibility with which they are endowed, which in turn magnifies their culpability. It may then be possible to accept an informed reading of Beare,[184] to which Hill says 'the point may be to give the maximum force to the subsequent denunciation of the actions of the scribes'.[185] Cook similarly concludes that the introduction gives force to the following material by 'methodologically dismantl[ing]' the references to the scribes and Pharisees.[186]

2.8. *The Problem of Hypocrisy as Deuteronomistic Curses*

An additional problem arises in our hypothesis if one accepts the language in Matthew 23 as reflecting, in a generalized sense, the Deuteronomistic curses of covenantal infidelity. One may legitimately question to what extent 'hypocrisy' per se is present at all in Deuteronomy 27-30, and as such, question its identification with the Matthean parallel. M.A. Powell has argued, following on from his discussion of the 'chair of Moses', that the ὑπόκρισις of Matthew 23 refers not to ones who do not 'practice what they preach',[187] but rather to 'a discrepancy between the inward nature observed by God and the outward appearance observed by others'.[188] This approach has particular merit because, in light of Matthew's narrative as a whole, it would be difficult to support the idea that Jesus affirms the teaching but not the practice of the scribes and Pharisees. As noted in our discussion above, both are condemned as inadequate. The εἴπωσιν of 23.3b should be understood as a reference to speaking or reading Torah, whereas the ἔργα αὐτῶν refer to their inadequate exegesis, and as such they are not to be followed (μὴ ποιεῖτε) as they make void the word of God for the sake of tradition (Mt. 15.6,

---

184 See above; Beare, *Matthew*, p. 448.

185 Hill, *Matthew*, p. 310; Stendahl, *School*, p. 792.

186 M. J. Cook, *Mark's Treatment of the Jewish Leaders* (Leiden: Brill, 1997), pp. 144–45.

187 See Powell, 'Do and Keep', p. 423. This interpretation has been made popular by certain modern translations of μὴ ποιεῖτε· λέγουσιν γὰρ καὶ οὐ ποιοῦσιν as 'for they do not practice what they preach', cf. NIV, (N)JB, RSV, TEB.

188 Powell, 'Do and Keep', p. 423.

cf. v. 2). Powell concludes: 'the popular notion of a hypocrite who says one thing and does another has no support in Matthew's Gospel even though, ironically, it probably derives from mistranslations and misrepresentations of this Matthean text (23.2-3)'.[189]

Although, in some regard, Powell satisfies our initial question of the charge of hypocrisy, there is still the residual problem of the remaining seven references to the scribes and Pharisees as ὑποκριταί in 23.13, 15, 23, 25, 27, 28, and 29. It seems that the most satisfactory response to this apparent tension involves understanding the words of condemnation in Matthew 23 as 'typical of that found among rival claimants to a philosophical tradition'.[190] L. T. Johnson has argued that this phenomenon 'is found as widely among Jews as among other Hellenists',[191] and that in antiquity 'the way the NT talks about Jews is ... the way all opponents talked about each other'.[192] We proceed with examples from both Hellenistic and Jewish primary sources.[193]

The most common context for rhetorical interaction in the Hellenistic world was between public preachers. At one poignant moment in Dio of Prussa's attack on the sophists, he refers to them as 'ignorant, boastful, self-deceived' (*Or.* 4.33), 'evil spirited' (*Or.* 4.38), and 'mindless' (*Or.* 54.1). The strong language employed is surprising, given that elsewhere the sophists are referred to as also embodying positive characteristics. Johnson suggests that this interplay indicates that the polemic 'has nothing to do with specific actions, but typical ones'.[194] Similarly, in Aelius Aristides' *Platonic Discourses* he attacks the philosophers saying that 'they despise others while being themselves worthy of scorn. They criticize others without examining themselves. They make a great show of virtue and never practice it' (*Plat. Dis.* 307.6), they have an outward appearance of virtue but are inwardly corrupt (307.10), and they are only after pleasure and wealth (307.15; 308.5).[195] A disciple of Epicurus, Colotes, attacked Plutarch, priest of Apollo, by labelling his philosophical forefathers 'buffoons, charlatans, assassins, prostitutes, nincompoops' (Plutarch, *Mor.* 1086E). Significant for our discussion is where Socrates is chastised as an 'arrogant boaster' (ἀλαζών) because he said one thing and did another. In like manner, Epictetus refers to the Platonists by saying, 'You will be no better than we who bear the name Stoics, for we too talk

189 Powell, 'Do and Keep', p. 423. This position, then, undermines the claim that the scribes and Pharisees are charged with hypocrisy per se.

190 L. T. Johnson, 'The New Testament's Anti-Jewish Slander and the Conventions of Ancient Polemic', *JBL* 108 (1989), pp. 419-41 (429).

191 Johnson, *Polemic*, p. 429.

192 Johnson, *Polemic*, p. 429.

193 For reference to these primary sources I am indebted to Johnson, *Polemic*, pp. 430-41 and Davies and Allison, *Matthew 3*, pp. 258-63.

194 Johnson, *Polemic*, p. 430.

195 Noted by Johnson, *Polemic*, pp. 430-31.

of one thing and do another; we talk of the noble and do the base ...'
(3.7.17).[196] Lucan of Samosata condemns the interactions of Apollonius
of Tyana and Euphrates as both 'proselytisers'[197] and 'hypocrites'.[198]
Johnson concludes that such diatribe formed a *topos*, in the sense that
'certain standard categories of vice were automatically attributed to any
opponent'.[199]

This is also evident in the polemics attested in extant sources of various
Jewish factions. Although other examples could be multiplied,[200] the
most expressive in this regard are references in the Dead Sea Scrolls to
those who did not belong to the community, otherwise known as the

---

196 At another point he says 'your doctrines are bad, subversive of the state, destructive of the family, not even fit for women' (*Diss.* 3.7.21).

197 Cf. Mt. 23.15 'for you cross sea and land to make a single convert', which is often quoted for supporting a widespread movement of Pharisaic proselytising. Others have taken the phrase idiomatically to refer to going to great lengths. There is also a relevant comment in Horace's *Satires* 1.4.138–43: 'like Jews we will command you to yield to our throng' (*veluti Iudaei cogemus in hanc concendere turbam*). However, the only evidence for an explicitly organized Jewish proselytizing campaign is found in the policies of the Hasmonaeans toward the Idumaeans and Ituraeans in the late second century BC (*Ant.* 13.257–258; 13.319). In 139 BC Jews were allegedly expelled from Rome 'because they attempted to transmit their sacred rites to the Romans', noted in Valerius Maximus 1.3.3 (cf. E. N. Lane, 'Sabazius and the Jews in Valerius Maximus: A Re-examination', *JRS* 69 [1979], pp. 35–38). Another similar incident occurred in 19 AD under Tiberius, in which Jews were expelled because they were 'converting many of the natives to their customs' (Cassius Dio *Historia Romana* 57.18.5a); Josephus blames four individuals who deceived a proselyte named Fulvia (*Ant.* 18.3.4 §65–84); cf. Tacitus *Annals* 2.85.5; Suetonius *Tiberius* 36.1. Apart from these limited references there is very slim evidence to suggest that Jewish missionaries were sent out from any central authority into the Greek or Roman world. This does not militate against proselytizing in a less formal way. Baron states 'although there were no professional missionaries, uninterrupted religious propaganda seems to have gone on throughout the dispersion. There must have been Jews among the itinerant preachers and rhetoricians who voyaged from city to city, propagandizing for one or another idea' (S. Baron, *A Social and Religious History of the Jews* [New York: Columbia University Press, 1952], p. 173). Although there is evidence of some proselytizing activity (and one would expect this since Israel was founded on the premise that it was to be a blessing to the nations Gen. 12.1-3), there was nothing like a missionary movement in the sense in which a Christian mission developed. Jewish proselytizing was sporadic and unorganized as far as our sources indicate (cf. *Ant.* 20.38–48).

198 *A True Story* 4; *The Carousal* 6–48; *Icanomenippus* 20–21; 29–34; *Timmon* 54–57; *The Fishermen* 29–38; *Double Indictment* 6–12; *The Parasite* 43–56; *Menippus* 3–5; *The Runaways* 12–21; *Hermotimus* 11; *Dialogues of the Dead* 369–70; *Dialogues of the Courtesans* 306–308.

199 Johnson, *Polemic*, p. 432. Hypocrisy and love of glory were two main categories of condemnation. For references to the love of glory see *Dio Oration* 32.10, 11, 19, 20, 24; 33.1, 9-10; Epictetus *Diss.* 1.21.3-4; 1.26.9; 2.16.11; 2.17.3; 2.21.9; 3.2.10–14; 3.12.1; 3.14.4; 3.23.10–14; 3.26.13; Lucan *Proteus Peregrinus* 1, 4, 20, 38, 42.

200 See multitudinous examples in Davies and Allison, *Matthew 3*, pp. 259–60, including accusations of 'hypocrisy' (Mt. 23.13-36), *Pss Sol.* 4.6-7; 1QS 4.14; *Ass. Mos.* 7.5-10; Philo *Em. Gai.* 25.162; *Apion* 2.142–44; and 'blindness' (Mt. 23.16, 17, 24), *1 En.* 90.7; *Wis.* 2.21; Philo *Vit con.* 2.10; *Apion* 2.142; *War* 5.572.

'sons of darkness' (1QS 1.10; 1QM 1.7) or 'sons of the pit' (1QS 9.16; 4Q265 6.15; 13.14). The Community Rule (1QS 4.9-14) refers to the outsiders in the following manner:

> The operations of the spirit of falsehood result in greed, neglect of righteous deeds, wickedness, lying, pride and haughtiness, cruel deceit and fraud, massive hypocrisy, a want of self-control and abundant foolishness, a zeal for arrogance, abominable deeds fashioned by whorish desire, lechery in its filthy manifestation, a reviling tongue, blind eyes, deaf ears, stiff neck and hard heart; to the end of walking in all the ways of darkness and evil cunning. The judgment of all who walk in such ways will be multiple afflictions at the hand of all the angels of perdition, everlasting damnation in the wrath of God's furious vengeance, never-ending terror and reproach for all eternity, with a shameful extinction in the fire of Hell's outer darkness. For all their eras, generation by generation, they will know doleful sorrow, bitter evil and dark happenstance, until their utter destruction with neither remnant nor rescue.

Davis and Allison note that 'the covenanters laid every sort of pejorative adjective upon the "sons of darkness," whom [also] they cursed in their rituals', so that 'the language of vilification was as stereotyped as the language of praise'.[201] Other Jewish writers similarly spare little courtesy. Josephus chastises Apion as having the 'mind of an ass' and the 'impudence of a dog' (*Apion* 2.86); as being ignorant (2.26; 2.130); a fool (2.37); stupid and blind (2.142). In *War*, Josephus condemns the Zealots as 'assassins' (2.255–58); 'imposters and brigands' (2.264); 'slaves, the dregs of society, and the bastard scum of the nation' (5.443–44). Philo mocks his Egyptian opponents in *The Embassy to Gaius* in referring to them as 'a seed bed of evil, in whose souls both the venom and the temper of the native crocodiles and wasps are reproduced ... ' (26.166).

In light of these parallels, one may plausibly conclude that Matthew presents Jesus using conventional condemnatory language, that is 'standard polemical *topoi*',[202] wherein the main 'thing that such slander indicated ... was that someone *was* an opponent'.[203] In this regard Davies and Allison conclude that 'the way the NT talks about its Jewish opponents is just the way all opponents talked about each other back then'.[204] If then, the language of hypocrisy, blindness, foolishness, etc. was conventional to the type of interaction,[205] we should not be surprised to find such vocabulary in Matthew's narrative when he records interactions between Jesus and his opponents. Thus, one need not discount the proposed parallel between the

---

201 Davies and Allison, *Matthew* 3, p. 260.
202 Davies and Allison, *Matthew* 3, p. 259.
203 Johnson, *Polemic*, p. 433.
204 Davies and Allison, *Matthew* 3, p. 258.
205 Although, interestingly blindness as a curse does occur in Deut. 28.28-29.

woes of Matthew 23 and the curses of Deuteronomy 27–30 based upon the apparent discrepancy in description of the polemic. Indeed, as Davies and Allison have noted, this technique 'emphasize[s] the conventional nature of the chapter's polemical rhetoric'.[206] Our attention will now be devoted to a similarly important issue: how other Jewish material, contemporary with Matthew, responded to and accounted for the destruction of the temple.

2.9. Significant Parallels in Jewish Literature[207]

Several commentators have noted the connection between Israel's covenantal infidelity and the destruction of the temple in inter-testamental Jewish literature. G. W. E. Nickelsburg notes that there are four major Jewish works which were written shortly after 70 AD and account for the temple's destruction in like fashion – the covenantal infidelity of Israel:[208] the *Apocalypse of Abraham*; *2 Baruch*; *4 Ezra*; and *Liber Antiquintatum Biblicarum*. To these can also be added *1, 3*, and *4 Baruch*, and *Josephus*. The manner in which this contributes to our discussion is relatively clear. Matthew joins a similar theological trajectory in associating the destruction of the temple, not ultimately to a pagan cause, but to inappropriate Israelite worship and cultic activity.

206 Davies and Allison, *Matthew 3*, p. 258. However, to see prophetic condemnation in the form of shared categories of denunciation as merely 'conventional name-calling ... simply a matter of convention, a touch of bravado', as Wilson, *When*, p. 103 suggests, is to miss the point. Here, Matthew's Jesus uses the available categories to denounce those who are opposed to him. A rather crass modern equivalent would to be call someone a 'bastard' or a 'bitch', without implying that the interlocutor is either a child born to unmarried parents or a female dog, wolf, fox, or otter. Although in some sense the scribes and Pharisees are condemned for their playacting (ὑπόκρισις) and ostentatious display of religiosity, this does not, as has been argued above, exclude the discourse from referring to the Deuteronomistic covenant.

207 See Davila's discussion as to what extent works preserved by Christian tradition can be considered Jewish: J. Davila, *The Provenance of the Pseudepigrapha* (Leiden: Brill, 2005).

208 G. W. E. Nickelsburg, *Jewish Literature between the Bible and the Mishnah. A Historical and Literary Introduction* (Minneapolis: Fortress Press, 1981), p. 77.

2.9.a. Apocalypse of Abraham[209]

R. Rubinkiewicz describes the Apocalypse of Abraham as concerned mainly with 'Israel's election and covenant'[210] presented in terms of a haggadic 'midrash based on the text of Genesis 15'.[211] The work displays some similarities with the Testament of Abraham but is differentiated by its 'greater sense of urgency that pervades its eschatological aspirations. This ... pondering of the ways of God and his justice ... is aroused by the reactions of the writer to the destruction of the Second Temple.'[212] The work falls into two distinct parts. Chapters 1–8 consist of a narrative concerned with Abraham's tragicomic discovery of God, in which he turns from making idols for his father's family business to worshipping God. Chapters 9–32 are an apocalyptic revelation granted to him in response to his prayer. The sequence is initiated with a vision of the divine court (God, his throne and attendants, chs 17–18), followed by scenes of the cosmic order (19–21). Chapters 22ff. go on to show what will happen to humanity. As Stone has commented, the 'later part of this revelation centers on the sin of Adam and its implications for mankind, as well as the destruction of the temple and its aftermath'.[213] Hall similarly concludes that 'the most obvious problem addressed by the ApAb concerns the destruction of the Temple in Jerusalem'.[214] Most modern discussions of *Apoc. Abr.* concern the redactional puzzle of ch. 29, which many have seen as a Christian interpolation.[215] Notwithstanding the complexities of this debate, our attention will

---

209 J. H. Charlesworth dates the *Apoc. Abr.* to the last two decades of the first century AD. J. H. Charlesworth, *The Pseudepigrapha and Modern Research* (Missoula: Scholars Press, 1981), pp. 68–69; also see discussion in R. G. Hall, *Revealed Histories* (Sheffield: Academic Press, 1991), pp. 75–79. *Apoc. Abr.* is preserved only in the Old Slavonic translation, but is unanimously believed to be derived from a Semitic original, see A. Kulik, *Retroverting Slavonic Pseudepigrapha: Toward the Original of the Apocalypse of Abraham* (Atlanta: Society of Biblical Literature, 2004), R. Rubinkiewicz, 'Apokalipsa Abraham', *Ruch Biblijny i Liturgiczny* 27 (1974), pp. 230–37; idem, 'La Vision de l'histoire dans l'Apocalypse d'Abraham', *ANRW* 2.19.1 (1979), pp. 137–51; idem, 'Apocalypse of Abraham', in *The Old Testament Pseudepigrapha*, ed. J. H. Charlesworth (2 vols; London: Darton, Longman & Todd, 1983), pp. 1.681–705 (681–88); idem, 'Les sémitismes dans l'Apocalypse d'Abraham', *Folia Orientalia* 21 (1989), pp. 141–48.

210 Rubinkiewicz, 'Apocalypse', p. 681.

211 R. Rubinkiewicz, 'Abraham, Apocalypse of', in *Anchor Bible Dictionary*, ed. D. N. Freedman (Vol. 1; New York: Doubleday, 1992), pp. 41–43.

212 M. Stone, 'Apocalyptic Literature', in *Jewish Writings of the Second Temple Period*, ed. M. Stone (Assen: Van Gorcum, 1984), pp. 383–441 (416).

213 Stone, 'Apocalyptic', p. 415.

214 Hall, *Revealed*, pp. 75–79.

215 See discussion in M. Philonenko, 'Le Poimandrès et la liturgie juive', in *Les syncrétismes dans les religions de L'antiquité*, ed. F. Dunand et al. (Leiden: Brill, 1975), pp. 204–11; Rubinkiewicz, 'La Vision', pp. 137–51; Stone, 'Apocalyptic', p. 415; R. G. Hall, 'The "Christian Interpolation" in the Apocalypse of Abraham', *JBL* 107 (1998), pp. 107–109.

focus upon the structural arrangement of material preceding ch. 27 (the destruction of the temple).

The depiction of the Fall of Adam and Eve (*Apoc. Abr.* 23) prompts Abraham's question of theodicy – why has God permitted Azazel to have such influence? God responds by saying that he has delivered those who do evil to the devil, who prods them to do evil.[216] Yet Abraham presses the question further: Why does God permit sin to be willed? The divine response is unfortunately obscured by a textual corruption at the beginning of ch. 24.[217] The material which follows in ch. 24 (or more specifically 24.3–25.2) is a catalogue of sins, presented as a series of seven (cf. seven woes of Matthew 23).[218] Each of the seven sins are introduced with the identical phrase 'And I saw … '. (1) The Fall of Adam and Eve (24.5a); (2) Cain's murder of Abel (24.5b); (3) fornication (24.6); (4) theft (24.7); (5) naked men bringing harm against their friends (24.8); (6) lawlessness (24.9); (7) idol of jealousy and infant slaughter (25.1-2). It is significant to note that the seventh sin is elaborated upon in ch. 25. What is immediately apparent is that this sin occurs within the temple and is related to the sacrificial system or, in this case, the sacrificial system's perversion.

Nickelsburg notes that, although Abraham is permitted to see an idealized vision of the temple and altar, it is marred by 'the presence of cultic abominations'.[219] Instructive in this regard are the religious authorities who are indicted for the desecration of the temple. M. McNamara concludes that 'God narrates to Abraham the fall of man and the idolatry of Abraham's own descendants … [in which] their infidelity will bring about the judgment.'[220] Nickelsburg suggests that the author may simply be following biblical tradition which held Jerusalem's former destruction in 586 BC as punishment for Manasseh's sin (2 Kgs 21.10-15).[221] Furthermore, the reference to idolatry could be a literary technique designed to recall Abraham's own past (*Apoc. Abr.* 1–8) as one in which he faithfully abandoned the idols of his father. When the nation later adopts Abraham's pre-encounter and rejection of idolatry, it does so at its own destruction. Given the time of writing and its proximity to the Roman destruction of the temple, this strongly suggests that the author was attempting to link the events of 70 AD with Israel's inappropriate cultic activity. This is certainly evident in the divine response to Abraham's anguished question, 'Why must it be so?' (*Apoc. Abr.* 27.6).

216 Nickelsburg, *Literature*, p. 296.

217 Nickelsburg, *Literature*, p. 296.

218 There is a similar situation portrayed in the *T. Abr.* 10 in which Abraham sees three different sins: murder, fornication, and thievery.

219 Nickelsburg, *Literature*, pp. 296–97.

220 M. McNamara, *Intertestamental Literature* (Wilmington: Michael Glazier, 1983), p. 84.

221 Nickelsburg, *Literature*, p. 298.

Apocalypse of Abraham 27.7 makes clear that the temple was destroyed because of false cultic worship.[222]

> And he [the Mighty One] said to me, 'Listen, Abraham, all that you have seen will happen on account of your seed who will (continually) provoke me because of the body which you saw and the murder in which was depicted in the Temple of jealousy and everything you saw will be so

In this regard James Mueller comments that 'heavy emphasis is placed on the cult ... Improper cultic practices have brought about the destruction of the Temple.'[223] The importance of an appropriate sacrificial system is emphasized in *Apoc. Abr.* 11–15, where Abraham perfectly fulfils all the requirements for the preparation of the sacrifice.[224]

In chs 27-29 the vision turns to the main eschatological section in its depiction of the consequent destruction of the temple and judgement of covenantal infidelity.[225] Licht notes that 'God has permitted this [destruction] for cultic abominations that Abraham had earlier witnessed [i.e. 24.3-25.2].'[226] And this, in a sense, somewhat alleviates the sharper question of 'Israel's status as God's people and its fate at the hands of the Gentiles'.[227] It seems to be no coincidence that the fate of Terah's house in *Apoc. Abr.* 8 and the fate of the Jerusalem temple in ch. 27 (see esp. vv. 3, 5) both suffer the same punishment of burning with fire because of their infidelity to God.

2.9.b. 2 (Syriac) Baruch

A similar theme is also found in *2 Bar.* in which the opening lines tell of the city being destroyed because of Israel's sin. In an ironic twist, emphasis is specifically averted from the tyrannical king. Responsibility lies with the people of Israel who oppress the king, 'for the former tribes were forced by their kings to sin, but these two have themselves forced and compelled their kings to sin'. *2 Baruch* 1.1-5 declares that in the twenty-fifth year of Jeconiah, God spoke to Baruch and showed him the great evil that was being perpetrated on the earth. The evil of the two tribes is described as outweighing the sinfulness of the ten which led to the Assyrian invasion.

As with several other late-first-century apocalypses, *2 Bar.* uses a fictional Babylonian setting as paradigmatic for the destruction of the temple in

---

222 See further discussion in Hall, *Revealed*, pp. 75–79.

223 J. R. Mueller, 'The Apocalypse of Abraham and the Destruction of the Second Jewish Temple', in *SBL Seminar Papers* (1982), pp. 341–49 (347).

224 Cf. *Apoc. Abr.* 17.10, 'Accept my prayer and delight in it, and (accept) also the sacrifice which you yourself made to yourself through me as I searched for you.'

225 The division of the present age into twelve parts is common to this type of material, cf. *4 Ez.* 14.12; *2 Bar.* 27; 53.6.

226 J. Licht, 'Abraham: Apocalypse of', *EJ* 2 (1972), pp. 126–27.

227 Nickelsburg, *Literature*, p. 297.

70 CE.[228] The main resolution to the question of theodicy consists of Israel being punished justly for her transgressions. The nation is presented as privileged, having Abraham as her father (78.4) and possessing God's promises (78.7), knowledge (14.5) and Law (48.24; 77.3). As such, the author stresses Israel's greater responsibility, 'But now, because he trespassed, having understanding, he will be punished because he has understanding' (*2 Bar.* 15.6); 'They, however, sinned and trespassed ... although they knew they had the Law to reprove them' (*2 Bar.* 19.3). Yet because they have now sinned (1.2; 77.8-10), deserved punishment will ensue (4.1; 6.9; 13.9; 78.3; 79.2) in the form of the destruction of the temple (1.4).

Baruch's lament begins with a beatitude to those who will not experience Jerusalem's fate and anticipates the horrendous nature of the destruction, 'Blessed is he who was not born, or he who was born and died ... (10.6-7). Baruch then summons all creation to mourn Jerusalem's punishment. Of particular significance is the reference to the priests being condemned for inappropriate leadership and cultic activity. In *2 Bar.* 10.18 Baruch exhorts 'You priests, take the keys of the sanctuary and cast them to the highest heaven, and give them to the Lord and say, "Guard your house yourself, because, behold, we have been found to be false stewards."'[229] The seriousness of this is emphasized by the motif of God and his angels acting as the agents of destruction. Rather than merely allowing Jerusalem to fall, the divine forces are said to have destroyed the city in *2 Bar.* 5.3; 6.8; 8.1-2. R. Marks concludes that the 'downfall [is] attributed to the will of God rather than its conqueror's strength or defenders' weakness'.[230] This is a common theme in various Old Testament, inter-testamental, and rabbinic sources,[231] and is employed here to emphasize the note of calamity.

2.9.c. 3 (Greek) Baruch

In similar manner to *2 Bar.* and *Apoc. Abr.*, *3 Bar.* is fictionally set against the Babylonian destruction of the temple in dealing with questions of theodicy after 70 AD. After an extensive lamentation on King Nebuchadnezzar plundering the city, Baruch poses the question as to why God has 'set fire to your vineyard?' Baruch defensively notes how the destruction of the city may result in the 'heathen ... reproach[ing] us saying "Where is their God?"' (*3 Bar.* 1.1-2).

---

228 Nickelsburg, *Literature*, p. 287; Charlesworth, *Pseudepigrapha*, pp. 616–17; P. M. Bogaert, *L' Apocalypse de Baruch* (2 vols; Paris: Editions du Cerf, 1969), pp. 1.294–95.

229 Also to note is *4 Bar.* 4.3-4, which has affinities with all those works attributed to Baruch in two regards: (1) Israel is justly punished because of transgression of the Mosaic covenant, and (2) the destruction is executed at God's will.

230 R. G. Marks, *Image of Bar Kokhba* (Philadelphia: Penn State Press, 2004), p. 35 n.48.

231 See similar themes in 1 Chron. 21.15-16; 2 Sam. 24.16; *1 En.* 56.5-8.

At various instances throughout the work the author lists several catalogues of sins. Chapter 4 is typical when it condemns drunkenness, lack of mercy, murder, adultery, fornication, perjury, and theft (*3 Bar.* 4.17). At one point the sinfulness of the people on earth is envisaged as so serious that it is said to defile the rays of the sun (*3 Bar.* 8.4-5; cf. 13.4).

Nickelsburg notes the significance of the allusion in *3 Bar.* 16.2 to Deut. 32.21 when he states 'the language of ... the divine sentence indicates that the author answers Baruch's question by interpreting the destruction of Jerusalem and the scattering of the people as punishment for their sins'.[232] Furthermore, in contradistinction to previous inter-testamental texts reviewed, *3 Bar.* does not refer to a future glorified national Jerusalem. Rather, Land and Temple are replaced with post-mortem personal blessings and cursings (i.e. individualized eschatology). And in this way the focus seems to be on the importance of Israel's sin, even to the level of personal accountability.

2.9.d. 4 Ezra *(2 Esd. 3–14)*

Although *4 Ezra* claims to be written by Ezra in Babylon thirty years after the destruction of 'our city' (Zion) (3.1), it is clearly an apocalyptic, pseudonymous piece of Jewish literature[233] written one generation after the destruction of the Jerusalem temple within the last decade of the first century AD.[234] Its main theme is the incongruency of the catastrophe which had come upon Israel in light of her election and covenantal status as Yahweh's chosen people (3.30, 32). *4 Ezra* is structured into seven visions/episodes, in which the seer has revelatory encounters in an attempt to explain this conundrum. The third vision (6.35–9.25) concludes Ezra's first series of triplicate lament/complaint by recounting the story of creation and asking 'If the world has indeed been created for us, why do we not possess the world for our inheritance?' (6.59). Although the

---

232 Nickelsburg, *Literature*, p. 302.

233 The original was written in a Semitic language yet has not survived, neither has it survived in its Greek translation of the Hebrew/Aramaic (or in Rabbinic tradition). See M. Stone, 'Esdras, Second Book of', in *Anchor Bible Dictionary*, ed. D. N. Freedman (vol. 2; New York: Doubleday, 1992), pp. 634–37 (611); see also R. P. Blake, 'The Georgian Version of Fourth Esdras from the Jerusalem Manuscript', *HTR* 19 (1926), pp. 299–375.

234 On the basis of external evidence it is difficult to be more definitive than to conclude anything before its citations (see above footnote). However, on the basis of the rather complex imagery in the fifth vision, the middle head has been identified as Domitian (81–96 AD). As there is no evidence that Domitian had died, many claim *4 Ezra* was written before 96 AD. M. Stone writes: 'The book stems from the last decade of the first century A.D. and was composed in reaction to the Roman destruction of Jerusalem in A.D. 70. Its primary concern, therefore, is to understand that traumatic event,' M. Stone, 'Fourth Ezra', in *Harper's Bible Commentary*, ed. J. L. Mays (San Francisco: Harper and Row, 1988), pp. 776–77. D. J. Harrington writes, 'the Babylonian exile of the sixth century B.C.E. becomes the literary occasion for exploring the theological issues raised by the recent destruction of Jerusalem and its temple in 70 C.E. under the Romans', D. J. Harrington, *Invitation to the Apocrypha* (Grand Rapids: Eerdmans, 1999), pp. 189–90.

author seems to conclude that God's ways are inscrutable and reserved for unique divine knowledge (4.21; 5.40), there are several hints that the rationale for Jerusalem's destruction rests at the feet of its inhabitants. Uriel, Ezra's angelic accompanier, reveals that Israel is under judgement for her sin (7.9-10): 'If now that city is given to a man for an inheritance, how will the heir receive his inheritance unless he passes through the danger set before him? I said, "He cannot, lord." And he said to me, "So also is Israel's portion."' Sin is defined as unfaithfulness to the law (9.36), which has consequently resulted in alienation and estrangement from God (7.48). At one point our author is a strong advocate for free will (3.8; 8.56-58); however, at other points he also affirms humanity's solidarity with Adam (7.118)[235] in sharing the *cor malignum* (evil heart, 3.20). This grain of evil seed (*granum seminis mali*) has been inherited by all descendants (4.30) and thus all are similarly responsible.[236] The fourth vision (9.26–10.59), although prefaced with echoes of a complaint (9.26-37), is a turning point in the narrative, in that Ezra accepts Israel's responsibility for her sin and consequent judgement: 'For we who have received the Law and sinned will perish, as well as our heart which received it' (9.36).

2.9.e. Book of Biblical Antiquities

The work entitled *Liber Antiquitatum Biblicarum* (*LAB*) is a 're-written bible'[237] which retells Israel's history from Adam to the death of Saul.[238] It is considered to be a 'product of the same school as the Fourth Book of Esdras and the Apocalypse of Baruch, and written, like them, in the years following the destruction of Jerusalem in 70 AD'.[239] It raises the crucial question of whether the destruction of Jerusalem because of Israel's sin dictated the end of her covenantal status. In this regard it is important to note that Israel's *sin*, particularly her idolatry, is presupposed as the cause of the city's destruction. Of Israel's apostasy in worshipping the golden calf, *LAB* 12.4-5a has God lament that the people, after they have entered the promised land, will commit further iniquity.

235 For the fascinating story regarding the lost Latin text of *4 Ezra* 7 see B. Metzger, 'The "Lost" Sections of II Esdras (IV Ezra)', *JBL* 76 (1957), pp. 153–56.

236 For a detailed discussion of responsibility for evil in *4 Ezra* see A. L. Thomson, *Responsibility for Evil in the Theodicy of IV Ezra* (Montana: University of Montana Printing Department, 1997).

237 G. Vermes, *Scripture and Tradition in Judaism: Haggadic Studies* (Leiden: Brill, 1961), compares it to *Jubilees*, *Genesis Apocryphon*, and Josephus' *Antiquities*.

238 D. J. Harrington, 'The Original Language of Pseudo-Philo's *Liber Antiquitatum Biblicarum*', *HTR* 63 (1970), pp. 503–14; idem, 'The Biblical Text of Pseudo-Philo's *Liber Antiquitatum Biblicarum*', *CBQ* 33 (1971), pp. 1–17; idem, *The Hebrew Fragments of Pseudo-Philo's Liber Antiquitatum Biblicarum Preserved in the Chronicles of Jerahmeel* (Cambridge: Harvard University Press, 1974).

239 G. Kisch, *Pseudo-Philo's Liber Antiquitatum Biblicarum* (Indiana: University of Notre Dame, 1949), p. 3; C. Perrot, and P.-M. Bogaert, *Pseudo-Philon: Les Antiquités Bibliques* (Paris, 1976), pp. 22–74.

Despite the prediction that 'a house may be built for me among them' (*LAB* 12.4), this will in turn 'be destroyed because they will sin against me. And the race of men shall be unto me as a drop of a pitcher and will be counted as spittle' (*LAB* 12.5).

This element of Israel's covenantal infidelity (and consequent destruction) is also emphasized in 19.7, where God explains why Moses is not permitted to enter the promised land. The main objection to Moses' entry into the promised land is that he might see 'see the graven images with which these people will start to be deceived and led off the path'. The result of this apostasy is plainly stated in terms of the Babylonian deportation: 'And after this it will be turned over into the hands of their enemies, and they will destroy it, and foreigners will encircle it.'[240] The whole scene is presented in terms which are reminiscent of the divine judgement when God 'smashed the tablets of the covenant ... that I drew up for you on Horeb' (*LAB* 19.7).

In this way *Liber Antiquitatum Biblicarum* strengthens the theological trajectory established thus far in Jewish documents written soon after the temple's destruction in 70 AD by attributing the calamity to Israel's moral failure.

2.9.f. Josephus

In somewhat different terms to the pseudepigrapha, Josephus accounts for the destruction of the temple on the basis of certain Jewish political revolutionaries, i.e. the Zealots. *War* 4.387–88 indicates a particular interest in emphasizing Israel's own culpability in the events culminating in the destruction of the temple in 70 AD: 'the Zealots caused the prophesies against their country to be fulfilled ... for there was an age-old saying of inspired men that the city would be taken and the most holy temple burnt to the ground by right of war if ever the citizens strove with each other and Jewish hands were first to pollute the house of God'.

Vicky Balabanski has traced Josephus' description of the vocabulary used to describe the actions of the Zealots and has 'identified how prominent the language of cultic transgression is'.[241] *War* 6.110 describes the Zealots in the following manner: 'And are not both the city and the entire temple now full of the dead bodies of your countrymen? ... It is God himself who is bringing on this fire, to purge that city and temple ... which is full of your pollutions (μιασμάτων).'[242] *War* 4.171 similarly states 'Will you bear, therefore, – will you bear to see your sanctuary trampled on? And will you lay steps for these profane wretches (ἀνοσίοις) upon which they may mount to higher degrees

---

240 *LAB* preserves a unique tradition, as the biblical narrative attributes it to Moses' former disobedience (Num. 20.7-13). See H. Jacobson, *A Commentary on Pseudo-Philo's Liber Antiquitatum Biblicarum* (2 vols; Leiden: Brill, 1996), pp. 1.622–23.

241 Balabanski, *Eschatology*, p. 124 n.41.

242 Cf. Lev. 7.18; Jer. 32.34; Ezek. 33.3

of insolence?'[243] Among other references,[244] these examples indicate that the actions of the Zealots, described by Josephus in negative cultic terminology, implicate them as the cause of the destruction of the temple, that is, rather than any Roman counterpart. In this way, Josephus offers a unique perspective on the culpability of Israel for the city's destruction. In so doing, this literature joins the theological trajectory of conceiving Israel's covenantal infidelity as the cause for the temple's fate.

2.10. Preliminary Conclusion

The above causes for Jerusalem's destruction could be duplicated with other first-century texts;[245] however, as can be seen from this brief survey of pseudepigrapha and Josephus, the reasons for Jerusalem's destruction are remarkably homogeneous.[246] The texts all seem to work within the parameters of Deuteronomy's blessing and curses, in that Israel's moral failure is linked with national destruction. Of particular note, *Apoc. Abr.* specifically links his discussion to the operations in the temple, and as such focuses in on aspects of cult and leadership.

These texts have significant implications for our current study. Matthew consistently presents Jesus' mission to the Jews as being met with rejection (Mt. 2.7-18; 8.5-13, 18-22; 12.38-42; 21.10; 23.37). Throughout the entire narrative Israel is sought, yet is portrayed as consistently turning away and rejecting. Matthew implies that because of this rejection Israel will be justly punished. The parable of the Wedding Banquet (Mt. 22.1-14) is instructive in this regard, in that the inappropriate response of the guests to the king's invitation resulted in 'their city' (v. 7) being burnt. In this sense Matthew can be centrally located in the stream of Jewish theological material which responded to the destruction of Jerusalem in 70 AD by laying the responsibility at the feet of the inhabitants.

---

243 See also *War* 4.261; 6.399; 7.379; cf. *War* 4.326; 2 Macc. 7.34; 8.32; 3 *Macc.* 2.2; 5.8; 4 *Macc.* 12.11; *Wis.* 12.4; Ezek. 22.9.

244 For example, ἀσέβεια is used of the Zealots' ungodliness and sacrilege eight times in *War* 4–7; ἀσεβέω occurs five times in *War* books 5–7 and refers to the Zealots on each occassion; τὸ ἀσέβημα also exclusively refers to the Zealots; ἀσεβής ἀσεβής occurs four times in *War* 4–6. The *BDAG*, p. 141 notes that the ασεβ- stem is to be 'understood vertically as a lack of reverence for deity and hallowed institutions as displayed in sacrilegious words and deeds'. Also see Balabanski, *Eschatology*, pp. 124–25.

245 For example, the Qumranic *Damascus Document* (4Q256) or the Habakkuk Commentary in which the Hasmonaean high priests are said to have polluted the sanctuary. The *Pss Sol.* 2.3; 8.11-13; 17.5-6 go beyond the scrolls in criticizing the Hasmonaeans' usurpation of the Davidic throne. There are other documents which recall the people's sins as the cause for God forsaking the temple; *T. Levi* 15.1; 16.4.

246 There are, however, alternative explanations. The introduction to 2 *Bar.* indicates that the destruction could be attributed to the tyrannical kings who consistently oppress God's people. It is in this context that the question of theodicy is sharpest.

Our discussion thus far has sketched the direction in which this study proposes to pursue the question of the 'abomination of desolation' in Matthew. In light of the possible Deuteronomistic framework of Matthew (chs 5–7 and 23), and the subsequent lament over Jerusalem, it will be argued that the coming of the Son of Man in ch. 24 is to be understood as referring to the destruction of Jerusalem because of Israel's rejection of her Messiah and her continuing abominations in the holy place.

2.11. A Residual Problem Concerning Dating

2.11.a. Introduction

A residual problem for the dating of Matthew's Gospel is whether our proposed date contributes, either positively or negatively, to the basic argument of our thesis, which maintains that the destruction of Jerusalem in 70 AD played a key role in the composition of Matthew's Gospel. We will assess the measure in which a possible later dating is inversely proportional to the plausibility of our central line of argument. That is, does a date in the mid-80s, which separates Matthew's composition from the destruction of Jerusalem by a decade and a half diminish the extent to which Matthew might have drawn on the event in a significant way in retelling his version of the Jesus story.

2.11.b. The problem of the inverse-proportional critique

In regard to the interpretive issues in Matthew 24, one may suppose that as the dating of the document gets later in the first century, the historical horizon of the Roman siege might diminish and the 'eschatological' perspective might increase. That is, the probability of Matthew using the historical occasion of the destruction of Jerusalem as a key interpretive feature of the narrative seems inversely proportional as the date extends further into the later part of the first century.[247]

This is a legitimate concern; however, there are three lines of evidence which would suggest that even a date in the mid-80s would not render our argument indefensible.[248] Below we turn to numismatic, architectural, and literary evidence which would suggest that the destruction of Jerusalem by the Romans in 70 AD was kept fresh in the minds of the inhabitants of the empire between the period 70 and 85 AD (and perhaps even beyond).

---

247 In personal discussion with Prof. Martin Goodman of Wolfson College, University of Oxford, he suggested, nonetheless, that the reverse might in fact be true. That is, the problem of the temple's destruction becomes *more* of a problem for Jews as it becomes increasingly obvious that the temple will not be rebuilt in the near future.

248 Needless to say, however, is that the closer the composition was to the destruction of the temple the greater literary impact and rhetorical effect Matthew 24 would have had.

2.11.b.i. Numismatic evidence

First, in regard to numismatic evidence, the eminent H. Mattingly has noted the relationship of coins and forms of propaganda in the Roman world: 'Coin types are constantly changing, and constantly emphasizing definite events and policies, and, as they change move in close agreement with the political changes of the time.'[249] He continues by stating, 'the possible influence of such coinage on public opinion could not possibly be overlooked or minimized by the Emperor. He must ... have censored, if not inspired it.'[250] In similar regard, W. Carter states that 'coins demonstrated Roman sovereignty ... [and] symbolized Roman accomplishments and the blessings of the gods which the emperor mediated to the people. There was no escaping Roman presence even in daily transactions.'[251] K. Dyer suggests that the circulation of coinage operated as one of the most efficient and concrete forms of communication in first-century Mediterranean village life.[252]

One of the most humiliating series of coins for Jewish communities in the first century were those of the *Judaea Capta* type minted by Vespasian.[253] It is generally assumed that the *Judaea Capta* coin was modelled on the victory coin of Herod and Sosius over Matthias Antigonus in 37 BC, which included a large trophy flanked by two seated prisoners. The *Judaea Capta* coins were minted throughout the empire as gold aurei,[254] silver denarii,[255] and brass sestertii.[256] Common features of the series includes (1) (on the obverse) a right-facing laureated bust of Vespasian, and (on the reverse) (2) reference to 'Iudea', usually symbolized as a woman bound, kneeling, sitting on a cuirass, or even blindfolded before Nike, (3) the presence of a Roman soldier or treasure of arms, and (d) a palm tree as a symbol of Judaea.

Significant for our own discussion is the fact that these coins were (1) minted throughout the entire empire during the reign of Vespasian (July 69 AD), but perhaps more importantly, (2) re-issued by Titus in June 79 AD and following. Examples of the re-issue under Titus include a gold

---

249 H. Mattingly, *Coins of the Roman Empire in the British Museum Vol. 3* (London: Trustees of the British Museum, 1936), p. xlv.

250 Mattingly, *Coins*, p. xlv.

251 W. Carter, *Matthew and the Margins* (Sheffield: Sheffield Academic Press, 2000), p. 38.

252 Dyer, *Concerning*, p. 112; Dyer, *Prophecy*, pp. 221–32. R. Oster, 'Numismatic Windows into the Social World of Early Christianity: A Methodological Inquiry', *JBL* 101 (1982), pp. 195–223, has also argued at length that coinage was one of the main methods of disseminated ideas and information in antiquity.

253 For a full catalogue of *Judaea Capta* coinage see H. B. Brin, *A Catalogue of Judaea Capta Coinage* (Minneapolis: Emmett Publishing, 1986), pp. 1–56.

254 H. Mattingly and E. A. Sydenham, *Roman Imperial Coinage: Vol 2 Vespasian to Hadrian* (London: Spink and Son, 1972), §15(a); §16; §301.

255 Mattingly and Sydenham, *Imperial*, §15(c); §16(s); §289; §363.

256 Mattingly and Sydenham, *Imperial*, §427(s); §426; §426(var); §425.

aurei,[257] silver denarii,[258] brass sestertii,[259] copper asses,[260] brass semis,[261] copper quadrans.[262]

One commentator summarizes the purpose of the issue as follows, 'minted throughout the Empire, the *Judaea Capta* series is a warning to all other groups within the Empire not to follow suit, so it can be seen as a propagandistic assertion of the greatness of the Flavians and the Flavian peace'.[263] There was, however, a very concrete historical motivation for the re-issue by Titus, namely, securing the line of Flavian succession. Of utmost significance for the Flavians was continued rule. Standing before the Senate, Suetonius records Vespasian's declaration, 'Either my sons will succeed me or nobody will.'[264] Indeed, as history records, Titus and Domitian, as children, would provide a secure line. However, at the outset of Titus' rule, no such security was evident. The *Judaea Capta* coinage was crucial to this endeavour. As Overman notes, 'the propaganda value of the victory in Judaea was especially in the case of Titus. Since establishing trust in a stable and peaceful succession was crucial, a line or gens had to be secured for the Flavians.'[265]

However, as R. Syme has observed, 'sacking Jerusalem was Titus' sole claim to glory'.[266] He had achieved little else in the decade preceding his rule that could be used as a valid form of securing his position. As such, 'the defeat of the Jewish rebels had to assume primacy within the Flavian propaganda program ... [and] had to be interpreted as having empire-wide implications, not a local disturbance'.[267] In presenting Titus in this fashion, the coinage celebrated and propounded one albeit significant event, as the 'paramount accomplishment of the Flavians'.[268]

In light of this, we may conclude that the coins that were produced over Vespasian's reign were of such significance that they were reissued by Titus. The coins then, enjoyed a minimum of twelve years of minting (69–81 AD), not including later circulation in the Mediterranean. This would have kept the event of the destruction of Jerusalem fresh in the minds of inhabitants of the empire, and as such, any use of the 'destruction of Jerusalem' theme by writers in the mid-seventh or eighth

---

257 Mattingly and Sydenham, *Imperial*, §160.
258 Mattingly and Sydenham, *Imperial*, §367.
259 Mattingly and Sydenham, *Imperial*, §638 (var.).
260 Mattingly and Sydenham, *Imperial*, §784.
261 Mattingly and Sydenham, *Imperial*, §141.
262 Mattingly and Sydenham, *Imperial*, §887.
263 A. Overman, 'The First Revolt and the Flavian Politics', in *The First Jewish Revolt Against Rome*, ed. A. Berlin and A. Overman (London: Routledge, 2002), pp. 213–20 (215).
264 Tacitus, *Vespasian* 25.
265 Overman, *Revolt*, p. 215.
266 R. Syme, 'The *Argonautica* of Valerius Flaccus', *CQ* 23 (1929), pp. 135–36 (135).
267 Overman, *Revolt*, p. 216.
268 Overman, *Revolt*, p. 216.

decades of the first century (in our case Matthew), would have at their disposal a well-known theme which Rome had used as a significant form of propaganda during the rule of Vespasian and Titus. As such, it may be argued that a later dating of Matthew does not impede our central claim.[269]

2.11.b.ii. Architectural evidence

Flavian building projects also emphasized the magnitude of the Jewish revolt and suppression by Titus. Situated in the south-east corner of the forum in Rome, the Pentelic marble triumphal arch of Titus was built by Domitian after the death of Titus and commemorated the sack of Jerusalem. Of particular significance is the relief sculpture depicting a parade of the victors carrying spoils from the temple. The inscription on the arch also reinforces the magnitude of the event.

> The Roman Senate and people [dedicate this] to the emperor Titus Caesar Vespasian Augustus, son of the deified Augustus, pontifex maximus, holding the tribunician power for the tenth year, acclaimed imperator seventeen times, consul eight times, father of this country, their princeps, because with the guidance and plans of his father, and under his auspices, he subdued the Jewish people and destroyed the city of Jerusalem, which all generals, kings, and peoples before him had either attacked without success or left entirely unassailed.[270]

As Overman notes, this 'sent a single powerful message promoting the Flavians in their monumental struggle with the Jews on behalf of Rome and Rome imperium'.[271] The celebration of Titus' accomplishment in this manner portrayed him as the greatest military hero in Rome's history. The phrase 'which all generals, kings, and peoples before him had either attacked without success or left entirely unassailed' illustrates the hyperbole. For either Pompey's triumph in Jerusalem was forgotten (Tacitus *His.* 5.9) or conveniently ignored for rhetorical effect.[272] In this light, it is evident that the memory of the destruction of Jerusalem was reinforced in the later part of the first century through Domitian's construction of the Arch of Titus.

269 Overman, *Revolt*, p. 215 concludes: 'by 75 CE ... the Flavian victory over the Jews was an event owned, as it were, by the entire Roman world'.

270 *CIL* VI, no. 994. N. Lewis and M. Reinhold, *Roman Civilization* II (New York: Columbia University Press, 1990), p. 15.

271 Overman, *Revolt*, p. 215.

272 See R. H. Darwell-Smith, *Emperors and Architecture: A Study of Flavian Rome* (Brussels: Latomus, 1996), p. 69.

2.11.b.iii. Literary evidence
Two kinds of literary sources also indicate that the destruction of Jerusalem was preserved in the psyche of potential readers/hearers of Matthew's Gospel in the first century, namely the texts relating to the *fiscus Judaicus*, and late-first-century pseudepigraphical texts. The *fiscus Judaicus* was instituted by Vespasian shortly after the end of the Jewish War in 70 AD. The law stated that all Jews, both male and female, were to pay an annual tax of two denarii to finance the rebuilding of the Temple of Jupiter Capitolinus.[273] Josephus makes reference to this in *War* 7.218, 'All Jews ... paid to the Capitoline god what they had previously paid to the Jerusalem Temple.' Similarly Cassius Dio 65.7.2 records:

> Thus was Jerusalem destroyed on the very day of Saturn, the day which even now the Jews reverence most. From that time forth it was ordered that the Jews who continued to observe their ancestral customs should pay an annual tribute of two denarii to Jupiter Capitoline. In consequence of this success both generals received the title of imperator, but neither got that of Judaïcus, although all the other honours that were fitting on the occasion of so magnificent a victory, including triumphal arches, were voted to them.

Furthermore, Ostraka from Appolinopolis Magna demonstrate that the tax was levied as far away as Egypt in as early as 71 AD.[274] The main difference in regard to the former temple tax and the new *fiscus Judaicus* was the range of people who were qualified to pay it. Whereas previously the temple tax was extracted only from free males aged twenty to fifty, the new law included both male and female, slaves and free, from the age of three to sixty-two. The Arsinoe papyrus includes a boy and a girl who were registered at the age of three to begin paying the tax,[275] as well as six sixty-one-year-old women who were liable for the tax.[276] Smallwood suggests an additional aggregate of quadruple the sum formally paid to the temple, that is, approximately 11 million denarii per annum.[277] Vespasian's heavier taxation (as well as Titus' [79–81] and Domitian's [81–96] enforcement of the *fiscus Judaicus*), served strongly to reinforce the event of the temple's destruction in 70 AD.[278]

---

273 M. Zetterholm, *The Formation of Christianity in Antioch* (London: Routledge, 2003), p. 185 notes that its original name was probably 'denarii duo Judaeorum' (the two denarii of the Jews).

274 *Corpus Papyrorum Judaicorum* 160–229. In some cases collected in arrears for 69 AD. See discussion in E. M. Smallwood, *The Jews Under Roman Rule: From Pompey to Diocletian* (Leiden: Brill, 1981), pp. 372–73.

275 *Corpus Papyrorum Judaicorum* 421.162–65; 170–74.

276 *Corpus Papyrorum Judaicorum* 421.183–84.

277 Smallwood, *Jews*, p. 374.

278 For further discussion see Smallwood, *Jews*, pp. 371–76; Carter, *Matthew*, p. 38; Overman, *Revolt*, p. 216.

The second form of literary texts which kept the memory of the destruction of the Jewish temple vividly alive in the late first century are pseudepigraphical texts which respond to the question of theodicy, that is, how could Yahweh allow his temple to become polluted? It is sufficient to note for our discussion here, that *all* the following works sought to respond in some measure to the events of 70 AD and *all* are dated, often considerably, after 70 AD. R. Rubinkiewicz notes that general scholarly opinion holds that the *Apocalypse of Abraham* was composed 'at the end of the first century'.[279] A. F. J. Klijn concludes similarly in regard to the *Apocalypse of Baruch*, stating that 'a data around A.D. 100 is probable'.[280] Similarly, *4 Ezra* (2 Esdras 3–14) is also accepted by the majority of scholarship to have been composed in or around the turn of the first century.[281] Other examples of similar dates are the *Liber Antiquitatum Biblicarum* and Josephus. All of these literary sources deal *in extenso* with events related to the destruction of Jerusalem, and therefore we maintain that if such parallel examples exist, a dating of Matthew beyond a decade after 70 AD does not diminish the possibility that the destruction of Jerusalem played a key motif in its composition and subsequent interpretation.

2.11.c. Conclusion

It might be argued that the further one moves Matthew's date from the destruction of Jerusalem, the likelihood decreases that the event was employed by Matthew in significant way to retell the story of Jesus, i.e. as distance increases, likelihood decreases. How then may we respond to the issue of Matthean dating and the potential problem of the inverse-proportional critique? First, we noted that, although difficulty surrounds the question, consideration of both external and internal evidence may suggest a date sometime in the Jamnian period (c. 80–85 AD). However, as was also recognized, this is by no means definitive.[282] In the second part of our discussion we noted that there is abundant evidence which suggests that the destruction of Jerusalem was well engrained into the psyche of inhabitants of the empire in the mid to late first century AD. Such evidence includes the numismatic (the *Judaea Capta* series of coins minted by Vespasian and re-issued by Titus), the architectural (the Arch

---

279 Rubinkiewicz, 'Apocalypse', p. 683. Of particular significance here is the apparent Christian interpolation in ch. 29 which shows a distinctly Christian interest in the question of the destruction of the temple.

280 A. F. J. Klijn, '2 (Syrian Apocalypse of) Baruch', in *The Old Testament Pseudepigrapha*, ed. J. H. Charlesworth (2 vols; London: Darton, Longman & Todd, 1983), pp. 1.615–52 (616).

281 B. Metzger, 'The Fourth Book of Ezra', in *The Old Testament Pseudepigrapha*, ed. J. H. Charlesworth (2 vols; London: Darton, Longman & Todd, 1983), pp. 1.516–613 (520).

282 However, as will be addressed in our final chapter, there are some modern scholars who have found precedent for a pre-70-AD dating.

of Titus built by Domitian to honour Titus' capture of Jerusalem), and the literary (the *fiscus Judaicus* and pseudepigraphical texts). As such, it is apparent that even if a slightly later date is accepted for the composition of Matthew's Gospel, this does not impede or diminish our central argument, that is, that (the conception or reality of) the destruction of Jerusalem played a central role in the composition of the Matthean text.

Chapter 3

'Eschatological' and 'Apocalyptic' Language in Matthew 24

3.1. Introduction

Our discussion thus far now raises the thorny issue as to how the language in ch. 24 should be understood. It is no understatement to suggest that more ink has been spilt on this chapter, with its synoptic parallels, than on any other in the Gospel narratives. Although consensus has consistently eluded scholars, there are some clues as to how we should frame the discussion of the vivid 'apocalyptic' descriptions in ch. 24. This chapter will tentatively suggest, that, given the introductory marker 'As Jesus came out of the temple' and the questions relating to the temple's buildings, there is no reason to suppose the author switches from a 'historical' to an 'end time eschatology'[1] at any point in ch. 24. As the following discussion will attempt to demonstrate, the language employed within this chapter finds its primary meaning with reference to the historical context of the temple's destruction on 9 Av, 70 AD.[2] In this schema, the parousia of the Son of Man refers to the city's destruction through Roman intervention. As will be discussed in a subsequent chapter, this theme is consistent with Jewish hopes of redemption, specifically in regard to the Danielic Son of Man who comes to destroy Israel's enemies. The irony in Matthew is that Israel is her own enemy and, as such, experiences divinely executed retributive justice.

It seems prudent to make a brief comment on the manner in which we will approach source-critical issues in our discussion. For the purposes of our research we are interested in the Matthean text in its extant form. We do not wish to deny that Matthew 24 is effectively rewriting Mark 13, which itself has a complex tradition history. We will adopt, what E. Haenchen has referred to as 'Composition Criticism'.[3] Bauer and Powell describe 'Compositional Criticism' as focusing on 'the total editorial achievement of the evangelist ... rather than the minute "process"

---

1   See definition of these terms below.

2   The related question as to whether or not there are any Matthean future final eschatological hopes will be addressed in our final chapter.

3   Haenchen, *Der Weg Jesu*. See discussion in Charette, *Recompense*, pp. 16–17; Moore, *Criticism*, p. 4; Wilson, *When*, p. 48.

according to which the evangelist brought about changes, omissions, and additions to his *Vorlage*'.[4] As such, reference will be made to Mark for redactional critical concerns. However, we will not pursue detailed discussion of source criticism and of redactional layers. Our concern is what the text *in its current form* has to say about the 'Abomination of Desolation'. We will focus on a holistic treatment of the Gospel, with special attention to the Gospel as a narrative, affirming that Matthew is a relatively coherent story of 'narrated series of events ... linked by temporal and causal connections'.[5] Matthew will be read as a unified story and not treated as a means to another end, such as attempting to identify strata in source material. Our working methodology will be akin to that of Gibbs' analysis, a 'text based study, [which will] attempt to describe the features of the text as it stands, and the interrelation of the parts of that text'.[6] As B. Childs has mentioned in a different context, 'the determination of its present function is exegetically far more important than recovering an earlier oral stage'.[7] Similarly, B. Charette states that:

> Composition criticism is the product of a recent trend in redaction criticism which, admitting the limitations of earlier forms of the method, recognizes that the concerns of an Evangelist are to be found not merely in the study of the changes he has made to his sources but also in the study of the completed work he has produced.[8]

In this regard R. E. Brown says that 'we cannot afford to lose sight of Matthew's highly effective narrative because of attention to comparative details'.[9] 'Compositional Criticism' is closely aligned with 'Narrative Criticism', and despite the conclusions of Moore,[10] they are effectively interchangeable when applied to our methodology.

---

4   D. R. Bauer and M. A. Powell, *Treasures New and Old* (Atlanta: Scholars Press, 1996), p. 3

5   T. R. Wolthuis, *Experiencing the Kingdom: Reading the Gospel of Matthew* (unpublished PhD dissertation; Duke University, 1987), p. 220.

6   G. A. Gibbs, *Let the Reader Understand: The Eschatological Discourse in Matthew's Gospel* (unpublished PhD dissertation; Union Theological Seminary, 1995), p. 34.

7   Childs, *Isaiah*, p. 16.

8   Charette, *Recompense*, pp. 18–19.

9   Brown, *Introduction*, p. 171.

10   Moore, *Criticism*, p. 4 argues that compositional criticism is 'a method aligned with *narrative criticism* but in the last analysis clearly distinguishable from it' (italics his). He also argues that 'Whereas compositional criticism extends the tradition of redaction criticism by reason in an overriding interest in the evangelists' theologies, narrative criticism represents a break with the tradition in the sense that the focus is no longer primarily on theology' (p. 7). It is not evident that such a nuance is adhered to by those who claim to be operating within either realm.

3.2. Matthew 24 in Recent Research

Before we launch into a full-scale discussion of the language of Matthew 24, it seems pertinent briefly to note the variegated approaches commentators have adopted in interpreting Matthew's 'apocalyptic/eschatological' discourse as a whole.

3.2.a. Cataclysmic eschatology[11]

The two figures who most significantly influenced the interpretation of the synoptic apocalypse in the late nineteenth and early twentieth centuries were J. Weiss and A. Schweitzer.[12] J. Weiss's work, *Die Predict Jesu vom Reich Gottes*, was first published in 1892 and later revised and expanded in 1900. His main contention was that the Kingdom of God was 'not an ethical society to be brought about by human effort, but a radical transformation to be effected by divine power'.[13] In other words, the proclamation of the Kingdom of God, of which Matthew 24 could be taken as typical (cf. 24.14 'and this good news of the Kingdom ... '), does not refer to a present spiritual state but rather an entirely future-oriented apocalyptic kingdom with Jesus functioning as *Messias designatus*.[14] Weiss concluded that, when the Kingdom comes, 'wird Gott diese alte, vom Teufel beherrschte und verdorbene Welt vernichten und ein neues Welt schaffen'.[15]

Building on Weiss's understanding of *kingdom*, A. Schweitzer argued that this would be inaugurated by the coming of the Son of Man who would apparently come during Jesus' ministry, which would signify the end of the present age.[16] Schweitzer argued that this was to occur during the time in which Jesus sent out the twelve disciples on their mission to Israel. Of particular importance was the key phrase in Mt. 10.23: 'For truly I tell you, you will not have gone through all the towns of Israel

---

11   Although in our later discussion we will find precedent to challenge the use of the word 'eschatology' in this fashion, we use it here for convenience in facilitating an understandable discussion of Matthew 24 in previous scholarship.

12   For a history of their influence see N. Perrin, *The Kingdom of God in the Teaching of Jesus* (London: SCM Press, 1963), pp. 16–23, 28–36; S. E. Porter, *The Criteria for Authenticity in Historical-Jesus Research* (Sheffield: Sheffield Academic Press, 2000), pp. 36–47.

13   A. Y. Collins, 'Apocalypticism and New Testament Theology', *New England Region of the Society of Biblical Literature* (Newton, MA, 22 April 2005), pp. 1–26 (5).

14   Although Weiss was referring to the historical Jesus rather than the Matthean Jesus, his view was (1) based upon (amongst other texts) Matthean material, and (2) has heavily influenced synoptic studies.

15   Trans.: 'God will destroy this old world, spoiled and controlled by the devil, and will create a new world.' Cited in T. F. Glasson, 'Schweitzer's Influence – Blessing or Bane?', *JTS* 28 (1977), pp. 289–302 (290).

16   A. Schweitzer, *The Mystery of the Kingdom of God: The Secret of Jesus' Messiahship and Passion* (trans. W. Lowrie; New York: Schocken, 1925).

before the Son of Man comes.' However, when this did not happen,
Jesus was compelled to attempt to usher in the *kingdom* by means of his
own person.[17] Schweitzer describes this 'final cosmical catastrophe'[18]
as follows:

> For the realisation of the Kingdom there remained but one way still open
> to him, – namely, conflict with the power which opposed his work. He
> resolved to carry this conflict into the Capital itself. There fate should
> decide. Perhaps the victory would fall to him. But, even if it should turn out
> that in the course of earthly events the fate of death awaited him inevitably,
> so long as he trod the path which his office prescribed, this very suffering
> must signify in God's plan the performance by which his work was to be
> crowned. It was then God's will that the moral state appropriate to the
> Kingdom of God should be inaugurated by the highest moral deed of the
> Messiah. With this thought he set out for Jerusalem ...[19]

Although this approach was challenged in subsequent years,[20] the
thoroughgoing influence of Weiss and Schweitzer is demonstrated in
the fifty-year period before anyone seriously took issue with this thesis.
In this regard, Wright comments that Schweitzer 'demolished the old
"Quest" so successfully – and provided such a shocking alternative –
that for half a century serious scholarship had great difficulty in working its way back to history when dealing with Jesus'.[21] In our current
discussion, we are operating within the framework of the Matthean
narrative and as such questions of the historical Jesus, while valid, lie
beyond the purview of this book. What is of importance for us is the

---

17   A. Schweitzer, *The Quest for the Historical Jesus: A Critical Study of its Progress
from Reimarus to Wrede* (trans. W. Montgomery; London: A&C Black, 1910), pp.
357–58. See G. Lundstrom, *The Kingdom of God in the Teaching of Jesus* (Richmond:
John Knox Press, 1963), pp. 35–81 for discussion and summary.

18   Schweitzer, *Mystery*, p. 114. Schweitzer suggested that this understanding of the
Kingdom of God was clear to hearers and that the mere mention of the phrase would
immediately bring to mind a cataclysmic end. Glasson, 'Influence', p. 291.

19   Schweitzer, *Mystery*, pp. 62–63.

20   R. H. Hiers attempted to revive Schweitzer's *konsequente Eschatologie* in his
1970 and 1973 volumes by contending that 'Jesus deliberately provoked the Jewish
authorities to bring about his suffering and death, so that he, himself, might bear the tribu-
lations prerequisite to the coming of the Kingdom of God' (R. H. Hiers, *The Kingdom of
God in the Synoptic Tradition* [Gainsville: University of Florida Press, 1970], p. 3). And
that 'the Judgement will take place soon, in the lifetime of at least some of those who
had heard Jesus' message' (R. H. Hiers, *The Historical Jesus and the Kingdom of God*
[Gainsville: University of Florida Press, 1973], p. 38). Hiers claims that there is nothing
in this message which can be understood as 'realized eschatology' (Hiers, *Historical*, p.
40); however, given the emphasis Hiers places on the motif of the consequent judgement
elsewhere, on those who reject Jesus, this may indicate some sort of unique relationship
between the so-called 'eschatological' discourse and the surrounding material of entry into
Jerusalem and rejection of Jesus as legitimate Messianic claimant.

21   Wright, *Jesus*, p. 21.

manner in which the above-stated conclusions have been uncritically applied by commentators to an interpretation of Matthew's text.

With specific regard to Matthew 24, there are a minority of scholars, including Gnilka, Hare, Harrington, Marxsen, and Walvoord, who have argued that the entire chapter refers to a cataclysmic end of the space-time continuum.[22] This approach is by no means unattested in antiquity,[23] and there have traditionally been three arguments used to argue for this particular interpretation. First, the 'eschatological' nature of the language which draws heavily on Daniel, has been interpreted as such in other contemporary literature. For 'eschatological' readings of Daniel 9 (vv. 24-27) and 11-12, commentators note 1QM1; 4Q174 and 11QMelch respectively.[24] In response, it can be noted that G. Caird has demonstrated that the word 'eschatology' has no fewer than eight nuanced meanings,[25] and thus must be defined much more carefully than finding general parallels with extant literature from Qumran. Furthermore, in terms of how Matthew hermeneutically employs his material, surely one must take serious consideration of the context *in Matthew*. A context which prefaces the following material with 'As Jesus came out of the temple and was going away, his disciples came to point out to him the buildings of the temple. Then he asked them, "You see all these, do you not? Truly I tell you, not one stone will be left upon another"' (Mt. 24.1-2). This would strongly suggest a reference to the destruction of the temple in 70 AD and indicate that at least *some* of the

---

22 Gnilka, *Matthäusevangelium*, pp. 2.309–333; Hare, *Persecutions*, pp. 177–79; D. J. Harrington, *The Gospel of Matthew* (Collegeville: Liturgical Press, 1991), pp. 331–41; W. Marxen, *Mark the Evangelist* (New York: Abingdon Press, 1969), pp. 198–204; J. F. Walvoord, 'Christ's Olivet Discourse on the Time of the End: Prophecies Fulfilled in the Present Age', *BSac* 128 (1971), pp. 206–14.

23 Cf. Did. 16.3-7 which uses Matthew 24 and speaks of the ἔσχατος καιρός ('the last time'); see also the Ethiopic *Apoc. Pet.* 1–2, 6 which seems to be functioning in an eschatological framework. Some early commentators also took a similar line of interpretation, including Irenaeus (*Adv. Haer.* 5.25.2), Hippolytus (*In Matthaeum* 24.198-204), Hilary and Cyril of Jerusalem (*Hilary* 25.2–26.1). U. Luz, *Matthew 21–28: A Commentary* (trans. J. E. Crouch; Minneapolis: Fortress Press, 2005), p. 185 traces the influence of this upon classical dogmatics. However, *pace* Luz, this is not the 'oldest type of interpretation' (Luz, *Matthew 21–28*, p. 185), as can be seen from Lk. 21.20-21; Mt. 24.15, 'when you see the desolating sacrilege standing in the holy place ... then those in Judea must flee to the mountains', is replaced with 'when you see Jerusalem surrounded by *armies*, then know that its desolation has come near'. Luke is one of the earliest attested instances of reception history of this saying and rather than supporting an 'eschatological' reading, actually reads Mk 13.14/Mt. 24.15 as a historical referent. The question of Luke's use of Matthew need not be invoked, as what is of importance is Luke's reception of the saying.

24 See for example J. J. Collins, *Daniel with an Introduction to Apocalyptic Literature* (Grand Rapids: Eerdmans, 1984), pp. 352–58, 377. Of particular interest is Josephus in *Ant.* 10, which interprets Daniel as referring to Jews under the rule of the Romans.

25 Or at least connotations in scholarly discourse. G. B. Caird, *Jesus and the Jewish Nation* (London: Athlone Press, 1965); idem, *The Language and Imagery of the Bible* (London: Duckworth, 1980).

following material responds to the opening sequence.[26] Davies and Allison object to this by noting that (1) the event was past and so the answer was known to all, and (2) Matthew elsewhere leaves his narrative material hanging in an unanswered sense.[27] In response it can be noted that (1) the relative significance of the destruction of the temple was sufficient that one would expect later reference to it, and (2) the examples provided by Davies and Allison for Matthew's characteristic of leaving material hanging is questionable. It seems highly suspicious to infer from Matthew's inconcinnities (Mk 6.17-29 = Mt. 14.3-12; Mk 15.6-10 = Mt. 27.15-18) that this forms a Matthean characteristic, which then legitimates a so-called 'eschatological' reading that is alien to its immediate context.[28] D. R. A. Hare, nonetheless, is quite content with this apparent contextual disjunction. He states that Matthew 'totally ignores the first question, which for his generation is no longer vital, and makes the discourse as a whole an answer to the second, viz. "What is the sign of your final coming and the consummation of history?"'[29] The implication of this serious inconsistency is not to be underestimated.[30]

A second argument forwarded for understanding the entirety of Matthew 24 as 'eschatological' is the linguistic unity of the discourse. Mainly drawing on Davies and Allison's analysis, we may note the following significant repetitions which bind the chapter together as a single whole: ταῦτα πάντα (vv. 2, 8, 33); σημεῖον (vv. 3, 24, 30); παρουσία (vv. 3, 27, 37, 39); πολλοὶ (vv. 5, 10, 11, 12); πλανάω (vv. 4, 5, 11, 24); (ψευδο)χριστός (vv. 5, 23, 24); (ψευδο)προφήτης (vv. 11, 24); τέλος (vv. 6, 13, 14; cf. συντέλεια v. 3); θλῖψις (vv. 9, 21, 29); τότε (vv. 9, 23, 30); ἔθνος (vv. 7, 9, 14); μισέω (vv. 9, 10); παραδίδωμι (vv. 9, 10); φεύγω / φύγη (vv. 16, 20); μέγας (vv. 21, 24, 31); αἱ ἡμέραι ἐκεῖναι (vv. 22, 29, 36[sg.]); ἐκλεκτός (vv. 22, 24, 31); ἰδού (vv. 23, 24, 31); μὴ πιστεύσητε (vv. 23, 26); υἱος τοῦ ἀνθρώπου (vv. 27, 30). It is argued that there is sufficient repetition across pericopes within ch. 24 to indicate that it is a single whole referring to a single eschatological entity. U. Luz similarly notes that the similar catchwords in vv. 9-14 and vv. 23-28 'demonstrate that the sections belong together'.[31] However, it is important

26   Furthermore, the opening of the discourse in ch. 24 is primarily orientated towards the postulation of questions. It would thus be most natural for these to occupy at least the first part of the response.

27   Davies and Allison, *Matthew 3*, p. 329.

28   Davies and Allison, *Matthew 3*, are right to note this as a sign of Matthew's redaction of Mark.

29   Hare, *Persecutions*, p. 179.

30   Hare, *Persecutions*, p. 178 also argues that 'that this is not out of character for Matthew; after the long discourse giving missionary instruction (ch. 10), no mention is made of the mission itself'. However, this seems to ignore Matthew 10 as the climax of the punctuated call narratives in Matthew 8–9. In that Mt. 10.1-4 is the culmination of Israel's restoration (i.e. Israel's twelve tribes).

31   Luz, *Matthew 21–28*, p. 181. We here find cause to agree with Luz that the verbal repetition does not only support the hypothesis of a single author, but also indicates the

to note that Davies and Allison's analysis of the distribution of vocabulary, which demonstrates a measure of linguistic unity, cannot exclusively be marshalled for an 'eschatological' reading. The analysis could also be used in support of a reading which took the entirety in reference to the historical events surrounding 70 AD, a reading which we will discuss in detail below.

The third argument used to support the 'eschatological' reading is the manner in which v. 29 is introduced; Εὐθέως (immediately). Davies and Allison note that 'if Matthew wrote much after 70 AD, he could not have thought the *parousia* would follow immediately upon the destruction of the temple, which in turn makes it unlikely that vv.15ff. depict that destruction'.[32] However, (1) this assumes that Matthew did write shortly after 70 AD, and (2) that the parousia refers to a literal reappearing of the resurrected Jesus. This problem is resolved by appreciating the appropriate semantic range of παρουσία, an issue to which we will shortly return.[33]

Hare offers additional argumentation for the purely 'eschatological' reading of Matthew 24 by stating: 'In opposition to the view that vv. 15-20 are understood by Matthew as referring to the events of AD 70, we would point out that the Matthean addition, μηδὲ σαββάτῳ (v20), would be inappropriate and indeed meaningless as a supplement to a fulfilled prophecy.'[34] Although J. P. Brown notes the possibility that the phrase 'may be a part of the remains of an M-apocalypse',[35] Hare counters this by arguing that:

> even if the phrase were pre-Matthean ... its retention by Matthew would be most improbable unless he regarded it as having reference to a future event ... We may suspect that the whole of v.20 would have been dropped had Matthew regarded the prophecy as fulfilled, since the exhortation to prayer would be pointless after the event.[36]

Hare concludes that Matthew's purpose is 'not to show that Jesus' predictions have been fulfilled in the events of A.D. 70 but to prepare the Christians for enduring faithfulness during the indefinite period that remains'.[37] However this presupposes two things: (1) that Matthew's

---

unified nature of the pericope and topic under discussion.

32   Davies and Allison, *Matthew 3*, p. 329. Although the authors do not accept the conclusions, Davies and Allison provide a helpful summary of this argument.

33   In our subsequent discussion we will argue that the coming Son of Man represents the forces of the Roman armies. See below for full discussion.

34   Hare, *Persecutions*, p. 178.

35   J. P. Brown, 'The Form of "Q" Known to Matthew', *NTS* 8 (1962), pp. 27–42 (30).

36   Hare, *Persecutions*, pp. 177–78.

37   Hare, *Persecutions*, p. 178. Interestingly, R. H. Gundry has argued on the basis of μηδὲ σαββάτῳ that Matthew is to be dated at some point between 65–67 AD, as a command to pray against fleeing on the Sabbath would be irrelevant to the Matthean community if it were written later (Gundry, *Matthew*, pp. 607–608). See below for discussion.

intention was *primarily* to instruct his community, and (2) that there is no other plausible explanation regarding μηδὲ σαββάτῳ (v. 20). In regard to the former it is necessary to note the persuasive case that has been made by Burridge on genre, which suggests the Gospel writers intended to offer some kind of biographical sketch rather than primarily addressing purely community-oriented issues.[38] Hare's presupposition cannot merely be assumed without further reasoning. In regard to Hare's second objection, G. N. Stanton has argued that the primary referent of μηδὲ σαββάτῳ is the destruction of Jerusalem in 70 AD and surrounding events, and is most plausibly understood as referring to the increased hardships which will potentially fall upon those who are fleeing.[39] Stanton's analysis more plausibly accounts for the Matthean addition and, as such, constitutes what Hare says is not forthcoming, a plausible explanation regarding μηδὲ σαββάτῳ (v. 20). U. Luz similarly concludes that a solely eschatological interpretation 'has greatest difficulty with vv.16 and 20, which are emphatically connected with Jewish and local realities … It [i.e. the eschatological reading] can scarcely make understandable the exhortations and words of comfort Matthew has woven into the text.'[40]

3.2.b. Historical-eschatological split

Schweitzer et al. found an antecedent to their 'end-of-the-world' understanding of 'apocalyptic' in certain pseudepigraphal sources including *Pss Sol.*, *1 En.*, *4 Ezra*, and *2 Bar.* However, in regard to *Pss Sol.* 17, wherein a son of David figure (v. 21) is presented as ruling over Israel and defeating Israel's enemies through God's power (vv. 7, 22), there is nothing to support Schweitzer's 'cataclysmic end-of-the-world' reading. Indeed, the description is one that imagines, not a cessation of the space-time continuum, but a Messiah acting within history to enact judgement on Israel's enemies.[41] Of particular note for our discussion is *Pss Sol.* 17.5, which attributes the former destruction of Jerusalem to Israel's covenantal infidelity: 'But, for our sins, sinners rose up against us.' Indeed, it was exactly this theme of divine recompense that was dis-

---

38   This has also been supported by the work of Bauckham et al. in R. Bauckham, *The Gospels for All Christians* (Grand Rapids: Eerdmans, 1998).

39   G. Stanton, '"Pray that your Flight May not be in Winter or on a Sabbath" (Matthew 24.20)', *JSNT* 37 (1989), pp. 17–30. Stanton notes that this could either refer to (1) people 'who perceive they are in danger of persecution keep the Sabbath so strictly that they would not attempt to escape and would therefore be in increased danger' (Stanton, 'Sabbath', p. 24), or (2) people who did flee on the Sabbath who would thus 'antagonize still further some of their persecutors' (Stanton, 'Sabbath', p. 25). On the basis of Mt. 12.1-15 the latter option is to be preferred.

40   Luz, *Matthew 21–28*, p. 186.

41   As we shall argue below, the irony in Matthew is that Israel's enemies are redefined, not as the pagan nations, but as Israel herself.

cussed in our former analysis of *4 Ezra* and *2 Bar.*, which were literary responses to the destruction of the temple *within history*.[42] Within the visions in *4 Ezra*, a man rises from the sea and rides with the clouds of heaven (ch. 13). T. F. Glasson emphasizes that this is an ascent from the sea not a descent from heaven: 'the picture should be taken as indicating in a symbolic way the emergence of the Messiah from concealment, as the writer himself explains (xiii.52)'.[43] Furthermore, in *2 Bar.* the Messianic figure is a warrior messiah (72.2, 6), which contributes to our subsequent discussion of the Son of Man imagery representing the invading Roman armies. Glasson concludes that the Messianic figure in these pseudepigrapha 'belongs to this world, he is an earthly king ruling over a victorious nation ... These writers give the exact opposite of what Schweitzer and his followers state.'[44]

The above-stated inter-testamental texts are not predominantly concerned with a Messiah figure. However, those that do address this issue simply describe him as a human king.[45] The only exception to this is *1 En.* 37-71, where there appears a transcendental pre-existent figure which accompanies God as judge. Nonetheless, it is to be noted that he is not described as 'coming on clouds' or even 'coming'. Furthermore, many have seen this section of *1 En.* as being formulated in the post-Christian era, and as such, of limited exegetical value.[46]

Yet certain sections of Matthew 24 have withstood the criticisms of the first Quest and modern commentators have, instead, accepted the narrative as switching from a primarily historical framework to a primarily eschatological setting. Although commentators differ in terms of where they locate the turning point of historical to eschatological, the consensus remains. *Some* of Matthew 24 refers to a historical reality and *other* parts are 'eschatological' in nature. Bultmann summarizes this general agreement during his presidential address to the SNTS in 1953 as follows:

> In later Judaism this hope for a prosperity on earth remained, a hope for a splendid future of the people ruled by the Messiah who will renew the kingdom of David, e.g. in the *Psalms of Solomon* and in the *Eighteen Prayers*. But besides this another hope arose, for a blissful future which is no longer of this

---

42   The same could also be said of Enoch.

43   Glasson, 'Influence', p. 292.

44   Glasson, 'Influence', p. 292.

45   Glasson, 'Influence', p. 293.

46   Among other arguments regarding the composition of these chapters at a later date, the absence of any fragments of Qumran is noted by J. T. Milik, *The Books of Enoch: Aramaic Fragments at Qumran Cave 4* (Oxford: Clarendon Press, 1976), and F. M. Cross, *The Ancient Library at Qumran* (Sheffield: Sheffield Academic Press, 1958), p. 150 as significant. For further discussion see J. T. Milik, 'Problème de la Littérature Hénochique à la Lumière des Fragments Araméens de Qumran', *HTR* 64 (1971), pp. 333–78; J. C. Hindley, 'Towards a Date for the Similitudes of Enoch. An Historical Approach', *NTS* 14 (1967–68), pp. 551–65.

earth and which shall not be realized by an historical crisis brought about by God, but by a cosmic catastrophe, the end of which will be the resurrection of the dead and the Last Judgement. The figure of the Davidic Messiah is superseded by the figure of the 'Son of Man', as far as there is reflection at all on a Saviour apart from God himself. This hope is connected with the conception of the two aeons which grew up in later Judaism.[47]

However, commentators display quite a range of variability concerning the place at which this eschatological turning point occurs within the narrative of Matthew 24. In sequential order, commentators have seen the division as follows; F. V. Filson notes that 'In all three Synoptic Gospels the discourse is composite ... Jesus speaks of both the fall of Jerusalem and the end of the age.'[48] He goes on to argue that in 'verses 15-22 ... The terrible final trial is described as an invasion of Palestine ... the final eschatological clash; it is a symbol of the conflict between the forces of good and evil.'[49] As such, Filson sees material in vv. 15ff. as referring to a future coming of Jesus.[50] C. Blomberg argues that the switch between 'history' and 'eschatology' occurs in v. 21, primarily on the basis of the association of the vocabulary θλῖψις μεγάλη with the culmination of salvation history.[51]

The majority of modern commentators, however, see the transfer from 'historical narrative' to 'eschatological discourse' in vv. 29-31. U. Luz argues that the disciples' second question (cf. v. 3) is answered in vv. 27-31, that is, 'verses 29-31 are formally separate from the preceding scenes'.[52] Augsburger similarly states that vv. 29-30 'close with a specific reference with the great judgement associated with the coming of the Lord',[53] which he equates with a physical return of the risen Jesus. Keener notes that 'the only *sign* of his immediate coming mentioned in the passage appears in the heavens when or just before Jesus appears', that is, v.30.[54] Whereas Kik, Tasker, France,

47   R. Bultmann, 'History and Eschatology in the New Testament', *NTS* 1 (1954–55), pp. 5–16 (6). Also see R. Bultmann, *Jesus Christ and Mythology* (London: SCM Press, 1960), p. 12 in which the Kingdom is described as 'a tremendous cosmic drama. The Son of Man will come with the clouds of heaven, the dead will be raised and the day of judgement will arrive ... God will suddenly put an end to the world and to history, and he will bring in a new world, the world of eternal blessedness.'

48   F. V. Filson, *A Commentary on the Gospel According to Matthew* (London: Adam and Charles Black, 1960), p. 253.

49   Filson, *Matthew*, pp. 254–55.

50   Filson, *Matthew*, p. 256: 'his coming means final divine judgement on all'.

51   C. Blomberg, *Matthew* (Nashville: Broadman, 1992), p. 359. Theophylact argued that the transition occurred in v. 23.

52   Luz, *Matthew 21–28*, p. 182.

53   M. S. Augsburger, *Mastering the New Testament: Matthew* (USA: Word, 1982), p. 273.

54   C. S. Keener, *Matthew* (Illinois: IVP, 1997), p. 343; Beasley-Murray, *Commentary*, p. 100 is in general agreement with this approach.

Brown and Garland argue for the turning point of v. 32,[55] France has the 'eschatological' section start at v. 36.[56]

In addition to these, there are many mediating views which see reference to the destruction of the temple as being intertwined with language concerning the supposed cataclysmic end of the space-time continuum. Albright and Mann argue that the attempt to piece Matthew 24 together chronologically, either 'historically or 'eschatologically', is 'in direct opposition to the confident assertions of many of the same commentators that the so-called "Sermon on the Mount" is in fact a miscellany'.[57] In regard to 24.29-44, Albright and Mann argue that 'the material in this section illustrates very well the miscellaneous character of the sayings grouped together in this chapter'.[58] Thus, rather than seeing Matthew 24 as a narrative whole, Albright and Mann, among others,[59] suggest that justice is not done to the sources of Matthew 24 if a strict chronology is imposed upon the material. This approach is evident in their discussion of 24.3: 'It is possible that the disciples' request, especially in view of the Matthean clause, may be in all three gospels a question introduced at this point in the narrative to gather together the apocalyptic and eschatological material.'[60] To this, one could point out that some sort of chronology is implied by Matthew's continued use of temporal markers in 24.9-10, 14, 16, 21, 23, 30, and 40. And although Albright and Mann suggest that these are 'no more than a stylistic device',[61] they are nonetheless a stylistic device which must be taken seriously in terms of how *Matthew* has crafted his narrative.

---

55   S. Brown, 'The Matthean Apocalypse', *JSNT* 4 (1979), pp. 2–27; J. M. Kik, *Matthew Twenty-Four* (Pennsylvania: Bible Truth, 1948); R. V. G. Tasker, *The Gospel according to St. Matthew* (London: Tyndale Press, 1961), pp. 223–28.

56   R. T. France, *Matthew* (Grand Rapids: Eerdmans, 1985), pp. 333–36. One interesting variation of this is Plummer, *Matthew*, p. xxxii, who holds that the destruction of Jerusalem and the future coming of Jesus were held closely together and that the Gospel of Matthew was written somewhere between 70 and 75 AD. J. Metcalfe, *Matthew* (Buckinghamshire: John Metcalfe Publishing Trust, 1995), pp. 43–44 is unspecified but nonetheless he sees a historical-eschatological split occurring at some point in the narrative: 'In the final chapter of this section [i.e. ch. 24] Jesus reveals the apocalyptic vision of the end of the temple, of Jerusalem, and of the world.'

57   W. F. Albright and C. S. Mann, *Matthew* (New York: Doubleday, 1971), p. 293.

58   Albright and Mann, *Matthew*, p. 298.

59   Ryle says of Matthew 24 that it is a 'chapter full of prophecy: prophecy of which a large portion is unfulfilled' from the modern standpoint (J. C. Ryle, *Matthew* [Illinois: Crossway Books, 1993], p. 225). It includes the 'destruction of Jerusalem … the second personal coming of Christ … and … the end of the world' (Ryle, *Matthew*, p. 225). Although he allows the material to be somewhat intertwined, it is claimed that the second coming of Christ is the subject of vv. 29-35, but also notes that vv. 15-28 could 'have a further and deeper application still', and that 'It is more than probable that they refer to a second siege of Jerusalem … ' (Ryle, *Matthew*, p. 229).

60   Albright and Mann, *Matthew*, p. 291.

61   Albright and Mann, *Matthew*, p. 298.

Albright and Mann also comment that, 'It is not likely to further our understanding of the gospels ... to examine every clause and sentence of the sayings in chapters xxiv–xxv for precise prediction, and then attempt to match this with known or supposed events after the passion.'[62] This, however, seems a somewhat premature statement, for if, after historical analysis of the period, some historical sense can be made of imagery used by Matthew, then this is strong support for a historical reading.[63]

J. A. T. Robinson previously argued that the early church misrepresented the material in Matthew 24. He suggests that Matthew's *parousia* is 'a term which is clearly editorial on its first appearance (24.3) and which evidently betrays the usage of the early Church'.[64] However, regardless of how one sees the development of Matthew 24 in the early church period, Robinson goes on to make a very insightful comment:

> What fails is the evidence that Jesus [or Matthew] thought of the messianic act as taking place in two stages, the first of which was now shortly to be accomplished, the second of which would follow after an interval and must in the meantime be the focus of every eye and thought.[65]

There is no internal evidence that such a shift occurs at any point in Matthew 24, and as such the discourse should be understood as a single narrative.

3.2.c. Historical reference only

One of the main exegetical figures who suggested the entirety of Matthew 24 is to be understood in reference to the destruction of Jerusalem in 70 AD was the seventeenth-century Hebraist, John Lightfoot (1602–75). Although we will have further opportunity to interact with Lightfoot's work in our subsequent discussion, it is important for us to note here his general interpretive framework. Lightfoot notes that 'the destruction of Jerusalem is very frequently expressed in Scripture as if it were the destruction of the whole world',[66] citing several strands of Old Testament tradition to illustrate this. Deuteronomy 32.20-21 threatens God's wrath consuming the people because they have been a 'perverse generation ... in whom there is no faithfulness', and then states in v. 22

---

62   Albright and Mann, *Matthew*, p. 286.

63   Although we will have occasion to interact with D. C. Allison below, it is significant to note that he argues against the apocalyptic language in Matthew 24 being understood non-literally (D. C. Allison, *Jesus of Nazareth: Millenarian Prophet* [Minneapolis: Fortress Press, 1998], p. 34). Instead he sees it as a theological phase with people coming to terms with various disappointed expectations (Allison, *Jesus*, pp. 152–69, esp. p. 167).

64   J. A. T. Robinson, *Jesus and His Coming* (London: SCM Press, 1957), p. 78.

65   Robinson, *Jesus*, pp. 81–82.

66   J. Lightfoot, *A Commentary on the New Testament from the Talmud and Hebraica* (Oxford: Oxford University Press, 1859), p. 318.

that 'a fire is kindled by my anger, and burns to the depths of Sheol; it devours the earth and its increase, and sets on fire the foundations of the mountains'. Likewise, Jer. 4.23 envisages the destruction of the nation in vivid metaphoric language: 'I looked at the earth, and it was formless and void; and at the heavens, and their light was gone' (cf. Isa. 65.17, 'For I am about to create new heavens and a new earth; the former things shall not be remembered or come to mind'). In this manner, Lightfoot interprets the 'apocalyptic' imagery associated with the 'coming Son of Man' as 'Christ's taking vengeance of that exceedingly wicked nation'.[67] Lightfoot argues that this takes historical expression in the Roman armies which 'compass around Jerusalem with a siege'[68] and that at this point 'most certain destruction hangs over it'.[69] In discussion of vv. 34-51, Lightfoot concludes that 'it appears plain enough, that the foregoing verses are not to be understood of the last judgement, but, as we said, of the destruction of Jerusalem'.[70]

A commentator of a more recent time has argued similarly. C. H. Dodd interprets the coming of the Son of Man in the synoptic eschatological discourses as follows:

> The coming of the Son of Man, in its aspect as judgment, is realized in the catastrophes which Jesus predicted as lying immediately in store – the persecution of Himself and His disciples, the destruction of the Temple and of the Jewish nation. These catastrophes He regarded as an immediately imminent development of the existing situation. Thus the care-free people eating and drinking at ease like the antediluvians are the men and women whom Jesus saw about Him, stupidly unaware that the judgments of God were in the earth, and destined at any moment to be overwhelmed with disaster.[71]

In a Festschrift for Dodd, A. Feuillet takes up this general approach and argues that, although it is difficult to avoid the impression of final judgement given the current academic presuppositions,[72] the coming Son of Man on the clouds does not refer to the physical return of the resurrected Jesus but 'sa venue sur les nuées n'est autre chose que l'établissement du règne messianique'.[73] As with others who share this view, Feuillet takes

---

67 Lightfoot, *Commentary*, p. 319.
68 Lightfoot, *Commentary*, p. 313.
69 Lightfoot, *Commentary*, p. 313.
70 Lightfoot, *Commentary*, p. 320.
71 C. H. Dodd, *The Parables of the Kingdom* (London: James Nisbet, 1936), pp. 126–27.
72 'Au premiere abord il semble bien difficile d'échapper à l'impression que la Parousia dont il ici question est le jugement final de l'humanité', A. Feuillet, 'Le sens du mot Parusie dans l'évangile de Matthieu', in *The Background of the New Testament and Its Eschatology*, ed. D. Daube and W. D. Davies (Cambridge: Cambridge University Press, 1956), pp. 261–80 (262).
73 Feuillet, 'Parusie', p. 262.

συντελείας τοῦ αἰῶνος as referring to the destruction of Jerusalem in 70 AD, in that it signified the end of the old dispensation. Although reference is made to a similar phrase (συντελείᾳ τῶν αἰῶνων) in Heb. 9.26, referring to the life of Jesus, which thus supports this reading, Feuillet's main contribution is his discussion of Jas 5.1-11. There Feuillet demonstrates that the phrase τῆς παρουσίας τοῦ κυρίου (v. 7) is used as an image of judgement and is directed towards those who 'have condemned and murdered the righteous one (τὸν δίκαιον), who does not resist you' (v. 6), which he takes as a reference to the Jews rejecting Jesus as messiah. Indeed this was the sense that Cassiodorus and Oec attributed to v. 6 in their early commentaries.[74] The New Testament itself provides evidence that τὸν δίκαιον could refer to Jesus, as Acts 3.14; 7.52; 22.14; 1 Pet. 3.18; 1 Jn 2.1, 29; 3.7 potentially indicate.[75] And as others have noted, Jesus could no doubt be considered under this *general* category of righteous sufferer.[76] However, even if one does not accept that τὸν δίκαιον refers to Jesus, Jas 5.1-11 still provides an early example of wicked behaviour and consequent judgement described in terms of the τῆς παρουσίας τοῦ κυρίου.

In regard to Matthew 24, although there have been positive signs of this overall historical understanding in contemporary discussions,[77] others have levelled criticisms against this approach. U. Luz argues that 'the greatest weaknesses of this type of interpretation lie in interpreting vv. 13-14 to refer to the time before the destruction of Jerusalem'.[78] We will attempt to address this objection below in our exegetical section. Furthermore, Davies and Allison argue that the entirety of ch. 24 cannot refer to the destruction of the temple because of the 'eschatological reference of vv.6-13, 21-22, and 27-31'.[79] And they conclude that there are no 'clear indications to the contrary'.[80] In our following discussion it is hoped that precedent will be found to question some criticisms of this kind,[81] and potentially provide some 'clear indications to the contrary'.[82]

---

74   See M. Dibelius, *James* (Philadelphia: Fortress Press, 1976), p. 239.

75   Cf. Isa. 53.11. Although, as Davids notes, only the first three aforementioned passages employ τὸν δίκαιον in a titular sense. P. H. Davids, *The Epistle of James: A Commentary on the Greek Text* (Exeter: The Paternoster Press, 1982), p. 179.

76   Davids, *James*, p. 180. See also S. Laws, *A Commentary on the Epistle of James* (London: SCM Press, 1980), pp. 204–206; J. Cantinat, *Les Èpîtres de Saint Jacques et de Saint Jude* (Paris: Gabalda, 1973), pp. 229–30.

77   Caird, *Imagery*, pp. 252–54; Wright, *People*; idem, *Jesus*; Wilson, *When*. These and other significant authors will be addressed in our exegetical analysis below.

78   Luz, *Matthew 21–28*, pp. 186–87.

79   Davies and Allison, *Matthew 3*, p. 329. We will take issue with this definition of eschatology in a later section of our discussion.

80   Davies and Allison, *Matthew 3*, p. 329.

81   In support, there have also been other developments in our understanding of Jewish eschatology of the period which lend weight to this hypothesis. See for example J. J. Collins, *The Scepter and the Star* (New York: Doubleday, 1995), who among others will be discussed in chapter 5.

82   A further interpretive approach envisages Matthew 24 as simultaneously refer-

3.3. The Language of Matthew 24

We will proceed with a detailed study to determine whether the afore-mentioned proposal of *Historical Reference* most thoroughly accounts for the type of imagery and the style of language used in Matthew 24.

3.3.a. Matthew 24.1-2

Matthew introduces the narrative sequence with the following words: Καὶ ἐξελθὼν ὁ Ἰησοῦς ἀπὸ τοῦ ἱεροῦ ἐπορεύετο ('And as Jesus came out of the temple and was going away ...'). Matthew previously noted Jesus' entry into the temple in 21.23, which indicates that all that has transpired from this point to 24.1 has occurred in the precincts of the temple,[83] including the subsequent disputations with the various groups of Jewish leadership: (1) the chief priests and elders (21.23ff.)[84] culmi-nating in the phrase 'Therefore I tell you, the kingdom of God will be taken away from you and given to a nation producing the fruits of the kingdom' (v. 43), which, significantly, is a unique Matthean addition; (2) the Pharisees/Herodians and paying tribute to Caesar (22.15-22); (3) the Sadducees and the resurrection (22.23-33); and (4) the seven woes against the scribes and Pharisees. Although very similar to the

---

ring to a historical *and* eschatological reality. That is, it is a single prophecy with two fulfilments. In this regard, Ephrem the Syrian, the fourth-century theologian and hymn writer said of Matthew 24, 'It is said that he [Jesus] was speaking of the punishment in Jerusalem and at the same time referring to the end of this world' (*Comm. Diat.* 18.14). This would be similar to the Antiochean school, founded by Lucian of Samosata in the late third century, which proposed the interpretive approach of *theoria*, whereby a single Old Testament prophesy can operate on multiple levels of fulfilment (cf. also Augustine's letter to Hesychius 901–13). Although J. P. Meier, a scholar of a more contemporary period, argues that a passage such as Mt. 24.14-22 could refer to the destruction of the temple as well as a future event (Meier, *Matthew*, p. 283), many have been reluctant to accept the entire chapter as operating in this regard. As to the legitimacy of this approach, the exegetical burden is upon those proposing this double fulfilment in identifying any specific indications (within the text itself) that this most plausibly makes sense of the narrative material. Whether such justification exists remains to be seen. To this issue we will return in due course.

83   Hagner, *Matthew 14–28*, p. 687 says the reference to departure from the temple is 'not to be correlated with a previously specified visit ... the intervening material presup-poses the passage of considerable time'. This however runs across the grain of the nar-rative which has been building towards the confrontation between Jesus and the Jewish leadership throughout the Gospel (3.14; 8.11-12 et al.). In terms of Matthew's narrative sequence the intervening events certainly do take place in the temple. Indeed, several of the events are only suitable in the confines of the temple; see for example the incident over paying tribute to Caesar.

84   The audience in v. 45 also includes Pharisees. But this may refer to a report brought before them by the initial audience. Perhaps the Chief Priests and elders sought the support of the Pharisees before attempting to arrest Jesus (again: see 21.23). However, it is important not to see these groups as involving mutually exclusive membership.

Markan parallel, Mt. 24.1 substitutes Matthean vocabulary,[85] and reveals important redactional activity. Matthew replaces Mark's present middle participle ἐκπορευομένου (to go out; to come out; Mk 13.1) with the aorist active participle ἐξελθών, and adds his own reference with the imperfect middle indicative ἐπορεύετο. In so doing, Matthew (1) eliminates Mark's genitive absolute, perhaps for the purpose of stylistic improvement,[86] (2) substitutes the plural οἱ μαθηταὶ αὐτοῦ (his disciples) for the singular εἷς τῶν μαθητῶν αὐτοῦ (one of his disciples) to widen the audience and hence magnitude of the following logion; and (3) eliminates the direct discourse while adding the purposive infinitive clause,[87] thus intensifying the dialogue.[88]

In Jesus' response (v. 2), Matthew changes Mark's simple question βλέπεις ταύτας ... ' ('Do you see these .... ?') to a slanted question expecting an affirmative answer: οὐ βλέπετε ταῦτα ... ; ('You see ... these don't you?'), by the addition of the particle οὐ. Emphasis is also added to Jesus' statement with the addition of (1) πάντα (Mark: 'You see these ...'; Matthew: 'You see *all* these ...')[89] and (2) the prefatory ἀμὴν λέγω ὑμῖν. Matthew omits the second double negative (μὴ) and changes Mark's aorist passive subjunctive (καταλυθῇ) to a future passive indicative (καταλυθήσεται).[90] Additionally, Matthew clarifies Mark's οἰκοδομάς (Mk 13.1) with οἰκοδομάς τοῦ ἱεροῦ (Mt. 24.1). Thus Matthew seems to bring together the previously stated woes (ch. 23) and the future oracle of judgement (ch. 24), and focuses specifically

---

85　Davies and Allison, *Matthew 3*, p. 334.

86　C. F. D. Moule notes 'the growing laxity of the Greek of the N.T. period, as compared with the Classical. It countenances the use of a clumsy Genitive Absolute where a phrase in agreement with an already present (or implied) Nominative, Accusative or Dative would be both correct and neat' (C. F. D. Moule, *An Idiom Book of New Testament Greek* [Cambridge: Cambridge University Press, 1959], p. 43). J. H. Moulton describes the genitive absolute as 'a violent use' (J. H. Moulton, W. F. Howard, and N. Turner, *A Grammar of New Testament Greek* [4 vols; Edinburgh: Clark, 1906–76], p. 1.74). M. Zerwick notes its absence is 'more elegant' (M. Zerwick, *Biblical Greek* [Rome: Pontifical Institute, 1963], p. 18). J. W. Wenham states that the 'genitive use of the participle is *not suitable* when the noun that goes with the participle is also the subject, object or indirect object of the main verb, since the participle *should* then itself take the case of the word with which it agrees' (J. W. Wenham, *The Elements of New Testament Greek* [Cambridge: Cambridge University Press, 1965], p. 155). F. Blass and A. Debrunner conclude that 'NT authors ... prefer the absolute construction in numerous instances where a classical author would not have admitted it even as a special license' (F. Blass, and A. Debrunner, *A Greek Grammar of the New Testament and Other Early Christian Literature* [trans. R. W. Funk; Cambridge: Cambridge University Press, 1961], §423).

87　Hagner, *Matthew 14–28*, p. 686.

88　Whereas in Mark a disciple merely points out their surroundings as they walk along, in Matthew the disciples (plural) specifically approach Jesus for the purpose of pointing out the buildings of the temple.

89　In so doing Matthew replaces Mark's μεγάλας οἰκοδομάς in v. 2, but this is readily explained by Matthew's reference to the τὰς οἰκοδομὰς τοῦ ἱεροῦ in the previous verse.

90　The parallel in Lk. 21.6 also displays similar variation to Mark at this point, which could be explained by the influence of Q or oral tradition.

on the temple. This comes to a climax with the saying in Mt. 24.2, οὐ μὴ ἀ φεθῇ ὧδε λίθος ἐπὶ λίθον ('not one stone will be left here upon another'). Jesus' response to his disciples' admiration of the temple buildings, possibly looking back towards Jerusalem as they climbed the Mount of Olives, is illuminated by a number of texts which celebrate the temple's grandeur and beauty.[91] This contextualizes Jesus' logion in v. 2 as particularly forceful.[92]

The manner in which this relates to our discussion is apparent in J. S. Kloppenborg's recent discussion of the Roman practice of the *evocatio deorum*, that is the 'calling out' of the tutelary deity of a city prior to its destruction ('devotion'). Kloppenborg proposes that it was commonly held that a city could not be destroyed while the deity was still present. This idea lead to the Roman siege tactic of calling out the deity. Kloppenborg argues that the practice was sufficiently attested in antiquity so as to form a literary *topos*.[93] Several examples are offered in support of his thesis,[94] including Livy's description of the destruction of the Etruscan city Veii in 396 BC;[95] Horace's retelling of Carthage's capitulation to Rome in 146 BC;[96] and

91   *War* 6.267 exclaims that the temple 'was the most admirable of all the works that we have seen or heard of, both for its curious structure and its magnitude, and also for the vast wealth bestowed upon it'. Similarly, *Ant.* 15.393 states, 'and the whole structure, as also the structure of the royal cloister, was on each side much lower, but the middle was much higher, till they were visible to those that dwelt in the country for a great many furlongs'. This is a theme which was also celebrated in the Talmud; *b. B. Bat.* 4a (b. Suk 51b) refers to the temple in the following manner: 'It used to be said "he who has not seen the temple in its full splendor has never seen a beautiful building."' The temple's renown for its beauty is attested in a variety of sources, and connected with it is the belief in its impenetrable status. See 2 Macc. 2.22; Philo *Spec. Leg.* 1.76; cf. Jer. 7.4.

92   There were, however, other prophetic figures who began prophesying the ruin of the temple during a time of peace. Jesus ben Ananias in 62 AD (*War* 6.300–309) is one example. Kloppenborg, *Excavating*, p. 87. Indeed, the Talmudic Chronicler notes that 'On the ninth day of the month Ab the city of Jerusalem was ploughed' (*Taanith* c. 5). Maimonides expands on this by noting 'On the ninth day of the month Ab, fatal for vengence, the wicked Turnus Rufus, of the children of Edom, ploughed up the Temple, and the places about it, that that saying might be fulfilled "Zion shall be ploughed like a field"' (*Taanith* c. 4. Hal. 6). Lightfoot, *Commentary*, p. 309 equates Maimonides' Turnus Rufus with Josephus' Terentius Rufus in *War* 7.31: Τερέντιος Ῥοῦφος οὗτος γὰρ ἄρχων τῆς στρατιᾶς κατελέλειπτο ('Terentius Rufus, who was left to command the army there'). Cf. also *War* 7.1: κελεύει Καῖσαρ ἤδη τήν τε πόλιν ἄπασαν καὶ τὸν νεὼν κατασκάπτειν ('Caesar gave orders that they should now demolish the entire city and temple'); *War* 7.3: οὕτως ἐξωμάλισαν οἱ κατασκάπτοντες ὡς μηδεπώποτ' οἰκηθῆναι πί στιν ἂν ἔτι παρασχεῖν τοῖς προσελθοῦσι ('it was so thoroughly laid even with the ground by those that dug it up to the foundation, that there was left nothing to make those that came thither believe it had ever been inhabited').

93   Kloppenborg, 'Evocatio', pp. 434–41.

94   For extensive secondary literature on this subject see Kloppenborg, 'Evocatio', p. 434 n.52. Kloppenborg also notes that this is not only a Roman belief but is also present in second temple literature and the Tanak. See chapter 2 of this book for further discussion in this regard.

95   Livy *Ab urbe condita* 5.21.1–3.

96   Horace, *Odes* 2.25–28.

general descriptions of the *evocatio* practice by Verrius Flaccus noted in Pliny's *Naturalis Historia*.[97] According to Kloppenborg, οὐ μὴ ἀφεθῇ ὧδε λίθος ἐπὶ λίθον in Mk 13.2 is the natural conclusion drawn from Q 13.35, that is, destruction is the only viable alternative subsequent to the desertion of God's house (temple). Following J. Lambrecht[98] and J. R. Donahue,[99] Kloppenborg notes (1) the 'verbal coincidence of the use of ἀφίεσθαι in [the] two sayings that pronounce doom on the temple …',[100] and (2) 'Mk 13.2 presupposes what Q 13.35a states expressly, that the deity has abandoned the "house" (= temple)'.[101] The connection of the destruction of the temple and the desertion of the deity[102] coheres well with our discussion of the textual issue in Mt. 23.38 and the departure of the *Shekinah*.[103] However, the crucial unknown element in Kloppenborg's thesis is whether Titus actually performed any such ritual. Although an explicit reference to the practice is lacking, there is some circumstantial evidence that may indicate the *evocatio* was employed. At one point in Josephus' description of the war, he notes Titus declaring 'I appeal to the gods of my own country, and to every deity who watched over this place (for now I believe that there is none. …'[104] And in *War* 6.323ff. Titus invoked the memory of Carthage, a siege which was known in the first century by Horace for the *evocatio* practice. More specifically, *War* 5.412 records: 'My belief, therefore, is that the Deity has fled from the holy places and taken his stand on the side of those with whom you are now at war.' Kloppenborg concludes that 'without actually describing the *evocatio* ritual, Josephus leaves sufficient hints in his account that it probably was performed'.[105] Josephus' omission can be attributed to his dual purpose of attributing the destruction of the temple to the Zealots.

Although Kloppenborg draws different conclusions relating to his discussion of the date of Mark and the parallel fates of Jesus and the temple,[106] his thesis is instructive in noting that 'Mark 13.2 should be read in concert with Q 13.35a.'[107] Surprisingly, Kloppenborg omits any reference to the Matthean parallel which, in fact, brings exactly these two traditions together in Mt. 23.38–24.2. This is surprising because it would seem that this phenomenon would support his overall reading in that it is supported by the earliest discernible stage in Mark's reception history.

---

97   Pliny *Nat. Hist.* 28.18–19. See Kloppenborg, 'Evocatio', pp. 434–41.

98   J. Lambrecht, *Die Redaktion der Markus-Apokalypse: Literarische Analyse und Strukturuntersuchung* (Rome: Päpstliches Bibelinstitut, 1967), pp. 77–78.

99   J. R. Donahue, *Are You the Christ?: The Trial Narrative in the Gospel of Mark* (Montana: Society of Biblical Literature, 1972), p. 108.

100   Kloppenborg, 'Evocatio', p. 448.

101   Kloppenborg, 'Evocatio', p. 448.

102   Kloppenborg, 'Evocatio', p. 442.

103   See chapter 2 above.

104   *War* 6.127.

105   Kloppenborg, 'Evocatio', p. 444.

106   Kloppenborg, 'Evocatio', p. 449.

107   Kloppenborg, 'Evocatio', p. 450.

In this light, Matthew seems to be drawing on the same conceptual idea that is present in the Old Testament, pseudepigrapha, and Rabbinic traditions.[108] The threat of Jerusalem's destruction is contingent on faithfulness to the covenant. Particularly striking are parallels that envision the consequences of disobedience as a reversal of the building process.[109] Haggai 2.15 threatens, 'But now, consider what will come to pass from this day on. Before a stone was placed upon a stone in the Lord's temple.' In addition, after the Solomonic dedication of the temple 1 Kgs 9.6-9 declares that 'If you turn aside from following me ... This house will become a heap of ruins; everyone passing by it will be astonished, and will hiss; and they will say, "Why has the Lord done such a thing to this land and to this house?"'[110]

In this way Matthew (1) draws on traditions (*evocatio deorum*), and (2) draws traditions together (Mk 13.2; Q 13.35), in order to present the woes of ch. 23 as climaxing in 23.38, which in and of itself demands the kind of narrative we find in Matthew 24. Within the context of our discussion, it is suggested that indeed this is the most appropriate way of understanding the introduction to ch. 24. Thus, one would need a strong incentive to switch from a 'historical' reading to an 'eschatological' reading part-way through the chapter. As we will find apparent, there is no such justification for this bifurcation. [111]

3.3.b. Matthew 24.3

Subsequent to the forecast of the temple's utter destruction, the disciples were perplexed and asked 'When will this be, and what will be the sign of your coming and of the end of the age?' Important for our discussion is Matthew's 'highly significant divergence'[112] from the synoptic parallel in his addition of τῆς σῆς παρουσίας ('... of your coming') to the Markan καὶ τί τὸ σημεῖον (Mk 13.4).

The παρουσία (vv. 3, 27, 37, 39), unique to Matthew, has traditionally been understood as the 'visible return of the resurrected and ascended Jesus'.[113] This is evident in the copious detail offered in commentaries of

---

108 For a discussion on the problems of dating Rabbinic material see *Introduction*.

109 Hagner, *Matthew 14–28*, p. 688.

110 Cf. Amos 9.1; Mal. 3.12; Jer. 7.13-14; 26.4-6; cf. *b. Ber.* 3a.

111 Jesus' departure per se may also have implicit symbolic action in representing Yahweh's departure from the temple. A point which Matthew emphasized through the duplication of Mark's singular reference to departure. Davies and Allison suggest that texts such as Jer. 12.7; Ezek. 8.12; 9.9; 11.23 and *LAB* 19.12 may be on the interpretive horizon. See Davies and Allison, *Matthew 3*, pp. 334–35. Although we do not have adequate scope to develop this here, it would indeed provide support for a very high Christology in Matthew.

112 Albright and Mann, *Matthew*, p. 290.

113 Wilson, *When*, p. 9. An example of this assumption is apparent in Kloppenborg's discussion of Mk 9.1; 13.30 where he refers to the parousia as a reference to an end time/ second coming event, even though Mark does not have a single reference to 'παρουσία, Kloppenborg, 'Evocatio', p. 421.

apparently similar 'instances of people asking for the time of the end'.[114] However, what is readily apparent in these lists of parallel biblical, rabbinic, and pseudepigraphical literature is the assumption that v. 3 does in fact refer to the end of the space-time continuum, a point with which we will take issue shortly. This kind of approach is so deeply entrenched in discussions of Matthew 24 that D. Patte states without any argumentation that 'This question ... concerned the time of the end ... the coming of the Son of Man and the end of the present age.'[115] Similarly, Hagner states that the παρουσία 'refers not to the visit or presence of an earthly king, as in the Hellenistic world, but is used technically to refer to the return of Jesus,[116] and that 'the disciples are not slow in recognizing the apocalyptic tone of the announcement [vv. 1-2], as their question in v 3 indicates ... the thought of the destruction of the second temple could ... only signal the time of final judgement'.[117] Similarly, Beasley-Murray states, 'The question of the disciples in v. 3 is inevitable: every Jew assumed that *that* temple would be the centre of the earth in the kingdom of God; its ruin then could only be in connection with the end of the age and the coming of the final kingdom.'[118] However, in response to both Beasley-Murray and Hagner's latter point, one could question the immediate association between the destruction of the temple and the final eschatological judgement on two grounds. First, there is no evidence that a response akin to this occurred after the destruction of the first temple, and second, there are similar themes of impending destruction of Jerusalem in both Jer. 9.11 and Mic. 3.12 without any reference to the 'end of time'. Jeremiah 9.11: 'I will make Jerusalem a heap of ruins, a lair of jackals; and I will make the towns of Judah a desolation, without inhabitant'; Mic. 3.12: 'Therefore because of you, Zion shall be plowed as a field; Jerusalem shall become a heap of ruins, and the mountain of the house a wooded height.' We shall argue that if such a reference to cataclysmic eschatology was not implicit in the prophetic literature, then justification is needed to import a different reading into Matthew, justification which up to this point has been lacking. In our following discussion we will (1) propose a revised model for understanding the παρουσία and (2) note how this relates to 24.3c καὶ συντελείας τοῦ αἰῶνος.

---

114 Davies and Allison, *Matthew 3*, p. 337.

115 Patte, *Matthew*, p. 334.

116 Hagner, *Matthew 14–28*, p. 688. Hagner also definitively states in the introduction to his commentary that 'The technical word παρουσία (*parousia*) ... refers to the eschatological return of Christ' (Hagner, *Matthew 1–13*, p. lxiii). See also J. Sherwood, 'The Only Sure Word', *MSJ* 7 (1996), pp. 53–74 (56), who states that 'παρουσία ... when used in relation to Christ in the NT, only describes His second coming'.

117 Hagner, *Matthew 14–28*, pp. 687–88.

118 G. R. Beasley-Murray, *Matthew* (London: Scripture Union, 1984), p. 99.

3.3.b.i. The parousia

The term παρουσία in its most basic sense refers to a person's presence, that is, as opposed to their absence. In 1 Cor. 16.17, Paul states, 'I rejoice at the coming (παρουσία) of Stephanas and Fortunatus and Achaicus, because they have made up for your absence.' Again in Phil. 2.12 Paul states, 'Therefore, my beloved, just as you have always obeyed me, not only in my presence (παρουσία), but much more now in my absence, work out your own salvation with fear and trembling.' Likewise in 2 Cor. 10.10, Paul's opponents claim that 'His letters are weighty and strong, but his bodily presence (παρουσία τοῦ σώματος) is weak, and his speech contemptible.'[119]

The term was also frequently employed more specifically. One common usage in the Hellenistic world was the use of παρουσία to refer to the visit of a ruler or a high official. Polybius *Hist.* 18.48.4 notes of Antiochus:

> and after speaking with him on the other matters about which they had instructions, they advised him to send an embassy to Rome, to ask for an alliance, in order to obviate all suspicion of being on the watch for an opportunity in expectation of the arrival of Antiochus (ἀποκαραδοκεῖν τὴν παρουσίαν Ἀντιόχου).

Polybius *Hist.* 16.25.1 also uses the term of Attalus' entry into Athens in 200 BC:

> The Athenian people sent envoys to king Attalus, both to thank him for the past, and to urge him to come to Athens to consult with them on the dangers that still threatened them ... . The Athenian people, being informed of his coming (τὴν παρουσίαν αὐτοῦ), passed very liberal votes as to the reception and general entertainment of the king. Arrived at the Peiraeus, Attalus spent the first day in transacting business with the Roman ambassadors, and was extremely delighted to find that they were fully mindful of their ancient alliance with him, and quite prepared for the war with Philip.

The Maccabaean literature also provides an illustrative parallel. *Third Maccabees* 3.14-18 records the following:

> When our expedition took place in Asia, as you yourselves know, it was brought to conclusion, according to plan, by the gods' deliberate alliance with us in battle ... and when we had granted very great revenues to the temples in the cities, we came on to Jerusalem also, and went up to honor

---

119 For other references to 'presence' see 2 Cor. 7.6-7; Phil. 1.26; P.Oxy 903.15; *Ant.* 3.80, 202–203; 9.55. A reference to simple presence is also attested in P. Wiscon. 74, which concerns a request for a brother to rejoin his family subsequent to his mother's death. This, however, does not negate the possibility that the term can be used in reference to an eschatological second coming as other New Testament references make clear: 1 Thess. 2.19; 3.13; 4.15; 5.23; 2 Thess. 2.1, 8; 2 Pet. 3.4, 12.

the temple of those wicked people, who never cease from their folly. They accepted our presence (παρουσίαν) by word, but insincerely by deed, because when we proposed to enter their inner temple and honor it with magnificent and most beautiful offerings, they were carried away by their traditional arrogance, and excluded us from entering; but they were spared the exercise of our power because of the benevolence that we have toward all.[120]

Of particular importance, in other extant literature, are the several instances of παρουσία linked specifically with kingship. The term can either be directly associated with kingship, such as in Ostraka 1481.2 (παρουσία τῆς βασιλίσσης, or more specifically related to a particular royal figure. Germanicus is recorded as saying εἰς τὴν ἐμὴν παρουσίαν ('in my coming'),[121] and of Ptolemy Philometor and Cleopatra it is said καθ' ὃς ἐποιεῖσθ' ἐν Μέμθει παρουσίας.[122]

In S. Llewelyn's discussion of the terminology of transport requisition in antiquity, he notes the phenomenon of the term παρουσία as that which can refer to soldiers or officials.[123] It is in this regard that we wish take the interpretation of παρουσία one step further than previously argued in the secondary literature. In an additional corpus of texts it is evident that παρουσία can refer not just to a royal military ruler, but to the presence of the military or army itself. Two references in Thucydides are significant in this regard. While denouncing the Syracusans, Thucydides, *The Peloponnesian War* 6.86.1–3, refers to military strength in the following manner: '[The Syracusans] live close to you, not in a camp, but in a city greater than the force we have with us (δὲ μείζονι τῆς ἡμετέρας παρουσίας ἐποικοῦντεσ ὑμῖν) ....'[124] While perhaps not a technical designation, in this particular narrative description παρουσία specifically refers to military presence. Similarly, in an earlier description of the Peloponnesian War, Thucydides uses the term in reference to the arrival of the military army. *The Peloponnesian War* 1.128.5 states:

> Some connections and kinsmen of the king had been taken in Byzantium, on its capture from the Medes, during the first invasion (τῇ προτέρᾳ παρουσιᾳ), after the return from Cyprus. These captives he sent off to the king with-

---

120 For other references of *parousia* as royal visit see *Corpus Inscriptionum Greacum* 4896, 8f.; *Sylloge Inscriptionum Graecarum* 3495, 85f.; 741, 21; 30; Ostraka II 1372; 1481. See A. Deissmann, *Light From the Ancient East* (Edinburgh: Kessinger Publishing, 1927), pp. 368–73.

121 Preisigke Sammel-buch, I. 3924, 3f. Cited in A. Oepke, 'Παρουσία, Πάρειμι', in *Theological Dictionary of the New Testament*, ed. G. Friedrich (trans. G. W. Bromiley; 10 vols; Grand Rapids: Eerdmans, 1970), pp. 5.858–71 (859).

122 P.Par., 26.1.18. Cited in Oepke, 'Παρουσία', p. 859.

123 S. Llewelyn, *New Documents Illustrating Early Christianity, Volume 7. A Review of the Greek Inscriptions and Papyri published in 1982–83* (Macquarie: The Ancient History Documentary Research Centre, 1994), p. 60.

124 English translation from E. C. Marchant, *Commentary on Thucydides Book 3* (London: MacMillan, 1909).

out the knowledge of the rest of the allies, the account being that they had escaped from him.

This semantic range of παρουσία is not limited to Thucydides, but is also attested in the Maccabaean literature. Second Maccabees 8.12 states that 'word came to Judas concerning Nicanor's invasion; and when he told his companions of the arrival of the army (παρουσίαν τοῦ στπατοπέδου)'. Also pertinent to our discussion are two letters from King Mithridates of Pontus to a Satrap in Caria, recorded in the *Sylloge Inscriptionum Graecarum*.[125] In both accounts it is said that Chairemon fled on hearing of the king's coming (παρουσία). The first letter records the following: ν[ῦν] τε τὴ[ν] ἐ[μὴ]ν παρουσίαν ἐπιγνοὺς τοὺς [τε υἱ]ους Πυθόδω[ρ]ον καὶ Πυθίων[α] ἐξέθετο καὶ αὐ[τος πέ]φευγεν ('And now having found out about my coming he has removed both his sons Pythodoros and Pythion to safety and himself fled').[126] The second letter similarly states: Νῦν τε τὴν εμὴν παρουσίαν πυθό[μενος], εἰς τὸ τῆς Ἐφεσίας Ἀρτέμιδος ἱερὸν καταπέ[φευγεν] ('And now having learnt of my coming he has escaped to the temple of the Ephesian Artemis').[127] Connolly says 'in this context *parousia* takes on connotations of retribution (the purpose and consequence of the king's coming) ...'.[128]

Within the Hellenistic world, παρουσία also took on a sacral meaning in referring to the presence of the deity, such as in the mystic cults of Hermes: ἡ παρουσία μου γίνεται αυτοῖς βοήθεια,[129] or of gods visiting the earth during times of sacrifice.[130] The combined royal and divine presence suggests some kind of similarity with the coming of Yahweh in the Old Testament, which always meant the defeat of Israel's enemies: Egypt (Isa. 19.1-2); Assyria (Isa. 30.27); the nations (Hab. 3.3-15); and even Israel herself when she had an apostate and disobedient people (Amos 5.18-24). It is our contention that this ironic reversal of the recipients of divine wrath permeates Matthew's presentation of his narrative.[131]

The manner in which this contributes to our discussion is relatively clear. This interpretation of the παρουσία, including military presence, royal retribution, and divine vengeance, coheres remarkably well with the contention that the Son of Man's presence represents the invading armies of the Romans in the war of 70 AD. Indeed, this is consistent with themes

---

125 Dittenberger 1915–24, noted by Connolly, 'παρουσία', p. 167.

126 SIG³ 741.21–23.

127 SIG³ 741.30–31.

128 A. I. Connolly, 'παρουσία', in *New Documents Illustrating Early Christianity*, Volume 4. A Review of the Greek Inscriptions and Papyri published in 1979 (ed. G. H. R. Horsely; Macquarie: The Ancient History Documentary Research Centre, Sydney, Australia), pp. 167–69 (167).

129 Corp. Herm. I.22, cited in Oepke, 'Παρουσία', p. 860.

130 Iambl. Myst. III.6 (cf. V.21). Oepke, 'Παρουσία', pp. 860–61.

131 Such is evident in Matthew's quotation of Isa. 7.14 in Mt. 1.23, which is referred to not as a word of encouragement but a threat of judgement (cf. Isa. 1–6).

in the Old Testament where Yahweh uses pagan forces to judge Israel's covenantal infidelity.[132] It would seem that the term in Matthew is employed to capture the above-mentioned aspects of 'presence', 'kingship', and 'military destruction'.[133] Precisely how this particular interpretation is to be understood with the surrounding material will ensue in the following discussion of Matthew 24.

In an interesting aside, C. K. Barrett contends that the 'Son of Man' sayings were originally alternatives to the resurrection narratives and were predictions of the final vindication of the crucified one.[134] This would indeed cohere well with our above-stated hypothesis which sees Matthew 24 as functioning as judgement upon those who did not offer an appropriate welcome to their legitimate king. Although, as Wilson has noted, 'Barrett goes too far in replacing the hope of the *Parousia* with the reality of the resurrection,'[135] the connection between vindication and judgement poses an appropriate parallel within its immediate context.

3.3.b.ii. The end of the age

As noted above, commentators often argue that Mt. 24.3's redaction of Mk 13.4 in the twofold τῆς σῆς παρουσίας καὶ συντελείας τοῦ αἰῶνος ('of your coming and of the close of the age') in place of Mark's single ὅταν μέλλῃ ταῦτα συντελεῖσθαι πάντα ('that all these things are about to be accomplished') indicates that the emphasis of what follows is 'not upon the destruction of the temple but upon the last things'[136] (see dis-

---

132 Such is the case in later reflection on the Babylonian exile (2 Chron. 36.15-21; 2 *Bar.* 1.1-5; *b.Pesah* 87b; *b.Sanh.* 37b).

133 Some may object that the personal pronoun in 24.3 excludes such an interpretation. However, it is important to note if Matthew intends to portray the 'Son of Man' as *representative* of the Roman armies then no real discontinuity exists. That is, the personal presence of the 'Son of Man' personifies Rome's destruction of Jerusalem. That the 'Son of Man' was understood in other literature of the day as representative of a larger entity is evident from *1 En.*, where the 'close connection between the individual Son of Man and the community of the righteous has led some scholars to invoke the allegedly Hebrew conception of corporate personality' (J. J. Collins, *The Apocalyptic Imagination* [New York: Crossroad, 1987], p. 185; also see T. W. Manson, 'The Son of Man in Daniel, Enoch and the Gospels', in *Studies in the Gospels and Epistles*, ed. M. Black [Manchester: Manchester University Press, 1962], pp. 123–45; D. S. Russell, *The Method and Message of Jewish Apocalyptic* [London: SCM Press, 1964], pp. 350–52). Although this identification has been slightly tempered by advances in anthropological theories of 'psychical unity' (J. W. Rogerson, 'The Hebrew Concept of Corporate Personality – A Re-Examination', *JTS* 21 [1970], pp. 1–16), Mowinckel has convincingly argued that 'representative unity and corporate conception of the leader as the bearer of the whole, and of the individual as a type of the race, is not the same as literal and actual identity. The fact that in the cult a person represents the whole, or in a symbolic sense is the whole, means that there is an intimate community ... between them' (S. Mowinckel, *He That Cometh* [trans. G. W. Anderson; Oxford: Oxford University Press, 1956] , p. 381).

134 C. K. Barrett, *Jesus and the Gospel Tradition* (London: SPCK, 1967), pp. 81–82.

135 Wilson, *When*, p. 14.

136 Davies and Allison, *Matthew 3*, p. 337.

cussion above). However, the most plausible way of understanding this verse was hinted at through Lightfoot's work in 1658–74 and Feuillet's later analysis in 1956 (noted above), which illustrate that the two questions are different sides of the same coin.

In this regard, although several manuscripts insert the definite article τῆς 'thereby suggesting a clear distinction between the coming of Jesus and the end of the age',[137] the external evidence favours its exclusion: τῆς is added in D W 0102 0138 f13 𝔐 but omitted in ℵ B C L Θ Ω f1 33 565 892 l2211. As such, Hagner has noted that 'the conceptual unity of the parousia and the end of the age is indicated by the single Greek article governing both [phrases]'.[138] Matthew 24.3b reads τὸ σημεῖον τῆς σῆς παρουσίας καὶ συντελείας τοῦ αἰῶνος. Instances of a single article with multiple substantives connected by καὶ were formulated into the following rule by Granville Sharp in the early nineteenth century: 'if a single article links two or more singular substantives (excluding personal names), the second and subsequent substantives are related to or further describe the first'.[139] This strongly suggests that the reference to τῆς σῆς παρουσίας and συντελείας τοῦ αἰῶνος is to the same event or entity.[140] As has been proposed above, this is the coming of the Son of Man represented by the invading Roman armies in 70 AD. Although Hagner accepts the 'conceptual unity' of these two constituent phrases, he attributes the latter to a deficiency in the question of the disciples and not something Matthew affirms. However, Hagner's conclusion has very little to support it and in the following section we will attempt to demonstrate the narrative coherence of taking the two phrases as mutually interpretive and consistent with Matthew's theological trajectory.[141]

Two further points may be noted in regard to understanding συντελείας τοῦ αἰῶνος in reference to 70 AD. First, the vocabulary of συντελεία is consistent with descriptions of military destruction in the LXX and is evidenced by the following: Judg. 20.40 states that a 'signal went up increas-

137 Hagner, *Matthew 14–28*, p. 686.

138 Hagner, *Matthew 14–28*, p. 688.

139 Cited in S. E. Porter, *Idioms of the Greek New Testament* (Sheffield: Sheffield Academic Press, 1992), pp. 110–11. Cf. D. B. Wallace, *Greek Grammar Beyond the Basics* (Grand Rapids: Zondervan, 1996), pp. 270–73; idem, 'The Semantic Range of the Article-Noun-Kai-Noun Plural Construction in the New Testament', *GTS* 4 (1983), pp. 59–84; G. B. Winer, *A Treatise on the Grammar of New Testament Greek* (trans. W. F. Moulton; Edinburgh: T&T Clark, 1882), pp. 162–63.

140 Gundry, *Matthew*, 476, *pace* P. F. Ellis, *Matthew: His Mind and His Message* (Collegeville: Liturgical Press, 1974), pp. 87–88. Keener, *Matthew*, p. 343, however, concurs with Gundry: 'Grammatically the coming of the close of the age are linked by the single sign and represent a single question; the single definite article governing them may identify them as well.' Similarly, Davies and Allison state that 'the disciples' question seemingly presumes a close logical connection between AD 70 and the end'. Davies and Allison, *Matthew 3*, p. 337. However, we will find precedent to disagree with the exact interpretation of 'the end'.

141 The manner in which the corresponding phrase in Mt. 28.20 is to be understood will be addressed in chapter 5.

ingly over the city as a pillar of smoke; and Benjamin looked behind him, and behold the destruction of the city (συντέλεια τῆς πόλεως) went up to heaven'. Although other examples are apparent,[142] Ezra 9.14 is instructive when it notes, 'whereas we have repeatedly broken your commandments, and intermarried with the people of the lands: do not be very angry with us to our utter destruction (συντελείας), so that there should be no remnant or one escaping'. Second, as noted above, Heb. 9.26 uses the plural construction in reference to Jesus: 'he has appeared once for all at the end of the age (συντελείᾳ τῶν αἰώνων) to remove sin by the sacrifice of himself'. This demonstrates that the potential semantic range of συντελείας τοῦ αἰῶνος includes it as an event very much within the space-time continuum of the first century. Thus, in Matthew, the phrase can be understood as a reference to the closure of the old dispensation. The way in which Lightfoot brings the two themes of τῆς σῆς παρουσίας and συντελείας τοῦ αἰῶνος together involves his reconstruction of Messianic expectations in the closure of the old age and the anticipation of the new age. 'What the apostles intended by these words is more clearly conceived by considering the opinion of that people concerning the times of the Messiah.'[143] Lightfoot goes on to define the expectation of the time of the Messiah's coming as involving,[144] (1) a resurrection of the just (the Messiah shall raise up those that sleep in the dust [*Midr. Tillin.* fol. 42.1]); (2) then shall follow the desolation of this world, the world shall be wasted a thousand years; (3) after which eternity shall succeed. Lightfoot concludes that Matthew presents the disciples as knowing that the Messiah is present with them, 'but do not ask the signs of his coming (as we believe of it) at the last day, to judge both the quick and the dead';[145] rather their question is to be understood to mean 'When will he come in the evidence and demonstration of the Messiah, raising up the dead, and ending this world, and introducing a new one; as they had been taught in their schools concerning his coming?'[146]

v.5 For **many**	will come in my name, saying, 'I am the Messiah!' and will **deceive** many.	
v.11 And **many**	false prophets will arise and	deceive many.
v.24 For false messiahs and **false prophets** will arise and produce great signs and omens,		deceive, if possible, even the elect.

Figure 3.1 Verse comparison

---

142 Nehemiah 9.31; Jer. 4.7; 5.18; 26.28; Ezek. 11.13; 13.13; 20.17; 21.33; Dan. 4.25, 28; 9.26-27; Amos 8.8; 9.5; Nah. 1.3, 8-9; Hab. 1.9, 15; Zeph. 1.18; 1 Macc. 3.42.
143 Lightfoot, *Commentary*, p. 309.
144 Lightfoot, *Commentary*, p. 311.
145 Lightfoot, *Commentary*, p. 311.
146 Lightfoot, *Commentary*, p. 311. For discussion of how Matthew employs the phrase elsewhere see discussion in chapter 5, section 5.6.

3.3.b.iii. Conclusion for Mt. 24.3

This section has attempted to demonstrate that both the phrases τῆς σῆς παρουσίας and συντελείας τοῦ αἰῶνος which have traditionally been understood as a reference to a physical return of the resurrected Jesus, are more plausibly understood in regard to the consequent judgement upon Jerusalem. The longevity of the former assumption has primarily been maintained by reading the synoptics through Pauline exegetical lenses which import ideas which are not immediately sustainable from the Gospel texts themselves. Oepke concludes in like fashion that the παρουσία 'as a technical term for the "coming" of Christ in Messianic glory seems to have made its way into primitive Christianity with Paul'.[147] In this sense, the aforementioned nuances of παρουσία as kingly ruler, military official, or even the military presence itself adds to the correspondence with the invading Roman armies in 70 AD. Of particular significance in this regard were the various connotations of retribution in the use of παρουσία in texts from King Mithridates of Pontus. Similarly, it was seen that συντελείας τοῦ αἰῶνος does not necessarily refer to a schism in the space-time continuum, but rather a reference to the changing from one dispensation to another in Yahweh's salvation-history timeline.

3.3.c. Matthew 24.4-5, 11, 24 and the Jewish 'sign prophets'[148]

3.3.c.i. Preliminary discussion

In Mt. 24.4-5 Jesus is presented as saying 'Beware that no one leads you astray. For many will come in my name, saying, "I am the Messiah!" and they will lead many astray.' Similar warning occurs in v. 11 and v. 24, and our following comments also relate to these verses.[149]

Within the history of interpretation, various commentators have understood the figures referred to in 24.4-5 as varieties of end time, eschatological antichrists.[150] Indeed, Davies and Allison have strongly argued that 'AD 70

---

147 Oepke, 'Παρουσία', p. 865. 'The hope of an imminent coming of the exalted Lord in Messianic glory is ... first found only in the later Church. A basic prerequisite for understanding the world of thought of primitive Christianity is that we should fully free ourselves from this notion, which, so far as the New Testament is concerned, is suspect both philologically and materially.'

148 The title 'sign prophets' is a modern designation adopted from P. W. Barnett, 'The Jewish Sign Prophets: A.D. 40–70', *NTS* 27 (1981), pp. 679–97.

149 There are two other Matthean passages which are relevant: 7.15, 'Beware of false prophets, who come to you in sheep's clothing but inwardly are ravenous wolves,' and 10.16, 'See, I am sending you out like sheep into the midst of wolves; so be wise as serpents and innocent as doves.' The context of these passages is related to a warning not to be deceived. Also to note in regard to Mt. 7.15-18 is the connection of inappropriate production of fruit and consequent judgement. Cf. the enacted parable of judgement of the withered fig tree in Mt. 21.19. For the fig tree narrative as a symbolic action of judgement see Wilson, *When*, p. 98.

150 See below.

does not exhaust the significance of vv.5ff., which plainly envisage eschatological events to come.'[151] Others have taken this argument further and claimed that there are no historical records of Messianic claimants *before* the destruction of Jerusalem in 70 AD.[152] By way of introduction, and in response to this type of approach, we will discuss Theudas, one of the attested 'prophetic pretenders' in Josephus, noting various characteristics of his claims. We will then address the issue of the 'anticipated prophet' (Deuteronomy 18) before returning to a discussion of other attested 'sign prophets' and their relationship to Mt. 24.4-5 within the context of 70 AD.

W. Marxen,[153] among others,[154] argues that the whole synoptic discourse, including vv. 4-8, is a *Parusierede* concerned with the period subsequent to the destruction of Jerusalem. However, as Reicke[155] has noted, there are various figures who could potentially fit this category in the period between Jesus' death and the beginning of the Jewish war. Several figures and groups concerned with revolution against Roman occupation of Judaea are discussed by Josephus. These individuals, finding considerable support in local villages, often present themselves as prophets, claiming an ability to perform signs and wonders. Josephus mentions seven prophetic figures who operate on this level.

During the procuratorship of Cuspius Fadus (44–48 AD), Theudas persuaded the people 'to take up their possessions and follow him to the Jordan River'.[156] Upon marching to the Jordan, Theudas claimed he would command the waters to part, thus allowing him and his faithful followers safe passage to the other side, at which point they would turn and besiege the Romans. Upon hearing rumours of these matters, Fadus, appropriately suspicious, dispatched cavalry against Theudas and his followers who were then attacked by surprise, and captured or killed the perpetrators. Theudas was decapitated and carried to Jerusalem, not only as a military trophy but also as a severe warning against insurrection against Rome.[157]

As was the case at Herod the Great's death (4 BC) and Archelaus' exile (AD 6), the most opportune time for political insurrection was during the transition of leadership, in Theudas' case the substitution of Jewish kings for Roman procurators.[158] Josephus refers to these failed revolutionary prophets with particular distaste. Not only are they described as the diseased parts of

151 Davies and Allison, *Matthew 3*, p. 331.

152 See for example H. A. W. Meyer, *Critical and Exegetical Handbook to the Gospel of Matthew* (2 vols; Edinburgh: T&T Clark, 1879), p. 2.128.

153 Marxen, *Mark*, pp. 138–40.

154 Gnilka, *Matthäusevangelium*, pp. 2.309-33; Hare, *Persecutions*, pp. 177-79; Harrington, *Matthew*, pp. 331-41; also see discussion in Marxen, *Mark*, pp. 198-204.

155 B. Reicke, 'Synoptic Prophecies on the Destruction of Jerusalem', in *Studies in New Testament and Early Christian Literature*, ed. D. E. Aune (Leiden: Brill, 1972), pp. 121-34 (130-34).

156 *Ant.* 20.97

157 *Ant.* 20.97-98.

158 Barnett, 'Sign Prophets', p. 681.

the Jewish body,[159] but Josephus terms Theudas[160] (and others as will be seen below) as both charlatans and deceivers. The term used is γόητες, which P. W. Barnett suggests recalls Josephus' own description of the Exodus where terms such as γοητεία and μαγεία refer to Pharaoh's court magicians.[161]

This does indeed lend support for a context very similar to Matthew's warning not to be πλανήσῃ ('led astray') through false prophetic activity, and may be related to the Mosaic prophet of Deut. 18.15-19. This is confirmed in an investigation of how Josephus employs γόης, γοητεία, or γοητεύω elsewhere in his work. Of the fourteen uses, six refer to Jewish sign prophets such as Theudas,[162] which firmly establishes this as a favoured description of these individuals. A further four are related to Moses (1) in defence of mighty deeds being of God;[163] (2) in the description of Pharaoh's mortification that he had allowed the Hebrews to go ὡς κατὰ γοητείαν τὴν Μωυσέος ('through Moses' deceptio),[164] and (3) in defence of Moses and his law as 'excellently designed to promote piety'[165] against Apollonius Molon and Lysimachus. These phenomena support Barnett's conclusion regarding 'Mosaic tone', for they are used in connection with Moses and the Exodus. Of the four remaining references, all are related to leadership in the Jewish War and three are specifically linked with insurrection.[166]

Although some may object that the apparent Mosaic typology is more in keeping with a new-Joshua schema, it can be simply said that, as Allison,[167] Alter,[168] Blenkinsopp,[169] Fishbane,[170] and other commentators have demonstrated, Joshua's presentation as a 'new-Moses' is one of the most clearly developed biographical literary typologies in the available corpus of ancient

159 *War* 2.264.

160 *Ant.* 20.97.

161 *Ant.* 2.286, 302, 332, 336. Barnett, 'Sign Prophets', p. 681. Also to note is Josephus' description of the practice in *Ant.* 2.286, when Moses addresses the Pharaoh; he says 'I will demonstrate that what I do is not done by craft, or counterfeiting what is not really true (πλάνην τῆς ἀληθοῦς), but that they appear by the providence and power of God.'

162 *War* 2.261, 264; *Ant.* 20.97, 160, 167, 188.

163 *Ant.* 2.286

164 *Ant.* 2.320

165 *Apion* 2.145, 161

166 John incited Gischala to revolt (*War* 4.85); Castor the Jew deceived a Roman invasion (*War* 5.317); and Justus, son of Pistis, incited a faction of the inhabitants of Tiberias to revolution through what Josephus calls 'deception' (*Life* 40). Josephus' description of the appointment of additional generals for the Jewish War refers to Eleazar, son of Simon, who is said to partake in deception. *War* 2.565

167 Allison, *Typology*, pp. 23–28.

168 R. Alter, *The Pleasures of Reading in an Ideological Age* (New York: Simon and Schuster, 1989), p. 118.

169 J. Blenkinsopp, *Prophecy and Canon: A Contribution to the Study of Jewish Origins* (Notre Dame: University Press, 1977), pp. 48–50.

170 M. Fishbane, *Biblical Interpretation in Ancient Israel* (Oxford: Clarendon Press, 1985), p. 359.

Jewish literature. And thus an event, such as the parting of the Jordan, which bears such close similarity with Moses' parting of the Red Sea, must be given its due.[171]

3.3.c.ii. Moses as prototypical prophet (Deut. 18.15-18)

In relation to Deut. 18.15-19, the expectation of (a) future Mosaic figure(s) can be understood in two broad categories. Von Rad argues that the passage envisions a single fulfilment of a figure in the future, that is, the coming of an individual eschatological figure.[172] A. F. Gfrörer argues that 'there is no verse in the books of the old covenant which ... refers so definitely ... to the Messiah as Deut. 18.15, 18'.[173] K. Bornhäuser more cautiously states that 'opinions vacillated whether the prophet and the Messiah would appear in one person or not'.[174] Although this seems to draw support from the indefinite translation 'a prophet', one must hesitate in leaning too heavily on this as there is no indefinite article in Hebrew, and hence any translation of א נבי׳ which suggests so, is potentially problematic.

Most scholars envision the 'prophet' contemplated not as a single individual belonging to a distant future, but Moses' representative, whose office it would be to supply Israel, whenever historical occasion should arise, with a prophetic guiding figure, of which Moses was the prototype. V. R. Steuernagel's translation, 'will raise up from time to time',[175] seeks to reflect this distributive interpretation of יָקִים (v. 15) and אָקִים (v. 18). In this sense, כָּמֹנִי (v. 15) and כָּמֹוךָ (v. 18) serve to illustrate Moses as the model for these prophets. Therefore, validation of prophetic legitimacy stems from continuity with Moses as the *canon* of authenticity. This could then be interpreted as either a continuous line of prophets, with each being succeeded by the next, in similar fashion to the monarchy, or a series of prophets emerging at specific moments in Israel's history to address a particular concern. It seems somewhat dubious to suppose, as Krause has suggested, that an institutional office of direct succession is in view, given that there are no indications that such a specified prophetic role was in operation. It is more plausible to suppose that Deuteronomy 18 anticipated specific individuals at specific moments for specific purposes being portrayed with specific Mosaic characteristics. This is also in accordance with the extant Old

---

171 For example, in the 'Song of Moses', which praises Yahweh for his wonders (פֶּלֶא Exod. 15.11), Moses describes the parted waters as נֵד 'a heap' (Exod. 15.8). Likewise, the waters of the River Jordan are described as 'rising up in a single heap (נֵד)' in Josh. 3.16. Assimilation is also strengthened by the explicit reference to and connection of the Red Sea event with the Jordan crossing in Josh. 4.23.

172 Von Rad cited in J. Jeremias, 'Μωυσῆς', in *Theological Dictionary of the New Testament*, ed. G. Friedrich (trans. G. W. Bromiley; 10 vols; Grand Rapids: Eerdmans, 1967), pp. 4.848–73 (858 n.125).

173 A. F. Gfrörer, *Kritische Geschichte des Urchristenthums* (Stuttgart, 1838), p. 324.

174 Bornhäuser, cited in J. Jeremias, 'Μωυσῆς', p. 858 n.125.

175 V. R. Steuernagel, *Der Rahmen des Deuteronomy* (Gesetzes, 1894).

Testament biblical text, which D. C. Allison has noted is replete with Mosaic figures.[176] Confirmation of this is also found in various inter-testamental Jewish documents. *Targum Jonathan* II Exod. 15.18 notes that:

> Moses will come out of the wilderness and the king Messiah will come out of Rome; the one will lead [the wilderness generation] at the head of a cloud, the other will lead the [diaspora] at the head of the cloud, and the memra of Yahweh will lead between both, and they will come in together, and the children of Israel will say 'to Yahweh belongs royal dominion in this world, and it is his in the world to come.'

Within the documents found at Qumran there were several texts which indicated expectations of an eschatological individual in Mosaic terms. 4QTest quotes Deut. 5.28-29 followed by Deut. 18.18-20; Num. 24.15-17; and Deut. 33.8-11 for the contribution they make to the portrait of the future eschatological figure who embodies Moses as prophet. Moses is so dominant within Samaritan thought as an 'eschatological' figure that when one assesses the body of Samaritan literature it is evident that they are expecting not only a restorer who is a Mosaic figure, but Moses *revividus* – back to life![177] These dominant expectations for a future Mosaic prophet, most plausibly finding antecedent in Deuteronomy 18, can be summed up in a later Rabbinic phrase which anticipates a prophet of Mosaic stature, 'As the first redeemer, so the last redeemer.'[178]

3.3.c.iii. Further discussion of Josephus' 'sign prophets'

In addition to Theudas, Josephus also notes that (an) unnamed person(s) during the reign of Antonius Felix, procurator in 52–60 AD, 'called upon the mob to follow him to the desert',[179] where he promised to perform 'unmistakable marvels'[180] and 'signs of freedom'.[181] Furthermore, in *Ant.* 2.286-87 Moses speaks of the signs (σημεῖα) he performed before Pharaoh in Egypt as κατὰ ... θεοῦ πρόνοιαν καὶ δύναμιν (from God's providence and power). It is significant to note that the signs promised by prophetic pretenders under Felix are described in *Ant.* 20.168 as τέρατα καὶ σημεῖα κατὰ τὴν τοῦ θεοῦ πρόνοιαν γινόμενα ('marvels and signs which would be wrought in accordance with God's providence'). Although Barnett concedes that no certain answer is possible in regard

---

176 Allison, *Typology*, pp. 1–94.

177 J. MacDonald, *The Theology of the Samaritans* (Philadelphia: Westminster Press, 1964), pp. 153–54. See the Samaritan *Memar Marqah* 6.6; also see 1.2 for Moses as God's vice-regent; 4.7 for the equating of belief in Moses and God; and 5.4 for Moses being attributed the divine name. Cf. Jos *Ant.* 18.85.

178 *Eccl. Rab.* 1.18.

179 *Ant.* 20.167–68; *War* 2.258–59.

180 *Ant.* 20.167–68.

181 *War* 2.258–59.

to what signs these prophets were expected to perform,[182] given (1) the close verbal parallel between *Ant.* 2.286 and 20.168, (2) Josephus' previous employment of the phrase τὴν ἐλευθερίαν αὐτοῖς σημείων in description of Israel at the Red Sea when they turned against Moses 'forgetful of all those signs wrought by God in token of their liberation',[183] and (3) our above discussion on Josephus' use of γοητ– as a description of activity in Egypt, it seems most plausible that the promised activities of the sign prophets would recall the Exodus event. This sentiment is also affirmed by Nicole, who concludes that the expression τέρατα καὶ σημεῖα, the repeated appearance of desert, and the content of the signs all make it clear that in some way or other all these prophets had in mind the Jewish expectations concerning the return of Mosaic times'.[184]

During the same period an Egyptian prophet arose and led thousands out into the wilderness,[185] after which they travelled to the Mount of Olives, where their leader claimed the walls of Jerusalem would collapse at his command. This would apparently facilitate the wholesale destruction of the Roman garrison and legitimize his own ascension to power. Given that Felix is described by Tacitus as practising 'every kind of cruelty and lust',[186] it is no surprise that he attacked, slaughtered, and scattered the Egyptian's followers before they even attempted their act of revolution.[187] On the basis of the presence of (1) wilderness, (2) a mountain, and (3) deliverance from oppression, Schürer's affirmation of a Mosaic scene is strongly supported.[188]

This particular figure is unique in that, in addition to laying claim to the title prophet, he also attempts to 'set himself up as tyrant of the people' (του δήμου τυραϲϲειϲν).[189] Meeks argues that this is a kingly designation, and as such also supports Mosaic allusion.[190] In this regard, Strack and Billerbeck conclude that 'both cases are concerned with an attempt to bring the people

---

182 Barnett, 'Sign Prophets', p. 683. He does not, however, rule it out.

183 *Ant.* 2.327.

184 W. Nicole, *The Sēmeia in the Fourth Gospel* (Leiden: Brill, 1972), p. 82.

185 The number of followers varies. According to Acts 21.38 it is 4,000 (Paul is confused with the leader of this particular group), yet according to *War* 2.261 it is 30,000. No figure is given in *Ant.* However, Josephus does say that 400 were killed and 200 were captured (*Ant.* 20.171).

186 *His.* 5.9. Barnett, 'Sign Prophets', p. 683.

187 *Ant.* 20.169–72. *War* 2.261–63 adds the detail of wilderness wanderings before the ascension on the Mount of Olives. Barnett notes 4QTest, where Joshua's curse on anyone who rebuilds Jericho (Josh. 6.26) is reapplied to Jerusalem. In this way the 'destruction of Jerusalem is an act of judgement on an apostate people'. Barnett, 'Sign Prophets', p. 683.

188 Schürer, cited in J. Jeremias, 'Μωυσῆς', p. 873.

189 Barnett, 'Sign Prophets', p. 683.

190 For Moses as king see W. A. Meeks, *The Prophet-King: Moses Traditions and Johannine Christology* (Leiden: Brill, 1967), p. 146; J. T. Porter, *Moses and Monarchy: A Study in the Biblical Tradition of Moses* (Oxford: Basil Blackwell, 1963); J. Lierman, *The New Testament Moses: Christian Perceptions of Moses and Israel in the Setting of Jewish Religion* (Tübingen: Mohr Siebeck, 2002), pp. 79–123.

to a revolt against the Romans. The men who pretend to be prophets desire to play the role of liberators, deliverers of Israel. From this one recognizes how closely related in the thought of the people in the last century before the destruction of Jerusalem is the conception of "a prophet who would come," and the redeemer.'[191]

Approximately a decade later, during the Procuratorship of Porcius Festus (60–62 AD), another unnamed individual promised (ἐπαγγελλομένου), salvation (σωτηρίαν), and rest from troubles (παῦλαν κακῶν), if the Israelites followed him into the wilderness.[192] Although there is no reference to signs, all three terms are used in Josephus' description of the redemption from Egypt.[193] In addition to σωτηρίαν being promised by most of the sign prophets,[194] *Ant.* 3.64 states that, 'Aaron and his family took Raguel, and sung hymns to God as the author and procurer of their salvation (σωτηρίας) and their liberty (ἐλευθερίας).' This indicates that these terms were, to some extent, synonymous and interchangeable. Furthermore, in *Ant.* 2.276 and 3.219, trouble (κακῶν) is the opposite to salvation (σωτηρία), in that God delivers (saves) Israel and brings judgement/disaster (κακοῖς) on her enemies, in this case, upon Egypt. In this light Barnett concludes that παῦλαν κακῶν is to be equated with σωτηρία and ἐλευθερία.[195] It seems inevitable to go one step further, in agreement with J. L. Martyn, and conclude that 'the signs referred to appear Mosaic ... they are, so to speak, wilderness signs',[196] and hence acknowledge the Exodus typology which plays such a significant role in Josephus' description of these individuals.

This is also confirmed in August of 70 AD when, during the temple's destruction through fire, 6,000 people fled to the only remaining portico in the outer court because they had been told by a 'prophet' that they would receive 'miraculous signs of their deliverance' and 'help from God' at such a time as this.[197] Josephus calls this individual a ψευδοπροφήτης ('false prophet'), and, in light of his presentation of Moses as a legitimate prophet elsewhere,[198] suggests that he most plausibly is understood as a false-Mosaic typological figure, that is, one who claims and attempts to operate in a Mosaic capacity, yet fails to do so. This may also be a clue as to why Josephus would pattern such deplorable individuals (in his view) on a type (i.e. Mosaic Exodus) which in all his other writing he reveres.[199] In two specific cases, Josephus notes that these γοητές claim prophetic status. In

---

191 Strack and Billerbeck, *Kommentar*, p. 2.480.
192 *Ant.* 20.188
193 Barnett, 'Sign Prophets', p. 685.
194 *Ant.* 2.237; 20.188; *War* 2.259; 6.286.
195 Barnett, 'Sign Prophets', p. 682.
196 Martyn cited in Barnett, 'Sign Prophets', p. 682.
197 *War* 6.284–86.
198 *Ant.* 2.327; *Apion* 2.145, 161; Barnett, 'Sign Prophets', p. 687.
199 It is also conceivable that Josephus here merely records the prophet's activities. However, the problem still remains that Josephus would include, in his mind, deplorable figures who attempt to pattern themselves on an event which he reveres.

Ant. 20.97 it is said of Theudas that he προφήτης γὰρ ἔλεγεν εἶναι. Likewise in *Ant.* 20.169 the Egyptian claimed προφήτης εἶναι λέγων.[200] Despite their claims, Josephus reveals their inauthenticity, because their failure to enact their promised signs automatically characterizes their non-belonging to the legitimate Mosaic-Exodus traditions.

J. Lierman,[201] following R. Gray's[202] analysis of σημεῖον in Josephus, suggests that in *Ant.* σημεῖον is specifically employed in reference to the authentication of a prophet. Lierman concludes that σημεῖον functions as a '*terminus technicus* denoting the authenticating miracle of a prophet'.[203] This finds general support in Ps. 74.9, where the post-exilic complaint is that 'we do not see our signs (σημεῖα); there is no longer any prophet'. This by no means diminishes Mosaic remembrance but intensifies it, as the would-be prophet is evaluated in the light of Moses' activities in Egypt. The legitimacy of his own prophethood is affirmed with reference to Moses as prototype. This is confirmed by *Sifre* Deut. 18.19, where it is stated that the words of a prophet may be accepted if he performs mighty deeds. Nicole argues that the passage from *Sifre* must have a fixed form in the first century because R. Akiba and R. Jose are attested to have had a discussion which presupposes it.[204] This strongly suggests that a literary category of Mosaic typology, based on his mighty deeds, was utilized by writers contemporary with Matthew.

Our discussion at this point could continue to document the shared features of other prophetic pretenders in Josephus.[205] However, it is sufficient to note that the undercurrent of prophetic/messianic activity has one common denominator: the promise of 'mighty deeds', 'signs of liberation', and 'rest from troubles'. When compared with the relevant material in Matthew 24 (i.e. vv. 5, 11, 24), it is apparent that these figures fit remarkably well with the period of time leading up to the destruction of Jerusalem in 70 AD. Thus there seems to be precedent to disagree with Davies and Alison who state that

200 This is echoed in *War* 2.261: προφήτου πίστιν ἐπιθεὶς ἑαυτῷ. Barnett, 'Sign Prophets', p. 683.

201 Lierman, *Moses*, p. 57.

202 R. Gray, *Prophetic Figures in Late Second Temple Jewish Palestine: The Evidence from Josephus* (Oxford: Oxford University Press, 1993), pp. 128–52.

203 Lierman, *Moses*, p. 58.

204 Nicole, *Sêmeia*, p. 83. *Sanh.* 89b, 90a; *Sifre* Deut. 13.3; *p.Sanh.* 18 (30c).

205 To the above can be added the example of Jonathan the weaver, who in 73 AD promised to accomplish 'signs and apparitions' (σημεῖα καὶ φάσματα) in the 'wilderness' (εἰς τὴν ἔρημον), *War* 7.438, a scenario which again recalls the figure of Moses and the event of the Exodus. Cited in Meeks, *Prophet-King*, p. 163. Furthermore, an unnamed Samaritan in 36 AD attempted to persuade large numbers of Jews to go with him to Mt. Gerizim, where he promised the temple vessels which Moses had hidden would be revealed (*War* 18.85–87). Samaritans believed that when these vessels were recovered this would signal the inauguration of the eschatological age. See MacDonald, *Samaritans*, p. 443. In addition, robbers (under Nero) persuaded a multitude to come to the desert to show them 'signs and wonders' (τέρατα καὶ σημεῖα) in *Ant.* 20.168; *War* 2.259 has the phrase 'signs of freedom' (σημεῖα ἐλευθερίας).

70 AD 'does not exhaust the significance of vv.5ff., which plainly envisage eschatological events to come'.[206] In our analysis, the events leading up to 70 AD do, in fact, account for the Matthean material without the necessity of further future fulfilment. Barnett suggests that the wonders promised by the sign prophets were intended to act as pledges of divine action.[207] This, he argues, was not considered as vague fulfilment in the distant future, but just as the 'Exodus signs'[208] were chronologically close to their fulfilment in the Exodus from Egypt, so too was it expected that Israel would be speedily redeemed when the 'the wheels of God ... [were] set in motion for a re-run of his great saving act'.[209]

3.3.d Matthew 24.6-8

Some commentators have seen in 24.6 an indication that Jesus acknowledges that his initial response has not addressed the 'eschatological' concerns of his disciples. One could argue that 24.6 demonstrates that the 'wars and rumors of wars' are in fact, indications of the reverse, i.e. not 'the end' (τὸ τέλος). This should give us pause in too hastily ignoring the possible 'eschatological' weight of this passage. However, it is certainly interesting to note that Matthew's phrasing is slightly more subtle. Matthew 24.6 says 'see that you are not alarmed; for this must take place, but οὔπω ἐστὶν τὸ τέλος (lit. "*not yet* is the end")'. Which may indicate that the wars and rumours of wars referred to here are in relation to the general unrest in Palestine in the generation after Jesus rather than the specific destruction of the temple. In this light, τὸ τέλος may refer (as συντελείας τοῦ αἰῶνος does in 24.3) to the end of one dispensation in Yahweh's salvation-history timeline.

---

206 Davies and Allison, *Matthew 3*, p. 331.

207 Barnett, 'Sign Prophets', p. 688. He points out *Ant.* 2.327 as characteristic in this regard.

208 Barnett, 'Sign Prophets', p. 688.

209 Barnett, 'Sign Prophets', p. 688. Some may object, however, that the figures mentioned above, such as Theudas et al., hardly come ἐμὶ τῷ ὀνόματί μου ('in my name', v. 5). As such, it is suggested that the claimants are some deviation of Christian adherence rather than Jewish per se. In response, it is important to note Matthew's redactional change in this regard. Matthew 24.5 follows Mk 13.6 verbatim (bar the addition of the postpositive γὰρ in Matthew): πολλοὶ γὰρ ἐλεύσονται ἐπὶ τῷ ὀνόματί μου λέγοντες· ἐγώ εἰμι. Whereas Mark concludes with ἐγώ εἰμι, Matthew adds ὁ χριστός so as to (1) alleviate the possible association with the same Septuagintal phrase used in the revelation of Yahweh's name in Exodus 3, and (2) link the phrase in v. 5 to general messianic fervour, rather than a necessarily Christian claim. As such, the sign prophets' promise of deliverance from foreign rule (*Ant.* 20.97–98 [Theudas]; *Ant.* 20.167–68 [unnamed individual]; *Ant.* 20.169–72 [Egyptian]; *Ant.* 20.188 [unnamed individual] et al. noted above) constitutes sufficient grounds for a comparison to be made with the Matthean text, and even more so because Matthew adds the titular ὁ χριστός to Mark's ἐγώ εἰμι. Thus, comparison is legitimate even if the referent in v. 5 is not explicitly a Christian deviation.

There are some considerations which may tip the balance slightly in favour of historical referent at this point. Verses 6-7a refer to there being wars and rumours of wars, with nation rising against nation and kingdom against kingdom. Although B. Reicke understands this as having 'nothing to do with Vespasian's local enterprise against the Jewish Zealots, because the reference is to a rumor [sic] coming from outside and concerning struggles between different nations and kingdoms of the commonwealth',[210] and as such is not related to 70 AD, his primary assumption is open to critique. The term ἔθνος (typically translating the MT's גּוֹי) can refer to both Jews (2 Macc. 11.25) and Gentiles (Gen. 10.5), and typically denotes a group of people living in the same geographical vicinity. It has a reasonably flexible semantic domain, including entities which are conceivably smaller than nations per se. In this light, the term could either refer to entities of civil unrest within a single political system[211] (such as the internal struggles preceding the Jewish War)[212] or a general unrest in the wider Mediterranean Gentile world.[213]

Verse 7b goes on to describe the scenario with vivid images of famines (λιμοὶ) and earthquakes (σεισμοὶ). In an interesting redaction, Matthew alters the Markan ordering of these calamities from σεισμοὶ ... λιμοὶ (Mk 13.8) to λιμοὶ ... σεισμοὶ (Mt. 24.7). R. Gundry notes that 'the putting of famines before earthquakes may indicate that famines result from the ravages of the warfare just mentioned'.[214] This redactional change, as well as the natural correspondence of famine with warfare, supports a historical reading (*War* 1.64; 4.62, 137, 361; 5.348, 418, 424, 449, 454).

Despite the fact that there is an active tectonic plate fault line in southern Judaea, which could refer to the prevalence of natural phenomena coinciding with the general period,[215] the σεισμοὶ might profitably be understood in reference to judgement language in the prophetic and related literature. Isaiah 29.6 declares 'you will be visited by the Lord of hosts with thunder and earthquake and great noise'. Isaiah 29 forms part of the larger unit of chs 28-33, in which Judah is rebuked and judged for her foolishness in trusting the nations instead of Yahweh. Interestingly, the whole section is unified by an introductory 'woe' formula in 28.1; 29.1, 15; 30.1; 33.1 (cf.

---

210 Reicke, 'Synoptic', p. 130.

211 For example, the campaign of the Romans against the Parthians (36 and 55 AD).

212 Or for that matter, the commotions of Galba, Otho, Vitellius, and Vespasian.

213 For example, in 60 AD, the British tribes rebelled against the overbearing Roman rule, only to have at least 150,000 fatalities. For ἔθνος as foreigners or Gentiles, also see Aristot., *Pol.* 1324b, 10; *Cass. Dio.* 36, 41; *Ps.-Callisth.* 2, 7, 4. For possible background in the Old Testament, see 2 Chron. 15.6; Isa. 19.2. See discussion below (v. 15) on Tacitus and the *Pax Romana*.

214 Gundry, *Matthew*, p. 478.

215 There are numerous recorded earthquakes; Antioch in 37 AD (Johannes Malalas *Chronographia* 10.243.10–15), Phrygia in 53 AD (Tacitus *Ann.* 12.58.3), Asia in 61 AD (Pliny *Hist. Nat.* 2.84–86), and in the Lycus Valley in 61 AD (including Laodicaea, Hierapolis, Colossae: Tacitus *Ann.* 14.27.1; Eusebius *Chron.* 183.1.20; Orosius *Hist.* 7.7). Cited in Luz, *Matthew 21–28*, p. 192 n.88.

Matthew 23).[216] Of particular importance in this scathing rebuke is Isaiah's condemnation of Ephraim's drunken leaders. Isaiah directly attributes their intended Egyptian alliance with the fall of the Northern Kingdom into foreign hands (Assyria).[217]

Similarly in Jeremiah 4, in the context of Yahweh imposing the sentence of death on Israel for her covenantal infidelity, Jeremiah concludes the climactic expression of judgement with a '"de-creation" of the cosmos, the world again became the chaos before creation began'.[218] Jeremiah 4.23-25 states:

> I looked on the earth, and lo, it was waste and void; and to the heavens, and they had no light. I looked on the mountains, and lo, they were quaking, and all the hills moved to and fro. I looked, and lo, there was no one at all, and all the birds of the air had fled.[219]

Interestingly, in a later passage of impending judgement in Jeremiah, the quaking σεισμοῦ is related to the approaching army of Philistine horses and chariots; Jer. 47.3 notes that 'At the noise of the stamping of the hoofs of his stallions, at the clatter of his chariots, at the rumbling of their wheels … .'[220] In regard to similar descriptions in Matthew, Luz asks, 'Did the readers think of concrete, historical experiences of their own?'[221] Based on the prevalence of earthquakes, and the common connection between wars and famines, Luz responds by noting that 'it is conceivable. The text does not forbid them.'[222]

In R. Bauckham's discussion of the 'eschatological earthquake in the apocalypse of John',[223] he argues that it is not the 'tired apocalyptic cliché so many commentators have thought it to be'.[224] Rather, he suggests that it functions as an image 'rich in Old Testament and contemporary allusion, and carries considerable theological weight'.[225] Among others, one of the

---

216 W. J. Dumbrell, 'The Purpose of the Book of Isaiah', *TynBul* 36 (1985), pp. 111–28 (120).

217 Isaiah 30.3, 7; 33.1, 3.

218 W. L. Holladay, *Jeremiah 1: Commentary on the Book of Jeremiah Chapters 1–25* (Fortress Press: Philadelphia, 1986), p. 164.

219 R. F. White notes that earthquakes are 'well known natural disturbances that accompany the παρουσία of the Lord'. R. F. White, 'Reexamining the Evidence for Recapitulation in Rev 20.1-10', *WTJ* 51.2 (1989), pp. 319–44 (337). White is, as expected, referring to a physical return of Jesus, but his insights are nonetheless relevant for our discussion. Cf. also R. Bauckham, 'The Eschatological Earthquake in the Apocalypse of John', *NovT* 19 (1977), p. 224–33.

220 On the association of earthquake and war see *War* 1.377.

221 Luz, *Matthew 21–28*, p. 192.

222 Luz, *Matthew 21–28*, p. 192.

223 Bauckham, 'Earthquake', pp. 224–33.

224 Bauckham, 'Earthquake', p. 232. In his opening remarks Bauckham states that, 'the earthquake is far too often passed over as a conventional apocalyptic image of no great interest'. Bauckham, 'Earthquake', p. 224.

225 Bauckham, 'Earthquake', p. 232.

significant horizons Bauckham sees behind the σεισμοὶ language is the theophanic arrival of God as warrior in military battle,[226] as ruler over the nations,[227] and in judgement upon the wicked.[228] Also to be noted is that 'the earthquake accompanies the expected coming of God as King and Judge ... [and] may also itself form part of the final judgement on the Gentiles, as in Sib. iii 675–693'.[229] This functioning of the earthquake as the judgement itself in *Sib. Or.* goes beyond the traditional meaning, as found in Ezek. 38.19-23, which refers only to God's coming.[230] There is some precedent for this, however, in Isa. 29.6 and Amos 9.1, where the σεισμόι are envisioned as instruments of divine judgement. In support of this general approach, there is further use of the imagery of 'earthquakes' in this fashion in Rev. 16.17-21, where 'the earthquake itself is part of the judgement'.[231]

Furthermore, that the prophetic oracles of judgement are on the horizon here is also confirmed by the following verse in Matthew 24 which describes these realities as the ἀρχὴ ὠδίνων ('beginning of birth pangs', v. 8). Although, Albright and Mann designate this phrase operating as 'an almost technical term for the sufferings which would immediately precede a new age',[232] that is somewhat of an overstatement.[233] What is of note are

---

226 Judg. 5.4-5; Joel 2.10; Mic. 1.4; Ps. 68.7-8.

227 Psalm 97.5; 99.1.

228 Isaiah 13.13; 24.18-20; 34.4; Jer. 51.29; Ezek. 38.20; Nah. 1.5.

229 Bauckham, 'Earthquake', pp. 225–26. We find insufficient Bauckham's passing note that in the synoptic 'eschatological' discourse, the earthquake 'has no special role as the accompaniment of the eschatological theophany'. Bauckham, 'Earthquake', p, 226.

230 Bauckham, 'Earthquake', p. 226. Cf. *Sib. Or.* 5.438 predicts that Babylon will be judged in the form of an earthquake; *Sib. Or.* 3.401–13, 449, 457, 459; 4.99f.; 5.128. Bauckham, 'Earthquake', p. 230 n.10. It is also apparent that in other traditions, the material in Ezekiel has been taken up and developed in different ways. In some pseudepigraphical works it does seem to refer to a cataclysmic end of the cosmos. However, there does not seem to be any trace of this theme in Matthew's presentation of the narrative.

231 Bauckham, 'Earthquake', p. 229. The earthquake mentioned in Mt. 27.51-54 seems not to refer to the above-stated scheme, but rather is included in Matthew's narrative to (1) account for the tearing of the temple's curtain; (2) as a metaphor for the crucifixion (J. I. H. McDonald, *The Resurrection: Narrative and Belief* [London: SPCK, 1989], p. 91); (3) as a variation of the story attested in the Gospel of Peter regarding the three men and cross which come out of the tomb (J. D. Crossan, *The Birth of Christianity: Discovering What Happened in the Years Immediately after the Execution of Jesus* [San Francisco: Harper San Francisco, 1998], p. 517); or (4) as a metaphor for Israel's return from exile based on Ezek. 37.12-13; Isa. 26.19; Dan. 12.2 (N. T. Wright, *The Resurrection of the Son of God* [Minneapolis: Fortress Press, 2003], pp. 632–36; cf. R. L. Troxel, 'Matt 27.51-54 Reconsidered: Its Role in the Passion Narrative, Meaning and Origin', *NTS* 48 [2002], pp. 30–47, who argues for allusion to *1 En.* 93.6, not in regard to the dawning of a new age, but specifically in regard to the centurion's confession).

232 Albright and Mann, *Matthew*, p. 292.

233 However several texts do speak of the coming new age in anthropomorphized language of birth pains: 1QH 3.7-10; *1 En.* 62.4; 1 Thess. 5.3; Rev. 12.2; *b.Sanh.* 98b; *Mek.* on Exod. 16.25; *b.Ketub.* 111a. Cf. Rom. 8.22. For further discussion see F. C. Grant, *Ancient Judaism and the New Testament* (London: Oliver and Boyd, 1960), pp. 68–95;

the parallel descriptions in Isaiah 13 of approaching national disaster upon Babylon because of their 'arrogance, cruelty and ruthless oppression of the weak'.[234] Isaiah 13.8 describes the punishment as follows: 'they will be in anguish like a woman in labor'.[235] H. Wildberger notes that this image 'has its roots in the oracles against foreign nations',[236] and, as such, its application to institutional Israel in Matthew is even more striking. As in Amos 1–2, Israel is presented as having abandoned her status as Yahweh's child and thus has become like one of the nations.

Comparable imagery is used by Jeremiah in description of the coming judgement on Jerusalem. Jeremiah 22.23 states: 'O inhabitant of Lebanon, nested among the cedars, how you will groan when pangs come upon you, pain as of a woman in labor!' W. L. Holladay states that this verse 'is all the judgement of Yahweh, to whom she did not listen'.[237] Similarly, Jer. 30.5-6 has Yahweh himself say 'We have heard a cry of panic, of terror, and no peace. Ask now, and see, can a man bear a child? Why then do I see every man with his hands on his loins like a woman in labor? Why has every face turned pale?' In a later section of Jeremiah's polemic, the impending destruction of Moab is described as, 'The towns shall be taken and the strongholds seized. The hearts of the warriors of Moab, on that day, shall be like the heart of a woman in labor' (Jer. 48.41).

In Mic. 4.9-10, the language of 'birth pangs' functions as a metaphor for exile to Babylon, the proto-typical historical event of covenantal curse:

> Now why do you cry aloud? Is there no king in you? Has your counsellor perished, that pangs have seized you like a woman in labor? Writhe and groan, O daughter Zion, like a woman in labor; for now you shall go forth from the city and camp in the open country; you shall go to Babylon.

Regardless of whether the reference to Babylon is a later gloss,[238] the imagery presented is one of reversal. Rather than the city being a place of refuge in a time of war, it has become deserted by its inhabitants. H. McKeating says that for people 'to flee in the other direction, from cities into the country, was a sign of complete hopelessness, an admission that the cities were not secure and their capture was inevitable'.[239] Depending on how one understands the reference to 'king' in 4.9a, various implications follow. Some commentators

J. Pryke, 'Eschatology in the Dead Sea Scrolls', in *The Scrolls and Christianity: Historical and Theological Significance*, ed. M. Black (London: SPCK), pp. 45–57.

234 A. S. Herbert, *Isaiah: Chapters 1–39* (Cambridge: Cambridge University Press, 1973), p. 95. For other oracles against Babylon in Isaiah see 13.1-22; 14.3-23; 21.1-10.

235 Cf. Isa. 26.17-18, where the metaphor is used of judgement on Israel.

236 H. Wildberger, *Isaiah 13–27* (Minneapolis: Fortress Press, 1997), p. 23.

237 Holladay, *Jeremiah*, p. 603.

238 H. McKeating, *The Books of Amos, Hosea and Micah* (Cambridge: Cambridge University Press, 1971), p. 174; F. Andersen and D. N. Freedman, *Micah: A New Translation with Introduction and Commentary* (London: Doubleday, 2000), p. 441–47.

239 McKeating, *Books*, p. 174.

have taken it as a reference to Yahweh, finding support for this in a similar theme in v. 7. Jeremiah 8.19 also attests to this idea through synonymous parallelism, 'Is the LORD not in Zion? Is her King not in her?' If this was the case, one could argue that Yahweh had indeed deserted Jerusalem and thus the city stood under judgement (cf. Mt. 23.38). Based on these attested similar references to 'child pangs', it is plausible to suggest that the phrase in Mt. 24.8, rather than implying an 'eschatological' cataclysm, drew on the prophetic descriptions of historical judgement to portray the Roman threat against Jerusalem in the first century.

3.3.e. Matthew 24.15[240]

Detailed discussion of how verse 15, and the βδέλυγμα τῆς ἐρημώσεως in particular, are to be understood, will be documented in the following chapter. Sufficient for our discussion at this point will be to discuss (1) the nature of the genitive case; (2) the hints which encourage further connection with the prophetic literature; and (3) a contemporary Roman author who describes Roman military action as 'desert making'.

3.3.e.i. Genitive construction

The genitive case is notoriously difficult to define. In his opening sentence on the use of the genitive, C. F. D. Moule states that 'This is so immensely versatile and hard-working a case that anything like an exhaustive catalogue of its uses would be only confusing and unnecessarily dull.'[241] Nonetheless, among other possibilities, the genitive in the construction βδέλυγμα τῆς ἐρημώσεως can be understood in two main ways which have significant interpretive implications. First, some commentators have suggested that the genitive is to be understood as an 'epexegetical genitive' or a 'genitive of apposition'. Wallace defines this use of the genitive as that which 'refers to the same thing as the substantive to which it is related'.[242] He goes on to suggest that the equation is not identical in the tautological sense, but that the genitive of apposition 'typically states a specific example that is a part of the larger category ... It is frequently used when the head noun is ambiguous or metaphorical.'[243] The implication of this would be that the 'desolation' is equated with the 'abomination'. That is, the phrase would be understood

---

240 The intervening material (vv. 9-15) is also most plausibly understood in reference to 70 AD. Parallels to the note in 24.9 regarding persecution are readily acquired (1 Thess. 2.14, 15; Heb. 10.33; Rev. 6.11-12). For the theme of Jewish persecution of Christians see Hare, *Persecutions*, p. 20. In a related point regarding Mt. 24.14, it can be seen from the narrative in Acts (ch. 8), that persecution precipitated the spread of the Gospel message. The τέλος in Mt. 24.14 should be understood in relation to our discussion of the συντελείας τοῦ αἰῶνος and the conclusion of a former dispensation.

241 Moule, *Idiom*, p. 37.

242 Wallace, *Grammar*, p. 95.

243 Wallace, *Grammar*, p. 95.

as 'When you see the abomination *which is* the desolation ...'. It was in this sense that J. Lightfoot understood the phrase in identifying the 'abomination' with the Roman army.[244] In favour of this interpretation is Lk. 21.20 which changes Mark's Ὅταν δὲ ἴδητε τὸ βδέλυγμα τῆς ἐρημώσεως (Mk 13.14) to Ὅταν δὲ ἴδητε κυκλουμένην ὑπὸ στρατοπέδων Ἰερουσαλήμ ('When you see Jerusalem surrounded by armies').

Alternatively, the genitive construction in Matthew can be understood as a 'causative genitive' or a 'genitive of result'.[245] The definition of this use is reasonably simple, in that the genitive expresses the result of the previous word or idea. It is in this sense that F. Blass and A. Debrunner refer to it as the 'genitive of purpose'.[246] Similarly, Wallace defines what he terms the 'genitive of product' as 'the *product* of the noun to which it stands related'.[247] Although this is a relatively rare use of the genitive, there are some clear examples in Koine usage.[248] The interpretive implication of understanding the genitive in this fashion in Mt. 24.15, in distinction to the former ('genitive of apposition'), is that the desolation (destruction of Jerusalem) is the direct result of the abomination (rejection of Jesus as legitimate Messiah).

Of these two differing ways of understanding the genitive, the latter more appropriately suits the context because (1) the above-stated reference to Luke's reworking of Mark does not necessarily have interpretive force for Matthew, and (2) the opposite may be true, for if Matthew wanted to express a similar sentiment to Luke's 'appositive' interpretation he was at liberty also to change the Markan tradition. He has, however, retained Mark's specificity in relation to the ἐρημός. The only redactional change in Mt. 24.15a.i (cf. Mk 13.14a.i) is Matthew's substitution of οὖν for Mark's δέ, which highlights the connection between the 'abomination' saying and the preceding material within the chapter. Furthermore, the 'causative genitive' not only concurs with the general thrust of Matthew's last main block of narrative (Matthew 19–22), in which the composite groups of Israel

---

244 Lightfoot, *Commentary*, p. 313. Similar in this regard is E. B. Elliott (cited in Lightfoot, *Commentary*, p. 617), who concludes that 'the abomination of desolation standing in the Holy Place at Jerusalem ... [is] a prophecy which doubtless had reference to the time of the consummated iniquity of the Christ-rejecting Jerusalem, and of the Roman besieging army with its idolatrous standards gathering into the sacred precincts of the Jewish city'.

245 This is distinct from (and actually opposite to) the genitive use known of as 'cause of state', in which the genitive is the cause of the referent (LXX Song 2.5). The 'causative genitive', in the sense that we are employing it, functions as expressing the result of the referent, and hence the cause of the genitive.

246 Blass and Debrunner, *Grammar*, §166.

247 Wallace, *Grammar*, p. 106.

248 John 5.29; 2 Macc. 7.14, cited in Blass and Debrunner, *Grammar*, §166. Romans 15.13, 33; 16.20; Heb. 1.9, cited in Wallace, *Grammar*, p. 106. In reference to ζωῆς in Rom. 5.18, C. E. B. Cranfield argues that it is 'to be explained as a genitive of result ... this righteous status has life, eternal life, for its result' (C. E. B. Cranfield, *The Epistle to the Romans* [Edinburgh: T&T Clark, 1975], p. 289).

are condemned and threatened with judgement (cf. Mt. 22.7), but the theme also fits very comfortably with the (previously mentioned) Deuteronomistic curses of covenantal infidelity and threats of judgement in the prophetic literature. It is to this potential prophetic echo that we will now briefly turn our attention.

3.3.e.ii. Prophetic literature as background to Mt. 24.15

Although this issue will comprise the central thrust of our following chapter, it seemed important at this point briefly to sketch the outline of how the argument will be developed, specifically noting those elements which would encourage an interpretation of Mt. 24.15, not only in reference to the book of Daniel but *also* in light of Israel's prophetic literature.

Given that Matthew specifically alerts the reader that the quotation is taken from Daniel, and that it is a unique Matthean redaction, one may plausibly ask what justification there is for suggesting that the prophetic literature is on the horizon per se. Our contention is that there is substantial interaction between the two bodies of literature (i.e. Daniel and the prophetic literature) and that Matthew employs them in mutual interpretation. It is interesting, however, that Matthew considers Daniel to be ὁ προφήτης. Davies and Allison suspect that this might indicate that Matthew's readers were more familiar with the LXX, in which Daniel belonged to the prophets, rather than the MT, where Daniel was grouped with the writings.[249] However, as Gundry has noted, Mt. 13.35 cites Ps. 78 as having prophetic derivation,[250] which is an unattested concept in the Hebrew Bible. Furthermore, 4Q174 refers to 'the book of Daniel the Prophet', and *Ant.* 10.249 refers to Daniel himself as τὸν προφήτην.[251] Perhaps Matthew was hinting at the connection between the themes present in these bodies of literature.

Turning our attention specifically to Mt. 24.15, we note that upon searching for the relevant cognates (βδελυγμα, βδελυγμος, βδελυκτος, βδελυρος, βδελυσσω, ερημα, ερημια, ερημικος, ερημιτης, ερημος, ερημοω, ερημωσις) within the same verse of the LXX, seven results are produced. Four of these refer to Antiochus Epiphanes IV (1 Macc. 1.54; Dan. 9.27; 11.31; 12.11), and three to Israel (Hos. 9.10; Jer. 44.22; Ezek. 33.29). Of particular note are Jer. 44.22, 'The Lord could no longer bear the sight of your evil doings, the abominations that you committed; therefore your land became a desolation and a waste and a curse, without inhabitant, as it is to this day,' and Ezek. 33.29, 'Then they shall know that I am the Lord, when

---

249 Davies and Allison, *Matthew 3*, p. 345 n.113.

250 Gundry, *Matthew*, p. 482.

251 J. Barton, *Oracles of God: Perceptions of Ancient Prophecy in Israel After the Exile* (Oxford: Oxford University Press, 1986), pp. 35–37. In *Apion* 1.7 Josephus claims that all scripture was written by prophets. Compare the tradition in the Babylonian Talmud that Daniel should not be included among the prophets, *b.Sanh.* 94a. Cited in J. J. Collins, *Daniel* (Minneapolis: Augsburg Press, 1993), p. 52.

I have made the land a desolation and a waste because of all their abominations that they have committed.' Both these oracles condemn Israel for their
abominations and threaten her with becoming a desolation, that is, they use
this language in an inter-Jewish polemic.

Further insight is gained when the unit of the LXX is widened to include
an entire chapter, which produces seventy-six results. Some of them are
particularly revealing.[252] One example from Jeremiah's temple sermon will
be sufficient.

> Jer. 7.10 and then come and stand before me in this house, which is called
> by my name, and say, 'We are safe!' – only to go on doing all these abomi-
> nations (βδελύγματα)? ... 30 For the people of Judah have done evil in my
> sight, says the Lord; they have set their abominations (βδελύγματα) in the
> house that is called by my name, defiling it ... 34 And I will bring to an end
> the sound of mirth and gladness, the voice of the bride and bridegroom in
> the cities of Judah and in the streets of Jerusalem; for the land shall become
> a waste (ἐρήμωσιν).

Our provisional thesis is that the phrase βδέλυγμα τῆς ἐρημώσεως,
given its background primarily in Daniel, but also taking into serious
consideration its intertextual echoes in the prophetic literature of the
Hebrew Bible (especially Jeremiah and Ezekiel), refers to Israel as the
abomination and the destruction of the temple as the desolation (i.e. an
ironic reversal of the perceived recipients of divine wrath). In this way
Matthew presents Jesus as thoroughly Jewish and standing in the long
line of Israel's prophets, uttering a divine oracle of judgement against
Israel. Although there was common expectation that the 'pagan' nations
would experience Yahweh's judgement, Matthew presents Jesus as the
mouthpiece announcing divine retribution (destruction of the temple)
which is to fall upon Israel for the rejection of her true Messianic King.
This interpretive approach is only possible if we allow Matthew to
have some literary sophistication – i.e. ironic reversal. Whereas in the
first instance the abomination which caused desolation was performed
by a wicked pagan (Antiochus Epiphanes IV), now Israel, who rejects
Yahweh's Messiah, typologically becomes 'the wicked, pagan nation'
and, as such, suffers the fate of Yahweh's wrath.

---

252 Exodus 8.20-28; Lev. 7.21, 38; 26.11, 22, 30-31; 26.33-35, 43; Deut. 7.22-26;
29.5, 17; 32.10, 16, 51; 1 Sam. 25.1-3; 2 Chron. 36.14-21; 1 Macc. 1.39, 49, 54; 2
Macc. 5.8, 27; Ps. 106.9, 14, 26, 40; 107.4, 18, 33, 35; Prov. 21.19-27 (temple religious
practice); Job 15.16, 28; Wis. 11.2, 24; Sir. 13.19, 20; 16.4, 8; 49.2, 6; Hos. 9.10; Amos
5.10, 25; Isa. 1.7-13; 14.17, 19, 23; 17.8-9; 41.18-24; 44.19-27; 49.7-8, 17-19; Jer. 2.6-7,
15, 24, 31; 4.1-7, 11, 26-27; 7.10, 30, 34 (temple sermon); 13.24-27; 44.2, 6, 22; Ezek.
5.9-11, 14; 6.9-14; 20.7-36; 33.24-29; 36.2-38; Dan. 9.17-18, 27; 11.24, 31; 12.11. Cf.
Isa. 13.9.

3.3.e.iii. Roman military action

In a famous passage in *De vita et moribus Iulii Agricolae*, Tacitus records a speech by Calgacus, the leader of the Caledonian Confederacy, which was spoken before the Battle of Mons Graupius in Northern Scotland in 83 AD.[253] In it, Calgacus attempts to rouse his troops to fight against the Agricola-led army of Rome. In his last exhortation, Calgacus laments the exploitation of Roman rule and the unquenchable thirst for conquest by stating, *Auferre, trucidare, rapere, falsis nominibus imperium; atque, ubi solitudinem faciunt, pacem appellant* ('They plunder, they slaughter, and they steal: this they falsely name Empire, and where they make a wasteland/desert, they call it peace').[254] Ogilvie and Richmond note that 'the epigram itself is an old jibe against the Romans; cf. Curtius 9.2.24 *"postquam solitudinem in Asia vincendo fecistis."*'[255] In an interesting and subversive wordplay, E. Brooks Jr notes that 'Peace given to the world' was a 'very frequent inscription on the Roman medals'.[256] The importance of the Tacitean passage is sufficient for fuller quotation:

> sed nulla iam ultra gens, nihil nisi fluctus ac saxa, et infestiores Romani, quorum superbiam frustra per obsequium ac modestiam effugias. Raptores orbis, postquam cuncta vastantibus defuere terrae, mare scrutantur: si locuples hostis est, avari, si pauper, ambitiosi, quos non Oriens, non Occidens satiaverit: soli omnium opes atque inopiam pari adfectu concupiscunt. Auferre trucidare rapere falsis nominibus imperium, atque ubi solitudinem faciunt, pacem appellant.[257]

253 It has been frequently noted that the speech itself is a 'rhetorical composition by Tacitus himself', M. Hutton, *Tacitus* (vol. 1; Cambridge, MA: Harvard University Press, 1970), p. 79.

254 Tacitus *Agr.* 30.6.

255 R. M. Ogilvie and I. Richmond, *Cornelii Taciti: De Vita Agricolae* (Oxford: Clarendon Press, 1967), p. 258. Also see discussion in V. D'Agostino, *Cornelii Taciti: De Vita et Moribus Iulii Agricolae Liber* (Florence: Biblioteca Della Rivista, 1962), p. 59.

256 E. Brooks, *The Germany and Agricola of Tacitus* (Whitefish, MT: Kessinger Publishing, 2004), p. 110. Ogilvie and Richmond note that the 'blessings of peace as the accompaniment of empire figured much in Roman literary propaganda', Ogilvie and Richmond, *Agricolae*, p. 258, citing Virg. *Aen.* 6.852–53; Vell. *Pat.* 2.131, 1; Sen. *de Prov* 4.14. A similar theme is also represented on Roman coins through the iconography of olive branches, cornucopiae, and the torch which sets fire to a pile of the enemies' weapons. See H. Mattingly, *A Catalogue of the Roman Coins in the British Museum: Volume II Vespasian to Domitian* (London: British Museum Publications Limited, 1976), pp. xlvi–xlvii, 98–103.

257 Tacitus *Agr.* 30.3b–6: 'But there are no tribes beyond us, nothing indeed but sea and cliffs and these more deadly Romans, from whose oppression escape is vainly sought by obedience and submission. Robbers of the world, having by their universal plunder exhausted the land, they rifle the deep. If the enemy be rich, they are rapacious; if he be poor, they lust for dominion; neither the east nor the west has been able to satisfy them. Alone among men they covet with equal eagerness poverty and riches. To robbery, slaughter, plunder, they give the lying name of empire; they make a desert and call it peace.'

Of particular interest here is the description of the Roman military's suppression of insurrection as 'desert making' (*solitudinem*). Indeed, this concurs remarkably well with our working hypothesis that the ἐρημώσεως in Mt. 24.15 refers to the destructive force of the Roman Empire due to the inappropriate attitude (βδέλυγμα) of the supplicants under their ruler. That the Latin *solitudinem* can be plausibly equated with the Greek ἐρημώσις is apparent from how the Vulgate and the LXX similarly render their Hebrew equivalents.[258]

In regard to the climactic *solitudinem* quotation, R. A. Bauman claims that it is 'more of a Tacitean *topos* than a serious statement of fact'.[259] However, as H. D. Weinbrot has noted, Calgacus' speech has been adapted 'for continuing rejection of Roman arbitrary government, cultural hegemony, and carnal imperialism',[260] and as such would lend itself more plausibly to a typological reappropriation based on context rather than style. D. R. Dudley notes that Calgacus 'delivers a fiery and eloquent speech on the evils of Roman imperialism'.[261] Dudley's subsequent sceptical question regarding the content of Agricola's critique – 'How much of this could conceivably be historical?'[262] – is directed towards the historicity of Calgacus and Agricola as speakers of the speeches rather than questioning the realities which they describe. R. Syme states that it is simply 'fervid denunciation of imperial conquest',[263] and although 'the actions of robbery and violence … [Tacitus] reports come from rhetorical stock-in-trade',[264] the objections of Bauman 'miss the mark … [as] annexation tended to provoke immediate rebellion in vassal kingdoms'.[265]

3.3.e.iv. Preliminary conclusion
In this light, our preliminary conclusion regarding Mt. 24.15 is that (1) the genitive construction in βδέλυγμα τῆς ἐρημώσεως functions as a causative genitive; (2) there are implicit hints in the vocabulary of this

---

258 Genesis 47.19 has *solitudinem* and ἐρημωθήσεται for the MT's תֵּשַׁם'. Exodus 5.3; 15.22; 16.10; 19.1; Lev. 16.10; Num. 33.8; Deut. 1.40; 2.1, 7 has *solitudinem* and ἔρημον for the MT's מִדְבָּר. Exodus 23.29 has *solitudinem* and ἔρημον for the MT's שְׁמָמָה. Leviticus 26.43 has *solitudinem* and ἐρημωθῆναι for the MT's הָשַׁמָּה. Numbers 23.38 has *solitudinem* and ἔρημον for the MT's הַיְשִׁימֹן. Leviticus 26.31 has *solitudinem* and ἔρημον for the MT's חָרְבָּה. Of note here is the theme of judgement through the destruction of the city: 'I will lay your cities waste, will make your sanctuaries desolate, and I will not smell your pleasing odors.'

259 R. A. Bauman, *Human Rights in Ancient Rome* (London: Routledge, 1999), p. 163.

260 H. D. Weinbrot, 'Politics, Taste, and National Identity: Some Uses of Tacitism in Eighteenth-Century Britain', in *Tacitus and the Tacitean Tradition*, ed. T. J. Luce and A. J. Woodman (Princeton: Princeton University Press, 1993), pp. 168–84 (181).

261 D. R. Dudley, *The World of Tacitus* (London: Secker & Warburg, 1968), p. 50.

262 Dudley, *Tacitus*, p. 51.

263 R. Syme, *Tacitus* (vol. 2; Oxford: Oxford University Press, 1958), p. 528.

264 Syme, *Tactius*, p. 529.

265 Syme, *Tactius*, p. 764.

verse which encourage further investigation as to the prophetic background of the ideas behind the text; and (3) there is at least one other Matthean contemporary author who describes the military action of the Roman army as 'desert making'.

3.3.f. Matthew 24.16

After Matthew's reference to the enigmatic ὁ ἀναγινώσκων νοείτω, the command is given to those in Judaea to φευγέτωσαν εἰς τὰ ὄρη. The exhortation has traditionally been understood as either an *ex eventu* reference to (1) the flight to Pella (Eusebius *Hist.* 3.5.3) or some other historical circumstance[266] or (2) an eschatological deliverance.[267] What is frequently overlooked is the common prophetic tradition of fleeing a city that has come under the wrath of God.[268] Genesis 19.17 states the following: 'When they had brought them outside, they said, "Flee for your life; do not look back or stop anywhere in the Plain; flee to the hills, or else you will be consumed."' In the light of this, Beasley-Murray suggests that Jerusalem is envisaged as 'another Sodom'.[269] Additionally, Ezek. 7.15-16 makes the connection between ὄρος and destruction: 'those in the city [Jerusalem] will be devoured by famine and pestilence. If any survivors escape, they shall be found on the mountains.' Significant in Zech. 14.2-5 is the reference to God gathering 'all the nations against Jerusalem to battle ... And you shall flee by the valley of the Lord's mountain for the valley.' Of particular note here is the connection between Jerusalem's destruction by pagan nations and salvation being achieved by fleeing to an adjacent mountain. Similar practice is adopted in the Maccabaean stories, wherein Mattathias fled with all those who were zealous for the law εἰς τὰ ὄρη.[270] Later in the narrative troops 'rushed on them from the ambush and began killing them. Many were wounded and fell, and the rest fled to the mountain.'[271] *Psalms of Solomon* 17.16 describes a similar circumstance where 'they that loved the synagogues of the pious fled from them, as sparrows that fly from their nest'. Although references to this common practice could be multiplied,[272] sufficient for our discussion is to note that Matthew

---

266 One of the factors which supports the idea that Matthew was not written *ex eventu* 70 AD is the way in which this detail does not correlate with the historical reality of the Jewish War, as all the nearby mountains were occupied by Roman troops.

267 C. S. Keener, *A Commentary on the Gospel of Matthew* (Grand Rapids: Eerdmans, 1999), pp. 586, 687.

268 The concept of fleeing into the mountains surrounding a city is not only attested in biblical and later Jewish literature, but also in Classical sources such as Plutarch *Mor.* 869B: 'the men, by fleeing to the mountain country, found safety'.

269 Beasley-Murray, *Matthew*, p. 100.

270 First Maccabees 2.28.

271 First Maccabees. 9.40.

272 *Ant.* 5.163; 17.218; 18.48; *War* 1.36; 1.95; 2.504; 2.511.

has employed conventional language used to describe the appropriate response of the inhabitants of a city during military invasion. This is not to advocate that Matthew had in mind the flight to Pella, etc. but only that he used conventional language, primarily taken from the prophetic literature in presenting his narrative. As such, this coheres well with a historical rather than a necessarily 'eschatological' reality.

3.3.g. The coming of the Son of Man with respect to the book of Daniel

The related question of the meaning of the coming of the Son of Man in Matthew and its background in Daniel will be discussed in detail in chapter 4 of this book. Sufficient for our discussion thus far is to note that, in Daniel 7, the Son of Man figure operates as Yahweh's representative, who comes to destroy Israel's political and religious enemies. It is argued in this work that Matthew picks up this tradition and weaves it into his story with one significant development – *irony*, a development for which there is justification from Israel's earlier prophetic tradition. The religious and political enemy of Israel in Matthew is institutional Israel herself. Matthew typologically applies the negative connotations of the idolatrous pagan nations to Israel, whom he presents as having flaunted her covenantal obligations, and as such standing under judgement and awaiting Yahweh's divinely executed retributive process.

3.3.h. Matthew 24.28: the Roman eagle and the destruction of a city

There is some uncertainty how best to understand Mt. 24.28 and surrounding verses. If this material was taken from Q 17.22-37, which most commentators have seen as embodying an eschatological perspective (bookending the false signs), how does it relate to our discussion of Matthew 24? Below we discuss this, including one possible manner in which 24.28 may pertain to the realities of 70 AD. Although some commentators have suggested that Matthew may have wanted to 'de-eschatologize' his source material but nonetheless left traces of the original perspective at this point, it is admitted that it would be somewhat strange that Matthew has retained these references. If we produce an interpretation which coheres with the wider narrative suggested thus far, then this seem methodologically preferable.[273]

One particularly fruitful avenue to pursue this question is the proverbial-like[274] saying of v. 28, ὅπου ἐὰν ᾖ τὸ πτῶμα, ἐκεῖ συναχθήσονται οἱ ἀετοί ('Where the corpse is, there the eagles will

---

273 It is important to note, however, that, as was noted in our opening discussion of assumptions, for the purposes of this research we are interested in the Matthean text in its extant form.

274 A. A. T. Ehrhardt, 'Greek Proverbs in the Gospel', *HTR* 46 (1953), pp. 68–72.

gather'). Commentators have often taken this in reference to the 'second coming' of Jesus, and related it to his visibility and obvious heavenly descent. Thus v. 28 functions in like manner to v. 27: 'For as the lightning comes from the east and flashes as far as the west, so will be the coming of the Son of Man.' The event which is spoken of will occur in plain sight for all to behold. Luz makes this connection by noting that 'people will be able to miss the parousia no more than vultures overlook a dead animal'.[275] The image 'merely wants to illustrate how impossible it will be not to see the parousia'.[276] Amid other interpretive possibilities,[277] Lightfoot, however, suggests the following:

> of pious men flying to Christ ... the discourse here is of quite a different thing: they are thus connected to the foregoing: Christ shall be revealed with sudden vengeance; for when God shall cast off the city and people, grown ripe for destruction, like a carcase thrown out, the Roman soldiers, like eagles, shall straight fly to it with their eagles (ensigns) to tear and devour it ... Jerusalem, and that wicked nation ... would be the carcase, to which the greedy and devouring eagles would fly to prey upon it.[278]

The connection between the ἀετοί ('eagles') and Roman troops was also referred to by J. J. Wettstein approximately a hundred years later.[279] In recent times W. Carter has developed this thesis at length by taking seriously the imperial symbolism. Crucial to this idea is the interpretation of the ἀετοί as eagles as opposed to vultures. As Carter has convincingly argued, the ἀετοί in Mt. 24.28 (Vulg. *aquilae*) should be understood in reference to eagles as there is a separate Greek word available if the author had intended to refer to vultures (γυψ, Lat. *vultur*). That the ἀετός and the γυψ should not be equated or collapsed

---

275 Luz, *Matthew 21–28*, p. 199. For the debate over what type of bird of prey ἀετός refers to, see below.

276 Luz, *Matthew 21–28*, p. 200. L. Mühlethaler understands it in reference to the false prophets of vv. 23-26. Luz, *Matthew 21–28*, p. 199 summarizes Mühlethaler, 'in this case the sense of the image would be: the coming parousia lures false prophets irresistibly to the plan'. Not surprisingly, the phrase has also been understood allegorically. Hippolytus' *In Matthaeum* 24, 205, argues that the carcass is a reference to the killed Christ and the eagles are the elect. Cf. also Origen frg. 478 μεγαλοφυῶς καὶ βασιλικῶς ... διὸ οὐ γῦπες, οὐ κόρακες, cited in Luz, *Matthew 21–28*, p. 200 n.153.

277 W. Carter, 'Are There Imperial Texts in the Class? Intertextual Eagles and Matthean Eschatology as "Lights Out" Time for Imperial Rome (Matthew 24:27-31)', *JBL* 122 (2003), pp. 467–87 (467 n.3) lists several main interpretations: (1) eschatological tribulation as vultures devour the flesh of the wicked dead; (2) as vultures come to a rotting corpse, so does the Son of Man come to a rotten world to judge it; (3) the saints will rise as eagles to be with Son of Man; (4) description of general resurrection; (5) the eagles are angels.

278 Lightfoot, *Commentary*, p. 319.

279 J. J. Wettstein, *Novum Testamentum Graecum* (vol. 1; Graz: Akademische Druck und Verlagsanstalt, 1962), p. 502.

into a single category of 'bird of prey' is apparent from ancient authors who went to lengths to distinguish the two.[280] Thus, one can conclude with reasonable confidence that Mt. 24.28 should be understood as referring to eagles.[281]

In that light, it is instructive indeed that a common metaphor in the LXX is that of the eagle as representative of the 'imperial powers whom God uses to punish sinful people'.[282] Hosea 8.1 portrays Assyria as the eagle who punishes Samaria in 722 BC, 'one like an eagle (ἀετός/כַּנֶּשֶׁר/ aquila) is over the house of the Lord, because they have broken my covenant, and transgressed my law'. A similar theme is evident in Deut. 28.49, which states 'The Lord will bring a nation from far away, from the end of the earth, to swoop down on you like an eagle (ἀετοῦ), a nation whose language you do not understand.'[283] Furthermore, of the twenty-two references to πτῶμα in the LXX, fourteen express God's judgement on the wicked (Job 15.23; 18.12; 20.5; Wis. 4.18-19; *Pss Sol.* 3.10), including Gentile tyrants (Ps. 110 [LXX 109].6; 2 Macc. 9.7). Πρῶμα is commonly associated with the person who has fallen in military battle.[284]

That the eagles of Mt. 24.28 are to be identified as Rome is supported by *4 Ez.* 11–12, a document contemporary with Matthew: 'On the second night I had a dream, and behold, there came up from the sea an eagle that had twelve feathered wings and three heads ... .' M. Stone has

---

280 Carter, 'Imperial', p. 469. Aristotle *Historia Animalium* 6.5–6; Pliny *Nat. Hist.* 10.3; Aelianus *Hist. Anim.* 2.46; 10.22; Job 39.26-30. Vultures feed on carrion (Homer *Illiad* 4.235; 11.162; 16.836; Euripides *Rhesus* 515; *Daughters of Troy* 599; Seneca *Ep.* 95.43; Martial *Epig.* 6.62.4), whereas, as Carter notes, eagles 'hunt their own living prey (so Job 9.26)'. Aelianus *Hist. Anim.* 2.39; Virgil *Aeneid* 11.752–56. Carter, 'Imperial', p. 470.

281 This renders some of the traditional parallels with this verse more tenuous. LXX Job 9.26; Cornutus *Nat. deorum* 21, 'the birds [vultures] ... gather together wherever there are (ὅπου ποτ' ἄν... ἦ) many corpses (πτώματα) slain in war'. Seneca *Ep.* 95.43, 'vultur est, cadaver expectat'; Martial 6.62.4 'cuius vultures hocerit cadaver'; Aelianus, *Hist. anim.* 2.46; Lucian *Navig.* 1; Lucian 6.550–51, 'Et quodcumque iacet nuda tellure cadaver Ante feras volucres sedet'; Prudentius Cathemer 10.41, 'Quae pigra cadavera pridem tumulis putrefacta iacebant, volucres rapientur in aures animas comitata priores.' See extensive discussion in D. C. Sim, *Apocalyptic Eschatology in the Gospel of Matthew* (Cambridge: Cambridge University Press, 1996), pp. 103–108.

282 Carter, 'Imperial', p. 473.

283 See Carter, 'Imperial', p. 473. Cf. Jer. 15.3; 48.40; 49.22 (apart from the reference to the eagle, of note here is the mention of labour pains [cf. Mt. 24.8]). Ehrhardt notes that Hab. 1.8 'lacks ... the mention of the carcase and is therefore rather unconvincing' (Ehrhardt, 'Proverbs', p. 68) as a parallel to Matthew. He may, however, be underestimating the force of φαγεῖν. The Matthean use of the plural ἀετοί could simply refer to Titus' multiple legions – V Macedonica, XII Fulminata, and XV Apollinaris on the western side, and X Fretensis on the Mount of Olives to the east.

284 In *Ant.* 7.16 and in ten of the thirteen references in *War*, πτῶμα denotes battle corpses (3.249; 5.16–18, 34, 516–17, 541, 570; 6.2, 29–30, 40, 405). Carter, 'Imperial', p. 479.

noted the eagle's three heads and has taken them to represent the three Flavian emperors, Vespasian and his two sons Titus and Domitian.[285] This identification of the eagle as Rome is strengthened by the multi-faceted use of the eagle as a symbol of authority and rule.[286] At various points in Josephus' *War* and *Ant.*, he refers to the events surrounding Herod's erection of an eagle on the temple in Jerusalem as a sign of political dominion.[287] In this regard *Ant.* 17.151 states ὁ βασιλεὺς ὑπὲρ τοῦ μεγάλου πυλῶνος τοῦ ναοῦ ἀνάθημα καὶ λίαν πολυτελὲς ἀετὸν χρύσεον μέγαν ('for the king had erected over the great gate of the temple a large golden eagle, of great value, and had dedicated it to the temple').

The most ancient military symbol employed by the Romans is said to have been a handful of straw fixed to the top of a spear or pole. This was succeeded by the figures of animals, of which Pliny the Elder (*Nat. Hist.* 10.4–5) enumerates five: the eagle, the wolf, the minotaur, the horse, and the boar. In the second consulship of Marius (104 BC) the four quadrupeds were laid aside as standards, the eagle (*Aquila*) being alone retained. Pliny *Natural History* 10.5 says:

> Caius Marius, in his second consulship, assigned the eagle exclusively to the Roman legions. Before that period it had only held the first rank, there being four others as well, the wolf, the minotaur, the horse, and the wild boar, each of which preceded a single division. Some few years before his time it had begun to be the custom to carry the eagle only into battle, the other standards being left behind in camp; Marius, however, abolished the rest of them entirely.

Representations of eagles (and their association with Jupiter, the chief god of the Roman state) were also common on coins which functioned as 'the handheld signs of propaganda that everywhere asserted Rome's power and authority bestowed by Jupiter'.[288] In first-century Mediterranean village life, K. Dyer suggests that the circulation of coinage operated as one of the most efficient and concrete forms of communication.[289] As such, in depicting eagles on the obverse of the

---

285   Stone, *Ezra*, pp. 363–66. For this and the following discussion I am indebted to Carter, 'Imperial', pp. 474–87.

286   L. J. Kreitzer notes that 'the legionary *aquilae* figured prominently in imperial propaganda', L. J. Kreitzer, *Striking New Images: Roman Imperial Coinage and the New Testament World* (Sheffield: Sheffield Academic Press, 1996), p. 67.

287   *War* 1.648–55; 2.5; *Ant.* 17.151–52, 155, 206.

288   Dyer, *Concerning*, p. 112.

289   Dyer, *Concerning*, p. 112; Dyer, *Prophecy*, pp. 221–32. Oster, 'Numismatic', pp. 195–223 has also argued at length that coinage was one of the main ways information was disseminated in antiquity.

coins of Nero,[290] Galba,[291] Otho,[292] Vespasian,[293] and Domitian,[294] the message was clear: the emperor of Rome had dominion as regent of Jupiter.[295] It was in this regard that numerous stories circulated of sightings of real eagles functioning as omens guaranteeing Roman victory in battle.[296]

There is, however, further evidence which links the ἀετοί directly with the Roman military. In his description of the military procession Josephus notes that, after certain horsemen 'came the ensigns encompassing the eagle (τὸν ἀετόν), which is at the head of every Roman legion, the king, and the strongest of all birds'.[297] Similarly *War* 5.48 describes the procession of Titus' army as follows: 'All these came before the engines; and after these engines, followed the tribunes and the leaders of the cohorts, with their select bodies; after these came the ensigns, with the eagle (ἀετὸν) ... .'[298]

In the light of this, it is certainly possible that the reference to ἀετοί in Mt. 24.28 refers to the ensign *aquilae* of the legions of Rome. As was noted above, this identification has been argued by W. Carter;[299] however, it is important to note the alternative way in which he developed his thesis in contradistinction to Lightfoot and Wettstein. Whereas Lightfoot and Wettstein had argued that the eagles represented Rome in the infliction of judgement on Jerusalem, Carter argues that the 'eagles are not doing something to the

290 A. Burnett, M. Amandry, and P. P. Ripollès, *Roman Provincial Coinage, Vol. 1, From the Death of Caesar to the Death of Vitellius (44 BC–AD 69)* (London: British Museum Press, 1992), nos 4176, 4177, 4180, 4184, 4185, 4186, 4188, 4189, 4191, 4192, 4197, 4198.

291 Burnett, *44 BC–AD 69*, nos 4193, 4194, 4195, 4196b, 4197, 4198.

292 Burnett, *44 BC–AD 69*, nos 4199, 4200.

293 A. Burnett, M. Amandry, and P. P. Ripollès, *Roman Provincial Coinage, Vol. 2, From Vespasian to Domitian (AD 69–96)* (London: British Museum Press, 1999), nos 1936, 1937, 1938, 1939/2, 1945–75 (excluding 1960).

294 Burnett, *AD 69–96*, nos 1976, 1977, 1978, 1979, 1980, 1981.

295 Appian *Bell. Civ.* 2.610 refers to the eagle as 'the symbol held in the highest honor by the Romans'. *Antiquities of the Jews* 12.227 records that the king's seal bore the sign of an eagle. For further discussion of the eagle as a symbol of Roman power see P. Richardson, *Herod: King of the Jews and Friend of the Romans* (Columbia: University of South Carolina Press, 1996), pp. 15–18.

296 Suetonius, *Aug.* 94.7; 96.1; 97.1; *Tib.* 14.4; *Claud.* 7.1; *Gal.* 1.1; 4.2; *Vit.* 9.1; *Ves.* 5.6; *Dom.* 6.2; Tacitus *Hist.* 1.62; *Ann.* 2.17; Pliny *Nat. Hist.* 15.136–37. Cited in Carter, 'Imperial', p. 475. Also to note are the 'eagle shaped supports for the roof of the temple of Jupiter Capitolinus', Carter, 'Imperial', p. 475; K. Scott, *The Imperial Cult under the Flavians* (Stuttgart: Kohlhammer, 1936), pp. 63–64. Cf. the Pentelic marble triumphal arch of Titus situated in the south-east corner of the forum in Rome, wherein the internal apex of the arch depicts an eagle. Significant in this regard is that this arch was built by Domitian after the death of Titus to commemorate the sack of Jerusalem.

297 *War* 3.123.

298 For other references of eagles as Roman standards (*aquilae*) see Appian *Bell. Civ.* 4.101, 1128; Caesar *Bell. Gal.* 4.25; 5.37; cited in Carter, 'Imperial', p. 476.

299 Carter, 'Imperial', pp. 476–87.

corpse but are "gathered with (συν) it"[300] and thus indicates that a 'complementary or parallel relationship exists in which both experience the same thing'.[301] That is, the passive verb συναχθήσονται indicates that Matthew intends to portray the similar fates of the two representative groups: 'what happens to the corpse happens to the eagle'.[302]

Although Yahweh often punishes the particular pagan nation he has used to inflict judgement on Israel,[303] this does not seem to be on the horizon for Matthew's narrative. This is apparent in two regards. First, the passive verb συναχθήσονται is used in the following chapter of Matthew in a way which suggests that the reference is to groups which do not endure the same fate. Matthew 25.32 notes that 'All the nations will be gathered (συναχθήσονται) before him, and he will separate people one from another as a shepherd separates the sheep from the goats.' From the context it is clear that the final destinations of the sheep and the goats are diametrically opposed. One group is sentenced to 'the eternal fire prepared for the devil and his angel' (v. 41), whereas the other is welcomed to 'inherit the kingdom prepared for you from the foundation of the world' (v. 34). Furthermore, as is suggested by Rev. 19.19, the passive participle form συνηγμένα can also refer to 'armies gathered to make war'.[304] The verb, specifically used to denote gathering together in opposition, is attested in the war narratives of King Saul. When introducing the Philistine war the LXX translator of 1 Sam. 13.5 notes the following: καὶ οἱ ἀλλόφυλοι συνάγονται εἰς πόλεμον ἐπὶ Ισραηλ ('And the Philistines were gathered together with Israel in war').[305] Significant for our discussion is the use of συνάγονται to refer to two entities gathered in opposition in a military context.

Second, problematic for Carter's interpretation, which takes Rome (οἱ ἀετοί) as gathered (συναχθήσονται) in judgement with Israel (τὸ πτῶμα), is the close connection of the two events in Matthew. If, as is commonly assumed, the Gospel of Matthew took its final form in the decade after the Jewish War, would not suspicion arise when a foreign invader did not overtake and punish Rome for her actions? In other words, the question can be asked as to when, in fact, Rome experienced judgement. Would not Matthew, had he imagined a mutual punishment of the punisher, have removed this glaring inconsistency from his final composition? Rather, it seems the imagery lends itself more plausibly to the eagles (Roman legions) and the corpse (Israel)

300 Carter, 'Imperial', p. 472.

301 Carter, 'Imperial', p. 472.

302 Carter, 'Imperial', p. 478.

303 *Fourth Ezra* 3.24-36; 4.22-25; 5.21-30; 6.55-59; 7.19-25; 9.26-37; *2 Bar.* 1.1-5; 4.1; 6.1-9; 32.2-4.

304 Although strictly speaking in Rev. 19.19 the passive participle form συνηγμένα does not refer to Gentiles gathered in opposition, they are 'to make war against the rider on the horse and against his army'. Cf. *Ant.* 12.366; Plato *Resp.* VII, 526d.

305 See H. W. Hertzberg, *I & II Samuel: A Commentary* (London: SCM Press, 1960), pp. 104–105; R. P. Gordon, *1 & 2 Samuel: A Commentary* (Exeter: Paternoster Press, 1986), p. 133.

being gathered together (συναχθήσονται) in opposition, a gathering which envisions the predatory traits of the eagle hunting and devouring the carcass of rebellious Israel[306] and picking dry the bones of destroyed Jerusalem.[307] In this way, Lightfoot and Wettstein's initial identification has been confirmed by our analysis *pace* Carter.[308] We therefore conclude that although it is possible that Matthew wanted to 'de-eschatologize' his source material but nonetheless left traces of the original perspective, we feel a reasonable case can be made for an interpretation that coheres with the wider narrative of the destruction of Jerusalem in 70 AD.

3.3.i. Matthew 24.29

The images and language of Mt. 24.29 – 'Immediately after the suffering of those days the sun will be darkened, and the moon will not give its light; the stars will fall from heaven, and the powers of heaven will be shaken' – has frequently been interpreted as referring to literal events accompanying Jesus' physical return. E. Schweizer states that here 'the appearance of the Son of Man is once more described ... Matthew is warning against the false prophets who state that Christ has already come ... [and] strengthening men's hope that the coming will be soon.'[309] Similarly, U. Luz envisions here a '"transcendental eschatology" that expects a cosmic catastrophe ... universal judgement at the end of the world'.[310]

However, what is readily apparent is that *all* of this imagery is used in the prophetic literature to describe military defeats of various nations.

306 The eagle was known as a hunter, both swift (Deut. 28.49; 2 Sam. 1.23; Job 9.26; 39.27; Prov. 23.5; Hab. 1.8; Jer. 4.13; 30.16; Lam. 4.19) and sharp-eyed (Horace *Sat.* 1.3.27, Philo *Post.* 161; *Abr.* 266, and Aelianus *Hist. Anim.* 1.42; 2.26). See Carter, 'Imperial', p. 471.

307 For other commentators who interpret this similarly see Tasker, *Matthew*, pp. 225–30; Dodd, *Parables*, p. 67 n.9; Brown, 'Apocalypse', p. 12; Draper, 'Development', pp. 16–17.

308 Also of note is Jer. 7.33 which states that 'The corpses of this people will be food for the birds of the air, and for the animals of the earth; and no one will frighten them away.' Significant in this regard is the similar context of judgement, temple, and devouring bird. There is also an older attested tradition which envisions eagles as executing military judgement on a nation's enemies. Currently housed in the Louvre, and documented as item no. 301 in J. B. Pritchard, *The Ancient Near East in Pictures* (Princeton: Princeton University Press, 1954), p. 95, a mid-third-millennium-BC cuneiform limestone fragment from Tello (ancient Girsu, Iraq) portrays eagles carrying away, in their beaks, the body parts (including heads and arms) of the slain, after a battle. Also from Tello is the 'stela of the eagle' (no. 298, Pritchard, *Pictures*, p. 94), which depicts the enemies of Ennatum (King of Lagash) caught in a net which is in the clasp of an eagle's claws. In the king's right hand is a mace, with which he strikes the nude figures with shaved faces and heads.

309 E. Schweizer, *The Good News according to Matthew* (trans. D. E. Green; London: SPCK, 1975), p. 455.

310 Luz, *Matthew 21–28*, p. 200. See similar approaches in Gundry, *Matthew*, p. 487; Hagner, *Matthew 14–28*, p. 709.

Such is the case in the oracle concerning the destruction of Babylon by the Medes in Isaiah 13, where military catastrophe is described as 'the stars of the heavens and their constellations will not give their light; the sun will be dark at its rising, and the moon will not shed its light' (Isa. 13.10, cf. Mt. 24.29b-c).[311] Likewise in Isa. 13.13 it is stated that Yahweh will 'make the heavens tremble, and the earth will be shaken out of its place' (cf. Mt. 24.29e). The imagery of falling stars is captured in Isa. 34.4 in description of the coming judgement on Edom: 'and all the stars (ἄστερα) shall fall (πίπτει) like leaves from a vine, and as leaves fall from a fig-tree' (cf. ἀστέρες and πεσοῦνται in Mt. 24.29d).[312] In all these cases, the Isaianic imagery and vocabulary is employed in descriptions of military conquests.[313] This is particularly evident in Isa. 34.5 which states of Yahweh's sword, 'Behold, it descends for judgment upon Edom, upon the people I have doomed.' As such, we suggest that the Matthean language is to be understood with direct reference to these common prophetic metaphors of military invasion which are then applied to Jerusalem's destruction.

3.3.j. The Lightning and the σημεῖον in reference to the Son of Man (Mt. 24.27, 30)

The surrounding description of Mt. 24.28 reveals two significant details: the reference to the ἀστραπή ('lightning') in v. 27, and the appearance of the σημεῖον in v. 30, both of which are directly connected to the παρουσία of the Son of Man. In various bodies of literature, ἀστραπή frequently functions as a metaphor for Yahweh's judgement on the nations and celebrates military triumph.[314] Zechariah 9.13-14 describes the victory of Judah over her enemies as follows: 'For I have bent Judah as my bow; I have made Ephraim its arrow. I will arouse your sons, O Zion, against your sons, O Greece, and wield you like a warrior's sword. Then the Lord will appear over them, and his arrow go forth like lightning (ἀστραπη).'

This theme is repeatedly used in other literature, including *Wisdom of Solomon* 5.21, which notes the following in description of the coming judgement on the ἐξθροι ('enemies', v. 17) of God, 'Shafts of lightning (ἀστραπῶν) will fly with true aim, and will leap from the clouds to the target, as from a well-drawn bow.'[315] In conjunction with our previ-

---

311 Isaiah 13.19 likens Babylon's destruction to that of Sodom and Gomorrah.

312 Carter, 'Imperial', p. 485 relates the 'falling stars with judgement on Satan and Satan's agents', *1 En.* 86.1-3; 88.1-3; 90.24; Jude 13; Rev. 12.4; Dan. 8.10 where falling stars are the defeat of celestial deities.

313 O. Kaiser, *Isaiah 13–39: A Commentary* (London: SCM Press, 1973), p. 353; Wildberger, *Isaiah*, p. 330.

314 Carter, 'Imperial', pp. 480–81.

315 *Wisdom of Solomon* 19.13 uses the alternative Greek word κεραυνῶν for lightning in a similar context of judgement, 'The punishments did not come upon the sinners

ously noted 'eagle' discussion, L. J. Kreitzer points out that 'in many coin representations of the eagle the creature is portrayed as clutching a bolt of thunder/lightning in its claws',[316] and its association is also 'well documented in literature, sculpture, paintings [and] cameos'.[317] The rationale for this seems to be the association of Jupiter and lightning and the emperor as Jupiter's agent. J. R. Fears says 'the god's thunderbolt epitomized the entire conception of divine power exerted against the forces of barbarous hubris and on behalf of civilized existence'.[318]

Second, the σημεῖον has been variously understood, from a literal 'cosmic cross appearing in the sky'[319] to direct identification with the Son of Man himself.[320] The former is unlikely as Matthew has omitted 'whom they have pierced' (cf. Rev. 1.7; Jn 19.37; Zech. 12.10),[321] and of the latter, Schweizer says that this interpretation is 'almost inconceivable, since it is explicitly stated that the Son of Man is seen only later'.[322] Taking his cue from T. F. Glasson 1964,[323] J. Draper argues that the background for 'sign' language in Matthew 24 'springs out of the Old Testament tradition of holy war'.[324] Draper argues that for those cases where geographical proximity was too great for the שׁוֹפָר as a signal for war, a 'totem' was raised on a hill to 'be a sign to the tribes to gather for war'.[325] Such is the case in Jer. 51.27, which calls for the raising of a נֵס/σημεῖον in the land'. Particularly instructive are the war narratives in Isaiah.[326]

---

without prior signs in the violence of κεραυνῶν, for they justly suffered because of their wicked acts; for they practiced a more bitter hatred of strangers.' Cf. also Philo *Abr.* 43; *Mos.* 1.118; *Ant.* 2.343–44; 6.27, 92.

316 Kreitzer, *Striking*, p. 66. Numismatic evidence includes Augustus (27 BC–14 AD), Tiberius (14–37 AD), Galba (68–69 AD), Domitian (81–96 AD).

317 Kreitzer, *Striking*, p. 66.

318 J. R. Fears, 'The Theology of Victory at Rome: Approaches and Problems', *ANRW* 2.17.2 (1981), pp. 736–826 (817).

319 *Barnabas* 12.4; *Odes Sol.* 42.1-2; cf. *Did.* 16.6. This was argued by Hippolytus *In Matthaeum* 24.206; Cyril of Jerusalem *Cat.* 15.22; but more recently by A. J. B. Higgins, 'The Sign of the Son of Man (Matt. XXIV.30)', *NTS* 9 (1962–63), pp. 380–82; L. Sabourin, 'l discorso sulla parousia e le parabole della vigilanza (Matteo 24–25)', *BeO* 20 (1978), pp. 193–212 (202–203).

320 Luz, *Matthew 21–28*, p. 202 takes the genitive phrase τοῦ υἱοῦ τοῦ ἀνθρώπου as an epexegetic.

321 Higgins, 'Sign', p. 281.

322 Schweizer, *Matthew*, p. 455. Hagner, *Matthew 14–28*, p. 713 similarly states that it is 'impossible to take the sign as ... an appositional genitive'.

323 Glasson, 'Influence', pp. 299–300.

324 Draper, 'Development', p. 2. This is an alternative approach to those who relate these celestial signs as portents of disaster which signalled Jerusalem's destruction. *War* 6.288–310; Tacitus *Hist.* 5.13.

325 Draper, 'Development', p. 2.

326 One could also note, however, Ps. 73.4 [LXX 74.4] and Jer. 6.1; 28.12, 27 [LXX 51.12, 27].

Isaiah 5.25-26 records Yahweh's anger kindled against his own people:

> He stretched out his hand against them and struck them; the mountains quaked, and their corpses were like refuse in the streets. For all this his anger has not turned away, and his hand is stretched out still. He will raise a signal (נֵס/σύσσημον) for a nation far away, and whistle for a people at the ends of the earth; Here they come, swiftly, speedily.[327]

The 'totem' however, can also refer to the mustering of troops for holy war against Babylon. Isaiah 13.2-4 declares, 'On a bare hill raise a signal (σημεῖον), cry aloud to them ... Listen, a tumult on the mountains as of a great multitude! Listen, an uproar of kingdoms, of nations gathering together! The Lord of hosts is mustering an army for battle.' Based on these and other Isaianic texts,[328] Draper concludes that the נֵס/σημεῖον functions as that which 'is to be raised on a mountain or some other prominent place to announce the beginning of war, either by God or on his behalf'.[329]

The implications for understanding how this functions in Matthew then are as follows, 'Matthew views the destruction wrought by Roman armies on Judaea and Jerusalem in his own day as a fulfillment of the prophesies concerning the נֵס in Isaiah. The nations are gathered together for war *against* Israel because of her sin.'[330] Draper goes on to interpret this sign as the crucifixion; however, given our former discussion concerning the eagles of Rome and their association with lightning and Jupiter, it seems more plausible to accept the referent as the Roman army. In this sense we concur with S. Brown, who notes, 'the sign of the *parousia* of the Son of man is given in the presence of Roman standards on the temple mount'.[331] As Brown goes on to argue, this idea becomes more convincing when one notices the Matthean redaction in closely connecting the Son of Man and the Jewish War.[332] Matthew 24.29 replaces the Markan introduction to the Isaianic language of ἀλλά (Mk 13.24) with εὐθέως ('immediately'). This is especially surprising given that εὐθέως is characteristically a Markan distinctive.[333] As T. L. Donaldson has noted, this 'appears to imply that for Matthew, the *parousia* and the destruction of the temple are bound together in a tight

---

327 Chilton, *Isaiah*, p. 13 has argued that the coming figure in the Targum is a Gentile king (מֶלֶךְ). It is also noteworthy that he is said to be coming 'as swift clouds', cf. Mt. 24.30. These elements are absent from the LXX and Vulgate. See discussion in Draper, 'Development', p. 6.

328 Isaiah 11.10-12 in reference to judgement on Assyria; cf. 18.3; 49.22; 62.10-11.

329 Draper, 'Development', p. 10. For Yahweh as warrior see Deut. 20.4; Exod. 14.14; Deut. 9.3; Judg. 4.14, R. de Vaux, *Ancient Israel: Its Life and Institutions* (London: Darton, 1967), pp. 259–67.

330 Draper, 'Development', p. 16. Italics original.

331 Brown, 'Apocalypse', p. 12.

332 Brown, 'Apocalypse', p. 12.

333 Mark 1.23, 28-30, 42-43; 2.8, 12; 3.6; 4.5, 15-17, 29; 5.2, 29-30, 42; 6.25, 27, 45, 50, 54; 7.25; 8.10; 9.15, 20, 24; 10.52; 11.2-3; 14.43, 45, 72; 15.1.

temporal sequence'.[334] In this light, 'the parousia of the Son of man ... is a sign of judgement against Jerusalem, now in ruins and occupied by a foreign power ... Matthew sees a coming Son of man which has already taken place in the temple's destruction.'[335] As Gaston concludes, 'the son of man really came on the clouds in A.D. 70'.[336]

3.3.k. Preliminary conclusion

In conclusion to our above discussion on Mt. 24.28 and 27, 30, one may call into serious question Luz's comments that 'in Matthew the saying about eagles hardly speaks of judgement'.[337] This is difficult to sustain, not only because of the strong links between the eagle as representative of Roman power, but also because of the Matthean context, in which there is no indication that the author has switched from a historical vantage point to an 'eschatological' discussion concerning the end of the space-time continuum. As has been noted by M. Stone, one the chief characteristics of an eagle in the Old Testament was the 'spreading of its wings', often as a metaphor for protection.[338] The reversal in Mathew, however, of the eagle as a force of destruction rather than protection (not unattested in the Old Testament Prov. 24.22e; 30.17; Hab. 1.7) emphasizes the picture as particularly jarring,[339] and as the consequence of an internal polemic against those who did not appropriately welcome their Messianic king. The consequence of this rejection is then described as the Son of Man returning in judgement, represented by the Roman legions with the corresponding military sign (σημεῖον).

3.3.l. Matthew 24.31 and the ἄγγελοι

It has been commonplace in Matthean studies to interpret Mt. 24.31 as referring to a final 'eschatological' event. Matthew 24.31 states, 'And he will send out his ἀγγέλους with a loud trumpet call, and they will gather his elect from the four winds, from one end of heaven to the other.' Luz is representative of commentators in saying that, at this point, 'Matthew portrays the end of the world,'[340] and that 'The Son of Man sends out

---

334 T. L. Donaldson, *Jesus on the Mountain: A Study in Matthean Typology* (Sheffield: Academic Press, 1985), p. 162.

335 Brown, 'Apocalypse', p. 14.

336 L. Gaston, *No Stone on Another* (Leiden: Brill, 1970), p. 484. Lightfoot comes to similar conclusions when he states that, 'many times they asked him for a sign; now a sign shall appear, that he is true Messias [sic], whom they despised ... namely his single vengeance and fury', Lightfoot, *Commentary*, p. 320.

337 Luz, *Matthew 21–28*, pp. 199–200.

338 M. Stone, *Fourth Ezra* (Minneapolis: Fortress Press, 1990), pp. 348–49; Exod. 19.4; Deut. 32.11; Ezek. 17.2.

339 See further discussion in Carter, 'Imperial', p. 471.

340 Luz, *Matthew 21–28*, p. 201.

his angels so that the final judgement can now begin.'[341] Similarly, W. Hendriksen envisions this verse to portray Jesus as appearing 'in majesty, surrounded by a multitude of angels upon clouds of glory'.[342] Specific reference to ἄγγελοι as non-human beings is assumed by Davies and Allison when they conclude that 'the use of "his angels" with reference to the Son of Man not only enhances his authority: it also reminds one of Hebrews 1, which rejects an angel Christology'.[343]

There is, however, a small but significant minority (including R. T. France, S. Brown, N. T. Wright, G. A. Gibbs, S. Hahn, and C. Mitch) who has argued that the ἄγγελοι could be interpreted as 'human missionaries'.[344] What support, if any, is there for this alternative interpretation? First, at the semantic level, the word ἄγγελος clearly has more than one possible referent; in particular, it can equally be applied to a human or a heavenly being. As noted by G. Kittel, the primary semantic domain of ἄγγελος is 'one who brings a message'.[345] The non-human angelic meaning derived from Hermes as *messenger* of the gods, and it is in this regard that J. Schniewind has remarked that 'the earthly sacral ἄγγελος is the prototype of the heavenly ἄγγελοι'.[346] In the New Testament the term is frequently used to refer to a human messenger delivering a message. Such is the case in (1) James's recollection of Rahab's hospitality towards the spies on their way to Jericho (ἀγγέλους, Jas 2.25); (2) the description of the men sent to Jesus by John (Lk. 7.24); and (3) Jesus sending messengers before him into the Samaritan village (Lk. 9.52). More importantly, however, within the context of Matthew, John the Baptist is referred to in the following manner: 'This is the one about whom it is written, "See, I am sending my messenger (τὸν ἄγγελόν μου) ahead of you, who will prepare your way before you"'

341 Luz, *Matthew 21–28*, pp. 202–203.

342 W. Hendriksen, *The Gospel of Matthew* (Edinburgh: The Banner of Truth Trust, 1973), p. 865.

343 Davies and Allison, *Shorter*, p. 431.

344 S. Brown asks 'What could have been more natural for someone ... to see in the sending out of the angelic messengers by the Son of man the heavenly counterpart to Jesus sending out the Twelve?' (Brown, 'Apocalypse', p. 13); see too Wright, *Jesus*, p. 361. R. T. France similarly states that the ἄγγελοι 'might be translated [as] "messengers" (as it is in 11:10), and refer ... to [the] human preaching of the gospel throughout the world ... The reference is not, therefore ... to the final judgement, but to the world-wide growth of the church ... which is consequent on the ending of Israel's special status, symbolized in the destruction of the temple' (France, *Matthew*, p. 345). S. Brown concludes that the function of the ἄγγελοι is 'to point to the final scene of the gospel, in which Jesus instructs the Twelve to "make disciples of all the nations" (28.19)' (Brown, 'Apocalypse', p. 13). Gibbs, *Understand*, p. 521; S. Hahn, and C. Mitch, *The Gospel of Mark* (San Francisco: Ignatius Press, 2001), p. 43.

345 G. Kittel, 'ἄγγελος, ἀρχάγγελος, ἰσάγγελος', in *Theological Dictionary of the New Testament*, ed. G. Friedrich (trans. G. W. Bromiley; 10 vols; Grand Rapids: Eerdmans, 1967), pp. 1.74–87 (74). This meaning is certainly the dominant one in the Homeric period (*Il.* 5.804; 18.2).

346 Cited in Kittel, 'ἄγγελος', p. 75. Plato *Crat.* 407e; *Od.* 5.29.

(Mt. 11.10). It is thus quite clear that Matthew can (and does) employ the word ἄγγελος to refer to a human messenger, a being quite distinct from an other worldly being. As Kittel clearly states, the term is 'linked with the concrete person of the Baptist'.[347] There is thus certainly precedent within Matthew's own Gospel for the possibility that the ἄγγελοι of 24.31 are also human messengers, not angelic figures.

Further, Matthew's usage in this regard is not unique in the first century. In Josephus' description of Absalom's death, the one who relays the message to David (in a military context of battle) is referred to as ἄγγελος three times in *Ant.* 7.249.[348]

> ... who said he was a good messenger (ἄγγελον). A little while after, he informed him, that another messenger (ἄγγελον) followed him; whereupon the king said that he also was a good messenger (ἄγγελον); but when the watchman saw Ahimaaz, and that he was already very near, he gave the king notice, that it was the son of Zadok the high priest, who came running.

Similarly, the messengers from Jezebel to Elijah in *Ant.* 8.347 are also described as ἄγγελοι: 'When Jezebel, the wife of Ahab, understood what signs Elijah had wrought, and how he had slain her prophets, she was angry, and sent messengers (ἀγγέλους) to him, and by them threatened to kill him, as he had destroyed her prophets.

Second, G. A. Gibbs notes that 'judgement on Jerusalem followed by mission to the Gentiles' is consistent with Matthean thought, in particular the parables of the wicked tenants (Mt. 21.33-41) and the wedding feast (22.1-14). After the vineyard is taken away from 'those wretches', the master leases the vineyard 'to other tenants who will give him the produce at the harvest time' (Mt. 21.41). Similarly, after the wrathful king has 'sent his troops, destroyed those murderers, and burned their city' (22.7), he sends slaves into the street in order that they might 'invite everyone ... [they] find to the wedding banquet' (22.9).[349] Gibbs concludes that 'the judgment upon Israel as a nation through the destruction of the temple ... is followed by the mission to the gentiles in its fullest expression'.[350]

Third, the verb ἐπισυνάγω occurs only three times in Matthew, once here in 24.31 and twice in 23.37. In 23.37, Matthew has Jesus use the term with reference to the gathering of Jerusalem's inhabitants to himself: 'Jerusalem, Jerusalem, the city that kills the prophets and stones those who are sent to it! How often have I desired to gather (ἐπισυναγαγεῖν) your children together as a hen gathers (ἐπισυνάγει) her brood under her wings, and you were not willing!' The use of ἐπισυνάξουσιν in 24.31, if indeed it does refer to mission to the Gentiles, provides an appropriate contrast with 23.37,

---

347 Kittel, 'ἄγγελος', p. 83.
348 Also cf. *Ant.* 7.246, 360.
349 Cf. Mt. 8.11-12.
350 Gibbs, *Understand*, p. 520.

'which fits well into Matthew's schema of the turning of the mission to the gentiles'.[351] Plummer echoes this sentiment in discussion of v. 31 when he states, 'Christ had again and again tried to gather together a congregation of those who believed in Him (xxiii.37), but had been thwarted by indifference and opposition.'[352] As Jerusalem's children οὐκ ἠθελήσατε ('were not willing'), his messengers accordingly turn to gather the elect from among the four corners of the globe, the activity of which Gibbs suggests is 'the widest possible, extending throughout the entire world'.[353]

Fourth, V. Balabanski[354] and T. L. Donaldson[355] have argued for paralleled themes between Matthew 24 and the missionary discourse in Mt. 28.16-20.[356] Although these two particular authors do not explicitly link the function of the ἄγγελοι in Mt. 24.31, their general conclusions on parallel contexts are significant for our discussion. Balabanski initiates her discussion by suggesting that the missionary discourse in Matthew 28 must be 'viewed against the broader canvas of the Gospel',[357] and in this sense she seeks to 'bring Mt. 28.16-20 into creative dialogue with another Matthean text that is of great importance for understanding mission in Matthew's Gospel, namely Mt. 24.1-31'.[358] The connections which Balabanski has identified between Mt. 24.1-31 and 28.16-20 are multifaceted and numerous. We will proceed by highlighting some of the more conspicuous examples. First, in both passages the settings are paralleled: the disciples come to Jesus on a mountain and the narrative emphasizes that they are alone with him (24.3; 28.16).[359] Second, the narrative contexts of chs 24 and 28 are paralleled in their projection from their present situation to an imminent future. Third, the phrase συντελείας τοῦ αἰῶνος is employed in both passages to refer to the end of a significant dispensation of Yahweh's salvation history. Fourth, Matthew refers to πάντα τὰ ἔθνη as recipients of the disciples' missionary activity (Mt. 28.19). Likewise, in Mt. 24.14 (cf. v. 31) it is stated that 'the good news of the kingdom will be preached to πᾶσιν τοῖς ἔθνεσιν'. Balabanski suggests that 'these various striking connections between Mt. 28.16-20 and Mt. 24.1-31 compel the careful reader to interpret them in

---

351 Gibbs, *Understand*, p. 522.
352 Plummer, *Matthew*, p. 336.
353 Gibbs, *Understand*, p. 522.
354 V. Balabanski, 'Mission in Matthew Against the Horizon of Matthew 24' (unpublished seminar paper at the Society of Biblical Literature Annual Meeting, Philadelphia, November 2005).
355 Donaldson, *Mountain*, pp. 157–58.
356 Bruner says in regard to v. 31, 'compare this passage with the Great Commission at the end of the Gospel. For at the end of the Gospel the Cosmocrator sends out messengers to the four winds to gather his elect ... there are striking parallels,' F. D. Bruner, *Matthew* (vol. 2; Grand Rapids: Eerdmans, 1990), pp. 513–14.
357 Balabanski, 'Mission', p. 1.
358 Balabanski, 'Mission', p. 1.
359 Cf. the presence of the ὄχλους in Mt. 5.1; 7.28-29.

close dialogue with one another'.[360] Donaldson affirms this mutual identification by noting that in 'Matthean thought these two mountain scenes were linked together'.[361] One could perhaps suggest that Mt. 28.16-20 offers some kind of intertextual horizon for Matthew 24 in general, and v. 31 in particular. [362]

There are, however, three corresponding problems with identifying the ἄγγελοι with human missionaries. First, several apocalyptic texts connect similar terminology in what is an 'eschatological' context. The *Testament of Abraham*, of which E. P. Sanders writes, 'is a Jewish work, probably of Egyptian origin ... is generally dated to the latter part of the first century AD'.[363] In Abraham's tour of the place of judgement 11.1–14.15, it is stated that:

> Before the front of the table sat an angel (ἄγγελος) of light, holding in his hand a balance, and on his left sat an angel all fiery, pitiless, and severe, holding in his hand a trumpet (σάλπιγγα), having within it all-consuming fire with which to try the sinners. The wondrous man who sat upon the throne himself judged and sentenced the souls.[364]

Similarly, in *The Life of Adam and Eve*, of which L. Rost writes regarding dating, 'The year A.D. 70 is the *terminus ante quem*, since the Temple ... is still standing. The author may have had affinities with Essene circles, as the ascetic features (especially the Apocalypse's description of the physical separation of the sexes, even for animals) suggest.'[365] Chapter 22.1-3 also uses the terminology under discussion in a distinctly 'eschatological' manner: 'and in that same hour, we heard the archangel (ἀρχαγγέλου) Michael blowing with his trumpet (σάλπιγγι) and calling to the angels (ἀγγέλους) and saying: "Thus says the Lord: 'Come with me to Paradise and hear the judgment, with which I shall judge Adam ...'"'[366]

These examples seem to indicate an eschatological/apocalyptic context for the terminology. The trumpet, however, is a piece of symbolism which occurs in varying biblical and extra-biblical contexts as a signalling device. The

---

360 Balabanski, 'Mission', p. 2.

361 Donaldson, *Mountain*, p. 158. Donaldson, however, rejects the hypothesis that the ἄγγελοι of v. 31 refer to missionaries (Donaldson, *Mountain*, p. 164). We draw on his work here to emphasize the paralleled settings of mountain-tops. See Donaldson, *Mountain*, pp. 157–58 for further discussion.

362 In regard to 28.20, Davies and Allison note a 'striking similar context: Jesus on a mountain giving instructions to his disciples for the period leading up to the close of the age', Davies and Allison, *Matthew 3*, p. 676.

363 E. P. Sanders, 'The Testament of Abraham', in *Outside the Old Testament*, ed. M. De Jonge (Cambridge: Cambridge University Press, 1985), pp. 56–70 (56).

364 *Test. Ab.* 12.9-11

365 L. Rost, *Judaism Outside the Hebrew Canon* (Nashville: Abingdon, 1976), p. 154.

366 Cf. 38.2-3.

trumpet can be used to (1) mark the beginning of Sabbath (*t.Sukk.* 4.11-12); (2) gather and direct armies (1QM; 1 Cor. 14.8; *Par. Jer.* 4.2); (3) frighten enemies (Jos. 6.5); (4) greet the new moon (Ps. 81.3); (5) warn of danger (Jer. 4.5); (6) herald a king's coronation (1 Kgs 1.34); (7) mark sacred occasions (Num. 10.10; *Ros.Has.* 26a); (8) signify an Old Testament theophany (Exod. 19.16); (9) signify the day of the Lord (Joel 2.1; Zeph. 1.16); and (10) signify the return from exile (Isa. 27.13; Zech. 9.14; *Pss Sol.* 11.1-3).[367] There is a fascinating parallel in *Shemoneh Esreh* benediction 10 which states 'sound the great sophar for our freedom, lift up the ensign to gather our exiles, and gather us from the four corners of the earth'. Beare suggests that the trumpet in Mt. 24.31 'is merely an incidental borrowing from the general stock' of imagery.[368] All this to note that an end to the space-time continuum would not be the only context in which someone might refer to a σάλπιγξ. In regard to Apocryphal texts, similar terminology is employed with striking similarity. *Apocalypse of James* 8.3 notes that after the σάλπιγξ κυρίου ('trumpet of the Lord') is sounded, heralds (οἱ κήρυκες) go out (ἐξῆλθον) to perform a particular mission, ἐξῆλθον δὲ οἱ κήρυκες καθ᾽ ὅλης τῆς περιχώρου τῆς᾽ Ἰουδαίας, καὶ ἤχησεν ἡ σάλπιγξ κυρίου, καὶ ἔδραμον πάντες ('and the heralds went out through the whole country of Judaea, and the trumpet of the Lord sounded, and all ran').

In the Matthean context, commentators have been particularly impressed by the unique combination of ἀγγέλους and σάλπιγγος, which seems to suggest an apocalyptic scenario. Recent scholarly work on apocalyptic, however, suggests that this need not be an insurmountable obstacle for the interpretation for 'human missionaries' in Mt. 24.31. Interestingly, Hagner notes that 'in 1 Cor. 15:52 the trumpet is associated with the resurrection of the dead, which Matthew makes no mention of here',[369] perhaps an indication that a different scenario is in mind.[370]

---

367 Davies and Allison, *Matthew 3*, p. 363.

368 Beare, *Matthew*, p. 130. Cf. F. W. Burnett, *The Testament of Jesus Sophia: A Redaction-Critical Study of the Eschatological Discourse in Matthew* (Washington, DC: University Press of America, 1979), p. 360. Also see *Test. Naph.* 8.3: 'for through their tribes God shall appear on earth to save Israel, and he shall gather together righteous ones from the Gentiles'.

369 Hagner, *Matthew 14–28*, p. 715.

370 Although it can be argued that in early Christian apocalyptic, this type of imagery did signify the arrival of Jesus in glory and resurrection of the dead (1 Thess. 4.16; 1 Cor. 15.51-56; Rev. 8.7-8, 10, 12; 9.1, 13-14; 10.7; 11.15), one could question whether Matthew is most plausibly understood as an apocalyptic text, contra a text with certain apocalyptic elements. Collins, *Imagination*, p. 4, defines apocalyptic as 'a genre of revelatory literature with a narrative framework, in which a revelation is mediated by an other-wordly being to a human recipient, disclosing a transcendent reality which is both temporal, in so far as it envisages eschatological salvation, and spatial in so far as it involves another, supernatural world'. Unless one see Jesus in angelic terms it is difficult to keep to this strict definition for Matthew 24.

C. Rowland has argued that individual eschatology is not an essential part of apocalypticism.[371] Rather, the apocalyptic genre 'is concerned with the knowledge of God, and the secrets of the world above, revealed in a direct way by dreams, visions or direct pronouncements'.[372] In this schema the essential element was the offering of 'a total view of history',[373] that is, a theological perspective on history. A. Y. Collins has argued that the apocalyptic genre primarily serves 'to interpret present, earthly circumstances in light of the supernatural world and of the future, and to influence both the understanding and behavior of the audience by means of divine authority'.[374] N. T. Wright brings this into sharper relief by suggesting that the language is frequently employed to 'invest history with theological meaning',[375] that is, 'writers borrowed all the appropriate imagery they could to show the immense significance with which the coming historical events would be charged'.[376] In this sense, the genre would allow a 'complex metaphor-system which invests space-time reality with its full, that is, theological significance'.[377] Wright's view may be summarized as follows: apocalyptic (1) uses complex and highly symbolic metaphors, (2) to invest real events within Israel's history for their true significance, which in turn (3) does not necessitate the end of a space-time universe. It is in this sense that we would agree with G. Caird when he quotes Ernst Jenni on eschatology and apocalyptic, where 'in the broader sense [they] refer ... to a future in which the circumstances of history are changed to such an extent that one can speak of a new, entirely different , state of things, without ... necessarily leaving the framework of history'.[378] We therefore suggest that those elements which have typically been understood as referring to an 'end-time scenario' and hence irreconcilable with our 'historical' reading, are more plausibly understood as Matthew undertaking a process whereby he invests historical circumstances with their true theological significance. By doing this, Matthew conceives the present in 'eschatological' terms in which the future hope is materialized in the present.

A second objection to understanding the ἀγγέλους as human missionaries is that it would imply that the implementation of the Gentile mission was only begun after 70 AD, which stands in tension with 28.16-20. It is important to note, however, that there is a remarkable tension within various 'missional' sections of Matthew's Gospel.[379] As Gibbs has noted:

---

371 C. Rowland, *The Open Heaven: A Study of Apocalyptic in Judaism and Early Christianity* (New York: Crossroad, 1982), pp. 14, 172.

372 Rowland, *Open*, pp. 9–10.

373 Rowland, *Open*, p. 145.

374 A. Y. Collins, 'Introduction: Early Christian Apocalypticism', *Semeia* 36 (1986), pp. 1–174 (7).

375 Wright, *People*, p. 284.

376 Wright, *People*, p. 284.

377 Wright, *People*, p. 299.

378 Caird, *Jesus*, p. 18.

379 See discussion regarding 10.5-6 in chapter 5.

on the one hand 21.43 and 22.7 give the following sequence: 1) rejection of God's Son, 2) judgement on those who reject him, and 3) mission to the Gentiles. On the other hand, the actual plot of the gospel gives this sequence: 1) rejection of God's Son, 2) vindication of God's Son, 3) mission to all nations, both Jews and gentiles, and 4) later judgement on the nation of Israel.[380]

Gibbs goes on to suggest that perhaps then the most appropriate manner in which to 'express the sequence that locates the mission to the gentiles after the judgement on the temple and the city is to say that the gentile mission reaches its "fullest expression" after the temple is destroyed'[381] – a fullness of expression that coheres remarkably well with Matthew's schema of 'salvation history';[382] that is, within the Matthean narrative itself, a new dispensation unfolds in which the nature of mission evolves.[383] D. R. A. Hare similarly concludes that,

> Matthew shows no interest in precision at this point, however. Matthew 22:7ff. suggest that the moment of rejection is the destruction of Jerusalem. If our analysis of the history of persecution is correct, the mission to Israel persisted with vigor beyond this point, and was not abandoned ten or fifteen years after this date. Although the abandonment of the mission could be regarded as the point of final rejection by God, it is probable that Matthew would say that the abandonment of the mission and the destruction of Jerusalem were both simply concrete signs of the divine rejection which occurred at the time of the death of Jesus and the birth of the church.[384]

Third, a minor residual problem with identifying the ἄγγελοι as the messengers of the Gospel is their linking with the Son of Man in quite a different capacity in Mt. 13.41; 16.27; and 25.31-32. Each of these references seems to envisage angelic beings and hence the question may be raised as to whether they support a similar reading in Mt. 24.31. However, despite Luz's scepticism,[385] these passages may be resolved on the basis that, as Luz himself acknowledges, the function and operation of the beings is quite distinct in the two groups of texts (Mt. 24.31 on the one hand and Mt. 13.41; 16.27; 25.31-32 on the other). It is apparent that the ἄγγελοι in the latter texts function as agents of judgement,

---

380 Gibbs, *Understand*, p. 520 n.234.

381 Gibbs, *Understand*, p. 520 n.234.

382 For further discussion see our concluding comments in chapter 5.

383 See Luz, *Matthew 21–28*, p. 16; D. Senior, 'Between Two Worlds: Gentile and Jewish Christians in Matthew's Gospel', *CBQ* 61 (1999), pp. 1–23 (16). P. Foster has noted, 'after chap. 15 there is almost without exception a positive attitude displayed to bringing Gentiles into the community', P. Foster, *Community, Law and Mission in Matthew's Gospel* (Tübingen: Mohr Siebeck, 2004), p. 220.

384 Hare, *Persecutions*, p. 155.

385 Luz, *Matthew 21–28*, p. 202 n.174.

whereas the former embody salvific hope.[386] The very different roles of the ἄγγελοι in 24.31, as compared with 13.41, etc., open up again the possibility, perhaps even probability, that the referents in the two sets of texts differ.

Although, some may consider this approach as an exegesis of despair, there is a minority of significant scholarship who have taken 24.31 with reference to human missionaries. When understood in the light of recent proposals in definitions of apocalyptic and eschatology, we suggest that this minority view is preferable and that the interpretation of ἄγγελοι as 'human missionaries' should be considered as a plausible alternative to the mainstream reading.

3.3.m. Additional support

Although we could continue this detailed analysis, we must restrict ourselves to those elements that are particularly striking. In this regard, there are four additional factors in Matthew 24 which suggest that the material refers to the destruction of Jerusalem in 70 AD. After a brief discussion of these elements we will respond to some recent questions raised in the secondary literature.

First, in an interesting parallel to Mt. 24.20 ('Pray that your flight may not be in winter or on a sabbath'), Rabbi Tanchum notes that as a measure of God's grace the first temple was destroyed in the summer and not in the winter:

> God vouchsafed a great favor to Israel; for they ought to have gone out of the land on the tenth day of the month Tebeth, as he saith, 'Son of man, mark this day; for on this very day ... If they shall now go out in the winter,' saith he, 'they will all die:' therefore he prolonged the time to them, and carried them away in summer.[387]

Furthermore, the context of v. 20 in Matthew 24 also supports this hypothesis; vv. 17-18 state 'the one on the housetop must not go down to take what is in the house; the one in the field must not turn back to get a coat'. The military invasion of a foreign power and consequent social mayhem are attested in Jeremiah's narration of the Day of Yahweh against the Philistines by the Chaldaeans: 'parents do not turn back for children, so feeble are their hands'.[388] Furthermore, if v. 20 did

---

386 Luz, *Matthew 21–28*, pp. 202–203. In Mt. 13.30, the positive element functions as a foil for the judgement saying.

387 Cited in Lightfoot, *Commentary*, p. 314.

388 Jerermiah 47.3b, cf. 14.5. This is also a common motif in Mesopotamian laments over the destruction of a city. Two examples from the lament over the destruction of Ur are as follows: 'The mother left before her child's eyes' (*LU* 233), 'The father turned away from his son' (*LU* 234), *ANET*[3] 459, cited in J. R. Lundbom, *Jeremiah 37–52* (New York: Doubleday, 2004), p. 236. For further parallels on the *lamentations of Ancient*

refer to the end of the space-time continuum, it would be rather optimistic, to say the least, to encourage one to flee from this cataclysmic event.

Second, in the following verse (Mt. 24.21), the situation is described as 'For at that time there will be great suffering, such as has not been from the beginning of the world until now, no, and never will be.' It is our contention that the phrase οὐδ οὐ μὴ γένηται ('nor ever again') implies that there is a continuation of the space-time continuum, otherwise such temporal language would be irrelevant. Likewise, θλῖψις rather than necessarily referring to an 'eschatological' perspective, can in fact refer to more earthly distress. Acts 19.11 refers to 'those who were scattered as a result of the persecution (θλίψεως) which took place over Stephen ...'. Although the term θλῖψις is commonly used to refer to normal suffering or trouble,[389] what of θλῖψις μεγάλη (Mt. 24.21) which is commonly linked with eschatological discussions, such as Rev. 7.14? The noun θλῖψις with corresponding adjective μεγάλη is attested in several other ancient sources with reference to hardship or suffering without reference to the 'eschaton'. In Stephen's speech to the Sanhedrin recounting Israel's narrative, he makes reference to the patriarch Jacob, as follows: 'Now there came a famine throughout Egypt and Canaan, and great suffering (θλῖψις μεγάλη), and our ancestors could find no food.'[390] Similarly, 1 Macc. 9.23-31, in the description of Jonathan assuming leadership after the death of Judas the Maccabaean, it is stated that 'there was great distress (θλῖψις μεγάλη) in Israel, such as had not been since the time that prophets ceased to appear among them'.[391]

Furthermore, in likening the coming of the Son of Man to the 'days of Noah' (Mt. 24.37-39), a circumstance is referred to where judgement occurred *within* history. It did not usher in a new or different kind of existence.[392] It was simply the historical point at which Yahweh executed judgement, and Matthew's inclusion of this was for the purposes of indicating its suddenness.[393]

Mesopotamia see M. E. Cohen, *The Canonical Lamentations of Ancient Mesopotamia* (Potomac: CDL Press, 1988), pp. 138, 166.

389 Other examples of a non-eschatological use of θλῖψις include Gen. 35.3; 42.21; Exod. 4.31; Deut. 28.53; as well as P.Oxy 939 *l*.13, where a dependent is writing to his master concerning illness.

390 Acts 7.11.

391 First Maccabees 9.27.

392 Genesis 5.29-30, 32; 6.8-10, 13, 22–7.1; cf. Sir. 44.17; 2 *Esd.* 3.11; Heb. 11.7.

393 The question as to why Matthew does not include the saying about Lot (Lk (Q) 17.28-29), which would seem to cohere well with the destruction of the temple by fire, is legitimate but contains several assumptions. The first is that Q exists as a literary source, and that the saying cannot be accounted for by Luke's special material commonly known as L. However, if Q did exist, perhaps Matthew chose to omit it because it was redundant after the Noah saying. See M. Myllykoski, 'The Social History of Q and the Jewish War', in *Symbols and Strata: Essays on the Sayings Gospel Q*, ed. R. Uro (Göttingen: Vandenhoeck & Ruprecht, 1996), pp. 143–99 (187); C. Tuckett, *Q and the History of Early Christianity* (Peabody: Hendrickson, 1996), p. 159. Furthermore, the idea of 'one taken the other left' in Mt. 24.40-41 is connected to the comparison with the generation

Third, Mt. 24.32-33 narrates the realities of these events as a παραβολήν of the συκῆς. The only other reference to a συκῆν in Matthew is the parable of the withered fig tree in 21.18-22. Far from being an immature outburst of anger because of Jesus' hunger, Matthew (21.18-22) presents Jesus as performing a symbolic act. The meaning of this has been almost unanimously accepted as a 'penal miracle with appended instruction ... What the fig tree represents – Jerusalem and the temple hierarchy – is symbolically punished in the fig tree for the Messiah's rejection.'[394] Similarly, Victor of Antioch states that this functions as 'an acted parable in which Jesus used the fig tree to set forth the judgement on Jerusalem'.[395] H. Alford has argued that both the fig tree parables in chs 21 and 24 function as a symbol of Israel (cf. Isa. 5).[396] It is our contention that the Matthean fig trees should be understood in a mutually interpretive sense; that is, the fig tree of ch. 24 should be understood in light of the fig tree of ch. 21. In such a schema, the following verse of Matthew 24 avoids the exegetical gymnastics often applied to it: 'Truly I tell you, this generation will not pass away until all these things have taken place' (v. 34), where γενεά is to be understood in the normal sense of Jesus' contemporaries (11.16; 12.39, 41, 42, 45; 16.4; 17.17)[397] rather than as an eschatological scenario in which the church is envisaged.[398] Furthermore, the close parallel in Mt. 23.36 is instructive. 'Truly I tell you, all this will come upon this generation', immediately precedes Jesus' lament over the destruction of Jerusalem, and thus the parallel here is helpfully read in that light.

Fourth, in regard to the Matthean material in 24.40-44, Davies and Allison[399] divide the stories into two units: vv. 40-42 and vv. 43-44. However, v. 42 is more plausibly to be understood with the material concerning ὁ κλέπτης in v. 43, mainly because of the repetition of the verb

of Noah. Therefore, the one taken is destroyed, the one who is left is saved. In light of this, the modern theological discussions of being 'raptured' seem to miss the entire point of the passage. See J. S. Kloppenborg, 'City and Wasteland: Narrative World and the Beginning of the Sayings Gospel (Q)', in *How Gospels Begin*, ed. D. E. Smith (Atlanta: Scholars Press, 1990), pp. 145–60 (152); Kloppenborg, *Excavating*, p. 119. In this regard Wright, *Jesus*, p. 366 says: 'It should be noted that being "taken" in this context means being taken in *judgement*. There is no hint, here, of a "rapture," a sudden "supernatural" event which would remove individuals from *terra firma*. Such an idea would look as odd, in these synoptic passages, as a Cadillac in a camel-train.'

394 Davies and Allison, *Matthew 3*, p. 148. For similar approaches see Gnilka, *Matthäusevangelium*, p. 2.123; Pesch, *Markusevangelium*, pp. 2.195–96.

395 Davies and Allison, *Matthew 3*, p. 150.

396 H. Alford, *The Greek New Testament, Volume 1: The Four Gospels* (Cambridge: Deighton Bell, 1968), p. 244. Surprisingly, Alford then proceeds to develop the idea of a promise of salvation. This development does not seem to be present in the context of Mt. 21.18-19. The ὄρος saying has been taken to represent the temple mount. See Wright, *Jesus*, pp. 494–95.

397 France, *Matthew*, p. 346.

398 Chrysostom, *Hom on Mt.* 77.1; Eusebius *Frag in Lc. Mt.* 24.31.

399 Davies and Allison, *Matthew 3*, pp. 382–83.

γρηγορέω (γρηγορεῖτε, v. 42; ἐγρηγόρησεν, v. 43) and the similar image it evokes.[400] Verse 42 exhorts the hearer to 'keep awake therefore, for you do not know on what day your Lord is coming', and offers the following parabolic illustration: 'But understand this: if the owner of the house had known in what part of the night the thief was coming, he would have stayed awake and would not have let his house be broken into' (v. 43). Matthean commentators have almost unanimously understood the parable of the 'thief coming in the night' in relation to a future physical return of Jesus. Davies and Allison suggest that 'this simple parable ... continues the twin themes of eschatological ignorance and vigilance'.[401] D. Wenham simply states that the parable concerns 'the future and second coming of Jesus'.[402] J. Jeremias likewise maintains that 'the parable of the House-breaker ... [is] a rousing cry to the crowd in view of the oncoming eschatological catastrophe'.[403] J. P. Meier concludes that 'the discourse tries to stir up proper eschatological fervor ... for the coming ... of the Son of Man'.[404]

Commentators have readily noted the difficulty of the negative image of the Son of Man as thief per se. In this regard, Wenham asks, 'Is Jesus then suggesting that the coming of the Son of Man will be a bad experience?'[405] To which he responds, 'Obviously not in general.'[406] Similarly, Jeremias states, 'the application of the parable to the Son of Man is strange; for if the subject of the discourse is a nocturnal burglary, it refers to a disastrous and alarming event, whereas the *Parousia*, at least for the disciples of Jesus, is

---

400 Also of significance to our discussion are the potential military overtones of γρηγορέω, understood as 'to keep watch'. See for example, 1 Macc. 12.27: 'So when the sun set, Jonathan commanded his men to be alert (γρηγορειν) and to keep their arms at hand so as to be ready all night for battle, and he stationed outposts around the camp'; Neh. 7.3: 'And I said to them, "The gates of Jerusalem are not to be opened until the sun is hot; while the gatekeepers are still standing guard (γρηγορούντων), let them shut and bar the doors. Appoint guards (προφύλακας) from among the inhabitants of Jerusalem, some at their watch posts, and others before their own houses'; Jer. 5.6: 'Therefore has a lion out of the forest smitten them, and a wolf has destroyed them even to their houses, and a leopard has watched (ἐγρηγόρησεν) against their cities; all that go forth from them shall be hunted: for they have multiplied their ungodliness, they have strengthened themselves in their revoltings.'

401 Davies and Allison, *Matthew 3*, p. 384. Immediately preceding these comments the following is stated in regard to v. 42: the reference to 'your Lord' 'underlies the communal dimension of eschatological vigilance and, followed by "comes," recalls the Aramaic, "*Maranatha.*"'

402 D. Wenham, *The Parables of Jesus* (London: Hodder & Stoughton, 1989), p. 74.

403 J. Jeremias, *The Parables of Jesus* (London: SCM Press, 1972), p. 49.

404 Meier clearly refers to an apparent second and visible return of Jesus and associates it with the passage in 1 Thess. 5.2-4. Meier, *Matthew*, p. 291. For a similar interpretation see Nolland, *Matthew*, pp. 91–96.

405 Wenham, *Parables*, p. 75.

406 Wenham, *Parables*, p. 76. Although Wenham does admit that the parable may concern 'the reality and seriousness of judgement ... an implication in our parable that the coming will be bad'.

the great day of joy'.[407] However, Jeremias makes two assumptions that we have cause to disagree with: first, that the *parousia* refers to a future second coming of the risen Jesus (see discussion above for the plausibility of an alternative hypothesis), and second, that Jeremias wrongly implies that the *parousia* would be a positive experience for even Jesus' disciples. Aside from details of one's interpretation of the *parousia*, the text of Matthew 24 is quite clear that it will be a devastating event for all involved. It is certainly not clear how Jeremias could consider an event which led to the desperate fleeing of Jesus' closest followers (v. 16) as a 'day of great joy'.[408] The main concern and thrust of the parable is on the unexpectedness and unpredictability of the Son of Man's arrival,[409] and there is ready acceptance of the overt and specific negative imagery associated with a thief. Despite accepting the aforementioned eschatological interpretation, E. Schweizer captures the essence of the negative judgement in the parable and its association with the Son of Man by noting that, 'the parable of the owner of the house and the thief emphasizes not the joyful nature of Christ's coming, but his coming in judgment'.[410]

Although Davies and Allison state that 'the likening of the eschatological end to an unexpected thief is unattested in ancient Jewish sources',[411] a parallel is to be noted with reference to Obad. 5a: 'If thieves (κλέπται; cf. Mt. 24.43 κλέπτης) came (εἰσῆλθον; cf. Mt. 24.43 ἔρχεται) to you, if plunderers by night – how you have been destroyed! – would they not steal only what they wanted?' What is of significance here is that the context is not one of eschatological consummation,[412] but rather a very specific threat of military invasion.[413] The book of Obadiah is predominantly composed of an oracle

---

407 Jeremias, *Parables*, p. 49.

408 Jeremias, *Parables*, p. 49.

409 For an interesting parallel see *Tg. Neof.* on Exod. 12.42, which notes that the Messiah will return at night. Also cf. *Exod. Rab.* 18.12, cited in S. T. Lachs, *A Rabbinic Commentary on the New Testament* (Hoboken: Ktav Publishing House, 1987), pp. 389–90.

410 Schweizer, *Matthew*, p. 462. Jeremias also states at a later point in his discussion that the image of a thief 'uses an alarming occurrence as a warning of the imminent calamity ... approaching', Jeremias, *Parables*, p. 49. It is not to be denied that the metaphor was applied to a future eschatological event in other Christian literature (1 Thess. 5.2; 2 Pet. 3.10; Rev. 3.3; 16.15). However, *Gos. Thom.* 21 (cf. 103) has significant parallels, including thieves and fields (cf. Mt. 24.40-41). G. Lüdemann, *Jesus After 2000 Years: What He Really Said and Did* (New York: Prometheus Books, 2001), p. 601 states of *Gos. Thom.* 121 that 'If we begin with the evident recognition that the children symbolize the Gnostics, it is manifestly being said that they are staying in a strange field, namely the evil world ... .' Thus it is apparent that in at least one Gnostic document, the thief is equated with hostile cosmic powers, rather than necessarily a traditional eschatological perspective. Davies and Allison, *Matthew 3*, p. 385, however, take this non-eschatological application as secondary.

411 Davies and Allison, *Matthew 3*, p. 384.

412 Thus in a very real sense Davies and Allison are accurate in not finding a parallel to an eschatological context.

413 Although Davies and Allison, *Matthew 3*, p, 384 n.74 admit that Obad. 5 is only

of doom against Edom for her cruelty, or more accurately her disregard towards Judah during the Babylonian conquest of Jerusalem in 588–86 BC. In v. 11 the author condemns Edom as partakers in the calamity which befell Jerusalem, 'On the day that you stood aside, on the day that strangers carried off his wealth, and foreigners entered his gates and cast lots for Jerusalem, you too were like one of them.' J. H. Eaton suggests that the introductory title, חֲזוֹן עֹבַדְיָה/Ὅρασις Ἀβδιου casts the subsequent words as a traditional prophetic text, and one which announces 'God's own disclosure of his forthcoming action',[414] and that a 'dread solemnity'[415] is added by including the common prophetic phrase, 'Thus says the Lord God' in v. 1b.

As the Edomites were Israel's closest southern neighbours (occupying the region between the Dead Sea and the Gulf of Aqaba), and also the descendants of Esau (Gen. 26.9), the twin brother of Jacob, they shared a unique and tendentious history with Israel. The Edomites are variously described as (1) the implacable enemies of Israel (Ezek. 35.5) and involved in constant military conflicts (1 Sam. 14.47; 2 Sam. 8.14; 1 Chron. 18.11, 13); (2) proud and self-confident (Jer. 49.16; Obad. 1.3); (3) strong and cruel (Jer. 49.19); (4) vindictive (Ezek. 25.12); (5) participating in idolatry (2 Chron. 25.14, 20); and (6) superstitious (Jer. 27.3, 9). As such, Edom featured in several oracles in the Old Testament prophetic literature including Isa. 21.11-12; 34.5-15; Jer. 49.7-22; Ezek. 25.12-14; 35.1-15; Amos 1.11-12; Joel 3.19 (cf. 'desolate wilderness').

Obadiah 1.1 introduces the coming military disaster upon Edom as a message sent out summoning Yahweh's forces to rise up for battle (לַמִּלְחָמָה/εἰς πόλεμον).[416] Despite the apparent security of Edom's location (v. 4a: 'Though you soar aloft like the eagle, though your nest is set among the stars'), divine retribution will nonetheless come to pass (v. 4b: 'from there I will bring you down, says the Lord"). Verse 5 follows: 'If thieves came to you, if plunderers by night – how you have been destroyed – would they not steal only what they wanted? If grape-gatherers came to you, would they not leave gleanings?' Whereas thieves normally only take what they require and those who collect grapes would typically leave some for the poor (Lev. 19.10), those who plunder Edom will leave nothing. J. H. Eaton describes Edom's imminent destruction in vv. 5-7 as utilizing 'the style of a funeral lament' and that it pictures the description in the past, and as such 'underlines its certainty'.[417] Although thievery can take place by day or night (Gen. 31.39), P. R. Raabe argues that 'the mention of night heightens the threat-

---

a 'very distant parallel', the similarity in vocabulary and context (previously unrecognized) invites further investigation.

414 J. H. Eaton, *Obadiah, Nahum, Habakkuk and Zephaniah* (London: SCM Press, 1961), p. 35.

415 Eaton, *Obadiah*, p. 39.

416 Cf. Obad. 8–10.

417 Eaton, *Obadiah*, p. 39. Also cf. Jer. 49.9: 'If thieves came by night, even they would pillage only what they wanted.'

ening force ... since the victims are asleep and therefore defenseless during the night, the plunderers have unlimited freedom to do as they please'.[418] Raabe also notes that the semantic domain of the plundered objects would include 'persons, homes, fields, cities and nations',[419] a description well suited to a military catastrophe.

Although there is no external attestation of Edom's eventual destruction,[420] what is of importance for our discussion is not the historical accuracy or inaccuracy of the prophetic description but the prophetic description itself. One which utilizes the idea of (1) 'thieves' and (2) 'night' in the context of (3) military destruction, and presented (4) as part of the divinely executed retributive process. It is in this light, we suggest, that the Matthean parable of the 'thief in the night' (Mt. 24.42-44) is to be understood. The concluding verse (Mt. 24.44) concerning the Son of Man, 'Therefore you also must be ready, for the Son of Man is coming at an unexpected hour' (v. 44), coheres (1) remarkably well within this Obadian context, and (2) with the hypothesis that this figure is representative of the invading Roman army against Jerusalem.[421]

Finally, in a recently published doctoral dissertation, A. I. Wilson's discussion of Jesus as judge in Matthew[422] raises various objections to reading the entirety of Matthew 24 in the light of the destruction of the temple in 70 AD. Like many before him, Wilson argues that Matthew 24 has two distinct parts: one referring to the destruction of the temple and the other referring to a future eschatological event or series of events.[423] One of the factors Wilson argues for in support of this twofold dichotomy is the use of *meshalim* (parables) in 24.36–25.46 but not in 24.1-35, concluding that 'it is largely composed of quite a different form to that found in 24.1-35, namely, *meshalim* of one kind or another'.[424] However, at a later point in his discussion of wisdom traditions, he seems to undermine his own argument by accepting C. H. Preisker's 'broad semantic field'[425] of the *meshalim*, including those categories noted by C. Brown: (1) figurative saying; (2) metaphor; (3) simile; (4) parable; (5) parabolic story; (6) illustrative story; (7) allegory.[426] Affirming this broad definition, Wilson goes on to quote B. Gerhardsson: 'they had in mind a short, carefully formulated text, which could be of many different kinds: a maxim, a proverb, a riddle, a taunt, etc., as well as a brief narrative, an illustration, a parable, an allegory, or even

418 P. R. Raabe, *Obadiah* (London: Doubleday, 1996), p. 140.

419 Raabe, *Obadiah*, p. 140.

420 C. E. Amerding, *Obadiah* (Grand Rapids: Zondervan, 1985), p. 347.

421 This interpretation also resolves those problems noted by commentators (Wenham, *Parables*, p. 75; Jeremias, *Parables*, p. 49) of associating a negative figure (thief) with the Son of Man.

422 Wilson, *When*.

423 See discussion above where these views were outlined and critiqued.

424 Wilson, *When*, pp. 134–35.

425 Cited in Wilson, *When*, p. 195.

426 Cited in Wilson, *When*, p. 196.

a pregnant prophetic or apocalyptic saying'.[427] If this broader definition of *meshalim* is taken for granted (and there seems no reason for not doing so), then Wilson's argument of dividing Mt. 24-25 on the parabolic/non-parabolic basis breaks down. For in 24.32-33, as noted above, the saying about the fig tree is specifically designated as a παραβολήν. But unfortunately for Wilson, this falls outside his parabolic eschatological discourse.

A second factor which Wilson sets forth for the discontinuity between 24.1-25 and vv. 36-51 is the theme of reward. He suggests that in vv. 36-51 there is a clear and obvious element of reward which one would be hard-pressed to equate with any aspect of the destruction of the temple in 70 AD. Three things should be noted in response: (1) there are two references before v. 36 which speak of the potential reward/salvation of individuals from the coming calamity (v. 13: 'the one who endures until the end will be saved', and the injunction in v. 16 to 'flee to the mountains' to escape the severity of the judgement); as such, a single parable (vv. 45-51) which includes an element of reward does not decrease the continuity between the two sections, but enhances it. (2) If an author intends to present a negative figure (κακὸς δοῦλος), then necessarily their argument is enhanced with a corresponding positive figure (πιστὸς δοῦλος), who may, for the purposes of the argument, be rewarded. (3) Given that the parable concludes with the climactic 'He will cut him in pieces and put him with the hypocrites, where there will be weeping and gnashing of teeth,' it seems most plausible to accept the dominant theme of the parable as one of judgement. In that light, it has several similarities with Matthew's earlier reference to the healing of the centurion's servant (παῖς) in 8.5-13. Not only are there similarities in vocabulary ('weeping and gnashing of teeth', 8.13), but the element of subversion is also present. Just as 'the heirs of the kingdom will be thrown into the outer darkness' (8.12) only to be replaced by the Gentiles (πολλοὶ, 8.11),[428] so too, responsibility is taken away from the κακὸς δοῦλος/ὑποκριτῶν (24.51; cf. 23.1-39).

3.4. Conclusion

This chapter has argued that the predominant use of language, metaphors, and images of Matthew 24 is most plausibly understood with primary reference to the destruction of the temple in 70 AD. As we noted above, given (1) the introductory marker 'As Jesus came out of the temple', and (2) that there is no identifiable switching point from 'historical narrative' to 'eschatology discourse', Matthew 24 is to be understood in light of 70 AD. Even such theologically loaded terms as παρουσία (vv. 3, 27, 37, 39), which have traditionally been interpreted in reference to

---

427 Gerhardsson, cited in Wilson, *When*, p. 96.
428 See chapter 5 for further discussion of the role of Gentiles in Matthew.

Jesus' physical return, are more suitably understood with reference to their royal and military motifs. Furthermore, far from the false prophets (24.4-5, 11, 24) indicating any interest in anti-Christ figures (cf. Thess.), a substantial parallel was substantiated from Josephus' 'sign-prophets'. Of particular significance in our findings was the attestation of at least one other Matthean contemporary author who describes the military action of the Roman army as 'desert making' (Tacitus *Agr.* 30.3b–6). A similar association was also seen in representing the Roman troops as the ἀετοί of 24.28. The so-called 'eschatological' language of sun, moon, and falling stars was seen to have background in the prophetic literature in reference to descriptions of military invasions. In the light of these multifaceted considerations, we contend that the imagery and language in Matthew 24 refer to the destruction of Jerusalem in 70 AD. In the following chapter we will turn our attention to the book of Daniel and the Old Testament prophetic literature with specific reference to the abomination saying.[429]

---

429 See our above discussion of the *evocatio deorum* in relation to Mt. 24.1.

Chapter 4

DANIEL AND INTERTEXTUAL PROPHETIC TEXTS

4.1. Introduction

This chapter is devoted to the Hebrew Bible's context of our Matthean quotation. After assessing Daniel's general influence on Matthew 24, we will provide a thorough contextual discussion of the more pertinent Danielic passages (9.27; 11.31). This will then provide an opportunity to discuss the intertextual relationship between Daniel and the prophetic literature. We will also briefly discuss those instances where a similar theological trajectory is attested in the Qumran literature.

4.2. Daniel's Influence on Matthew 24

A great deal has been and could be said on the literary influence of Daniel upon Matthew's narrative.[1] We will, however, restrict our discussion to ch. 24 in general, and material related to the βδέλυγμα specifically. As demonstrated by Davies and Allison's comparative analysis, Matthew 24 is clearly indebted to Daniel at several key points:[2] (1) temple destroyed (Mt. 24.3; Dan. 9.26); (2) time of the end (Mt. 24.3; Dan. 12.6-7); (3) rumours of wars (Mt. 24.6; Dan. 9.26; 11.44); (4)

---

1   For the discussion see J. Bowker, 'The Son of Man', *JTS* 28 (1977), pp. 19–48 (26); M. Casey, 'The Use of the Terms "Son of Man" in the *Similitudes* of Enoch', *JSJ* 7 (1976), pp. 11–29 (29); M. Casey, *Son of Man: The Interpretation and Influence of Dan. 7* (London: SPCK, 1979), p. 112. For the extensive influence of Daniel on Matthew 24 see the thorough study of L. Hartman, *Prophecy Interpreted: The Formation of Some Jewish Apocalyptic Texts and of the Eschatological Discourse Mark 13 par.* (Lund: Gleerup, 1966), pp. 145–77. For the influence of Daniel on the New Testament, particularly the Gospel traditions, see A. Y. Collins, 'The Influence of Daniel on the New Testament', in *Daniel*, ed. J. J. Collins (Minneapolis: Augsburg Press, 1993), pp. 90–123. For the general influence and pervasiveness of the book of Daniel in the first century see 1 Macc. 2.59-60 (where Matthias uses Hannaniah, Azariah, and Mishael as exhortatory examples); *Sib.Or.* 3.397 (ten horns and another sprouting on the side cf. Dan. 7.7); *3 Macc.* 6.6-7 (reference to the three youths in the furnace and Daniel in the lions' den); as well as multiple copies of the work at Qumran see the Prayer of Nabonidus; 4QPsDan; Son of God Text (4Q246); and 4QFlor 2.3 (4Q174).

2   Davies and Allison, *Matthew 3*, p. 332.

persecution of saints (Mt. 24.9-11; Dan. 7.25; 11.33); (5) abomination (Mt. 24.15; Dan. 8.13; 9.27; 11.31; 12.11); (6) time of tribulation (Mt. 24.21; Dan. 12.1); and (7) Son of Man on clouds (Mt. 24.30; Dan. 7.13). On the basis of these and other parallels,[3] L. Hartman notes that Matthew 24 displays an 'association with Daniel which ... upholds and inspires the main part of this "discourse,"'[4] and that they 'overlap to a great extent ... [and are] concerned with similar matters'.[5] An instance which is particularly revealing concerns Matthew's redactional addition of ἐν τόπῳ ἁγίῳ in 24.15 (cf. Mk 13.14). E. Klostermann has rightly argued[6] that Matthew added this phrase to assimilate his text to Dan. 9.27 [LXX and Theodotian] which reads καὶ ἐπὶ τὸ ἱερὸν βδέλυγμα τῶν ἐρημώσεων ἔσται ('and on the temple shall be the abomination of desolation').[7] Other Danielic elements in Matthew 24 have raised the question for D. Ford as to whether Matthew 24 should be understood as a *midrash* on Daniel, a view to which he is sympathetic.[8] Hartman is somewhat more sceptical in stating that this 'designation would not be completely inappropriate'.[9] However, in order to substantiate even this more modest claim, Hartman proposes that 'many things must have happened to this "midrash" before the eschatological discourse took on the form it has now'.[10] In regard to our extant text of Matthew, J. Z. Lauterbach, R. Bloch, and B. Gerhardsson have all argued that there are too few 'distinct connections with the text interpreted'[11] for Matthew 24

---

3 Hartman, *Prophecy*, pp. 172–74.

4 Hartman, *Prophecy*, p. 145.

5 Hartman, *Prophecy*, p. 145.

6 Klosterman, *Matthäusevangelium*, p. 193.

7 In regard to the variation in the Greek versions, Hartman, *Prophecy*, p. 162 states that 'it is probable that Daniel supplied this adverbial phrase, for the context of both 9.27 and 11.31 makes clear that the abomination is in the Temple'. Also see D. Daube, *The New Testament and Rabbinic Judaism* (London: The Athlone Press, 1956), pp. 418–37.

8 Ford, *Abomination*, pp. vii–viii. For a similar view see F. Gils, *Jésus prophète d'après les Évangiles synoptiques* (Louvain: Publications Universitaires, 1957), p. 128. A. G. Wright, *The Literary Genre of Midrash* (New York: Alba House, 1967), p. 74 is somewhat generalized in stating that *midrash* is 'a work that attempts to make a text of scripture understandable, useful and relevant for a later generation'. G. Porton, 'Midrash: Palestinian Jews and the Hebrew Bible in the Greco-Roman Period', *ANRW* 2.19.1 (1979), pp. 103–38; J. Neusner, *What is Midrash?* (Philadelphia: Fortress, 1987).

9 Hartman, *Prophecy*, p. 174.

10 Hartman, *Prophecy*, p. 174. He describes the extant text of Matthew in the following manner, 'to continue with the rabbinic terminology, the original "midrash" is well on the way to becoming a "Mishnah."' Also to note is that the Danielic text itself has often been envisioned as a *midrash* on Joseph in Pharaoh's court (L. A. Rosenthal, 'Die Josephgeschichte, mit der Büchen Ester und Daniel verglichen', *ZAW* 15 (1895), pp. 278–84; C. Gaide, *Le Livre de Daniel* (Paris: Mame, 1969), pp. 19–20. However, Collins, *Daniel*, p. 39 concludes that the apparent similarities could equally be attributed to the similarities in Near Eastern court settings and an interest in dreams.

11 Hartman, *Prophecy*, p. 174. See J. Z. Lauterbach, 'Midrash and Mishnah. A Study in the Early History of the Halakah', *JQR* 5 (1915), pp. 503–27; R. Bloch, 'Écriture

to be conceivably a *midrash* on the book of Daniel. Davies and Allison concur in concluding that 'it is too much to say that Matthew 24 (or its main source) is a midrash upon Daniel'.[12] Nonetheless, Daniel is clearly on Matthew's interpretive horizon, and, as with the specific reference to Dan. 9.27, Matthew makes explicit what Mark leaves implicit.

4.3. The Abomination of Desolation in Its Danielic Context

At the broadest level, the literary context of Daniel concerns the Babylonian exile, as the introductory verse indicates, 'In the third year of the reign of King Jehoiakim of Judah, King Nebuchadnezzar of Babylon came to Jerusalem and besieged it.' On this literary level, Daniel's work falls into two halves.[13] Chapters 1–6 narrate (in the third person) the exploits of Daniel[14] and his companions after being deported in the Babylonian exile, and consist of an emphasis on Daniel as interpreter of dreams and pagan kings confessing to the greatness of Israel's God (1.17, 2.24, 47; 3.28; 4.9, 31-34, 37; 5.17; 6.26-28). The second half of the work, chs 7–12, consists of three Danielic visions (narrated in the first person) regarding the future of Israel. Within this second half there is a discernible difference in emphasis. Whereas previously Daniel was capable of interpreting other people's dreams, he now requires a divine mediator for explanation of his own dreams. Furthermore, rather than the pagan kings willing to confess the legitimacy of Yahweh's rule, they are instead portrayed as ravaging beasts devouring the people of God.[15] Of particular interest for our discussion is the commonly noted concentric structure of chs 2–7. Chapters 3 and 6

---

et Tradition dans le Judaïsme', *CahSion* 8 (1954), pp. 9–34 (19–21); B. Gerhardsson, *Memory and Manuscript* (Uppsala: Copenhagen, 1961), pp. 83–85.

12   Davies and Allison, *Matthew 3*, p. 332. For broader critiques on understanding Matthew as *Midrash* see G. N. Stanton, 'Matthew as Creative Interpreter of the Sayings of Jesus', in *Das Evangelium und die Evangelien*, ed. P. Stuhlmacher (Tübingen: Mohr), pp. 273–87; R. T. France, 'Jewish Historigraphy, Midrash and the Gospels', in *Gospel Perspectives III: Studies in Midrash and Historiography*, ed. R. T. France and D. Wenham (Sheffield: JSOT), pp. 99–127.

13   We refer here to the author of Daniel as Daniel out of convention rather than implying a sixth-century date for its composition. See further discussion below.

14   For the prominence of Daniel in early Jewish literature see 1 Macc. 1.60; Ezek. 14.14; 28.3. Also see M. Noth, 'Noah, Daniel und Hiob in Ez 14', *VT* 1 (1951), pp. 251–60; W. Zimmerli, *Ezekiel 1* (Philadelphia: Fortress Press, 1979), pp. 314–15.

15   Benedikt Spinoza (1674) envisioned these two sections as displaying such dissimilarity that he proposed multiple authorship, cited in C. Gebhardt, *Theologisch-Politischer Traktat* (Hamburg: Meiner, 1955), p. 207. This approach is eclipsed by L. Berthodt, *Daniel aus dem Hebräisch-Aramäischen neu übersetzt und erklärt mit einer vollständigen Einerleitung und einigen historischen und kritischen* (Erlangen: Palm, 1808), who argued that Daniel consisted of at least nine authors from the Seleucid period. A similar view is suggested by Corrodi, cited by Collins, *Daniel*, p. 27 n.265.

both narrate stories of miraculous deliverance: Shadrach, Meshach, and Abednego from Nebuchadnezzar's furnace and Daniel's rescue from the lions' den. Chapters 4 and 5 function as admonitions to the pagan kings (Nebuchadnezzar and Belshazzar), and are paralleled in terms of their consequent positive or negative results.[16]

There has been considerable discussion on the relationship of ch. 2 to ch. 7, more specifically whether the stone (2.34) should be equated with the Son of Man (7.13). Collins notes several aspects that would seem to detract from the parallelism: (1) ch. 2 consists of the king's dream, whereas ch. 7 is Daniel's dream; (2) the different metals in ch. 2 refer to the decline of the succeeding kingdoms, but in ch. 7 'the beasts from the sea... are [the] symbols of rebellious chaos'.[17] (3) Collins states that 'chapter 2 has no counterpart to the heavenly judgement scene of chapter 7, and its symbolism is quite different'.[18] However, in response to this, and in support of A. Lenglet,[19] several points can be noted: (a) Both chs 2 and 7 have a four kingdom schema. (b) The reception of the vision is presented in similar fashion, with Collins himself admitting that 'the manner in which Daniel receives his revelation in 2.14-23 resembles the apocalyptic revelation of chaps. 7 and 8'.[20] (c) Other specific numeric elements from the vision are paralleled, such as the ten toes in 2.41-42 which are to be compared to the ten horns of the beast in ch. 7. (d) In regard to Collins' objection noted in point (b) above, it is important to recognize that ch. 7 is related to the ultimate decline and defeat of the chaotic nations that oppress Israel. (e) At a later point in Collins' discussion he notes that 'the kingdom prophesised in chap. 2 was presumably understood in light of chap. 7'.[21] (f) Finally, it is important to note that symbolism, by virtue of its being symbolism, necessarily departs from exact correspondence. Implicit in the use of any paradigm is the abandoning of some features to highlight or represent others. This issue is well captured by Chrysostem, who states: 'The type must not have nothing in common with the antitype, for then there would be nothing typical. Nor on the other hand must it [the type] be identical with the other [the antitype], or it would be the reality itself.'[22] We will return to the implications of Dan. 2.7's mutually interpretive structure after our discussion of the function and context of chs 9 and 11.

Chapter 9 introduces Daniel as reflecting on Jer. 29.10, which concerns the duration of the Babylonian exile, 'For thus says the LORD: Only when Babylon's seventy years are completed will I visit you, and I will fulfil to

16   A. Lenglet, 'La Structure littéraire de Daniel 2–7', *Bib* 53 (1972), pp. 169–90 has suggested that chs 4 and 5 are directed towards Antiochus Epiphanes IV.

17   Collins, *Daniel*, p. 34.

18   Collins, *Daniel*, p. 34.

19   Lenglet, 'Structure', pp. 176–80.

20   Collins, *Daniel*, p. 36

21   Collins, *Daniel*, p. 60.

22   *PG* 51.248

you my promise and bring you back to this place.'[23] In this light, A. G. Wright suggests that Daniel 9 is thus presented as a *midrash* on Jeremiah in that it 'make[s] a text of Scripture understandable, useful, and relevant for a later generation'. The vision is set in the first year of Darius son of Ahasuerus, which some commentators have suggested corresponds well to the Persian conquest of Babylon (518 BC) and thus exciting Israel's hope of an end to the exile.[24] The reason for Daniel's apparent cognitive dissonance is the irreconcilable historical timeframe in Jeremiah and his (i.e. Daniel's) current situation. In response, Daniel turns to prayer in order to resolve this difficulty. His prayer is accompanied by fasting, sackcloth, and ashes, all of which denote a posture of repentance.[25] Although debates concerning the authenticity of Daniel's prayer in 9.4b-19 continue to feature in contemporary academic discussions,[26] for the purposes of our analysis it is sufficient to note that the theme is consistent with our previous analysis of various pseudepigraphical literature which draws on the Deuteronomistic tradition of blessing for obedience and cursing for infidelity. In this regard, O. H. Steck has noted the pervasive element of Deuteronomistic theology,[27] which J. J. Collins summarizes as 'a confession of Israel's sin and affirmation of God's justice and appeal for mercy, not because of Israel's merit but for God's own sake'.[28] Israel has ignored their covenantal obligations, wilfully sinned and done wrong (v. 5), consistently not listened to Yahweh's servants and prophets (v. 6),[29] and thus stands under the Mosaic curse of judgement (v. 11).[30] Daniel's specific supplication in 17b, 'Lord, let your face shine upon your desolated sanctuary', ties the 'abomination' passages together (8.13; 9.26; 11.31; 12.11) through the common use of שָׁמֵם in regard to the profanation of the temple. Interestingly, in Lam. 5.18, שָׁמֵם becomes

23   Jeremiah 29.10; cf. 25.11; Zech. 1.7, 12; 7.5. Interestingly, the context of Jer. 25.11 is the 'desolation (לְשַׁמָּה) of this land'. A seventy-year period of punishment is a common motif in the Ancient Near East. Collins, *Daniel*, p. 349 notes a relevant parallel in the *Black Stone of Esar-haddon*, where it is recorded that Marduk 'decreed seventy years of desolation for Babylon, when it was destroyed by Sennacherib in 689 BCE'. Holladay, *Jeremiah*, pp. 668–69 argues that seventy years commonly refer to one lifetime.

24   J. E. Goldingay, *Daniel* (Dallas: Word Books, 1988), pp. 231–32; Collins, *Daniel*, p. 349. Second Chronicles 36.20-22 interprets Jeremiah's prophesy as continuing from the destruction of the temple in 586 BC to its restoration under Cyrus, cf. Ezra 1.1.

25   Jonah 3.6; Esth 4.1-4; Ezra 9.3-4; Neh. 9.1. Cf. Ezra 9.6-15; Neh. 1.5-11; 9.5-37; Ps. 79.

26   Commentators arguing that the prayer is secondary include E. W. Heaton, *The Book of Daniel* (London: SCM Press, 1956), pp. 203–204; L. F. Hartman and A. A. DiLella, *The Book of Daniel* (New York: Doubleday, 1978), pp. 245–46.

27   O. H. Steck, *Israel und das gewaltsame Geschick der Propheten* (Neukirchen: Neukirchener Verlag, 1967), pp. 110–28.

28   Collins, *Daniel*, p. 350.

29   Cf. Jer. 26.5; 29.19; 35.15; 44.4-5; Mt. 23.37.

30   Of which the ultimate expression was exile from the land, cf. Lev. 26.14-39; Deut. 28.15-68. Also see Jer. 7.20; 42.18; 44.6; 2 Chron. 12.7; 34.25; Ps. 79.6.

a synonym for the temple's destruction, which echoes earlier traditions in Lev. 26.31: 'I will lay your cities waste, will make your sanctuaries desolate (וַהֲשִׁמּוֹתִי), and I will not smell your pleasing odours.'

While Daniel is in mid-supplication (v. 20, 'While I was speaking …'), Yahweh responds through his angel Gabriel. To Daniel's dismay he learns that rather than the punishment lasting seventy years, the exile will last seventy weeks of years, or 490 years (vv. 24-27).[31] This extension of punishment seems to find rationale in the Sabbatical theology of Lev. 25-26, in which there is a sevenfold punishment of sins. Leviticus 26.18 states: 'And if in spite of this you will not obey me, I will continue to punish you sevenfold for your sins.' The sin and iniquity of 9.24 is most plausibly that which has been previously mentioned in Daniel's prayer.[32] The historical situation envisioned within these verses (i.e. Dan. 9.24-27) is most plausibly the events surrounding the Maccabaean revolt. Several aspects correspond well to other documented sources of the period. (1) Daniel 9.24's reference to the 'anointing of a holy place' conceivably refers to the re-dedication of the Jerusalem temple by Judas Maccabee in 164 BC (1 Macc. 4.36-59). (2) Daniel 9.26 refers to 'an anointed one, being cut off' and would cohere well with the murder of Onius III (2 Macc. 4.23-28; cf. Dan. 11.22). (3) V. Tcherikover[33] argues that the 'host of the ruler who is to come' in 9.26 is a reference to the Syrian soldiers under Antiochus who settled in Jerusalem (1 Macc. 1.29-40; cf. Dan. 11.39). (4) Daniel 9.27 refers to a certain figure making 'a strong covenant (διαθήκη) with many for one week'. A parallel can be found with Antiochus Epiphanes' alliance with certain Hellenizing Jews in 1 Macc. 1.11: 'In those days certain renegades came out from Israel and misled many, saying, "Let us go and make a covenant (διαθήκην) with the Gentiles around us, for since we separated from them many disasters have come upon us."' While this historical scenario of the Maccabaean revolt is accepted by the majority of modern commentators, the specific identity of the abomination of desolation has evaded scholarly consensus and deserves further discussion. It is to this issue we now turn our attention.

4.3.a. The specific identity of the abomination in Daniel

The comments of Albright and Mann, that 'Matt xxiv 4-36 … is free commentary on Daniel (vii 8-27, viii 9-26, ix 24-27, and xi 21–xii 13) both in ideas and actual quotations, seems to be generally agreed.

---

31 Such divisions of history were common in antiquity. For examples see *1 En.* 10.12, 90.1-17, 93.1-10; 4Q180 1.9; *T.Levi* 16.1, 17.1, cited in Goldingay, *Daniel*, p. 232.

32 O. H. Steck, 'Weltgeschehen und Gottesvolk im Buche Daniel', in *Kirche*, ed. D. Lührmann and G. Strecker (Tübingen: Mohr), pp. 53–78 (69–70), *pace* Collins, *Daniel*, p. 354.

33 V. Tcherikover, *Hellenistic Civilization and the Jews* (New York: Athenaeum, 1959), p. 189.

Beyond that there is no large consensus of opinion,'[34] amount to quite an overstatement when it comes to the identity of the 'abomination of desolation' in Daniel. The view which has dominated scholarship, however, as to the referent of the abomination, is characterized by E. Nestle, who in 1884 argued for a statue of the Phoenician deity *Baal-samem* (the 'Lord of Heaven') which Philo of Byblos associated with the Greek Zeus.[35] A similar approach was adopted by E. Bickermann, who not only accepted that the 'abomination of desolation' functioned as a dysphemism,[36] but also argued that it was a synchronistic attempt to associate the Phoenician deity and Zeus with the God of Israel.[37]

In a recent study by J. Lust,[38] both these views have suffered substantial critiques, especially in identifying the 'abomination' as a statue of Zeus. Lust notes that although שִׁקּוּצִים/βδέλυγμα can refer to a statue of a deity such as Milkom, Molek, Kemosh, or Ashtoret,[39] the semantic domain goes beyond a simple identification with a statue. The terms are more frequently linked with cultic activity. Second Chronicles 15.8 associates the terms with the altar of the Lord, stating that 'Asa put away the הַשִּׁקּוּצִים/βδελύγματα ... and repaired the altar of the Lord'. Similar linking together of הַשִּׁקּוּצִים/βδελύγματα and the altar occurs in Jer. 7.30-31 and 32.35 [LXX 39.35] (cf. μιάσματα for βδελύγματα in Jer. 32.34). One could also note Zech. 9.7, which narrates Yahweh's words concerning the Philistines: 'I will take away their blood from their mouth, and their abominations (וְשִׁקֻּצָיו/βδελύγματα) from between their teeth.' Lust[40] notes that 'in this context the abominations can hardly be gods or their images but are probably pagan sacrifices'. A similar theme is also attested in the Isaianic condemnation (66.17) of those 'eating swine's flesh and the abomination (שֶׁקֶץ/βδελύγματα) and mice'.

When one turns to the relevant non-Danielic data, however, quite a distinctive picture emerges. First Maccabees 1.47-48 describes Antiochus' command to the Israelites to cease offering sacrifices, and as such

---

34   Albright and Mann, *Matthew*, p. 289.

35   E. Nestle, 'Zu Daniel', *ZAW* 4 (1884), pp. 247–50. For a representative modern proponent see Goldingay, *Daniel*, p. 263.

36   See discussion in A. Geiger, *Ursprung und Überstezungen der Bibel* (Breslau, 1875); M. Tsevat, 'Ishbosheth and Congeners: The Names and Their Study', *HUCA* 46 (1975), pp. 71–87.

37   E. Bickerman, *Der Gott der Makkabaäer* (Berlin: Schocken, 1937), pp. 107–108. A related interpretive approach is that of J. A. Goldstein, *I Maccabees* (New York: Doubleday, 1976), pp. 139–40, who argues for the identification of the abomination of desolation in Daniel as meteorites fashioned into idolatrous objects of worship which Antiochus ordered to be affixed to the temple altar to be worshipped. See discussion in Lust, 'Cult', pp. 285–86.

38   In the following discussion we are indebted to the analysis of Lust, 'Cult', pp. 283–99.

39   First Kings 11.5, 7; 2 Kgs 23.13. Cf. Ezek. 20.30

40   Lust, 'Cult', p. 289.

'making themselves abominable'. First Maccabees 1.54 goes on to say that Antiochus erected the 'abomination of desolation' (βδέλυγμα ἐρημώσεως) on the altar (θυσιαστήριον) and idol-altars (βωμούς) in the surrounding towns of Judah. When Judas 'tore down the abomination that he [Antiochus] had erected on the altar in Jerusalem' (1 Macc. 6.7), there is no mention of a statue of a pagan deity or the like. The βωμούς are to be understood as some kind of structural embellishment to the original θυσιαστήριον. [41] Josephus mentions that Antiochus 'spoiled the temple, and put a stop to the constant practice of offering a daily sacrifice of expiation' (*War* 1.32) and that he 'sacrificed swine's flesh upon the altar'. When Judas restores the cult, he is recorded as having repaired the altar (βωμόν) and reinstalled the sacrifices (ἐναγισμῶν). [42] On this basis Lust concludes that the abomination in Daniel is to be understood not as a pagan statue, but as 'a pagan altar set up upon the altar of the Lord'. [43] It is in this regard that Kloppenborg concludes that 'the phrase τὸ βδέλυγμα τῆς ἐρημώσεως in Mt. 24.15 is clearly indebted to Dan. 9.27, where Daniel described the erection of an altar ... by Antiochus IV Epiphanes in 167 B.C.E'. [44] In fact, the βδέλυγμα τῆς ἐρημώσεως in biblical literature is never associated with a statue. Those who point to 2 Macc. 6.2 as evidence, neglect to appreciate that when Antiochus dedicated the temple to Zeus Olympios, there is no indication that this implied the erection of a statue. It was only four centuries later in a commentary on Daniel that Jerome mentioned a figure by the name of Porphyry who apparently understood the Danielic phrase in this way. [45]

In our previous discussion of the Matthean τὸ βδέλυγμα τῆς ἐρημώσεως phrase, we argued that the construction was a causative genitive, in that the 'desolation' was caused by the 'abomination'. The question is then raised as to how the genitive functions in Daniel. Lust argues for a 'genitive of possession or belonging', [46] based on other Old Testament attestations of שִׁקּוּץ linked with a personal pronoun or proper noun. [47] As such, Lust maintains that the construction refers to either (1)

[41] The account is repeated in *Ant.* 12.251–53, but again the reference is to a βωμούς rather than an εἴδωλον.

[42] Also of relevance is 1 Macc. 4.43, which notes that the priests who purified the temple 'removed the defiled stones to an unclean place'. Based on parallels with how stones were used in Canaanite and Syrian cultic contexts, various commentators have suggested that the abomination consisted of sacred stones placed on the altar. See above discussion. Goldstein, *Maccabees*, pp. 144–51; N. W. Porteous, *Daniel: A Commentary* (Philadelphia: Westminster, 1965), p. 143; Collins, *Daniel*, p. 358.

[43] Lust, 'Cult', p. 295.

[44] Kloppenborg, 'Evocatio', p. 422.

[45] *PL* 25.569. See discussion in Lust, 'Cult', p. 285. Modern proponents include Hartman and DiLella, *Daniel*, pp. 252–53.

[46] Lust, 'Cult', p. 297.

[47] Ezek. 7.20; 11.21; 20.30; 37.23; 1 Kgs 11.5, 7; 2 Kgs 23.13. Cf. the more ambiguous 4QpNah 3.1 because of a lacuna in the text.

the 'collectivity of those who use or venerate the abomination … in their cultic practices',[48] or (2) Antiochus IV Epiphanes himself who imposed the שִׁקּוּץ/βδέλυγμα. Although we agree with Lust that the phrase is not a *genitivus qualitatis* (genitive of quality), cf. RSV 'the desolating sacrilege', nonetheless, we will argue that understanding the genitive construct as of 'possession' or 'belonging' fails to convince. First, in all three references to the 'abomination of desolation' in Daniel, the phrase is composed of a noun followed by a participle. In Dan. 9.27 and 11.31 the Hebrew construction שִׁקּוּצִים מְשֹׁמֵם is composed of the common masculine plural noun of שִׁקּוּץ and the Poel masculine singular participle of שָׁמֵם.[49] In Dan. 12.11, the author uses the masculine singular noun with a Qal masculine singular participle. The Poel verb is typically used in place of the Piel in conjunction with hollow verbs by morphological necessity,[50] and a double-ayin verb would not be attested as a Poel if it could naturally be expressed as a Piel.[51] The implication of this is that the semantic possibilities of the Poel are identical to the semantic possibilities of the Piel. Although Hebrew grammarians suspect a unifying understanding of the Piel, as is evident in the work of Kaufman and Joosten,[52] one of the primary categories of the Piel is generally accepted as factitive.[53] As such Joüon and Muraoka have noted that the Piel is the 'causative … active'[54] stem, and Arnold and Choi conclude that 'the Piel frequently expresses the bringing about of a state … [and] focuses on causation and the outcome of the action'.[55] Examples of factitive Piels

---

48   Lust, 'Cult', p. 297.

49   It is important to note, however, that in all three passages in the LXX a genitive construction is used: Dan. 9.27, βδέλυγμα τῶν ἐρημώσεων; 11.31, βδέλυγμα ἐρημώσεως; 12.11, τὸ βδέλυγμα τῆς ἐρημώσεως.

50   A. E. Cowley, *Gesenius' Hebrew Grammar as Edited and Enlarged by E. Kautzsch* (28th edn; Oxford: Clarendon, 1970), pp. 55, 671.

51   B. Waltke and M. O'Connor, *An Introduction to Biblical Hebrew Syntax* (Winona Lake: Eisenbrauns, 1990), treat the Poel as a irregular subset of the Piel. Also see discussion in P. Joüon and T. Muraoka, *A Grammar of Biblical Hebrew* (2 vols; Rome: Biblical Institute Press, 1993), pp. 52d, 59a, 82e.

52   S. A. Kaufman, 'Semitics: Directions and Re-Directions', in *The Study of the Ancient Near East in the Twenty-First Century*, ed. J. S. Cooper and G. M. Schwarz (Winona Lake: Eisenbrauns), pp. 273–82 (282) states, '[I]t is pointless to try to find a single … explanation to account for all of the transformative power of the … [Piel] stem. It is simply a form.' J. Joosten, 'The Functions of the Semitic D Stem: Biblical Hebrew Materials for a Comparative-Historical Approach', *Or.* 67 (1998), pp. 202–30 (227) concludes similarly that the Piel cannot be understood as a single underlying function. See discussion in B. T. Arnold and J. H. Choi, *A Guide to Biblical Hebrew Syntax* (Cambridge: Cambridge University Press, 2003), pp. 41–45.

53   Arnold and Choi, *Syntax*, p. 44. Other categories suggested include denominative, frequentative, and declarative.

54   Joüon and Muraoka, *Hebrew*, p. 151.

55   Arnold and Choi, *Syntax*, pp. 42–43. E. Jenni, *Das hebräische Pi'el: Syntaktisch-semasiologische Untersuchung einer Verbalform im Alten Testaments* (Basel: Helbing und Lichtenhahn, 1968), distinguishes between the Piel and the Hiphil, as an imposition of a

are relatively common in the MT:[56] 1 Chron. 29.12, וּבְיָדְךָ לְגַדֵּל ('and it is in your hand *to make great*'); Gen 12.2, וַאֲגַדְּלָה שְׁמֶךָ ('and I will *make* your name *great*'); Exod. 31.13, אֲנִי יְהוָה מְקַדִּשְׁכֶם ('I, Yahweh, *sanctify* you'); 1 Sam. 2.6, יְהוָה מֵמִית וּמְחַיֶּה ('Yahweh kills and *brings to life*'); Deut. 11.4, וַיְאַבְּדֵם יְהוָה ('Yahweh *destroyed* them'); 2 Kgs 18.4, שִׁבַּר אֶת־הַמַּצֵּבֹת ('*he broke down* the pillars'); Deut. 4.5, וּמִשְׁפָּטִים לִמַּדְתִּי אֶתְכֶם חֻקִּים ('*I have taught* you statues and ordinances). In this light, the phrase שִׁקּוּצִים מְשֹׁמֵם in Dan. 9.27 and 11.31 is most plausibly understood as a factitive, that is 'the abomination which causes desolation'.[57] This supports our prior discussion of the Matthean βδέλυγμα τῆς ἐρημώσεως as a causative genitive. However, the question still remains as to the identity of the figure who causes the desolation, and it is to this question we now turn our attention.[58]

The main protagonist in the book of Daniel is presented as living in the sixth century BC during the Persian and Babylonian eras. As was noted in our above discussion of Jewish pseudepigrapha, 'apocalyptic' works such as Daniel were characteristically pseudonymous.[59] Coupled with this common pseudonymity, 'apocalyptic' works were often depicted in an alternate time period to their actual composition.[60] So, although originally presented as a sixth-century literary setting, in the foreign courts of the Babylonians (Dan. 1.1) and the Medes (Dan. 5.30, 9.1), the consensus of scholarship is that the latter half of Daniel's composition was a response to the Maccabaean crisis. In such a schema chs 7-11 are

state versus an imposition of a process. Arnold and Choi offer the example of הָיָה ('live' in the Qal), where the Piel would be 'to cause to be alive' and the Hiphil would be 'to cause to live', that is, a distinction between being and doing. There has been both support (T. Lambdin, *An Introduction to Biblical Hebrew* [London: Prentice Hall, 1971], pp. 388–89) and criticism (S. E. Fassberg, 'The Movement from *Qal* to *Pi'el* in Hebrew and the Disappearance of the *Qal* Internal Passive', *Hebrew Studies* 42 [2001], pp. 243–55 (243–44)) of Jenni's proposal. However, it suffices for our discussion to note the Piel's factitive sense. For examples see below.

56   Examples are taken from Lambdin, *Hebrew*, pp. 193–95; Waltke and O'Conner, *Introduction*, pp. 400–404; Joüon and Muraoka, *Hebrew*, pp. 154–56; C. L. Seow, *A Grammar for Biblical Hebrew* (Nashville: Abingdon Press, 1995), pp. 173–75; and Arnold and Choi, *Syntax*, p. 44.

57   *Pace* Hartman, *Prophecy*, p. 147, who interprets the entire phrase in reference to the desecration of the temple rather than its destruction.

58   We will argue that the historical situation of Daniel would suggest that the figure associated with the abomination is Antiochus IV Epiphanes.

59   Pseudonymity was a common feature of various genres in antiquity. For discussion see B. Metzger, 'Literary Forgeries and Canonical Pseudepigrapha', *JBL* 91 (1972), pp. 3–24. For a discussion of the genre of Daniel see Collins, *Daniel*, pp. 38–61; Goldingay, *Daniel*, pp. 320–22.

60   Some of the examples noted above were the *Apocalypse of Abraham*, *1–3 Baruch*, and *4 Ezra*, all of which are purportedly written concerning the Babylonian destruction of the temple. However, they came into being as a reasonably homogeneous response to the destruction of Jerusalem in 70 AD. In regard to Daniel, see Collins, *Daniel*, pp. 24–33.

not history prophesied but prophesy historicized, that is, material written with the benefit of hindsight.[61]

The historical context of the events leading up to the Maccabaean crisis can be sketched as follows with particular reference to Daniel's narrative.[62] In 336 BC Alexander the Great (Dan. 11.3) succeeded his father Philip and began his campaign across Asia Minor, crushing the Persians at the battle of Issus (333 BC) and was consequently welcomed by the Egyptians as Pharaoh (332 BC). After conquering Babylon, Susa, and Persepolis, Alexander reached as far as India in 331 BC; however, on his westward homebound journey he fell ill and died in Babylon. The empire was then divided among his generals (Dan. 11.4; cf. 8.8).[63] Of interest to Daniel is the southern kingdom which arose from this situation; the king of the south (Dan. 11.5) should be identified with Ptolemy I Soter at Alexandria. Seleucus, under Ptolemy and as such one of his commanders, ruled Babylonia for a short period before retreating to Alexandria when challenged by the ruler of Asia, Antigonus Monopthalmos. Ptolemy and Seleucus defeated Antigonus and Seleucus returned to Babylonia and extended his control over Syria and Persia. It was in this sense that Seleucus could be said to have dominion over a greater kingdom than Ptolemy (Dan. 11.5).[64] During the period 253–41 BC, Ptolemy II Philadelphus offered his daughter Berenice to be Antiochus II's wife (Dan. 11.6), but after a complex series of events, Antiochus reinstated the legal status of his first wife Laodice. Berenice was supported in opposing this decision by her brother Ptolemy III Euergetes. Consequently, military invasion ensued and both Berenice and her son were killed. In this regard Dan. 11.6 seems to refer to their murders and vv. 7-8 to Ptolemy III's campaign in her support. During this time Ptolemy took his father's place, entered the Seleucid capital in northern Syria, and successfully campaigned, perhaps as far as Babylon. In 242 BC Seleucus II attempted an unsuccessful counter-attack before agreeing to a peace treaty (Dan. 11.8-9).

---

61   A second-century date is argued by Goldingay, *Daniel*, p. xxvi; Collins, *Daniel*, pp. 87–88; and the majority of scholars. However, one could also argue that even if a sixth-century date was accepted, eg. A. Hill and J. H. Walton, *A Survey of the Old Testament* (Grand Rapids: Zondervan, 1991), pp. 349–51, the proleptic nature of the text would nonetheless invite comparison with the Maccabaean period. Our own analysis does not stand or fall on the dating of Daniel 7–12; either way the referent seems to be Antiochus IV.

62   I am here indebted to Collins, *Daniel*, pp. 376–85.

63   The description in Dan. 11.4 of the kingdom divided 'toward the four winds of heaven' need not strictly refer to the later situation in 301 BC where Asia Minor is under Lysimachus, Syria and Babylon under Seleucus, Macedonia under Cassander, and Egypt under Ptolomy; rather וְתֵחָץ לְאַרְבַּע רוּחוֹת is to be understood as a general description of the fracturing of Alexander's kingdom. See F. E. Peters, *The Harvest of Hellenism: A History of the Near East From Alexander to the Triumph of Christianity* (New York: Simon and Schuster, 1970), p. 77.

64   Arrian, *Expedition of Alexander* 7.22. Also see discussion in A. A. Bevan, *The House of Seleucus* (New York: Barnes and Noble, 1902), pp. 50–60.

The succeeding Seleucid king (Antiochus III) took advantage of the instability of the Ptomelaic kingdom after Ptolemy III's death in 222 BC and initiated his opportunity for revenge. This culminated in the Fourth Syrian War (219 BC) which found Antiochus occupying the entirety of Palestine (Dan. 11.10). However, in 217 BC at Raphia, on the southern boarder of Palestine, Antiochus suffered a significant defeat despite his military strength (Dan. 11.11).[65] This victory was not final (Dan. 11.12) for in the subsequent years (202–199 BC) Antiochus III took advantage of the turmoil within the infrastructure of the Ptolemaic kingdom (Dan. 11.13-14) and made subsequent attempts to regain control.

There is also evidence of a pro-Seleucid party in Jerusalem, which, by the time of Antiochus' conquest of Palestine, was in the majority. The central figure in this party was Simon II 'The Just', who was in continued conflict with the Ptolemaic supporters in Jerusalem, such as Hyrcanus. The anti-Jewish policies of Ptolemy also contributed to opposition. The third book of Maccabees (*3 Macc.* 2.28b-30a) records the attempts of mass conversion to the cult of Dionysus. Antiochus III took advantage of the decline of the Ptolemaic kingdom in Egypt, especially after the mysterious circumstances surrounding the death of Ptolemy IV in 204 BC, and instigated the Fifth Syrian War (202–200 BC). Gaining victory at Panium, the remnants of the defeated army fled to Sidon, where they suffered final defeat (Dan. 11.15). After the surrender of Sidon, Antiochus consolidated his control over Palestine, 'the beautiful land' (Dan. 11.16),[66] but was nonetheless under pressure on the western borders.

In the period of 194–88, Antiochus III was keen to win the sympathy of his new subjects (Dan. 11.17-19), some sources mentioning his support for the rebuilding of the temple, and of his respect for the Law of Moses, in particular that foreigners should not enter the sanctuary. Daniel 11.17 seems to understand the royal marriage (in 194–93 BC) of Ptolemy V and Antiochus' daughter Cleopatra as intended to overthrow the kingdom, that is, Egyptian control over Palestine. It was meant to give Antiochus the freedom to address the Roman threat on the western boundary ('the coast lands' of western Asia Minor and Greece, v. 18). However, this plan was frustrated with defeats at Thermopylae in Greece (191 BC) and Magnesia in Asia Minor (190 BC) by the Romans and their allied forces (Dan. 11.18b). On account of the peace treaty of Apamea in 188 BC, Antiochus III was forced to surrender much of his land and pay an indemnity of 12,000 talents. In characteristic fashion he attempted to recover this from a temple treasury in Elymais (187 BC); however, he consequently met his untimely end when the residents of that particular area were enraged by his defiant actions (Dan. 11.19).[67]

---

65   Polybius 5.79; 3 Macc. 1.
66   See *Ant.* 12.2.3; cf. Dan. 8.9; 11.41; Jer. 3.19; *1 En.* 89.40; 90.20.
67   Diodorus 28.3; 29.15; Strabo 16.1.8.

Heliodorus was then sent to Jerusalem by Seleucus IV (Dan. 11.20)[68] in order to recover further funds from the temple treasury. Upon returning to the royal court, Heliodorus murdered Seleucus with premeditation (v. 20b, 'not in anger or in battle'). Antiochus IV then arose in 175 BC to rule over a Palestine that was internally divided on the issue of embracing or resisting elements of Hellenistic culture. Facing external pressures from Egypt in the south and the Romans in the west, Antiochus IV made an executive decision to impose the worship of Greek gods which he hoped would unify his new domain (Dan. 11.21). He bestowed on himself the honorific title 'Epiphanes' (god manifest) and produced coinage to the same effect. His debts were regularly repaid with money taken from the various temples under his juris-diction. Obviously many in Jerusalem would have vehemently opposed such actions. Meanwhile, further division and tension was building in Jerusalem when, in 175 BC, Jason purchased the high priesthood from Antiochus IV and displaced his brother Onius III (Dan. 11.22; cf. 9.26). Jason subsequently built a gymnasium and promoted Hellenistic sports, dress, and customs. Menelaus usurped Jason as high priest by outbidding him (Dan. 11.22) and had Onius III murdered.[69]

After Antiochus IV's second Egyptian campaign (Dan. 11.25-30) and continued opposition to his policy of unification under Greek religion in Jerusalem, he sent Apollonius, accompanied by a large army, to Jerusalem (Dan. 11.30-34). The results were devastating for a large number of Jerusalem's inhabitants. Many were massacred and sacrifices in the temple were suspended. The Sabbath and traditional festivals were outlawed, as was circumcision. Copies of the law were destroyed and the temple suffered ultimate desecration when a swine was sacrificed on the altar.[70] It was at this point that the Maccabaean revolt began.[71]

In light of our above discussion, we may affirm, with J. J. Collins, that Dan. 11 'presents a remarkably accurate portrayal of Hellenistic history down to the time of Antiochus Epiphanes'.[72] For the purposes of our own discussion, it is important to highlight the near consensus view among commentators that the figure alluded to in Dan. 11.31 – 'Forces sent by him shall occupy and profane the temple and fortress. They shall abolish the regular burnt offering and set up the abomination that makes desolate' (cf. 9.27) – is that of Antiochus IV Epiphanes.[73] Thus, Lust concludes that

---

68   See description of his despoiling of the temple in 2 Maccabees 3.

69   See 2 Macc. 4.7, 13, 34-35. In regard to Dan. 11.24, see *Polybius* 26.10 'in the sacrifices he furnished to cities and in the honors he paid to the gods he far surpassed all his predecessors'. Cf. Dan. 11.37, 38; 1 Macc. 3.30; *Ant.* 12.7.2.

70   First Maccabees 1.20-61; 2 Macc. 5.11-26; 6.1-5; *Ant.* 12.253.

71   Daniel 11.34, 'they will receive little help'. Both Porphyry and Jerome argued that the 'little help' referred to the premature death of Mattathias and his sons. See Collins, *Daniel*, p. 386.

72   Collins, *Daniel*, p. 377. Collins also notes that 'chapter 11 presupposes a detailed knowledge of Hellenistic history'. Collins, *Daniel*, p. 69.

73   Collins, *Daniel*, pp. 384–85; Goldingay, *Daniel*, pp. 301–302, 309–310.

'this encourages us to recognize ... a reference to Antiochus as the desolator or appaller on whom God's final wrath is going to be poured out'.[74] It is in this sense that stronger parallel is found with Daniel's vision in ch. 9 and the identification there also of the מְשֹׁמֵם שִׁקּוּצִים/βδέλυγμα τῆς ἐρημώσεως as Antiochus IV Epiphanes.[75]

4.4. The Son of Man, the Stone, and the Defeat of the Beasts

It is no understatement to suggest that the book of Daniel, in particular ch. 7, has captivated the minds of writers from antiquity to the present. In contemporary works, discussion often has more than half of each printed page devoted to footnotes. Thus it is rather ambitious to attempt a comprehensive analysis of the complexities of the debate in the context of our own discussion. We will, however, focus upon the pertinent elements which demonstrate that the presence of the Son of Man leads to the destruction of Israel's enemies, a theme which is also attested in *1 Enoch* and *4 Ezra*. As will be discussed below, the structure of the book of Daniel has also prepared the reader/hearer for such a schema by chiastically introducing similar themes in ch. 2.

Daniel 7 can be roughly divided into vision (vv. 2-15) and interpretation (vv. 16-27), with vv. 1 and 28 functioning as introduction and conclusion. The vision consists of four beasts arising from the sea: a lion, a bear, a leopard, and a beast with ten horns. Of the ten horns, three were 'plucked up by the roots' (v. 8) to make room for a κέρας ... μικρόν/זְעֵירָה אָחֳרִי קֶרֶן ('little horn', v. 8), which was exceedingly arrogant. The fourth beast is then put to death (v. 11) as the Son of Man is presented before the Ancient of Days (v. 13) and receives dominion, glory and kingship (v. 14). Interpretation of these images is then offered by 'one of the attendants' (v. 16), who identifies the four beasts with four kings (v. 17). Verses 19-22 focus attention upon the fourth beast and the arrogant horn who made war with the holy ones, and who is finally destroyed by divine judgement (v. 22).

There has been considerable debate recently over the source-critical evaluation of ch. 7.[76] E. Sellin argued that various portions of the chapter related to Antiochus Epiphanes ('little horn') and were thus second-century redactional insertions.[77] However, as stated previously, for the purposes of our

---

74 Lust, 'Cult', p. 298.

75 Hartman, Prophecy, p. 153.

76 G. Hölscher, 'Die Entstehung des Buches Daniel', *Theologische Studien und Kritiken* 92 (1919), pp. 114–38, contends that 7.7b, 8, 11a, 20-22, 24-25 were not attested in the pre-Maccabaean version of Daniel. See also L. Dequeker, 'The Saints of the Most High in Qumran and Daniel', *OTS* 18 (1973), pp. 108–87. Casey, *Son*, pp. 11–17 discusses the rather dubious criteria used in many of these discussions.

77 E. Sellin, *Einleitung in das Alte Testament* (Leipzig: Quelle & Meyer, 1910), pp. 233–34.

research, prime consideration is given to the final form of the text as would have been available to Matthew during the first century. Given that Sellin et al. agree that the text had evolved into its current shape by the time of the first century, this issue goes beyond the interest of this book. However, what is interesting to note are the suggested parallels with the Greek empires which strengthen the identification of the little horn with Antiochus Epiphanes.[78]

F. J. Murphy notes that one of the key aspects in Daniel's vision is that the 'chapter represents successive empires oppressing Israel as supernatural beasts ... [in which] Daniel witnesses a judgement scene in the heavenly court that results in [the] defeat of Israel's enemies'.[79] The representation of Israel's enemies as beasts is well attested in the Old Testament. One particularly vivid example occurs within Ezekiel's discussion of 'good and bad shepherds'.[80] Ezekiel 34.28 states the following: 'They shall no more be (A) plunder for (B) the nations, nor shall (B˙) the beasts of the land (A˙) devour them.' The author presents a chiastic synonymous parallelism, in which the readers/ hearers are invited to identify the pagan nations as beastly animals.[81] Verse 8 is also helpful in that it parallels בַּז ('plunder') and אָכְלָה ('food'), the former syntactically functioning as the protasis. צֹאנִי ('sheep') is the subject of both clauses, and both are nominal forms with a prefixed לְ. This idea is also strengthened by threats of animals in vv. 5 and 25.[82] It is for this reason that Collins is justified in arguing that 'there was a tradition of applying this [beastly] imagery to the historic enemies of Israel'.[83]

Of significance for our discussion are those places in the Old Testament (for example Isa. 17.12-14), where beasts/monsters from the sea are identified as powers that are hostile to God. Furthermore, Isa. 27.1 records that 'On that day the Lord with his cruel and great and strong sword will punish Leviathan the fleeing serpent, Leviathan the twisting serpent, and he

---

78   Casey, *Man*, p. 20 comments that the identification of the little horn as Antiochus Epiphanes is 'rightly unquestioned among serious critical scholars'. H. H. Rowley, *Darius the Mede and the Four World Empires in the Book of Daniel* (Cardiff: University of Wales Press, 1964) has convincingly argued that the four kingdoms in chs 2 and 7 are that of Babylon, Medea, Persia, and Greece. See further discussion below.

79   F. J. Murphy, 'Second Temple Judaism', in *The Blackwell Reader in Judaism*, ed. J. Neusner and A. J. Avery-Peck (Oxford: Blackwell Publishing, 2000), pp. 42–59 (48).

80   Ezekiel 34.1-31.

81   For the combination of chiasm and synonymous parallelism see R. E. Murphy, *The Wisdom Literature* (Grand Rapids: Eerdmans, 1981), p. 65. Although the technical term 'synonymous parallelism' is typically reserved for literary works of poetry rather than prose, the style of the chapter is discernibly parallelistic (v. 6, mountain/hill; v.27, 'The trees of the field shall yield their fruit, and the earth shall yield its increase'), and thus would invite such a reading.

82   Wild animals as hostile entities towards God's chosen people is also apparent in Genesis 2; Deut. 7.22; 8.15; Num. 21.5-6; Zeph. 2.13-14. Also note Wis. 16.5 'For when the terrible rage of wild animals came upon your people and they were being destroyed by the bites of writhing serpents, your wrath did not continue to the end.'

83   Collins, *Daniel*, p. 288.

will kill the dragon that is in the sea.'[84] Similarly, Ps. 74.13 recalls the Exodus from Egypt and the defeat of Pharaoh's army as follows, 'You divided the sea by your might; you broke the heads of the dragons in the waters.'[85] It is in this regard that Casey states that 'the sea has mythological overtones – it is the domain of all that is opposed to God'.[86]

In relation to Daniel, Casey goes on to argue that the image of mythological beasts from the waters forms an appropriate contrast to the Son of Man riding on the heavenly clouds.[87] However, his conclusion that 'in using the sea as a symbol of hostility to God ... [the author] was drawing on native Israelite imagery',[88] is only partially accurate, as there are some features of the vision which bear no antecedent in the Old Testament. In an attempt to explain these, Gunkel[89] argued that the closest parallel was attested in the Sumerian *Enuma Elish*, where the Son of Man functioned in similar capacity to Marduk and Canaanite Baal in pagan myths. Although this view has been met with considerable opposition,[90] it did encourage subsequent commentators to look for closer Near Eastern parallels with visionary elements compared with Daniel 7. Attempts have included (1) the Iranian figure of Gayomart, the Primordial Man,[91] and (2) the Babylonian Akkadian *Vision of the Netherworld*.[92] However, the view which has found

---

84   Cf. Isa. 30.7.

85   Cf. Job 26.12-13; Ps. 87.4; 89.9-11; Isa. 51.9-10; Ezek. 29; 32.

86   Casey, *Son*, p. 18. In an interesting development Hos. 13.7-8 uses the images of lion, bear, and leopard as a divine threat: 'So I will become like a lion to them, like a leopard I will lurk beside the way. I will fall upon them like a bear robbed of her cubs, and will tear open the covering of their heart; there I will devour them like a lion, as a wild animal would mangle them.' This may have granted Matthew the theological precedent for taking up the imagery in Daniel and applying it ironically to Israel herself in Matthew 24. Also see J. Day, *God's Conflict with the Dragon and the Sea* (Cambridge: Cambridge University Press, 1985), p. 157; Collins, *Daniel*, 1993, p. 295.

87   Casey, *Son*, p. 18.

88   Casey, *Son*, p. 18.

89   H. Gunkel, *Schöpfung und Chaos in Urzeit und Endzeit: Eine religionsgeschichtliche Untersuchung über Gen 1 und Ap Joh 12* (Göttingen: Vandenhoeck & Ruprecht, 1895), pp. 323–35. Although there is some doubt that there is a *Menschensohnvorstellung* ('son of man concept') prior to Daniel 7, Gunkel also argued for the existence of a 'Son of Man' as a mythological figure pre-dating our Daniel narratives (Gunkel, *Schöpfung*, p. 331). In arguing this, Gunkel supports the titular usage of the phrase.

90   J. A. Montgomery, *A Cricitcal and Exegetical Commentary on the Book of Daniel* (Edinburgh: Clark, 1927), p. 323; Hartman and DiLella, *Daniel*, p. 212; Casey, *Son*, pp. 35–38.

91   Richter 1819, cited in J. M. Schmidt, *Die jüdische Apokalyptik* (Neukirchen-Vluyn: Neukirchener Verlag des Erziehungsvereins, 1969), p. 51; K. Koch, *Das Buch Daniel* (Darmstadt: Wissenschaftliche Buchgesellschaft, 1986), p. 231.

92   H. S. Kvanvig, *Roots of Apocalyptic: The Mesopotamian Background of the Enoch Figure and of the Son of Man* (Neukirchen-Vluyn: Neukirchener Verlag, 1988), pp. 389–441; objections by C. Colpe, ὁ υἱὸς τοῦ ἀνθρώπου, in *Theological Dictionary of the New Testament*, ed. G. Friedrich (trans. G. W. Bromiley; 10 vols; Grand Rapids: Eerdmans, 1970), pp. 8.403–81 (409); Collins, *Daniel*, pp. 284–86.

most positive reception is that argued by Collins for a Canaanite background based on recently published texts from Ugarit[93] regarding the conflict between Ba'al and Yamm (Sea), in which Ba'al is aided by the craftsman Kotar-wa-Hassis.[94] Following O. Eissfeldt,[95] Collins notes *CTA* 2.4: 'Truly I say to you, O Prince Ba'al, I repeat [to you], O Rider of the Clouds (תפר:בכרל:תנת): Behold your enemy, Ba'al, behold, your enemy you will smite, behold you will smite your foe. You will take your everlasting kingdom, your dominion forever and ever.'[96]

Although there are a limited number of distinctive features between the Ugaritic texts and Daniel 7 (*four* beasts, beast defeated in judiciary court rather than slain in combat), the similarities of (1) sea, (2) the rider on clouds, as well as (3) the theme of the inheritance of everlasting dominion suggest that 'the old story has been given a new literary form, and adapted to fit a new historical situation'.[97]

The majority of the beastly vision and interpretation in Daniel 7 is devoted to the enigmatic fourth beast (7.7-8, 19-27). Distinctive elements include the iron teeth (cf. 2.40), and the ten horns representing power.[98] Casey argues that these horns refer to the Seleucid line: (1) Alexander the Great; (2) Seleucus I Nicator; (3) Antiochus I Soter; (4) Antiochus II Theos; (5) Seleucus II Calilinicus; (6) Seleucus III Ceraunus; (7) Antiochus III the Great; (8) Seleucus IV Philopator; (9) Demetrius I Soter; and (10) Antiochus younger son of Seleucus IV.[99] The latter three were suppressed by Antiochus Epiphanes.[100] Regarding the identity of the 'little horn', Casey notes that its 'identification as Antiochus Epiphanes is rightly unquestioned among serious critical scholars'.[101]

In the subsequent throne vision (7.9-14),[102] although we are not told how or by whom the beast is slain, it is evident that the Son of Man's

---

93   CTA 1–6; KTU 1.1-6.

94   Collins, *Daniel*, p. 287.

95   O. Eissfeldt, *Baal Zaphon, Zeus Kasios und der Durchzug der Israeliten durchs Meer* (Halle: Niemeyer, 1932), pp. 25–30.

96   Also see discussions in Day, *Conflict*, p. 13; F. M. Cross, *Canaanite Myth and Hebrew Epic* (Cambridge: Harvard University Press, 1973), pp. 118–19.

97   J. J. Collins, 'Stirring up the Great Sea: The Religio-Historic Background in Daniel 7', in *Seers, Sybils and Sages in Hellenistic-Roman Judaism*, ed. J. J. Collins (Leiden: Brill), pp. 139–56 (146). A. A. Bevan, *A Short Commentary on the Book of Daniel* (Cambridge: Cambridge University Press, 1892), p. 122; Hartmann and DiLella, *Daniel*, p. 213 et al. have argued that the third beast is to be understood as Persia. Its four heads are explained as the four kings (Dan. 11.2). Montgomery, *Daniel*, p. 290 notes that the reference to wings as the four corners of the earth refers to the immeasurable spread of the Persian Empire. As Collins notes, universal rule was also 'predicated of the third kingdom in Dan. 2.39', Collins, *Daniel*, p. 298.

98   Zechariah 2.1-4; Ps. 92.10; 132.17-18; *1 En.* 90.9; 1QSb 5.26.

99   Casey, *Son*, p. 20.

100 Casey, *Son*, pp. 20–21.

101 Casey, *Son*, p. 20.

102 Cf. 1 Kgs 22.19; Isa. 6; Ezek. 1; 3.22-24; 10.1; *1 En.* 14.18-23; 60.2; 90.20.

presence means the defeat of the beastly enemies of Israel.[103] S. Mowinckel argues that the text of Daniel 7 has the Son of Man figure 'play a part in the judgement'.[104] Mowinckel finds justification for his argument in that within the vision, '"thrones (plural) were placed": but afterward only one (the Ancient of Days) is mentioned as taking his seat'.[105] The additional throne, it is argued, is for the Son of Man to bestow judgement from. Mowinckel concludes that 'the retention of the plural, "thrones," shows that, in the original conception, the one in human form took part in the judgement … He was thought of as sharing God's throne.'[106] Casey, however, argues that this resolution of the plural of thrones in v. 9b should be doubted because 'this left him [the author] with nowhere for the court to sit'.[107] In response to Casey, it should be noted that if this were the case, the reader/hearer is left with the awkward image of the entire divine court huddled on one throne. The absence of such heavenly furniture does not pose a problem for Job 1 or Ps. 82, both of which envision a divine court. Thus we may concur with Collins when he argues that the plural thrones in 7.9 would naturally invite the interpretation that one was for the Son of Man. It is then only a short exegetical inference to consider that the Son of Man had a role in the judgement sequence,[108] and 'since the "one like a son of man" receives dominion after the death of the beast, it is reasonable to assume that he has in some way triumphed over it'.[109]

Despite the fact that Collins claims that 'there is nearly universal consensus that the phrase "one like a son of man" means simply "one like a human being,"'[110] he readily concedes that there is no discernible homogeneous

---

103 It is important to note that Dan. 7.13 does not indicate 'whether the figure is ascending, descending or moving horizontally', Collins, *Daniel*, p. 311. This is significant to our above discussion on the presence (παρουσία) of the Son of Man in Matthew 24. The OG of Dan. 7.13 has 'he came as the ancient of days', reading ως for εως. However, if the OG is accurate, there is an awkward element in that there is no other figure for the Ancient of Days to be presented to. The divergent manuscript tradition at the point seems to be a scribal oversight.

104 Mowinckel, *Cometh*, p. 352.

105 Mowinckel, *Cometh*, p. 352. In Ps. 122.5 and 11Q17 *Songs of the Sabbath Sacrifice* (2.1.9, 'the thrones of his glory'), multiple thrones seem to refer to the court (v. 10) sitting in judgement. Collins, *Daniel*, p. 301 suggests that the background to this image 'lies in ancient traditions about the council of 'El, where the gods sit on their "princely thrones,"' Collins, *Daniel*, p. 301, citing *CTA* 2.1.19-27; Cross, *Myth*, p. 98. In Matthew a similar image occurs in 19.28; cf. Rev. 20.4.

106 Mowinckel, *Cometh*, p. 352. Rabbi Akiba resolved the difficulty of two thrones in a messianic sense: 'One for Him (i.e. God) and one for David (i.e. the Messiah)', *b.Hag* 14a; *b.Sanh.* 38b). Also see discussion in A. Segal, *Two Powers in Heaven: Early Rabbinic Reports about Christianity and Gnosticism* (Leiden: Brill, 1977), p. 38.

107 Casey, *Son*, p. 23.

108 Collins, *Daniel*, p. 81.

109 Collins, 'Stirring', p. 146.

110 Collins, *Daniel*, p. 304.

philological concept.[111] There are, in fact, various possibilities, of which one commends itself as most probable in the context of Daniel 7, namely that of 'a messiah warrior figure'.

The 'Son of Man' as a messianic figure has been frequently argued by commentators.[112] The primary rationale for this view has been found in the generalized symbolism of the chapter. Just as the beasts are interpreted as symbols for various pagan nations, so too is the 'Son of Man' representative of his kingdom. Such is the case in Ps. 8, which has frequently been interpreted messianically due to the royal themes within.[113] J. J. Collins, however, objects: 'the decisive objection against the messianic interpretation is that nowhere in the book do we find either support for or interest in the Davidic monarchy'.[114] In response to this it should be noted that Israel's national vindication was a key concept in the earlier chapters of Daniel, and indeed the opening verses portray Israel's exile as the historical background to the ensuing dramas. Collins also objects that the 'Son of Man' is never attributed the title 'Messiah'.[115] However, any figure who liberates Israel from her political enemies and is described as having 'dominion', 'glory', and 'kingship' (Dan. 7.14) has clear messianic overtones.

In this light we may conclude as follows with regard to the 'Son of Man' figure in Daniel 7. In the Genesis creation story, human beings exercise dominion over the beasts of the field. The picture in Daniel 7 inverts this and presents humanity struggling for integrity while being ruled by beastly empires. The ultimate defeat of Israel's enemies is thus presented as a parabolic echo of Genesis where right order is restored in human–beastly relations. In this regard Casey concludes that 'the author made use of the traditional Israelite idea that man is superior to the beasts, an idea which is expressed with great clarity in the creation narrative of Gen. 1 and in Ps. 8.6-8'.[116]

---

111 Proposals include (1) Judas Maccabee (G. Archer, *Jerome's Commentary on Daniel* [Grand Rapids: Baker, 1958], pp. 80–81; H. Sahlin, 'Antiochus IV Epiphanes und Judas Mackabäus', *StTh* 23 [1969], pp. 41–68); (2) Daniel cf. Dan. 8.17 (H. Schmid, 'Daniel der Menschensohn', *Judaica* 27 [1971], pp. 192–221); (3) a collective symbol to be equated with the holy ones, i.e. God's people; (4) an angelic being; or (5) not to be invested with theological significance (G. Vermes, 'The Use of *bar nash/bar nasha* in Jewish Aramaic', in *An Aramaic Approach to the Gospels and Acts*, ed. M. Black [Oxford: Clarendon Press, 1967], pp. 310–28; G. Vermes, 'The "Son of Man" Debate', *JSNT* 1 [1978], 19–32).

112 Koch, *Daniel*, pp. 217–18; H. Gese, 'Die Bedeutung der Krise unter Antiochus IV. Epiphanes für die Apokalyptik des Danielbuches', *ZTK* 80 (1983), pp. 373–88 (380).

113 P. G. Mosca, 'Ugarit and Daniel 7: A Missing Link', *Bib* 67 (1986), pp. 496–517 (516).

114 Collins, *Daniel*, p. 309.

115 Collins, *Daniel*, p. 309.

116 Casey, *Son*, p. 25. Cf. Daniel 4 and the story of Nebuchadnezzar's beastly transformation.

In relation to the points made above regarding the mutually interpretive nature of chs 2 and 7,[117] Collins has argued against such parallelism on the basis of differing emphases. Whereas ch. 7 presents the fourth kingdom as a more severe threat than the ones preceding it, in ch. 2 'the emphasis on strength here initially ignores the theme of decline'.[118] Additionally, Collins argues that the vision in ch 2 does not present Israel's situation as urgent. Daniel serves those to whom Yahweh has given power, for the time being. 'Consequently, the author tones down the revolutionary implication of the four-kingdom schema by placing it in a context where its fulfilment does not appear imminent ... Eschatology is not denied but deferred.'[119] M. Casey, however, validly highlights that 'none of this is sufficient to upset the basic literary structure ... Dan. 2 and 7 broadly correspond in all important matters; there is no reason to imagine that they should have corresponded at the level of more precise detail.'[120] While Collins provides a helpful insight, it is important to remember that one of the key features in the vision in ch. 2 is that the pagan kingdoms *are* transitory. Collins' analysis, however, does not seem to give due weight to the function of both the visions. Both Daniel 2 and 7 present a reality which envisions that even the current human powers and world empires will be made subject to the rule of Yahweh. The emphasis is on wholesale final defeat and vindication rather than differences in minutiae. Casey thus concludes that the dreams in chs 2 and 7 contribute to 'embodying the four kingdom theory, according to which, the destruction of the fourth world kingdom will be followed by the divinely ordained triumph of the kingdom of God'.[121]

Nebuchadnezzar's vision in Daniel 2 consists of a frightening statue (v. 31) with a head of gold (v. 32a), chest and arms of silver (v. 32b), middle and thighs of bronze (v. 32c), legs of iron (v. 33a), and feet partly iron and partly clay (v. 33b). This imposing figure is destroyed by a stone (v. 34) which strikes the statue on the lower part, then itself becomes a great mountain and fills the whole earth (v. 35).[122] The interpretation granted to Daniel understands the various metals as being representative of various successive pagan kingdoms (vv. 36-45).[123]

---

117 In summary these are (1) four kingdom schema; (2) similar reception of vision; and (3) numeric elements paralleled within the vision.

118 Collins, *Daniel*, p. 170.

119 Collins, *Daniel*, p. 175.

120 Casey, *Son*, p. 9.

121 Casey, *Son*, p. 7. Casey also notes that Daniel 7 has a narrative framework which corresponds to Dan. 2.1-30, 46-49. Casey, *Son*, p. 8.

122 In Daniel's prayer of thanks and praise in response to God's revelation of King Nebuchadnezzar's dream, 2.21 includes the following: 'He changes times and seasons, deposes (μεθιστῶν) kings and sets up kings.' This periodization of history encourages the reader that there is some measure of determinism in the cosmic order and that world events are ordained by God and expressed by the visionary. See Collins, *Daniel*, pp. 55, 352–53.

123 In regard to the imagery in Nebuchadnezzar's dream, Collins, *Daniel*, p. 163 notes various parallels in ANE in regard to the statue and the metals as representative

Although the stone has normally been interpreted as the Maccabaean state,[124] there has been some debate as to how the successive empires are to be understood. The traditional view from antiquity has been (1) Babylon; (2) Medea; (3) Persia; and (4) Greece. In support of this are the narratives in Maccabees, especially 1 Macc. 1.54, where the 'abomination of desolation' is correlated with successions of kingdoms and the action of Antiochus. This progression was also the view of the Syrian church in Antioch, and Porphyry seems to have depended on Syrian interpretation as a way of refuting claims by others. Moreover, modern commentators have noted that the progression in the book of Daniel implies this fourfold structure. Stories relating to Nebuchadnezzar and Belshazzar give way to Darius the Mede, and then Cyrus the Persian. The focus subsequently shifts to the Greeks. Additionally, the content of 2.36-45 coheres well with the known histories of the corresponding empires.[125] The image of mixed iron and clay fits well into the Seleucid and Ptolemaic divide with the Greek empire, with the Seleucids having greater military strength than the Ptolemies.[126] In this way, ch. 2 prepares the reader for the expanded and more explicit vision of the defeat of Israel's enemies in ch. 7.[127]

of kingdoms which are to come; for example, Hesiod *Works and Days* 1.109–201; *BahmanYashi* 1, originally noted by F. Delitzsch, 'Daniel', *Realencyklopädie für protestantische Theologie und Kirche* 3 [1855], pp. 271–87. Also cf. *Lev. Rab.* 13.5; Gen. 2.10; and the river from Eden.

124 Other interpreters (E. F. Siegman, 'The Stone Hewn from the Mountain (Daniel 2)', *CBQ* 18 [1956], pp. 364–79; J. Steinman, *Daniel: Text français, introduction et commentaries* [Bruges: Desclée de Brouwer, 1961], p. 53) have taken the stone with reference to Jesus and the relevant New Testament material (Mk 12.10-11; Mt. 21.42; Lk. 20.17-18; 1 Pet. 2.7). The messianic interpretation is also extant in rabbinic literature; for example, *4 Ezra* 13 where the man from the sea carves out a mountain which is identified as Zion.

125 Regarding the inter-dynastic marriage between Ptolemies and Seleucids in Dan. 2.43, most commentators either refer to Antiochus II and Berenice (252 BC) or that of Ptolemy Epiphanes to Cleopatra (daughter of Antiochus III, 193–92 BC (cf. Dan. 11.6; 17).

126 The second way of understanding the progression of empires is (1) Babylon; (2) Medea/Persia; (3) Greece; and (4) Rome. The association of Rome with the fourth kingdom is first attested in *4 Ezra*. However, in Daniel 2, the history of the Roman Empire does not correspond as well to the details mentioned above. The text of *4 Ezra* acknowledges that Rome as the fourth kingdom is a new interpretation. In this light, the beastly kingdom destroyed is that of Antiochus Epiphanes IV. However, it is important to note that *4 Ezra* 13–14 is commonly taken as a reference to Daniel 7.

127 In further association between chs 2 and 7 it can be noted that the first beast (a lion with wings which becomes a man [Dan. 7.4]) can be compared to the first kingdom in Daniel 2 as Nebuchadnezzar is described as a lion in Jer. 4.7; 49.19; 50.17 and his army as eagles Hab. 1.8; Ezek. 17.3. Various commentators, as early as Hippolytus and Jerome, saw this transformation between lion/eagle to man related to Nebuchadnezzar's restoration in Daniel 4 (Kvanvig, *Apocalyptic*, p. 487).

Although the 'Son of Man' tradition is conspicuously absent from the Qumran literature, it did play an important role in other Jewish traditions, particularly *1 Enoch* and *4 Ezra*.[128] Within *1 Enoch*, the 'Son of Man' figure appears within chs 37-71, that is, the *Similitudes of Enoch*. Of particular importance for our own discussion is the role assumed in ch. 46 (the second parable). C. Caragounis has argued at length that one of the most prominent roles of the Son of Man in *1 Enoch* is that of judge.[129] Not only is this a prominent feature in ch. 46, but the Son of Man's judgement of kings, the mighty and the strong is also prominent in later sections of the work, in particular 62.1-3, 5, 9 and 69.26c-29.[130] Although we will find reason to disagree with Caragounis regarding the implications of these findings for the interpretation of the Gospels,[131] he validly highlights one of the main roles/functions of the Son of Man in *1 Enoch*, that is, executer of judgement. *Pace* P. M. Casey who argues that within *1 Enoch* 'the "Son of Man" would naturally be read as the equivalent of "man"',[132] J. J. Collins suggests that this is not a warranted conclusion on the basis of two considerations. First, apocalyptic literature often employs this figure as representative (cf. angel in Dan. 8.15; 9.21; 10.5; 12.6), and second, the phrase is generally considered to be an allusion to Daniel 7, wherein it is something more than a 'man'.[133] Collins concludes that 'whenever the expression "Son of Man" is repeated, it is not simply equivalent to "the figure you saw" but also implies that this figure carries the eschatological associations of Daniel 7'.[134]

---

128 Collins, *Daniel*, p. 79 n.38 dates the *Similitudes* before the mid first century because 'it is difficult to imagine that a Jewish author would have made such use of "Son of Man" after it had become a title of Jesus, or that a Christian author would have identified Enoch with the Son of Man (*1 En.* 71.14). Accordingly a date before the middle of the first century is highly probable.' E. Isaac, '1 (Ethiopic Apocalypse of) Enoch', in *The Old Testament Pseudepigrapha*, ed. J. H. Charlesworth (2 vols; London: Darton, Longman & Todd, 1983), pp. 1.5–89 (7), argues for a date somewhere between 105 and 64 BC.

129 C. Caragounis, *The Son of Man* (Tübingen: Mohr, 1986), pp. 116–20. Other roles include (1) vindicator; (2) universal ruler; (3) revealer; and (4) object of worship.

130 The obvious dual motif here is also the vindication of the righteous who have been oppressed by the kings and the mighty. See also 1 En. 48.4; 62.12; 71.17

131 When Caragounis, *Son*, p. 117 states in regard to the *Similitudes of Enoch*, 'The mentality of the author of the *Parables* is quite different from that found in the Gospels,' this prejudices any discussion of the Gospel texts. In favour of Enochic and Matthean similarities are (1) terminology; (2) date; and (3) similar contexts of judgement. We will return to this issue below.

132 Casey, 'Enoch', pp. 14–18; Casey, *Son*, pp. 100–102.

133 Collins, *Imagination*, p. 184. Additionally, it can be noted that when the 'Son of Man' is introduced it is qualified with 'this/that Son of Man' or 'the son of man who ...', the only exception to this being 69.27. Some commentators have suggested that this indicates that the text refers to a previously mentioned or known figure. However, as G. W. E. Nickelsburg, 'Son of Man', in *Anchor Bible Dictionary*, ed. D. N. Freedman (New York: Doubleday, 1992), pp. 4.137–150 (139) has noted, 'as is often the case in Ethiopic, which has no definite article, the demonstratives "this" and "that," very likely reproduce the article in the earlier Greek form of the Parables'.

134 Collins, *Imagination*, p. 184. For the use of Daniel in relation to other Hebrew

Also important for our discussion is the figure of the 'Son of Man' in *4 Ezra*.[135] *Fourth Ezra* 3-14 is a Jewish apocalypse composed towards the end of the first century AD,[136] consisting of seven visions.[137] Although the exact terminology 'Son of Man' is not attested within the sixth vision (13.1-58), there does appear 'something like the figure of a man' (v. 3) rising from the sea. *Fourth Ezra* 13.1-3 states:

> After seven days I dreamed a dream in the night; and behold, a wind arose from the sea and stirred up all its waves. And I looked, and behold, this wind made something like the figure of a man come up out of the heart of the sea. And I looked, and behold, that man flew with the clouds of heaven; and wherever he turned his face to look, everything under his gaze trembled.

The vast majority of commentators have seen this figure as closely associated with the 'Son of Man' figure in Daniel 7,[138] and influential in this regard is *4 Ezra*'s knowledge and use of Daniel in 12.11-12: 'The eagle which you saw coming up from the sea is the fourth kingdom which appeared in a vision to your brother Daniel. But it was not explained to him as I now explain or have explained it to you.' Of particular significance for our own discussion is the representation of the 'Son of Man' as 'judge'. In *4 Ezra* 13 it is announced that 'all those who were gathered against him to wage war with him' (v. 8) are annihilated without the 'Son of Man' lifting 'his hand, nor holding a spear nor any weapon of war' (v. 9). The enemies are annihilated when the 'Son of Man' 'sends forth from his mouth as it were a stream of fire, and from his lips a flaming breath, and from his tongue he shot forth

Bible allusions in *1 En.* 46–47 see G. K. Beale, *The Use of Daniel in Jewish Apocalyptic Literature and in the Revelation of St.John* (Lanham: University Press of America, 1984), pp. 97–100.

135 It is generally accepted by contemporary scholarship that *4 Ezra.* was originally composed in a Semitic language. Collins, *Daniel*, p. 82 argues for Hebrew, and Kvanvig, *Apocalyptic*, p. 521 for Aramaic. It is currently extant predominantly in the Latin and Ethiopic traditions.

136 H. H. Rowley, *The Relevance of Apocalyptic* (London: Lutterworth Press, 1947), p. 115; Russell, *Method*, p. 63; B. Metzger, *An Introduction to the Apocrypha* (Oxford: Oxford University Press, 1957), p. 22.

137 3.1–5.20; 5.21–6.34; 6.35–9.25; 9.26–10.59; 11.1–12.51; 13.1-58; 14.1-48.

138 Collins, *Imagination*, pp. 142–54, 210–12; Collins, *Daniel*, p. 82; Caragounis, *Son*, pp. 119–20; Casey, *Son*, pp. 122–29; Stone, *Ezra*, pp. 383–87. Although note the dissenting voice of Kvanvig, *Apocalyptic*, pp. 522–23 who finds stronger parallel with *4 Ezra* to the Akkadian *Vision of the Netherworld*. Collins, *Daniel*, p. 83, however, has shown how 'very forced' the proposed parallels are. Association between Daniel and Ezra seems to have influenced the rabbinic interpretation to identify the 'Son of Man' as a messianic figure; *b.Sanh* 98a; *Num. Rab.* 13.14; '*Aggadat Ber 'esit* 14.3; 23.1. See further discussion in Casey, *Son*, p. 80; Caragounis, *Son*, p. 131–36; W. Horbury, 'The Messianic Associations of "The Son of Man",' *JTS* 36 (1985), pp. 34–55.

a storm of sparks' (v. 10).[139] Verse 11 summarizes this as follows:

> All these were mingled together, the stream of fire and flaming breath and the great storm, and fell on the onrushing multitude which was prepared to fight, and burned them all up, so that suddenly nothing was seen of the innumerable multitude but only the dust of ashes and the smell of smoke ...

As the subsequent interpretation makes clear, the 'Son of Man' functions with strong overtones of the warrior motif:

> And he, my Son, shall reprove the assembled nations for their ungodliness (this was symbolized by the storm), and will reproach them to their face with their evil thoughts and with the torments with which they are to be tortured (which were symbolized by the flames); and he will destroy them without effort by the law (which was symbolized by the fire).[140]

As is evident from numerous examples, fire often indicates the divine destruction of enemies. Psalm 97.2-3 notes that 'Clouds and thick darkness are all around him; righteousness and justice are the foundation of his throne. Fire goes before him, and consumes his adversaries on every side.' Similar is 2 Sam. 22.9 which states 'Smoke went up from his nostrils, and devouring fire from his mouth; glowing coals flamed forth from him.' Caragounis concludes that these 'ideas ... confirm most conclusively the Son of Man's ... function as Judge'.[141]

4.4.a. Preliminary conclusion

The purpose of our discussion thus far has not been to solve every exegetical riddle of Daniel 7, but rather to sketch the appropriate background necessary to understand why Matthew may have explicitly directed the reader to the book of Daniel. Our above analysis has established that Daniel as a whole had a significant influence on the Gospel of Matthew as a whole and ch. 24 in particular. Daniel is presented within the literary context of the Babylonian exile, and ch. 7 has functioned as a crucial point in the development of the plot – Israel's enemies are destroyed and 'burnt with fire' (Dan. 7.11) by the coming/going of the

---

139 Cf. Dan. 7.11, 'and its body destroyed and given over to be burned with fire'. Also cf. 'the mountain' in 4 Ez. 13.6 with Dan. 2.45.

140 Vv. 37-39. Also see 12.32-33, where the 'The Anointed one ... will ... speak with them, upbraid them for their wickedness, condemn them for their injustices, and confront them directly with their insults. First he will present them alive for judgement, and then, after upbraiding them, he will destroy them.'

141 Caragounis, *Son*, p. 131. For further discussion of the Son of Man as judge see N. Perrin, 'The Son of Man in Ancient Judaism and Primitive Christianity: A Suggestion', *BR* 11 (1963), pp. 17–28 (23); Jeremias, *Theology*, p. 268; A. J. B. Higgins, *The Son of Man in the Teaching of Jesus* (Cambridge: Cambridge University Press, 1980), p. 8.

Son of Man. Furthermore, there are several indications that the close parallel of Daniel 9 and 11, to the Maccabaean history in the second century BC, identifies the main opponent as Antiochus IV Epiphanes. Further analysis demonstrated that the 'abomination of desolation' is not associated with pagan altars erected in honour of Zeus, but rather to the idolatrous and inappropriate behaviour of Antiochus' forces in the temple. In confirmation of our former discussion on the genitive construction in Matthew, the שִׁקּוּץ מְשֹׁמֵם/שִׁקּוּצִים מְשֹׁמֵם was found to have a factitive sense. Therefore the contribution to our discussion in relation to Matthew is relatively clear: Matthew makes more explicit what Mark leaves implicit, that the 'abomination' (at least in Daniel) is to be identified with Antiochus IV Epiphanes. In our next section we will investigate where this language has prior attestation in the Hebrew Bible and how this contributes to Matthew's unique reworking of both these traditions.

4.5. Relevant Prophetic Texts as Background for the Abomination of Desolation

The following section will seek to establish three matters concerning our discussion thus far. First, that the language of βδέλυγμα/שִׁקּוּצִים (abomination) and ἐρήμωσις/מְשֹׁמֵם (desolation) is attested in the prophetic literature and used in the description (i.e. abomination) and consequence (i.e. desolation) of Israel's covenantal infidelity. Second, to demonstrate the pervasive and thoroughgoing influence of the prophetic tradition on the book of Daniel. Third, that these two issues potentially provided Matthew with the theological trajectory and impetus to employ the Danielic material ironically in description of the destruction of Jerusalem in Matthew 24.

4.5.a. Prophetic literature

Although other examples could be generated, for the following discussion we have focused attention upon Isaiah, Jeremiah, and Ezekiel.[142] As noted in our discussion above, these examples are rarely, if ever, mentioned by commentators on the phrase βδέλυγμα τῆς ἐρημώσεως in Daniel or Matthew because the phrase is expected verbatim. However, if the natural literary division of the relevant pericope is taken into account, that is, a unit delimited by syntactical markers, or a scene, plot or narrative change of some sort, with appropriate attention to vocabulary, there are significant results. We have no interest in challenging the valuable caution and critique offered by J. Barr in the opening years of

---

142 For other possible examples see discussion of Jeremiah 7 in chapter 3 above.

the 1960s.[143] Barr's contributions stand firm. The approach that we are suggesting which may prove fruitful, is one which keeps a keen eye on the manner in which significant terminology is used in conjunction *within* a pericope or natural literary division. That is, examples of similar description of Israel's behaviour as an 'abomination' (βδέλυγμα) and the consequent punishment as 'desolation' (ἐρήμωσις). The reason this is necessary for the exegesis of the passage is that it does greater justice to the unity of the work's final literary form. The importance of this approach is highlighted by W. Kaiser when he states:

> Words belong to sentences, and sentences usually belong to paragraphs, scenes, strophes, or larger units within the grammar of a genre. This is why I urge ... never take less than a full paragraph, or its literary equivalent (e.g., a scene, a strophe, or the like), as a basis. The reason is clear: Only the full paragraph, or its equivalent, contains the full idea or concept of that text. To split off some of its parts is to play with the text as it could be bent in any fashion in order to accomplish what we think is best.[144]

4.5.a.i. Isaiah 1.7-17

The opening chapter of Isaiah's work presents Yahweh's lawsuit concerning Israel as rebellious child and Yahweh as disappointed father.[145] The litigation includes the customary witnesses (v. 2a), litigant (v. 2b), charges (vv. 2c-3), and the accused (v. 3c).[146] The witnesses summoned are none less than the created order itself (i.e. the 'heavens'[147] and 'earth'), a rhetorical effect that strengthens the charge. H. Wildberger suggests that Yahweh summoned these powers as 'those who had witnessed the ratification of the covenant [and] are also witnesses who attest that the covenant has been violated'.[148] J. Blenkinsopp argues that this legal setting is 'suggestive of the indictment or arraignment following covenant violation',[149] and is supported by the use of the

---

143 J. Barr, *The Semantics of Biblical Language* (Oxford: Oxford University Press, 1961). One of Barr's most significant contributions was his 'root-fallacy' critique, wherein he argued against 'that of supposing that the root of a word is necessarily determinative of its meaning throughout its history and that the root-meaning links it semantically with all other words of the same root', N. W. Porteous, 'The Present State of Old Testament Theology', *ET* (1963), pp. 70–74 (71). Barr would not, of course 'deny that in many cases the etymology of a word does indeed furnish an important clue for determining its meaning', Porteous, 'Present', p. 71.

144 W. Kaiser, *Preaching and Teaching From the Old Testament* (Grand Rapids: Baker Academic, 2003), p. 54.

145 For a similar theme see Isa. 3.12-15; 5.1-7.

146 See G. E. Mendenhall, 'Ancient Oriental and Biblical Law', *BA* 17.2 (1952), pp. 26–46; H. B. Huffmon, 'The Covenant Lawsuit', *JBL* 78 (1959), pp. 285–95.

147 The Mt. has the plural שָׁמַיִם, whereas the LXX has the singular οὐρανέ.

148 H. Wildberger, *Isaiah 1–12* (Minneapolis: Fortress Press, 1991), p. 10. For similar judgement speeches see Deut. 32.1; 31.28; Mic. 6.2; Ps. 50.4.

149 J. Blenkinsopp, *Isaiah 1–39* (London: Doubleday, 2000), p. 182.

verb פָּשְׁעוּ ('rebelled') in the description of Israel's infidelity, as 'it fits the parent-child analogy as well as it does the king-subject pattern'.[150] Vivid illustration is then offered in presenting Israel as more ignorant than an ox or a donkey. Although these household animals are able to remember to whom they belong, Israel is incapable: 'The ox knows its owner, and the donkey its master's crib; but Israel does not know, my people do not understand.'[151]

Verse 4 has commonly been identified as a 'woe speech'.[152] J. D. W. Watts has demonstrated that the metre is intentionally uneven for emphasis.[153] A. S. Herbert has contributed to this discussion by noting that the opening word (הוֹי) is typical of funeral laments (cf. Jer. 22.18), and in this way 'Isaiah sees the nation as virtually dead because they have forsaken the living God'.[154]

Important for our discussion are the consequences of this rebellion, which are described in vv. 7-9 as 'your country lies desolate (שְׁמָמָה/ἔρημος)' because it has been devoured by aliens (v. 7); it is a besieged city and partly compared to Sodom and Gomorrah (v. 9). This language is particularly relevant as it 'comes from a setting within the context of blessings and threats of curses which are found in the covenantal tradition'.[155] Regarding the reversal of judgement, it is noteworthy that 'what had once happened to their enemies when Israel was still under the blessing of Yahweh was now happening to them, as part of the curse'.[156] Although J. Hayes and S. Irvine have argued that this imagery is that of an earthquake,[157] their analysis has failed to convince the majority of scholars who clearly see the hostile military overtones of the countryside devastated and cities burnt.[158] There has consequently been much debate as to which military invasion vv. 7-9 speak of. Wildberger claims that the historical referent behind these verses 'can be determined with great accuracy'[159] to that of the siege of the city by Sennacherib in the year 701 BC (cf. 2 Kgs 18.13-16). Although this is

---

150 J. D. W. Watts, *Isaiah 1–33* (Waco: Word, 1985), p. 16. Gen. 31.36; Exod. 22.8; 23.21; 34.7; Lev. 16.16, 21; Num. 14.18; Josh. 24.19; 1 Sam. 24.12; 25.28; 1 Kgs 8.50; Lam. 1.5, 14, 22; Dan. 8.12-13; 9.24.

151 Cf. Num. 22.21-30, where Baalam's donkey has more insight than Balaam.

152 J. Hayes, *Old Testament Form Criticism* (San Antonio: Trinity University Press, 1974), p. 164. See other woes in Isaiah 5, 10 culminating at 10.25.

153 Watts, *Isaiah 1–33*, pp. 16. The seven key words of the speech are presented as three pairs, with one to summarize their effect at the end. See Watts, *Isaiah 1–33*, p. 18.

154 Herbert, *Isaiah*, p. 26.

155 Wildberger, *Isaiah 1–12*, p. 27. Cf. Exod. 23.29; Lev. 26.33; Deut. 38.27. Also see Isa. 6.11; 17.9.

156 Wildberger, *Isaiah 1–12*, p. 28. For Canaanite cities destroyed by fire, Wildberger notes Josh. 6.24 (Jericho), Josh. 8.28 (Ai), and Josh. 11.11, 13 (Hazor).

157 J. Hayes and S. Irvine, *Isaiah the Eighth-Century Prophet: His Times and His Preaching* (Nashville: Abingdon, 1987), pp. 69–73.

158 Blenkinsopp, *Isaiah 1–39*, p. 182.

159 Wildberger, *Isaiah 1–12*, p. 21.

the most plausible contender,[160] it is also evident that the description could refer to a number of historical catastrophes.[161] Verses 10-15 then go on to castigate Israel for the abhorrence of her religious practices. In v. 13, *Israel's* inappropriate temple activity is described as '[your] incense is an abomination[162] (βδέλυγμα) to me'.[163]

The importance and significance of this analysis is strengthened by how commentators have seen Isaiah 1 functioning in the context of and relationship to the entire work. G. Fohrer[164] argued that Isaiah 1 served as a *Zusammenfassung* (compendium) of Isaianic thought, presenting the salient message of the book as a 'foyer' to the rest of the work.[165] To use the words of D. Carson in a different context, this has the effect of 'simultaneously drawing the reader in and introducing the major themes'.[166] In similar fashion R. E. Clements suggested Isaiah 1 functions as a 'general preface and guide'.[167] H. G. M. Williamson has reinforced this hypothesis by demonstrating the parallels between 1.2b-3 and 30.9; 1.4 and 5.7; and 1.5-9 and 30.15-17.[168] As such, any theme in the opening part of Isaiah should be given special attention, all the more if similar vocabulary (ἔρημος and βδέλυγμα) is employed in subsequent prophetic literature.[169]

4.5.a.ii. Jeremiah

Jeremiah's reckoning of the cause for Jerusalem's destruction is clearly expressed in several important passages throughout his work.[170]

---

160 J. A. Emerton, 'The Historical Background of Isaiah 1:4-9', in *Avraham Malamat Volume*, ed. S. Ahituv and B. A. Levine (Jerusalem: Israel Exploration Society), pp. 34–40.

161 Childs, *Isaiah*, p. 16.

162 Most commentators have taken 'incense' (קְטֹרֶת/θυμίαμα) in the absolute state and 'abomination' (βδέλυγμα / תּוֹעֵבָה) as predicate. However, one could also take תּוֹעֵבָה קְטֹרֶת to be in a construct relationship (Wildberger, *Isaiah 1–12*, p. 35), which would have the meaning 'it is an abominable offering to me'.

163 Although a different Hebrew root is used in this example (תּוֹעֵבָה), comparison can be made on the basis of the Greek word in the LXX (cf. Mt. 24.15). For the Matthean preference of the LXX in Old Testament citations see M. J. J. Menken, *Matthew's Bible* (Leuven: Peeters, 2004). One important exception is Isa. 53.4 in Mt. 8.17. We are not, however, presuming a fixed textual form of the LXX in the first century, rather only pointing out that Matthew predominantly sides with what we know as the LXX rather than the Mt. in citation and allusion.

164 G. Fohrer, 'Jesaja 1 als Zusammenfassung der Verkündigung Jesajas', *BZAW* 99 (1967), pp. 148–66.

165 D. A. Carson, *The Gospel According to John* (Leicester: IVP, 1991), p. 111 uses a similar phrase in description of the prologue of John.

166 Carson, *John*, p. 111.

167 R. E. Clements, *Isaiah 1–39* (Grand Rapids: Eerdmans, 1980), p. 21.

168 H. G. M. Williamson, 'Relocating Isaiah 1:2-9', in *Writing and Reading the Scroll of Isaiah*, ed. C. C. Broyles and C. A. Evans (Leiden: Brill), pp. 263–77 (164–65).

169 See further discussion in J. Jensen, *The Use of Torah by Isaiah. His Debate with the Wisdom Tradition* (Washington, DC: Catholic Biblical Association, 1973), pp. 68–84.

170 Note, however, that some have attributed the following passages to Deuteronomistic redaction.

Jeremiah 5.19 notes that when people ask, '"Why has the Lord our God done all these things to us?" the response will be "As you have forsaken me and served foreign gods in your land, so you shall serve strangers in a land that is not yours."' Jeremiah 9.12-16 poses a similar rhetorical question, 'Why is the land ruined and laid waste like a wilderness (ἔρημος)?' The response given is that 'they have forsaken my law that I set before them, and have not obeyed my voice … but have stubbornly followed their own hearts and have gone after the Baals, as their ancestors taught them'. Further consequence is described in vivid exilic terminology: 'I will scatter them among nations that neither they nor their ancestors have known; and I will send the sword after them, until I have consumed them'. Jeremiah 16.10-11 states:

> 'Why has the Lord pronounced all this great evil against us? What is our iniquity? What is the sin that we have committed against the Lord our God?' … It is because your ancestors have forsaken me, says the Lord, and have gone after other gods and have served and worshipped them, and have forsaken me and have not kept my law.[171]

Of particular importance for our analysis are the no fewer than four passages within the book of Jeremiah in which Israel's covenantal infidelity is described as an 'abomination' (βδέλυγμα). Furthermore, within the same 'concept unit', Israel's consequent punishment for this disobedience is described as 'desolation' (ἐρήμωσις). This clearly illustrates that the application of such terminology in the context of an internal Jewish polemic was not unique to Matthew but, rather, well attested in the scriptural tradition.

4.5.a.ii.1. Jeremiah 4.1-7

Jeremiah 4 opens with an offer of hope to God's people in the form of multiple conditional clauses; vv. 1-2 state that 'If you return, O Israel, says the Lord, if you return to me, if you remove your abominations from my presence, and do not waver, and if you swear, "As the Lord lives!" then blessing will ensue, for both Israel and the nations.' It is important to note for our discussion, that the description of covenantal infidelity in 4.1b is described in similar vocabularic fashion to the Hebrew and Greek in Dan. 9.27 and Mt. 24.15 respectively: 'if you remove your abominations (שִׁקּוּצֶיךָ/βδελύγματα) from my presence …'.[172] Several commentators have seen this divine offer as Yahweh's response to the confession of the people in the last words of the previous chapter

---

171 Cf. Jer. 22.8-9.

172 D. R. Jones, *Jeremiah* (Grand Rapids: Eerdmans, 1992), p. 105 finds Canaanite sexual imagery behind this term in Jeremiah, particularly in light of Jer. 13.26. Here, however, it seems to have a more general sense of violation of Yahweh's covenant.

(3.22b-25).[173] Indeed, J. R. Lundbom entitles it a 'profound remedy'[174] for Israel's return to Yahweh. However, as becomes clear in the ensuing oracle, Yahweh's conditional offer is not accepted, and judgement ensues. The 'declaration of this disaster'[175] is expounded in 4.5-10, with the oracle comprising the poetic vv. 5-7.[176] H. Cunliffe-Jones summarizes this section as follows: 'the alarm is sounded. The destroyer from the north is on his way, and this is God's judgement on Israel.'[177] P. C. Craigie argues that in its present literary form 'the Northern foe was almost certainly identified as the Babylonian Empire',[178] and, as Lundbom has noted, 'this foe will carry out Yahweh's judgement against Judah for breach of covenant'.[179] The key clause for our analysis is found in v. 7: 'A lion has gone up from its thicket, a destroyer of nations has set out; he has gone out from his place to make your land a waste (ἐρήμωσιν/לְשַׁמָּה); your cities will be ruins without inhabitant.'[180] The image of a lion as Israel's enemy is a common metaphor,[181] and in at least two other prophetic works, Yahweh is portrayed as a lion attacking unfaithful Israel (Amos 3.8; Hos. 5.14).

Similar to our Isaianic conclusion, the importance of this oracle is enhanced by its functioning as a 'lead oracle'.[182] J. R. Lundbom suggests that just as Jer. 2.2b-3 functions as a 'lead oracle for the apostasy-repentance collection'[183] (2.1-3) and Ps. 1 is made a 'lead psalm' for the Psalter, so too does Jer. 4.5-10 become a 'lead oracle', thus enhancing the impact of Jeremiah's choice of vocabulary.

4.5.a.ii.2. Jeremiah 7.1–8.3

As was argued in chapter 3 of this book, if one searches for the relevant cognates within the same verse of the LXX, seven results are produced.[184]

---

173 J. M. Berridge, *Prophet, People, and the Word of Yahweh* (Zürich: EVZ-Verlag, 1970), pp. 168–69; W. Baumgartner, *Jeremiah's Poems of Lament* (Sheffield: Almond Press, 1988), pp. 88–89.

174 J. R. Lundbom, *Jeremiah 1–20* (New York: Doubleday, 1999), p. 327.

175 This is the title P. C. Craigie, *Jeremiah 1–25* (Dallas: Word Books, 1991), p. 70 gives Jer. 4.5-10.

176 Craigie, *Jeremiah 1–25*, p. 70.

177 H. Cunliffe-Jones, *The Book of Jeremiah* (Naperville: Northumberland Press, 1960), p. 65.

178 Craigie, *Jeremiah 1–25*, p. 72.

179 Lundbom, *Jeremiah 1–20*, p. 333.

180 Terminology from 4.6-7 is employed again in 10.22. 4.6-7: 'I am bringing from the north (מִצָּפוֹן/ἀπὸ βορρᾶ) ... to make ... a desolation (לְשַׁמָּה/ἐρήμωσιν), your cities (עָרַיִךְ/πόλεις)'; 10.22, 'it is coming ... from a land of the north (צָפוֹן/βορρᾶ) ... To make the cities (עָרֵי/πόλεις) ... a desolation (שְׁמָמָה/ἀφανισμὸν).'

181 Jeremiah 2.15; 5.6; Isa. 5.29; Ezek. 32.2. Although the image is also used in a positive Messianic sense in some sources (Rev. 5.5), in Jeremiah, however, this is clearly a context of negative judgement.

182 Lundbom, *Jeremiah 1–20*, p. 333.

183 Lundbom, *Jeremiah 1–20*, p. 333.

184 First Maccabees 1.54; Dan. 9.27; 11.31; 12.11; Hos. 9.10; Jer. 44.22; Ezek. 33.29.

However, if the context is broadened to the level of pericope or natural literary division, with attention to description of Israel's behaviour as an 'abomination' (βδέλυγμα) and the consequent punishment as 'desolation (ἐρήμωσις), one of the most explicit appears in Jeremiah 7: v. 10, 'and then come and stand before me in this house, which is called by my name, and say, "We are safe!" – only to go on doing all these abominations (βδελύγματα)?'; v. 30, 'For the people of Judah have done evil in my sight, says the Lord; they have set their abominations (βδελύγματα) in the house that is called by my name, defiling it'; v. 34, 'And I will bring to an end the sound of mirth and gladness, the voice of the bride and bridegroom in the cities of Judah and in the streets of Jerusalem; for the land shall become a waste (ἐρήμωσιν).' The significance of this chapter in Jeremiah for our discussion should not be underestimated. First, Jeremiah 7 narrates the prophet's introduction into public life, which is his first public act. As R. E. Watts has noted, first public acts often 'alert the reader to a key feature' of the protagonist's agenda.[185] Lundbom has noted that Jeremiah's denunciation of 'abominations' (v. 10) describes the 'covenant violations of v. 9 [Will you steal, murder, commit adultery, swear falsely, make offerings to Baal, and go after other gods that you have not known?]'.[186] J. Bright argues that this constitutes 'an almost total breach of the covenantal stipulations'.[187] Second, that this event is recorded as occurring *within* the temple strengthens the association and makes it even more pertinent to our discussion of Matthew 24's use of Daniel, both of which explicitly refer to temple activity. Jeremiah 7.2 notes that Yahweh instructed Jeremiah to 'Stand in the gate of the Lord's house and proclaim there this word.' Third, it is evident that Jeremiah's temple sermon was a 'prose address ... coloured by the Deuteronomistic editorial tradition'.[188] We have repeatedly seen these Deuteronomistic elements come up in our discussion thus far. This was considered in relation to the overall literary structure of Matthew's Gospel (Deuteronomistic blessings in Matthew 5–7 and Deuteronomistic curses in Matthew 23–25), as well as the content of the Matthean woes (Matthew 23) and the warnings of destruction (Matthew 24). Among other possibilities, Deuteronomistic elements in Jeremiah 7 include v. 12, 'where I made my name dwell at first' (cf. Deut. 12.11; 14.23; 16.2, 11; 26.2), and vv. 6, 9, 18, 'go after other gods' (cf. Deut. 4.28; 5.7; 6.14; 7.4; 8.19; 11.16, 28; 13.2, 6, 13; 17.3; 18.20; 28.14, 36, 64; 29.26; 30.17; 31.18, 20).[189] In the light of this, Craigie has concluded that 'it is clear that there is some degree of common ground between

---

185 Watts, *New*, pp. 154; cf. p. 343.
186 Lundbom, *Jeremiah 1–20*, p. 467.
187 J. Bright, *Jeremiah* (New York: Doubleday, 1965), p. 56.
188 Cunliffe-Jones, *Jeremiah*, p. 81.
189 For further analysis of this phrase see J. Bright, 'The Date of the Prose Sermons of Jeremiah', *JBL* 70 (1951), pp. 15–35.

... Jeremiah and the language of the Deuteronomic corpus'.[190] Fourth, a shorter account of the same event is given in Jeremiah 26, which sets the sermon as occurring at the beginning of Jehoiakim's reign (608–597 BC). Cunliffe-Jones notes that the people had most probably gathered in the temple 'to be reinforced in their belief that God would protect them in their difficult situation'.[191] Josiah had been killed, Jehoahaz had been exiled, and the newly enthroned Jehoiakim was both a subject and ally of Egypt.[192] At the very moment the people were expecting comfort and encouragement amid turbulent times, they received dire warnings about the consequences of disobedience and covenantal infidelity. As such, the rhetorical effect of the discourse was enhanced and would have had a greater impact.[193]

4.5.a.ii.3. Jeremiah 13.24-27

Jeremiah 13.20-27 is the climactic seventh pericope of judgement on God's people in Jer 12.7–13.27, and concerns Jerusalem's coming shame. Dated to the reign of Johoiakim after 605 BC,[194] Jerusalem is personified as a woman and instructed to anticipate her devastation from the northern enemy (vv. 20-22). The shame that Jerusalem will endure is described in v. 22 which Cunliffe-Jones translates as 'your skirts are torn from you, and your heels are laid bare'.[195] 'Skirts' is a simple euphemism for what is under skirts, and indeed, this is the manner in which it has been understood in both the Septuagint (τὰ ὀπίσθιά σου, 'your hinder part') and the Vulgate (*verecundiora tua*, 'your private parts'). Nahum 3.5 describes a similar fate to Yahweh's punishment of his exiled people: 'I am against you, says the Lord of hosts, and will lift up your skirts over your face; and I will let nations look on your nakedness and kingdoms on your shame.'[196] Cunliffe-Jones concludes that 'the image is a sexual one, indicating extreme public humiliation'.[197] The reason for this is plainly stated in v. 22: 'it is for the greatness of your iniquity' (cf. Jer. 5.6; 30.15) – an iniquity that Lundbom defines as 'unfaithfulness to Yahweh and the covenant'.[198] Far from any contribution to theological debate regarding free will and the like, vv. 23-27 simply illustrate the depth of sin to which Judah has plummeted: 'Can Ethiopians change their skin or leopards their spots?'

---

190 Craigie, *Jeremiah 1–25*, p. 118.

191 Cunliffe-Jones, *Jeremiah*, p. 81.

192 Cunliffe-Jones, *Jeremiah*, p. 82.

193 Strengthening our above suggestion of Deuteronomistic elements is Reventlow (cited by Jones, *Jeremiah*, p. 143), who argues that the summary in ch. 26 is given in 'Deuteronomistic commonplaces'.

194 Cunliffe-Jones, *Jeremiah*, p. 113.

195 Jones, *Jeremiah*, p. 203.

196 Cf. also Amos 1.13; Isa. 3.17; 20.4; 47.2-3; Ezek. 16.39-40.

197 Jones, *Jeremiah*, p. 203.

198 Lundbom, *Jeremiah 1–20*, p. 686.

These two paralleled rhetorical questions are addressed to Judah in the second person plural and intend to illustrate that it is not possible for Judah to behave appropriately because their sinful behaviour has become engrained in them to the extent that it is part of who they are.

Verse 24 goes on to further describe this punishment as chaff being scattered (cf. Isa. 40.24; 41.2; Ps. 83.13). Whereas the Mt. has 'I will scatter you like chaff, *by* the wind of the wilderness' (וָאֲפִיצֵם כְּקַשׁ־עוֹבֵר לְרוּחַ מִדְבָּר), the LXX has 'I scattered them as sticks carried by the wind *into* the desert' (καὶ διέσπειρα αὐτοὺς ὡς φρύγανα φερόμενα ὑπὸ ἀνέμου εἰς ἔρημον). Thus, whereas the Mt. has מִדְבָּר ('desert') adjectivally modifying רוּחַ ('wind'), the LXX has ἔρημον as part of the prepositional phrase εἰς ἔρημον which indicates the location of the blown chaff, rather than a description of the type of wind (i.e. desert wind). In this way, the LXX provides a clear example of ἔρημος as the locus of judgement, a theme which is evident in the rationale for Israel's forty-year wanderings (Num. 14.33; 32.13).[199]

After further reiteration of the shameful consequences of Judah's unbelief (v. 26), Yahweh catalogues additional charges against his people (v. 27). At the head of the list are the 'abominations' (βδελύγματα/ שִׁקּוּצָיִךְ). Again, it is important to note that the association of sin (βδελύγματα) and consequent judgement (ἔρημον) in this pericope would have been overlooked had the only verbatim phrase βδέλυγμα τῆς ἐρημώσεως been sought. By expanding the 'textual unit' to include the 'pericope unit' we have identified the association of these two concepts in the context of an internal critique of Israel's idolatrous practices. Craigie, therefore, legitimately concludes that 'the passage appears to give the reason for the exile threatened in the preceding verses'.[200]

4.5.a.ii.4. Jeremiah 51.22 [LXX]

The close terminological association of βδέλυγμα with ἐρήμωσις is also supported by the oracle attested in Jer. 51.22 [LXX] against the diaspora Jews in Egypt: 'And the Lord could no longer bear you, because of the wickedness of your doings, and because of your abominations (βδελυγμάτων) which you wrought; and so your land became a desolation (ἐρήμωσιν) and a waste, and a curse as at this day.'[201] The threat of punishment as ἐρήμωσις recalls earlier portions of the same chapter which describe the consequences of Israel's covenantal infidelity. Jeremiah 51.2 describes this reality as, 'Thus says the Lord God of Israel: You yourselves have seen all the evils that I have brought on Jerusalem and on all the towns of Judah. Look at them; today they are

---

199   This corresponds to our analysis regarding 4Q179. See below.

200   Craigie, *Jeremiah 1–25*, pp. 192–93.

201   The same passage is found at Jer. 44.22 in the MT. For discussion of the complex relationship between the Mt. and LXX texts of Jeremiah see S. Soderlund, *The Greek Text of Jeremiah* (Sheffield: JSOT Press, 1985).

a desolation (ἔρημοι), without inhabitants.' In similar fashion v. 6 states, 'and my anger and my wrath dropped upon them, and was kindled in the gates of Judah, and in the streets of Jerusalem; and they became a desolation (ἐρήμωσιν) and a waste, as they still are today'.

4.5.a.iii. Ezekiel
The book of Ezekiel provides three further examples of similar description of Israel's behaviour as an 'abomination' (βδέλυγμα) and the consequent punishment as 'desolation' (ἐρήμωσις).[202]

4.5.a.iii.1. Ezekiel 5.9-14
The larger oracle of Ezek. 5.5-17, of which vv. 9-14 are central, provides the justification for Ezekiel's symbolic threats in 4.1–5.4. Ezekiel 4.1-2 symbolize Jerusalem's coming destruction as an inscribed clay tablet besieged by a foreign army. Any escape from the city is prevented by its being (מָצוֹר/περιοχὴν ('shut up'/'besieged'),[203] with προμαχῶνας ('ramparts'), χάρακα (' barricade'), and παρεμβολὰς ('enemy camps'). After the city is secured, βελοστάσεις ('war engines') are brought against it, presumably on ramps constructed from surrounding timber lands (2 Sam. 20.15; 2 Kgs 19.32; Isa. 37.33; Jer. 6.6; 32.24; 33.4).[204] L. C. Allen argues that this description of military warfare is consistent with the neo-Babylonian adoption of Assyrian tactics, in which 'the destructive feature was its metal ramming rod, the end of which was shaped like a spear head or an ax blade. It rammed between the stones of the city wall and then would be levered from side to side so that a section of the wall would collapse.'[205] To this depiction of symbolic depiction, two further figurative images are added. In this light, Zimmerli notes that 'eight independent verbal clauses, preserved in three acts, follow each other in particularly rigid form'.[206] (1) Ezekiel's horizontal lying position, 390 days on the left side for the sins of Israel, and forty days for the sins of Judah (Ezek. 4.4-17), and (2) the shaving of Ezekiel's head and the division of his hair into thirds – one-third burnt, one-third struck with the sword, and one-third scattered into the wind (5.1-4).

After these three vivid depictions of coming judgement, divine rationale is offered in 5.5-17, introduced by divine speech: 'Thus says the Lord God: This is Jerusalem; I have set her in the centre of the nations, with countries all around her. But she has rebelled ... .' Significant for our own discussion is the description of Israel's sin as βδελύγματά ('abominations') in 5.9 and 11, which Allen argues 'functions as an equivalent of general sins or iniquities'.[207]

---

202 In addition to the texts discussed below see Ezek. 20.7-36.
203 Cf. 2 Kgs 25.1; Jer. 52.4.
204 See discussion in Block, *Ezekiel*, pp. 164–217.
205 L. C. Allen, Ezekiel 1–19 (Dallas: Word Books, 1994), pp. 64–65.
206 Zimmerli, *Ezekiel*, p. 161.
207 Allen, *Ezekiel*, p. 74. Cf. Ezek. 18.13, 24; 20.4; 22.2. Allen however argues for a

Additionally, P. Humbert has argued that הִנְנִי עָלֶיךָ (lit. 'behold above', v. 8) has its derivation in a summons to a contest in background Babylonian literature of the period, and 'always has a threatening meaning'.[208] Zimmerli concludes that 'in its present connection [this saying] contains a wholly threatening divine announcement'.[209] Within this context M. Greenberg notes that the first divine הִנְנִי עָלֶיךָ ('I am coming to you', v. 8) which announces retribution is attested in Nah. 2.14 against Nineveh and is of some consequence in that it is a 'phrase originally used of divine judgement on the nations ... here turned against Israel'.[210] Furthermore, in the same pericope, the consequent judgement of Jerusalem destroyed is described as Yahweh making the people εἰς ἔρημον ('a desolation') (5.14). The seriousness with which this oracle is presented is again underlined by divine speech in the closing words of the oracle: 'I, the Lord, have spoken' (5.17, cf. 5.15).[211]

4.5.a.iii.2. Ezekiel 6.8-14

The theme of coming judgement is continued in the following chapter of Ezekiel through the presentation of a prophecy in 6.1-14 against the אֶל־הָרֵי יִשְׂרָאֵל/τά ὄρη Ἰσραηλ (mountains of Israel).[212] This has the effect of presenting the previous symbolic actions (Ezekiel 4–5) as the epicentre for the coming judgement, and the following material in ch. 6 extending this 'so as to make it overtake the whole land and all the sanctuaries'.[213] This ripple effect of sorts is described in the following verses as the destruction of high places (v. 3),[214] altars (v. 4), incense altars (v. 4), and the slaughtering of people (v. 4), with their bones scattered (v. 5) and towns laid waste (v. 6, ἐξερημωθήσονται). In response to these devastating events, the writer notes that the scattered exiles will remember Yahweh and loathe their previous 'abominations' (v. 9, βδελύγμασιν). The pertinent warning in v. 10, 'I did not threaten

---

different, more specified usage in 5.11, where he links it to cultic transgression.

208 Cited in Zimmerli, *Ezekiel*, p. 175.

209 Zimmerli, *Ezekiel*, p. 175.

210 M. Greenberg, *Ezekiel 1–20* (New York: Doubleday, 1983), p. 113.

211 Cf. Ezek. 4.1 (cf. 6.1), where Yahweh addresses Ezekiel as 'Son of Man' (υἱὲ ἀνθρώπου) before instructing him symbolically to lay siege to Jerusalem. Although commentators are generally in agreement that the term in Ezek. 4.1 lacks a titular usage, it is of some significance that the Son of Man's role here is very similar to his proposed role in Matthew 24. That is, including Matthew's representation of the Son of Man as Roman military troops in Matthew 24, and the symbolic action in Ezek. 4.1–5.4. Although this identification is not to be overstated, it is mentioned here only to note that it could potentially have provided Matthew with the theological impetus for the association we have proposed in our above discussion.

212 For parallels of material in Ezekiel 6 see Lev. 26.14-39.

213 D. M. G. Stalker, *Ezekiel* (London: SCM Press, 1968), p. 76. Zimmerli, *Ezekiel*, p. 182 argues that the expressive gestures in vv. 2 and 11 'undoubtedly belong in close proximity to the prophetic sign-acts'.

214 See Ezekiel's condemnation of high places in 18.6, 11, 15; 22.9.

in vain to bring this disaster upon them,' is followed by a particularly vivid expressive gesture: 'Clap your hands and stamp your foot, and say, Alas for all the vile abominations (βδελύγμασιν) of the house of Israel!' The clapping of hands has attestation in relation to royal celebration (Ps. 47.2), eschatological jubilation (Ps. 98.8), and military triumph over the fall of Nineveh (Nah. 3.19). On this basis, Zimmerli argues that this action is not one of a 'gloating onlooker'[215] but the 'action of Yahweh himself in which he triumphantly settled accounts with his enemies'.[216] Likewise Greenberg concludes 'the prophet is to represent God's satisfaction at venting his rage upon Israel'.[217] Verses 13-14 reiterate this threat and thus add emphasis to the seriousness of Israel's predicament. In this description, a theme that we have previously noted as prominent in the prophetic tradition surfaces again. As is evident from v. 14, 'I will stretch out my hand against them, and make the land desolate and waste (שְׁמָמָה/ἐρήμου),' what was initially described as inflicted on Israel's enemies is now inflicted upon Israel. This is evident when v. 14 is read in the light of the Exodus tradition, where an 'outstretched arm' brought plague and destruction on the Egyptians: Exod. 3.20, 'So I will stretch out my hand and strike Egypt … .'[218] In this ironic twist of fate, Stalker notes that now 'Yahweh has become the enemy of his people.'[219]

Thus, in this process of describing Israel's sin as 'abominations' (βδελύγματα) and the consequent judgement as 'desolation' (ἐρήμος), Ezekiel effectively argues that the Canninization of Yahwehism, which has resulted in reducing the Sinai covenant to a pagan fertility cult, 'can only be cured by the devastation of the land and the extermination of its inhabitants'.[220]

4.5.a.iii.3. Ezekiel 33.21-29 [221]

Ezekiel 33.21-33 is an explanation of Jerusalem's fall. Verse 21 clearly states, 'In the twelfth year of our exile, in the tenth month, on the fifth day of the month, someone who had escaped from Jerusalem came to me and said, "The city is taken (ἑάλω ἡ πόλις)."' Those who were not deported in the Babylonian exile had remained in Judah and possessed the unoccupied land, arguing that since Abraham was one man and they, in fact, were many, *a fortiori* they had legitimate claim over the

---

215 Zimmerli, *Ezekiel*, p. 184.

216 Zimmerli, *Ezekiel*, p. 184.

217 Greenberg, *Ezekiel 1–20*, pp. 135.

218 Also see Exod. 7.5,19; 8.5; 9.22; 10.12, 21; 14.16, 26; cf. Zeph. 2.13, where the stretching out of Yahweh's hand results in Nineveh becoming like the desert (ὡς ἔρημον).

219 Stalker, *Ezekiel*, p. 81.

220 Stalker, *Ezekiel*, p. 77.

221 Various similar thematic elements are also present in Ezek. 36.16-21 regarding the reason for Jerusalem and the surrounding mountains having suffered desolation.

land:[222] 'Abraham was only one man, yet he got possession of the land; but we are many; the land is surely given us to possess' (v. 24b).[223] As K. W. Carley has noted, 'Those who remained comforted themselves with their continued possession of the land.'[224] However, as the text goes on to explicate, these people had neglected their covenantal obligations and lived in ways that were contrary to Yahweh's law. The catalogue of sins includes (1) eating meat with blood still in it (v. 25);[225] (2) practising idolatry (v. 25); (3) murder (v. 25); and (4) defiling one's neighbour's wife (v. 26), including the description βδέλυγμα (Θ LXX Ezek. 33.26).[226] In the light of this, Ezekiel rhetorically asks, 'Should you then possess the land?' To which the expected response is a definitive 'no!'.

The resultant consequences are three plagues in v. 27 (sword, wild animals, and plague) summarized in v. 28 as desolation: 'And I will make the land desert (ἔρημον), and the pride of her strength shall perish; and the mountains of Israel shall be made desolate (ἐρημωθήσεται).' This is repeated in v. 29 with the following: 'And they shall know that I am the Lord; and I will make their land desert (ἔρημον), and it shall be made desolate (ἐρημωθήσεται) ... .' Of significance for our own discussion is the description of the above catalogue of sins as 'abominations': 'when I have made the land a desolation and a waste because of all their abominations (βδελύγματα) that they have committed'. In light of this, Carley notes that Ezekiel rather forcefully 'reaffirms the complete destruction of the inhabitants'.[227] Zimmerli similarly concludes that 'this devastation [is] brought about by the atrocities committed by the people'.[228]

---

222 For the use of *a fortiori* in the New Testament see Mt. 6.26, 28-30; 7.9-11; 10.25, 29-31; Rom. 5.8-10, 15-17; Heb. 7.1-10; cf. Mk 2.23-28, which operates as a reversal of the normal *a fortiori*, in that it argues not from smaller to greater, but greater to smaller. Also see the humorous example in Aristophanes' comedy *Clouds* 382–94. Thematic parallel of Ezek. 33.24 is evident with Mt. 3.7-10.

223 See Stalker, *Ezekiel*, p. 240.

224 K. W. Carley, *The Book of the Prophet Ezekiel* (Cambridge: Cambridge University Press, 1974), p. 225.

225 Cf. Priestly law in Gen. 9.4.

226 Theodotian is in agreement with the Mt. in including v. 26; cf. omission by Symacchus and Aquila.

227 Carley, *Ezekiel*, p. 225. Other relevant passages which link Israel's abominations (βδελύγματα) with her desolation (ἐρημος) include the following: Lev. 26.11-43; Deut. 7.22-25; 2 Chron. 36.14-21; 1 Macc. 1.39-48; Job 15.16-28; Sir. 49.2-6.

228 Zimmerli, *Ezekiel*, p. 200.

4.6. A Similar Trajectory at Qumran

Before concluding with our final observations, it is important to note a particularly striking parallel in the literature of Qumran. In a recent article, H. Najman notes that there are predominantly three usages of the concept of 'wilderness' in ancient Judaism: (1) wilderness as punishment; (2) wilderness as purification; and (3) wilderness as a locus for revelation.[229] Of particular significance for our study are those instances where the concept is used in the first-mentioned category of punishment/exile. In this light, one of the fragments from Cave 4 (4Q179) is instructive.[230] A. Berlin entitles 4Q179 a 'poem' rather than a '*pesher*',[231] and argues that it is an example of what D. Dimant calls 'anthological style, which makes use of biblical allusions, reminiscences, and semi-citations as a literary feature'.[232] The closest biblical parallel is the book of Lamentations, which consists of five laments. H. L. Ellison has noted that within this fivefold lament, 'all but the third [are] explicitly based on the destruction of Jerusalem by the Chaldeans in 587 BC and its aftermath'.[233] Indeed, 4Q179's similarity to Lamentations afforded it the title 4Q*Lamentations* in the early period. In this light, M. P. Horgan has suggested that 4Q179 was a 'poetic reminiscence of the fall of Jerusalem in 587 BC'.[234] And although it is excluded by virtue of palaeographical evidence, as being a literary response to 70 AD,[235] it has significant thematic similarities with Antiochus IV Epiphanes' two attacks upon Jerusalem, one in 169/68 BC and the other in 168/67 BC. The first is recorded in 1 Macc. 1.20-28 and refers to Antiochus' plundering of the temple. The second incident is subsequently narrated in 1 Macc. 1.29-32 regarding Apollonius (commander of Antiochus' forces) and his extensive destruction of Jerusalem.[236] Horgan also notes that, 'not only are the details of the destruction as presented in I Macc. similar to the content of 4Q179, but also following the account of each

---

229 H. Najman, 'Towards a Study of the Uses of the Concept of Wilderness in Ancient Judaism', *DSD* 13.1 (2006), pp. 99–113.

230 The following English translations are from M. O. Wise, M. G. Abegg Jr, and E. M. Cook, *The Dead Sea Scrolls: A New English Translation* (New York: HarperCollins Publishers, 1996).

231 A. Berlin, 'Qumran Laments and the Study of Lament Literature', in *Liturgical Perspectives: Prayer and Poetry in Light of the Dead Sea Scrolls*, ed. E. G. Chazon (Leiden: Brill, 2003), pp. 1–18 (3).

232 Cited in Berlin, 'Lament', p. 3.

233 H. L. Ellison, 'Lamentations', in *The Expositors Bible Commentary Vol. 6*, ed. F. E. Gaebelein (Grand Rapids: Zondervan, 1986), pp. 693–733 (695).

234 M. P. Horgan, 'A Lament Over Jerusalem (4Q179)', *JSS* 18.2 (1973), pp. 222–34 (222).

235 Horgan, 'Lament', p. 222.

236 Horgan, 'Lament', p. 222.

attack is a brief poetic lament comparable to the Qumran document'.[237] The comparative element which Horgan finds impressive is the attribution of the cause for destruction, namely 'the sins of the people'. This is evident in 4Q179 1i lines 2 and 15: 'all our misdeeds and it is not within our power; for we did not obey ... our offences ... our sins'.[238] Of further significance for our discussion is the description of the lamentable destruction as 'desolation'. 4Q179 1i 10 records that 'all her fine buildings are desolate (שממו)' and 1i 12 reinforces this with '[Judah ...] our inheritance has become like the wilderness (כמדבר) ... .'[239] As Najman has noted, 'the experience of wilderness is a result of the punishment of exile',[240] and this text portrays Jerusalem as a 'wilderness' *because* of the lawlessness of the people.[241] And thus, in this rewritten lament text, we find all the essential ingredients for our discussion: (1) a description of the destruction of Jerusalem; (2) this destruction resulting in a 'desolation' (שממו) and 'wilderness' (כמדבר); (3) the cause for this destruction being Israel's covenantal infidelity; and (4) displaying particular interest in scriptural intertextuality.

4.7. The Influence of Prophetic Material on Daniel

We now turn to briefly assess the extent to which the prophetic literature has demonstrably influenced the Danielic traditions. As J. J. Collins has argued, most commentators have considered G. von Rad's argument of radical discontinuity between the genres of 'prophecy' and 'apocalyptic' to be exaggerated.[242] Collins later notes that, in Daniel, 'the development of historical type of apocalypses is associated with the crisis of the Maccabean period and involves an extensive reappropriation of the prophetic tradition'.[243] Thus, rather than any

---

237 Horgan, 'Lament', pp. 222–23.

238 This is a similar theme to which we saw operative in Dan. 9.4-20. See Bickerman, *Makkabaâer*, pp. 24–27.

239 Also of note is the strengthening of this idea in 1ii 1: 'Woe to us, for the wrath of God has come upon [...]'; 1ii 5: 'her young men are desolate (שוממו), the children of [... fleeing]'; and 2 5: '[...] the princess of all the nations is as desolate (שוממה) as an abandoned woman, and all her daughters are likewise abandoned'. Adding to this devastating military imagery of destruction is the reference to 'fire' in 1i 5: '[...] has become burned by fire and overthrown'.

240 Najman, 'Wilderness', p. 103.

241 Najman, 'Wilderness', p. 101. For parallels in the DSS regarding wilderness as punishment for transgressions see 4Q169 3–4ii, 3–4iii, so that 'It is clear that the Qumranic texts appropriate and continue the use of the word *midbar* as the *wilderness of suffering* that is a result of God's wrath.' Najman, 'Wilderness', p. 104.

242 Collins, *Daniel*, p. 59 n.481. For further discussion on the definition of 'apocalyptic' see our concluding chapter.

243 Collins, *Daniel*, 71.

discontinuity between the 'prophetic' and 'apocalyptic', there is cause to infer that the two genres had considerable overlap. This is made all the more plausible when one accepts J. Dines' modest proposal that if 'Daniel is to be dated to c.164 BCE, it is likely that the author had access to most of the now canonical Latter Prophets in some written form'.[244]

The prime example of prophetic influence on Daniel is the use of Jer. 25.11-12 and 29.10 in Dan. 9.24-27. As was noted above, chapter 9 introduces Daniel as reflecting on Jer. 29.10, which concerns the duration of the Babylonian exile: 'For thus says the Lord: Only when Babylon's seventy years are completed will I visit you, and I will fulfil to you my promise and bring you back to this place.' It is also worth repeating, for the sake of emphasis, A. G. Wright's comment that Daniel 9 is presented as a kind of *midrash* on Jeremiah in that it 'make[s] a text of Scripture understandable, useful, and relevant for a later generation'.[245] Jeremiah's influence is apparent on two levels: first, the explicit reference to Jeremiah in Daniel 2, 'according to the word of the Lord to the prophet Jeremiah', which indicates to what the following material in Daniel is indebted, and second, and somewhat expectedly, the thematic similarity between the two texts, that is, the desolation of Jerusalem.

Modern commentators have also readily noted the pervasive influence of Isaianic material in Daniel. Among many possible examples,[246] H. L. Ginzberg has demonstrated that the Danielic heroes (*maskilim*) are conspicuously modelled on the Suffering Servant of Isaiah 53.[247] Collins suggests that 'the term *maskil* itself may be adopted from the opening verse of the Servant poem (Isa. 52.13)',[248] and that 'when the *maskilim* are said to make the *rabbim* ("many") understand and especially when the *maskilim* are also described as *masdiqe harabbim* (lit. "those who justify the many") in [Dan.] 12:3, there is a direct

---

244 J. Dines, 'Greek Daniel's Debt to Isaiah – But Which Isaiah?' (unpublished paper presented at the Summer Meeting of the Society for Old Testament Study, University College, Durham, July, 2006), pp. 1–13 (1).

245 Wright, *Midrash*, p. 74.

246 Isaiah 59.3 and 65.4 in Dan. 1.8; Isa. 10.22-23 in Dan. 5.27; Isa. 41.3 in Dan. 8.5; Isa. 10.6 in Dan. 8.13; Isa. 48.11 in Dan. 9.17; Isa. 10.33, 28.22 in Dan. 9.27; Isa. 6.7, cf. Jer. 1.9 in Dan. 10.16; Isa. 11.1 in Dan. 11.7; Isa. 8.8 in Dan. 11.10; Isa. 26.19 and 66.24 in Dan. 12.2; Isa. 30.18 in Dan. 12.12. I. L. Seeligmann, *The Septuagint Version of Isaiah: A Discussion of its Problems* (Leiden: Brill, 1948), p. 75 argues that it is 'incontestable' that Daniel used the LXX rather than the Mt. for Isa. 10.22-23 in Dan. 5.27.

247 Cited in Collins, *Literature*, p. 100. For the interpretation of the Suffering Servant in Daniel 12 see J. Day, 'Da'at "Humiliation" in Isa. liii 3 in the Light of Isa. liii and Dan. xii 4 and the Oldest Known Interpretation of the Suffering Servant', *VT* 30 (1980), pp. 97–103.

248 Collins, *Literature*, p. 100.

allusion to Isa. 53:11 ("my servant shall justify the many")'.[249] It is for this reason that J. Day is justified in concluding that 'the apocalyptic book of Daniel is in certain respects a reinterpretation of earlier Old Testament prophecies'.[250]

The book of Ezekiel has also influenced Daniel, particularly in the vivid symbolic imagery in the visionary scenes. M. J. Cook has noted the varied similarities between Daniel 7 and Ezekiel 1, including thrones, beasts, winds, wheels, and clouds.[251] D. S. Russell records the following:

> In each case there appears a throne set on wheels and aflame with fire (Ezek. 1:4, 15f., 21, 26, and Dan. 7:9f.) on which sits God himself in appearance like a man (Ezek. 1:26f.) and one Ancient of Days (Dan. 7:9f.); this chariot-throne is accompanied by a great cloud (Ezek. 1:4) and the Son of Man comes with the clouds of heaven (Dan. 7:13); in each case there appear four great beasts (Ezek. 1:5f., and Dan. 7:3f.) which, though their appearance and functions are different, emphasize, as in Ps. 8:4, the distinction between man and the animal creation.[252]

In discussing the symbolism of the human figures in Daniel, particularly the influence of Ezekiel 1, 8, and 9–10 on Daniel, Collins notes that 'the influence of these passages on Dan. 8–12 is obvious'.[253] Furthermore, the description of Israel as צְבִי ('beautiful') in Ezek. 20.6 and Dan. 8.9, the recipient's prostrate response (Ezek. 1.28; Dan. 8.17) and the manner of address ('son of man') are derived from Ezekiel.[254] Collins has also argued that Daniel's location by the river in Dan. 8.2, 'In the vision I was looking and saw myself in Susa the capital ... and I was by the river Ulai,' recalls the opening of Ezekiel (1.1): 'In the thirtieth year, in the fourth month, on the fifth day of the month, as I was among the exiles by the river Chebar'.[255]

The above analysis of Isaiah, Jeremiah, and Ezekiel has attempted to demonstrate the distinct possibility of the prophetic tradition influencing Daniel's choice of vocabulary for τὸ βδέλυγμα τῆς ἐρημώσεως. As such, in regard to Daniel's employment of the 'abomination of desolation' phrase, he portrays Israel's fiercest contemporary enemy (Antiochus IV Epiphanes) through the use of two terms which were originally applied to apostate Israel and the consequences of disobedience. In this light, Collins states that 'there

---

249 Collins, *Literature*, p. 100.

250 J. Day, 'The Dependence of Isa. 26:13–27:11 on Hos. 13:4–14:10 and Its Relevance to some Theories of the Redaction of the "Isaiah Apocalypse"', in *Writing and Reading the Scroll of Isaiah*, ed. C. C. Broyles and C. A. Evans (Leiden: Brill, 1997), pp. 357–69 (357).

251 M. J. Cook, *Mark's Treatment of the Jewish Leaders* (Leiden: Brill, 1997), p. 95.

252 Russell, *Method*, p. 341.

253 Collins, *Daniel*, p. 306.

254 Collins, *Literature*, p. 87.

255 Also see Collins, *Daniel*, p. 58 where it is stated that 'Daniel 10.1–12.4 is in itself a complete "Historical" Apocalypse in the form of an Epiphany with an angelic discourse. The Epiphany is influenced by Ezekiel 1, 8–10.'

is no doubt that Daniel stands in continuity with the prophetic tradition, especially as it is developed in the post-exilic period'.[256] J. Dines similarly concludes that that 'one of the fascinations ... [of] Daniel is its capacity to evoke, allude to and reinterpret earlier prophecy'.[257]

4.8. Conclusion

As noted in our introduction to this chapter, our aim was to investigate the context of the Matthean quotation. It was seen that Daniel, as a whole, had influenced various aspects of Matthew's narrative, particularly the 'apocalyptic discourse' in Matthew 24. It was also seen that the literary context of the βδέλυγμα της ἐρημώσεως in Daniel (i.e. Daniel 9 and 11) accurately reflected (if partially) the Hellenistic period of the Maccabaean crisis. Thus, the referent of the βδέλυγμα της ἐρημώσεως was clearly identified as Antiochus IV Epiphanes. In our discussion regarding the 'Son of Man', a sketch of the appropriate background was offered to explore why Matthew may have explicitly directed the reader to the book of Daniel. Of importance for previous discussions of Matthew 24 is the reality which envisaged Israel's enemies destroyed by the coming/going/presence of the Son of Man (cf. *1 Enoch* and *4 Ezra*). This then provided the opportunity to discuss the intertextual relationship between Daniel and the prophetic literature, a relationship which identified considerable interest on Daniel's behalf in themes and vocabulary from the prophetic literature. Of particular interest was the similar theological trajectory attested in 4Q179.

We suggest that the well-attested vocabulary of βδέλυγμα της ἐρημώσεως, in appropriation of language applied to Israel as an internal polemic, could potentially have provided Matthew with the theological trajectory and impetus for ironically employing Daniel's material. In other words, the evolution of the βδέλυγμα της ἐρημώσεως concept is first attested in the prophetic literature and refers to Israel's covenantal infidelity and consequent punishment. This vocabulary was then re-used in Daniel's presentation of Antiochus as Israel's arch-enemy. In Matthew, however, the two stages of evolution are amalgamated into an image which ironically portrays Israel *herself* as Israel's arch-enemy. L. Hartman has suggested that, within Matthew's Gospel, the Hebrew Bible 'associations may be interwoven in the most complicated patterns'.[258] However, the hypothesis being put forward here is *not* overly complicated or esoteric. It is simply an ironic twist of to whom/to what the βδέλυγμα της ἐρημώσεως refers.

---

256 Collins, *Daniel*, p. 59.
257 Dines, 'Greek', p. 1.
258 Hartman, *Prophecy*, p. 145.

What, however justifies this more complex textual background in the prophetic literature, rather than reference to Daniel alone? There are seven cumulative points which, when taken together, perhaps provide an alternative to be taken seriously. First, in our discussion of the proposed connection between Matthew and Daniel, we sought to highlight two key aspects: (1) that Israel is identified as the 'Antiochus' figure in Matthew, as indicated through the explicit mentioning of τὸ ῥηθὲν διὰ Δανιὴλ τοῦ προφήτου; and (2) the ironic implementation of this Danielic figure through a prophetic lens. So in a very real sense, it was necessary for Matthew to refer to Daniel to establish the primary referent with which he was to compare Israel, namely Antiochus IV. Matthew then goes on from here to appropriate the ironic application of this basic identification.

Second, an interpretation which takes into account the theological emphasis of the prophetic background to Daniel is remarkably coherent with Matthew, in particular emphasis on the reversal of recipients of God's blessing. As will be discussed below,[259] several commentators have suggested, on the basis of 8.12; 12.21; and 21.28 that one of Matthew's leading themes was 'the definite and final rejection of Israel by her God'.[260] In this schema, the Gentiles are granted special status, or more accurately, Israel's status is demoted to that of the Gentiles. That this is a significant theme in Matthew is evident from the outset of the Gospel. John the Baptist's initial proclamation attacks the Jewish authorities by stating: 'God is able from these stones to raise up children to Abraham' (Mt. 3.9). This trajectory is continued throughout the Gospel and comes into particularly sharp focus in the story regarding the centurion's paralysed servant (Mt. 8.5-13) and the Canaanite woman and the loaves (Mt. 14.13-21; cf. 15.22-28, 29-39).[261] Similarly, the phrase in 8.11, 'Many will come from east and west and will eat with Abraham ...' is instructive.[262] The language of 'east and west', although originally applied to the dispersed Jewish exiles (Ps. 107.2; Isa. 43.5; Zech 8.7-8), is used in Matthew specifically in relation to Gentiles (cf. Isa. 2.2-3; Mal. 1.11) and a polemic against Israel: 'while the heirs of the kingdom will be thrown into the outer darkness, where there will be weeping and gnashing of teeth' (Mt. 8.12). Matthew records the element of reversal and irony in Israel's special status, soon to be displaced by the open invitation to the nations (Mt. 28.16-20). The concentration of such threats is particularly high in the parables Jesus narrates subsequent to his arrival in Jerusalem (ch. 21).

Of particular significance is the parable of the wicked tenants (21.33-45), which is generally seen to be dependent on Mk 12.1-12. The conclusion of the parable in Matthew is without parallel in Mark and as such is to be

---

259 See chapter 5, section 5.4.

260 Clark, 'Gentile', p. 65. Also Strecker, Trilling, Meyer, and Hare, cited in B. Repschinski, *The Controversy Stories in the Gospel of Matthew* (Göttingen: Vandenhoeck & Ruprecht, 2000), p. 35.

261 See chapter 5 for further discussion.

262 See extended discussion in chapter 5, section 5.4.a.

identified as a redactional addition. Matthew concludes with the following: 'Therefore, the Kingdom of God will be taken away from you and given to a people (ἔθνει) who produce fruit' (Mt. 21.43). Rather than conclude with v. 41 (as per Mark), which would indicate a general threat (cf. 1 Sam. 15.28), Matthew has specified that the Kingdom of God will be given to another ἔθνει. The use of ἔθνος highlights not the individual, but the collective nation. In doing so, Matthew clearly focuses on the transference of the Kingdom to Gentiles. In light of this, our proposal of the ironic implementation of Daniel within Israel's story, that is, Israel as her own enemy, coheres well with the sustained polemic in Matthew in regard to unfaithful Israel and the future reversal of perceived reward and punishment.

Third, the use of irony is widespread in Matthew and has been often noted by various commentators. Witherington is typical when he notes over twenty examples of irony in Matthew.[263] Of the story of the Magi (2.1-12), Witherington notes that it is 'laced with irony',[264] which 'of course is that non-Jews were more likely to properly recognize Immanuel for who he was than Jews'.[265] In 15.1-20, 'ironically the Law becomes an obstacle to real encounter with God because the means has been mistaken for the end'.[266] Witherington notes that in the story of paying taxes to Caesar (22.15-22), 'Jesus is said here to be "true" and to "teach the way of God in truth." This is a clear example of irony because the inquisitors do not believe this, but the Evangelist's audience clearly knows this is an accurate characterization.'[267] And it is significant that there is 'considerable irony in the last few stories that lead up to the Passion Narrative, for it is others such as the blind men who more nearly model discipleship, knowing that their relationship with Jesus amounts to depending on his mercy and then following him ... .'[268] Even the name 'Matthew', which means 'gift of Yahweh' (cf. 2 Kgs 24.17; Neh. 11.17), could be an ironic play on the soliciting of 'gifts' by tax collectors.[269] Furthermore, the titulus on the cross, ὁ βασιλεὺς τῶν Ἰουδαίων, is often seen as one of the more conspicuous examples of ironic motif. If then, Mt. 24.15 was ironically appealing to Daniel, in light of the prophetic literature, it would be utterly consistent with such literary devices found throughout the Gospel.

Fourth, although Matthew draws the attention of the reader to Daniel rather than the prophetic literature (Mt. 24.15, 'as was spoken of by the prophet Daniel ...'), as was noted in previous discussion, Matthew identifies Daniel as ὁ προφήτης, which could indicate the influence of the LXX, where

---

263 Witherington, *Matthew*, pp. 56, 61, 149, 186, 212, 224, 238, 269, 282, 297, 305, 321, 381–82, 411, 413, 445, 477, 482, 485, 500, 508–509, 516, 528, 530, 541.
264 Witherington, *Matthew*, p. 56.
265 Witherington, *Matthew*, p. 61.
266 Witherington, *Matthew*, p. 297.
267 Witherington, *Matthew*, p. 411.
268 Witherington, *Matthew*, p. 382.
269 Witherington, *Matthew*, p. 212.

Daniel belonged to the prophets rather than the writings, as per the MT.[270] The connection of Daniel as a prophetic figure is a relatively well attested theme in second temple literature (4Q174; *Ant.* 10.249)[271] and perhaps hints of a possible connection between the themes present in both bodies of literature.

Fifth, several streams of the prophetic literature have demonstrably influenced Daniel's narrative (Isa. 53.11 and Dan. 12.3; Jer. 25.11-12 and 29.10 in Dan. 9.24-27; Ezek. 1 and Dan. 7; Ezek. 20.6 and Dan. 8.9; Ezek. 1.28 and Dan. 8.17; Dan. 8.2 and Ezek. 1.1). In this light, one might suggest some kind of interrelationship.

Sixth, it is possible that the textual marker ὁ ἀναγινώσκων νοείτω ('Let the reader understand') in 24.15 may function to alert the reader that there is something more at work than simply substitution of the pagan referent (Antiochus IV Epiphanes) in the Danielic context. That is, perhaps Matthew potentially offered a clue to the more subtle interplay of the prophetic tone of the saying.

Seventh, it may be the case that identification of the referent is problematic for the proposed typology. In Daniel, Israel suffers violence at the hands of Antiochus IV Epiphanes. Israel is not an active agent in inflicting desolation. Antiochus IV Epiphanes is the abomination *and* inflicts the desolation. In contrast, in Matthew, Israel is the abomination and a second party inflicts the desolation (namely, the Roman armies). It is important to note that one must be careful not to overestimate the criteria for assessing correspondence in a typological association. As noted in our earlier discussion, implicit in the use of any paradigm is the abandoning of some features to highlight or represent others. In this regard Chrysostom concludes: 'The type must not have nothing in common with the antitype, for then there would be nothing typical. Nor on the other hand must it [the type] be identical with the other [the antitype], or it would be the reality itself.'[272] Comparable in both Daniel and Matthew are the twin themes of Yahweh using a foreign power (Seleucid/Roman), and the culpability of the recipients of divine wrath: 'Seventy weeks are decreed for your people and your holy city: to finish the transgression, to put an end to sin, and to atone for iniquity ... desolations are decreed. ... an abomination that desolates' (Dan. 9.24-27); 'You snakes, you brood of vipers! ... I send you prophets, sages, and scribes, some of whom you will kill and crucify, and some you will flog in your synagogues ... "You see all these, do you not? Truly I tell you, not one stone will be left here upon another; all will be thrown down"' (Mt. 23.33–24.2).

These seven considerations when taken together might not necessarily provide a watertight case for understanding the βδέλυγμα τῆς ἐρημώσεως phrase in the proposed manner, but perhaps when taken together provide a plausible and persuasive alternative to be taken seriously.

---

270 Davies and Allison, *Matthew 3*, p. 345 n.113.
271 See above discussion, chapter 3, section 3.3.e.ii.
272 PG 51.248.

Chapter 5

IMPLICATIONS, SUMMARY, AND CONCLUSIONS

5.1. Introduction

This chapter seeks to bring to an appropriate conclusion our discussion of the βδέλυγμα τῆς ἐρημώσεως in Mt. 24.15. In so doing, we shall discuss several pertinent implications of our research for Matthean studies. Given that we have argued that Matthew typologically portrays Israel as the 'new Antiochus', we will begin with (1) a brief discussion of the possible rationale for the typological and metaphorical association in Matthew's Gospel. This then provides us with a helpful introduction to issues relating to (2) the Matthean Jesus' representation in similar manner to Hebrew Bible prophets, and (3) the role and presentation of the Gentiles in Matthew's Gospel, who seem at points to function as the 'true Israel' (Mt. 8.5-13). We will further pursue this line of enquiry in relation to the mutually interpretive stories in Mt. 14.13-21 and 15.22-28. Of corresponding significance is (4) the issue of Matthew 25 and the multifaceted use of 'Son of Man' language in Matthew.

5.2. Rationale for Typological and Metaphorical Association in Matthew

The question of an author's motivation for typological association, although addressed to some degree in our discussion thus far, deserves further consideration. D. C. Allison summarizes Plato's pedagogical maxim as being a process where 'the new is invariably apprehended through the old'.[1] Ludwig Josef Wittgenstein, a philosopher of a more recent century, approaches human understanding in like fashion, arguing that the human mind can only grasp the nature of the present in terms of his/her experience of the past.[2] In the theological realm, Ernst

---

1   Allison, *Typology*, p. 12.
2   N. Malcolm, 'Wittgenstein, Ludwig Josef Johann', in *The Encyclopedia of Philosophy*, ed. P. Edwards (8 vols; London: Macmillan, 1967), pp. 8.327–40; J. Heal, 'Wittgenstein, Ludwig Josef Johann', in *The Shorter Routledge Encyclopedia of Philosophy*, ed. E. Craig (London: Routledge), pp. 1057–71 (1067), states in regard to Wittgenstein's philosophy of mind, specifically in relation to language, that 'for a word to

Troeltsch expressed a similar sentiment when he reasoned that historians or theologians, ancient or modern, can only narrate events which have some kind of analogy in their own or community's experience.[3] It seems quite evident that one need not accept the totality of Platonic, Wittgensteinian, or Troeltschian thought to appreciate their contribution on this pedagogical matter. These three writers validly highlight one of the important facets of human understanding, which in many respects is moulded on prior experience and existing memory.

It is no surprise then that both historical and biographical authors typologically recall prior concepts, persons, or events to communicate their message. Documents from the Ancient Near East, particularly those from Mesopotamian sources, frequently reconstruct history on the basis of prior memory. In one place, the invasion of Babylon by the Seleucids is described in similar language to the Guti invasion of Ur and the corresponding lament expressed by Samaria.[4] In regard to Graeco-Roman literature, D. C. Allison notes there was even a technical term for biographical comparison, συγκρίσις.[5] In one such case Porphyry esteems Pythagoras by noting his Odyssean features and Socratic disposition.[6] Within the realm of Biblical Studies, M. Fishbane has traced this theme of literary typology throughout the Old Testament in various directions. Noah as a new Adam,[7] David as a new Abraham,[8] and Joshua, Elijah, and Ezekiel as 'new Moses' figures.[9] It seems that Matthew is on sure ground in drawing on Israel's prior traditions and experiences, and contemporaneously reappropriating them in regard to the material relating to the temple's destruction. This however raises the important issue of the date of Matthew's Gospel, i.e. whether it is pre or post 70 AD. However, before addressing this particular matter, we will briefly assess the extent to which the Matthean Jesus functions in similar trajectory to prophets as presented in the Hebrew Bible.

5.3. Jesus as Prophet in Matthew

J. D. Kingsbury's *Matthew. Structure, Christology, Kingdom*,[10] published in 1975, offered a new and fresh approach to Matthean studies.

---

have meaning there must be some extended practice in which its use has a point'.

3   Troeltsch 1912–25, cited in Wright, *Resurrection*, pp. 16–18.

4   Pinches 1901, cited in Fishbane, *Interpretation*, p. 360 n.109. For historical assimilation in cuneiform literature see J. H. Tigay, *The Evolution of the Gilgamesh Epic* (Philadelphia: University of Pennsylvania Press, 1982), pp. 81–103, 170–74.

5   Allison, *Typology*, p. 12.

6   Vita Phythagorae; cited in Allison, *Typology*, p. 12.

7   Genesis 1.26-31/9.1-9; Gen. 3.17/5.29. See Fishbane, *Interpretation*, p. 372.

8   Genesis 17.6; cf. 1 Kgs 3.14; 9.4; 11.4, 6, 38; 15.11; 2 Kgs 14.3; 16.2; 18.3; 22.2. Fishbane, *Interpretation*, p. 373.

9   Fishbane, *Interpretation*, p. 373.

10   Kingsbury, *Structure*.

His initial discussion entails a critique of fivefold division of the Gospel (proposed by Bacon) in analogy with the Pentateuch. Kingsbury proposes an alternative structure based on the dual redactional phrase Ἀπὸ τότε ἤρξατο ὁ Ἰησοῦς ('from that time Jesus began ...') in 4.17 and 16.21, thus forming three main divisions in Matthew's Gospel: 1.1–4.16, 'The Person of Jesus Messiah'; 4.17–16.20, 'The Proclamation of Jesus Messiah'; and 16.21–28.20, 'The Suffering, Death and Resurrection of Jesus Messiah'.[11] Kingsbury suggests that this structural schema indicates that Jesus is not primarily a prophetic figure in Matthew. He offers two further supporting points. First, the title 'prophet' is inadequate. Kingsbury proposes that when Matthew applies the term 'prophet' to Jesus, 'he does not even raise it to the rank of what may properly be construed as a Christological title'.[12] He offers the analogy of John the Baptist, claiming that, even for him, the title was inadequate (Mt. 11.9). Kingsbury also argues that the title has 'only negative value'[13] because it is frequently found on the lips of 'some men' (16.13b-14) or the 'crowds' (21.11, 46). At one point Kingsbury even attributes it to a title of 'scorn which Matthew imbues'.[14] Second, Kingsbury argues that at the traditional junctures where many commentators have seen strong prophetic influences (particularly new-Moses typology) on the narrative,[15] Matthew has in fact gone to 'pains to develop his Son-of-God Christology'.[16] For example, the identification of the child who escapes death as 'my son' (2.15) or the temptation of the 'Son' in ch. 4. On the basis of these objections, Kingsbury concluded that the interpretation of Jesus as a primarily prophetic figure 'is to import into Matthean Christology a category Matthew himself repeatedly refused to make'.[17] B. Witherington has similarly come to sceptical conclusions regarding the prophetic influence on Matthean Christology. At one point he states rather emphatically: 'In Matthew Jesus is Emmanuel,

---

11   Kingsbury then goes on to argue that the primary Christological title in Matthew is 'Son of God' and this is reflected not only in Matthew's structure, but also in its leading theological concept, the 'kingdom of heaven'. In this way Kingsbury offers a twofold critique of former Matthean scholarship, first in terms of challenging writers such as Bornkamm and Frankemölle, who argued for 'Son of David', 'Lord', and 'Son of Man' as of primary interpretive significance, and second against the likes of Bultmann et al., who envisaged Matthew's primary concern with the church rather than the person of Jesus. Kingsbury concludes that Matthew 'poses for his church the central question of who Jesus Messiah is', Kingsbury, *Structure*, p. 126. After a long discussion of the 'Son of God' designation, Kingsbury considers other minor Christological titles including 'Son of Abraham', 'The Coming One', and 'Prophet'.

12   Kingsbury, *Structure*, p. 88.

13   Kingsbury, *Structure*, p. 88.

14   Kingsbury, *Structure*, p. 88.

15   Particularly the infancy narrative, temptation, and the Sermon on the Mount.

16   Kingsbury, *Structure*, p. 90.

17   Kingsbury, *Structure*, p. 91.

Wisdom, the Davidic Messiah, God's Son, the Son of Man, but there is hardly a mention of Jesus as a prophet. "Prophet" does not seem to have been seen by this evangelist as either a christological or an eschatological term.'[18]

What then can be said regarding these criticisms of Jesus as 'prophet' in Matthean Christology? In regard to Kingsbury's first objection, it is important to note that Jesus does in fact refer to John as a prophet (11.9), but that he also states that John transcends this prophetic category, fulfilling the role of the expected return of Elijah (Mal. 4.5). Furthermore, to argue that the title 'prophet' is in some way diminished by being offered as a confession of the 'crowds' denies the positive role of the 'crowds'' confession in 21.9, 'Hosanna to the Son of David', which immediately precedes their further designation of Jesus as 'prophet' in 21.10-11. There need not be any antithesis which denies the possibility of a multifaceted portrait of Jesus in which the titles function complementarily. In Kingsbury's attempt to identify Jesus as 'Son of God', he collapses all Matthean Christological titles into one monolithic entity. One wonders if these concerns have not caused him to overdraw its place within the entire Gospel. Furthermore, no rationale seems to be provided for the understanding that his one Christological title needs to be understood as 'most exalted', 'foremost', 'principal', or 'preeminient',[19] yet Kingsbury seems simply to assume this is the case without further argument.[20] On at least three occasions this adversely influences his exegetical discussion. In reference to Mt. 1.16b, Kingsbury argues that the neutral ἐγεννήθη should be interpreted as 'was born (by a special act of God)'.[21] Second, in discussion of Mt. 5.1 and 15.29 the mention of a mountain is taken 'to point to Jesus as Son of God',[22] with nothing other than his claim to support it. And in regard to Mt. 27.46, Kingsbury precariously suggests that 'Matthew proposes to construe "my God" as synonymous with "my Father"',[23] again a claim that cannot bear the interpretive weight Kingsbury attempts to attribute to it.

We will, at this point, continue our discussion of 'Jesus as prophet' in Matthew in two directions. (1) By primarily drawing on the specific vocabulary in Matthew, we will attempt to demonstrate that the concept *was* significantly employed in the narrative and (2) that Jesus is presented as a prophet in his words and deeds, particularly in prophetic symbolic action.

18   B. Witherington, *Jesus the Seer* (Peabody: Hendrickson, 1999), p. 339.
19   Kingsbury, *Structure*, pp. 67, 99, 101, 162.
20   Given that the title 'Son of God' does not appear in Mt. 1.1, one may ask to what extent it can be made normative for Matthew's Christology.
21   Kingsbury, *Structure*, p. 43.
22   Kingsbury, *Structure*, p. 57.
23   Kingsbury, *Structure*, p. 75.

5.3.a. Vocabulary in Matthew

First, it is important to note that the vocabulary of 'prophet' is not inconspicuous in Matthew's narrative.[24] In no fewer than three instances, the crowds acknowledge Jesus as having prophetic status. In Mt. 16.13-20, Jesus asks his disciples what rumours are circulating about his work and ministry. The initial response is as interesting as it is informative: 'Some say John the Baptist, but others Elijah, and still others Jeremiah or one of the prophets.' What is of significance here is that all the suggested figures have strong prophetic overtones, particularly Jeremiah for his woes against the temple institution.[25] As Davies and Allison have noted, 'the common denominator is the prophetic office'.[26] Although the narrative continues to affirm that Jesus is more than a prophet, 'You are the Messiah, the Son of the living God' (v. 16), he is certainly nothing less. And indeed, Matthew's narrative regarding Jesus' words and deeds coheres remarkably well.[27]

At the climactic point of Jesus' entry into Jerusalem, 21.11 notes that the ὄχλοι ('crowds') were saying 'This is the prophet Jesus from Nazareth in Galilee.' Luz has argued that this confession does 'not express a conclusive recognition of who Jesus actually is, [but nonetheless does] … say something positive'.[28] Although Schweitzer similarly concludes that 'the jubilant crowd accompanying Jesus does not get beyond the testimony that he is a prophet',[29] he is also open to the possibility that the reference may refer to 'the prophet' of Deut. 18.18. If this is the case, then there are more significant Christological implications than commentators have commonly acknowledged. Indeed, Gundry suggests that within this story 'the Jewish leaders are ignorant; but the crowds know who Jesus is, and their understanding marks them as disciples'.[30]

Matthew 21.23-27 also narrates the instance where the chief priests and elders question Jesus on the basis of his authority. Jesus offers a

---

24   In addition to the material covered below, other references to προφήτης are used in reference to fulfilled Scripture (1.22; 2.5, 15, 17, 23; 3.3; 4.14; 8.17; 12.17; 13.14, 35; 15.7; 21.4; 24.15; 26.56; 27.9); Scripture (5.17; 7.12; 11.13; 22.40); unidentified historical figures (5.12; 13.17; 23.29-31; 23.34); John the Baptist (11.9; 21.26); Jonah (12.39).

25   Furthermore, the reference to Jeremiah is unique to Matthew. A similar redactional insertion of 'Jeremiah' occurs in 2.17; 27.9. Matthew is unique among New Testament authors in mentioning Jeremiah. M. J. J. Menken, 'The References to Jeremiah in the Gospel According to Matthew', *ETL* 60 (1984), pp. 5–25 (17–24) suggests that Matthew has in view here the idea of the suffering prophet. See discussion in U. Luz, *Matthew 8–20: A Commentary* (trans. J. E. Crouch; Minneapolis: Fortress Press, 2001), pp. 361.

26   W. D. Davies and D. C. Allison, *The Gospel according to Matthew* (vol. 2; Edinburgh: T&T Clark, 1991), p. 617.

27   For further discussion see Hill, *Matthew*, pp. 48–69.

28   Luz, *Matthew 21–28*, p. 10.

29   A. Schweitzer, *The Kingdom of God and Primitive Christianity* (trans. L. A. Garrard; London: A&C Black, 1967), p. 405.

30   Gundry, *Matthew*, p. 411.

counter-question in defence (vv. 24-25): 'I will also ask you one question; if you tell me the answer, then I will also tell you by what authority I do these things. Did the baptism of John come from heaven, or was it of human origin?' In so arguing, Jesus' authority is seen to be 'indissolubly bound up with John',[31] who was also considered to be operating as a prophet. In this regard, v. 46 is instructive. Again it is stated that although the chief priests 'wanted to arrest him ... they feared the crowds (ὄχλους), because they regarded him as a prophet (προφήτην)'. It is significant to note that both of these instances (21.11; 21.46) are unique Matthean redaction, which indicates Matthew's special interest in presenting Jesus as a prophetic figure. Thus *pace* Kingsbury, J. R. C. Cousland concludes that 'while the appellation [prophet] hardly discloses the full spectrum of Jesus' identity, the ... remark is accurate'.[32] And, as Allison has noted, 'the crowds which hail Jesus as the Son of David speak the truth while those in the guilty capital hold no opinion'.[33]

In addition to the crowds identifying Jesus as prophet, there are two instances where Jesus equates himself within the prophetic trajectory, once explicitly and once implicitly. (1) Within the polemical context of synagogal teaching, Jesus accounts for the lack of reception with the following proverb: 'Prophets are not without honor except in their own country and in their own house.'[34] Luz has argued that the category of prophet expresses 'an inadequate understanding of Jesus',[35] for support citing 16.14; 21.11, 46. As was noted above, these texts were employed by Matthew to contrast Jesus as legitimate prophet amid the criticism of Jewish authorities. As Luz himself has noted of 21.11, the reference to ὁ προφήτης 'do[es] say something positive'.[36] Our view herein does not claim that Matthew's Christology is limited solely to the category of prophet (specifically related to Deuteronomy 18 or otherwise), but rather it is a legitimate designation supported by both Jesus' followers and Jesus himself.[37]

---

31   Hill, *Matthew*, p. 49.

32   Cousland, *Crowds*, p. 222.

33   Allison, *Typology*, p. 314. The crowds are often described as following Jesus (4.25; 5.1; 8.1, 18; 12.15, 46; 13.2, 34, 36; 14.13-15; 15.30; 19.2; 20.29), being astounded by his words and deeds (7.28; 9.8, 33; 12.23; 22.33), or functioning as the backdrop for a story or event (9.23, 25, 36, 11.7). For further discussion regarding the mostly neutral, but sometimes positive portrayal of the crowds in Matthew see Cousland, *Crowds*. The negative portrayal of the crowds in 26.47, 55; 27.15, 20, 24 as participants in Jesus' arrest and execution is identified by Cousland as dependent on Ezekiel 34, which depicts Israel's suffering at the hands of corrupt leadership (cf. Mt. 27.20); indeed the crowds are 'the present exemplars of the covenant people of God, who ... have suffered from bad leadership and await divine intervention' (Cousland, *Crowds*, p. 98).

34   Matthew 13.57. For the use of οἰκία as city see Jer. 22.5; Mt. 23.38; T.*Levi* 10.4. The saying also occurs in Mk 6.4; Lk. 4.24; Jn 4.44; *G.Th.* 31; P.Oxy 1.

35   Luz, *Matthew 8–20*, p. 302.

36   Luz, *Matthew 21–28*, p. 10.

37   See also M. Hooker, *The Signs of a Prophet* (London: SCM Press, 1997), pp. 9–16.

Furthermore, an implicit personal claim made by Jesus which associates him with the prophetic category is his concluding speech in ch. 23: 'Jerusalem, Jerusalem, the city that kills the prophets and stones those who are sent to it! How often have I desired to gather your children together as a hen gathers her brood under her wings, and you were not willing!' (v. 37). That the tradition of 'rejected prophet' was well attested during this time is evident from the following. Second Chronicles 24.19: 'Yet he sent prophets among them to bring them back to the Lord; they testified against them, but they would not listen'; 2 Chron. 36.15:

> The Lord, the God of their ancestors, sent persistently to them by his messengers, because he had compassion on his people and on his dwelling place; but they kept mocking the messengers of God, despising his words, and scoffing at his prophets, until the wrath of the Lord against his people became so great that there was no remedy.

Jeremiah 25.4: 'And though the Lord persistently sent you all his servants the prophets, you have neither listened nor inclined your ears to hear'. Nehemiah 9.26: 'Nevertheless they were disobedient and rebelled against you and cast your law behind their backs and killed your prophets, who had warned them in order to turn them back to you, and they committed great blasphemies.' Similar sentiment is expressed in Jub. 1.12: 'and I shall send to them witnesses so that I might witness to them, but they will not hear. And they will even kill the witnesses. And they will persecute those who search out the Law, and they will neglect everything and begin to do evil in my sight.' 4Q166.2.3-6 records:

> that [they ate] and were satisfied and forgot God who [gives them the blessings, because] they left behind his commandments that He had sent them [through] his servants, the prophets. Instead they listened to those who deceived them. They honored them and revered them in their blindness as if they were gods.

In this light, Mt. 23.37 can be seen as an implicit attempt in the Matthean narrative to associate Jesus' rejection (and consequent denunciation of the temple institution) as being in line with former prophetic activity.[38]

5.3.b. Jesus as prophet in word and deed: prophetic symbolic actions

Second, both the broader narrative cues of Matthew and the prophetic symbolic actions are attributed to Jesus by Matthew. However, it is

---

38   Also to note is the link of Mt. 23.37 with 10.41: 'Whoever welcomes a prophet in the name of a prophet will receive a prophet's reward; and whoever welcomes a righteous person in the name of a righteous person will receive the reward of the righteous.' Hill, *Matthew*, p. 52 notes that the reference in Mt. 26.28 implies that 'even his enemies thought of Jesus in terms of a "prophet", albeit a false one'. That this is accurate is supported by the other mockery and corresponding charges, including royal humiliation and the charge of kingship.

important at this point to acknowledge the potential bias in discussions of the prominence of prophetic categories in Matthew based on the 'word-concept-fallacy'. That is, 'the idea ... may be present and intended even where the technical vocabulary is lacking'.[39] Nowhere is this danger greater than in symbolic action where the emphasis is on the enacted parable rather than the spoken word. With this precaution in mind we proceed by sketching the idea of enacted parable in the Hebrew Bible, before turning to the relevant portions of Matthew's narrative.

W. D. Stacey's monograph, *Prophetic Drama in the Old Testament*,[40] addresses the lacunae in scholarly discussion regarding the pervasive and multifaceted aspect of performing strange or dramatic actions to support or clarify a message.[41] The theme is traced through the prophetic drama in the Deuteronomistic history to the major and minor prophets. In this study he found that one of the hallmark traits of prophetic figures in the Hebrew Bible were their enacted parables which vividly portrayed the threat of Yahweh's judgement on unfaithful Israel. Among many possible examples[42] we will focus on those which most illustrate the role and function of enacted parable in the clearest and most succinct fashion.

One of the most striking prophetic acts in the Hebrew Bible is Hosea's instruction to take a whore in marriage to symbolize the manner in which Israel had forsaken Yahweh: 'Go, take for yourself a wife of whoredom and have children of whoredom.'[43] As the ensuing narrative indicates, it is clear that this action was to exemplify Israel's inappropriate behaviour towards God 'for the land commits great whoredom by forsaking the Lord'.[44] Wolff describes this symbolism as a 'fully allegorized metaphor of

39   C. D. Marshall, *Beyond Retribution* (Grand Rapids: Eerdmans, 2001), p. 146. This idea is a different side of the same coin Barr vehemently argued in 1961, where he proposed that the mere presence of 'words' did not imply conceptual meaning. Barr argued that vocabularic meaning should be derived from context rather than etymology.

40   W. D. Stacey, *Prophetic Drama in the Old Testament* (London: Epworth Press, 1990).

41   See also H. W. Robinson, 'Prophetic Symbolism', in *Old Testament Essays*, ed. D. C. Simpson (London: C. Griffin), pp. 1–17, who particularly explores the historical question of whether such enactments actually occurred; G. Fohrer, 'Die Gattung der Berichte über sumbolische Handlungen der Propheten', *ZAW* 64 (1952), pp. 101–20, is more concerned with the form-critical shape of the extant narrative.

42   The robe tearing at Gilgal (1 Sam. 15.27-35); Ahijah's cloak (1 Kgs 11.29-31); Elijah on Carmel (1 Kgs 18.20-46); Elijah invests Elijah (1 Kgs 19.19-20); Elisha's farewell rite (1 Kgs 19.21); Zedekiah's horns (1 Kgs 22.1-12; 2 Chron. 18.1-11); tearing of Elisha's clothes (2 Kgs 2.12-18); Elisha's arrows (2 Kgs 13.14); Shear-jashub (Isa. 7.3); Immanuel (7.10-17); Maher-shalal-hash-baz (8.1-4); Isaiah's nakedness (20.1-6); Micah's nakedness (Mic. 1.8); the coronation (Zech. 6.9-16); the shepherd (11.4-17). See other references below.

43   Hosea 1.2a.

44   Hosea 1.2b. Cf. 2.4-7; 3.3; 4.10-18; 5.3; 6.10; 9.1. See G. A. F. Knight, *Hosea: Introduction and Commentary* (London: SCM Press, 1960), p. 41.

Yahweh as the loving yet rejected husband'.[45] In this prophetic action the naming of Hosea's children symbolized Yahweh's judgement: Jezreel, 'for in a little while I will punish the house of Jehu for the blood of Jezreel, and I will put an end to the kingdom of the house of Israel' (1.4); Lo-Ruhamah, 'for I will no longer have pity on the house of Israel or forgive them' (1.6); and Lo-Ammi, 'for you are not my people and I am not your God'. As such D. Stuart notes that the 'divine command to perform a symbolic act is followed by divine explanation of the act's symbolic importance. The act itself is then done in obedience to the command and in service of the symbolism.'[46] J. L. Mays concludes by highlighting the consequential corollary of judgement in this process: 'Yahweh's command [is] undertaken to dramatize the divine indictment of Israel.'[47]

The book of Jeremiah also frequently employs the enacted parable to aid in the delivery of the prophetic message.[48] One vivid example is that in 13.1-11, where Israel is portrayed as a rotting loincloth. Stacey notes that the threefold structure indicates a 'deliberate and formal structure':[49] (1) the command to buy and wear a loincloth (vv. 1-2); (2) the command to bury it in the cliff near Perath (vv. 3-5); and (3) the command to retrieve it after 'many days' (vv. 6-7). The divine interpretation, provided in vv. 8-11, directly associates Israel's wickedness, idolatry, and the rotten uselessness of the loincloth, the association made explicit in v. 11: 'For as the loincloth clings to one's loins, so I made the whole house of Israel and the whole house of Judah cling to me, says the Lord, in order that they might be for me a people, a name, a praise, and a glory. But they would not listen.'[50] R. K. Harrison concludes that this enacted parable 'made clear that idolatry, with its attendant moral corruptions, would be the ruin of the people'.[51]

We note a final example of interrelated prophetic dramas in Ezek. 4.1–5.4,[52] wherein Jerusalem's destruction is symbolized in a clay tablet (4.1-3), then explicated with further parable (4.4–5.5).[53] Of significance is

---

45   H. W. Wolff, *Hosea* (Philadelphia: Fortress, 1974), p. xxvi.

46   D. Stuart, *Hosea-Jonah* (Waco: Word, 1987), p. 24.

47   J. L. Mays, *Hosea: A Commentary* (London: SCM Press, 1969), p. 25.

48   In addition to our discussion below, see Jer. 16.1-13 (celibacy); 18.1-12 (potter's clay); see J. A. Thomson, *The Book of Jeremiah* (Grand Rapids: Eerdmans, 1980), pp. 443–56; 19.1-13 (broken earthenware jug); and 27.1-22 (Nebuchadnezzar's yoke).

49   Stacey, *Prophetic*, p. 131.

50   Interestingly, Stacey notes that the intimate nature of the loincloth represented Israel's privileged status as covenant people. Stacey, *Prophetic*, p. 131.

51   R. K. Harrison, *Jeremiah and Lamentations* (Leicester: IVP, 1973), p. 99.

52   See also Ezek. 2.8–3.3 (scroll); 3.22-27; 24.25-27; 33.21 (dumbness); 6.11-14 (stamping); 12.1-16 (exile); 12.17-20 (eating and drinking); 21.6-7, 12 [Mt. 21.11–12, 17] (sighs of grief); 21.8-17, 28-32 [Mt. 21.13-22, 33-37] (sword); 21.18-22 [Mt. 21.23-27] (Nebuchadnezzar); 24.1-2 (inscribing the date); 24.3-15 (cooking pot); 24.15-27 (mourning, cf. Jer 16.1-13); 37.15-28 (joining sticks).

53   Stacey, *Prophetic*, pp. 180–1-92; J. Blenkinsopp, *Ezekiel* (Louisville: John Knox Press, 1990), pp. 33–39.

the description that the inscribed miniature of the siege is to be a אוֹת/σημεῖον for the house of Israel, which might suggest an actual visual representation.[54] Thus B. Lang has suggested that the scene is reminiscent of a 'prophetic street theatre'.[55] Ezekiel 4.4-17 then expands this initial enactment to include various other scenes: the prophet lying on his left (4.4-6) then right (4.6-8) side in order to symbolize the sin of Israel and Judah respectively; while eating a bread cooked over cow manure (4.9-17); and finally for Ezekiel to shave his head and to equally burn, cut, and scatter his hair as a symbol of what will happen to Jerusalem. The divine interpretation in 5.5-8 makes clear that it is Yahweh himself who is punishing his people for their rebellion: 'You have not followed my statutes or kept my ordinances ... therefore ... I myself, am coming against you; I will execute judgments among you in the sight of the nations.'

Thus it becomes evident that the prophetic parable or enacted drama was utilized by various authors in multifaceted ways. Despite the variety of dramatic expressions, the underlying theme is invariably negative judgement because of covenantal infidelity. The manner in which this brief survey contributes to our discussion is relatively clear; the examples noted will help to contextualize similar enacted parables of retribution in the Matthean narrative. Indeed, it is in this regard that Hill states that 'a further indication that Jesus may have set himself within the prophetic tradition is provided by his performance of symbolic acts'.[56] It is to these issues we now turn.

A tendency of both historical Jesus studies and discussions of Matthean Christology has been to focus on the 'words of Jesus' in preference to the 'actions of Jesus'.[57] As such, M. Hooker has noted, 'detailed discussion of Jesus as a prophet has usually concentrated on his words'; she then goes on to conclude, however, that 'what he [Jesus] *did* was surely quite as important as what he *said*'.[58] Similar in this regard is J. P. Meier, who advocates that 'one cannot hope to interpret the actions without a context of interpreting words, just as the words float in a vacuum without an interpretive context of deeds ... [and that] any dichotomy in the treatment of Jesus' words and

---

54   Parallels of such ground plans are attested in the Babylonian reliefs, Pritchard, *Pictures*, pp. 129–32.

55   B. Lang, *Monotheism and the Prophetic Minority* (Sheffield: Almond, 1983), p. 81.

56   D. Hill, *New Testament Prophecy* (London: Marshall, Morgan & Scott, 1979), p. 63. Hill also notes that Jesus' parabolic prophetic speech is partly derived from the Hebrew Bible (2 Sam. 12.1-7; Isa. 5.1-7). Hill, *Prophecy*, p. 58.

57   E. P. Sanders, *Jesus and Judaism* (London: SCM Press, 1985) has been criticized for the opposite, that is over-emphasizing the actions of Jesus without appropriate consideration of his words. See J. P. Meier, *A Marginal Jew: Rethinking the Historical Jesus: Mentor, Message, and Miracles* (New York: Doubleday, 1994), pp. 464–65. On prophetic action see A. E. Harvey, *Jesus and the Constraints of History* (London: Duckworth, 1982), pp. 57–62, 120–53.

58   Hooker, *Prophet*, p. 1. Italics original.

deeds [is] questionable in theory and unworkable in practice'.[59] Thus, while not neglecting the interrelation of Jesus' words and deeds in Matthew, we proceed by analysing (1) the temple incident (21.12-17), and (2) the withering of the fig tree (21.18-22), with special attention to the manner in which this portrays Jesus as a prophetic figure.

5.3.b.i. The temple incident

After Jesus' rather lukewarm reception into Jerusalem (Mt. 21.1-11), he proceeded to the temple and 'drove out all who were selling and buying in the temple, and he overturned the tables of the money changers and the seats of those who sold doves ...' (Mt. 21.12-17).[60] Commentators have typically understood this incident in two broad categories.[61] First, that Jesus endeavoured to perform a 'temple cleansing', that is, a restoration of the true cult and holiness of the temple by driving out those who were conducting business in the outer court. Jeremias suggests that the polemic lay in the misuse of the system 'by carrying on business to make profit'.[62] Similar is A. Edersheim, who argues 'the whole of this traffic – money-changing, selling of doves, and market for sheep and oxen – was in itself, and from its attendant circumstances, a terrible desecration'.[63] G. Aulén concurs in stating that, 'To transform the court of the temple to a market place ... was a violation of the law concerning the holiness of the temple.'[64] In addition to the various contemporary texts which polemically suggest that the Sadducees benefited economically through the operation of the temple,[65] Luz notes that the description of the money-changers in 21.12 is not in neutral terms of ἀργυραμοιβοί or τραπεζῖται but κολλυβιστῶν, literally 'those who take a commission'.[66] However, it is important to note that (1) the commission rate was needed for those selling animals, as this was how they

---

59 Meier, *Marginal*, p. 465.

60 For parallel accounts see Mk 11.15-17; Lk. 19.45-46; cf. Jn 2.13-17.

61 This twofold categorization does not intend to over-simplify the interpretive issues. Most views are some kind of variation of these two categories. For other views such as Jesus' action as political endeavour to establish his messianic rule see H. S. Reimarus, *Fragments* (trans. R. S. Fraser; Philadelphia: Fortress Press, 1970), p. 146; S. G. F. Brandon, *Jesus and the Zealots: A Study of the Political Factor in Primitive Christianity* (New York: Scribner's, 1967), pp. 332–40.

62 Jeremias, *Theology*, p. 145.

63 A. Edersheim, *The Life and Times of Jesus the Messiah* (2 vols; Grand Rapids: Eerdmans, 1936), p. 1.370.

64 G. Aulén, *Jesus in Contemporary Historical Research* (Philadelphia: Fortress, 1976), p. 77.

65 *Ass.Mos.* 7.6 (greedy priests); *Ant.* 20.205-206 (high priest Ananias as a hoarder of money); *t.Menah* 13.22 (533) (temple destroyed because of greediness). See also C. A. Evans, 'Jesus Action in the Temple: Cleansing or Portent of Destruction?', *CBQ* 51 (1989), pp. 237–70.

66 Luz, *Matthew 21–28*, p. 12.

gained their livelihood,[67] and (2) if the animals were sold outside the temple there was a danger they would be polluted, and hence rendered ineffectual for temple sacrifice.[68] Although it is granted that any economic system is open to abuses and potential exploitation of consumers, and that there was both a need for sale and commission of animals in the temple, one questions how these might function as the appropriate sole motivation for Jesus' action in the Matthean narrative.[69]

It seems that an alternative proposal is more plausible in this regard. E. P. Sanders has influentially argued at length that Jesus' action was performed as a symbolic act of destruction against the temple.[70] Sanders particularly highlights the action of Jesus' overturning (κατέστρεψεν); he notes, 'had Jesus wished to make a gesture of symbolizing purity, he doubtless could have done so. The pouring out of water comes immediately to mind. The turning over of even one table points towards destruction.'[71] In support of this are the many instances in the LXX where καταστρέφω is employed to denote Yahweh's destruction of a city. Prototypical in this regard was the description of Sodom and Gomorrah's destruction: 'Then the Lord rained on Sodom and Gomorrah sulfur and fire from the Lord out of heaven; and he overthrew (κατέστρεψεν) those cities, and all the Plain, and all the inhabitants of the cities, and what grew on the ground.'[72] This event is also remembered in tradition history in similar terms. Amos 4.11: 'as when God overthrew (κατέστρεψεν) Sodom and Gomorrah ...'; Isa. 13.19: 'And Babylon, the glory of kingdoms, the splendor and pride of the Chaldeans, will be like Sodom and Gomorrah when God overthrew them'; Jer. 27.40 LXX [Mt. 50.40]: 'As God overthrew (κατέστρεψεν) Sodom and Gomorrah and their neighbors, says the Lord, so no one shall live there.'[73] In addition to the term καταστρέφω being used in regard to the general destruction of pagan cities,[74] in Deut. 29.23 (covenantal curses) Israel is threatened with a similar fate should she flaunt her covenantal status.

This theme also finds attestation in 2 Kgs 21.13-15 regarding the consequences of Manasseh's 'detestable practices of the nations':[75]

---

67   Shekalim 1.6.

68   Jeremias has demonstrated that *Berakoth* 9.5 does not support the idea that money was never changed in the temple precincts, but rather referred to visitors to the temple area and not those who came to offer sacrifices; Jeremias, *Theology*, p. 179.

69   This view, however, has some merit and contributes to the theme of inappropriate temple activity in Matthew's Gospel.

70   Sanders, *Jesus and Judaism*, pp. 61–76. Also see Gnilka, *Matthäusevangelium*, p. 278.

71   Sanders, *Jesus and Judaism*, p. 70.

72   Genesis 19.24-25.

73   Also see Gen. 13.10; Lam. 4.6.

74   Ezra 6.12; Hag. 2.23 [Mt. 2.22]; Jer. 20.16; Sir. 10.16, 'The Lord overthrew the lands of the nations and destroyed them to the foundations of the earth.' Also see Jon. 3.4 (Nineveh) and Mal. 1.4 (Idumaea).

75   Second Kings 21.2.

I will stretch over Jerusalem the measuring line for Samaria, and the plummet for the house of Ahab; I will wipe Jerusalem as one wipes a dish, wiping it and turning it upside down (καταστρέφεται) ... they shall become a prey and a spoil to all their enemies, because they have done what is evil in my sight ...

Similarly, Isa. 1.7 speaks of threat, interestingly combining several key theological terms: 'Your country lies desolate (ἔρημος), your cities are burned with fire; in your very presence strangers devour your land; it is desolate, as overthrown (κατεστραμμένη) by strangers.'

In regard to Jesus' action in the temple, C. Moule questions whether this would be self-evident.[76] M. Hooker expresses similar concern by stating that 'Jesus' action is by no means an obvious symbol of coming destruction',[77] making the comparison with Jeremiah breaking the clay jar. However, it should be noted that these comments by Moule and Hooker refer to a discussion related to the historical Jesus rather than the extant form of Matthean narrative.[78] Despite Luz's scepticism,[79] there are several converging lines of evidence that indicate Matthew understood this event as a symbolic act of destruction. In support of this we may note the following. First, within the Matthean narrative, Jesus later prophesies the temple's destruction (24.2), and this would cohere remarkably well with his temple action being understood as a prophetic act of judgement. Second, as Jer. 26.1-11 indicates, there was Old Testament precedent for Jesus' action (v. 2 being a declaration in the 'house of the Lord'), and indeed it would be consistent with the aforementioned enacted parables in the prophetic literature. Third, *pace* Luz who states, 'Of course ... Mt. 21.13 speak[s] *against* this interpretation',[80] the quotation from the Old Testament in Matthew actually offers strong support for our view.[81] The quotation in 21.13 combines Isa. 56.7, ὁ γὰρ οἶκός μου οἶκος προσευχῆς κληθήσεται ... ('For my house will be called a house of prayer ...'), and Jer. 7.11, μὴ σπήλαιον λῃστῶν ὁ οἶκός μου, οὗ ἐπικέκληται τὸ ὄνομά μου ('Has this house, which is called by my name, become a den of robbers?'). Mark 11.17 retains the extended Isaianic phrase πᾶσιν τοῖς ἔθνεσιν ('to all nations'), whereas Matthew omits it. The reason for this may be twofold. First, as noted by Gundry, 'Though he favors the Gentiles, their mention here would have diverted the attention from the accusatory point he wants to make

---

76   Moule cited in Sanders, *Jesus and Judaism*, p. 70.

77   Hooker, *Prophet*, p. 46.

78   Thus in later comments regarding the narrative of the Gospels, Hooker notes, 'the incident was seen ... as a sign of the temple's future destruction', Hooker, *Prophet*, p. 44.

79   'It is scarcely possible to say how Matthew understood the episode', Luz, *Matthew 21–28*, p. 12.

80   Luz, *Matthew 21–28*, p. 12.

81   Luz further questions why 'a particular action of Jesus against representatives of the financial operation in the temple has in any way indicated the end of the temple?', Luz, *Matthew 21–28*, p. 12. In response, it should be noted that without the buying and selling of sacrifices, the temple is not able to operate.

against unbelieving Jewry.'[82] Second, as noted in our previous discussion, in Matthew's conception, there is no future role for the temple in legitimate worship. Israel has sinned, Yahweh has departed from the temple, and now it faces imminent destruction. It is at this point that we find cause to disagree with Sanders' otherwise convincing reading of the temple incident. He goes on to argue that the intended outcome of the action was 'that the end was at hand and that the temple would be destroyed, so that the new and perfect temple might arise'.[83] As Hooker has noted, there is no indication that the temple is destroyed for the purposes of a new one to arise, rather 'God had judged his people and found them guilty.'[84]

In regard to the quotation from Jeremiah, it is significant to note that the context of Jeremiah 7 is a prophecy of the temple's destruction; v. 14 declares 'therefore I will do to the house that is called by my name, in which you trust, and to the place that I gave to you and to your ancestors, just what I did to Shiloh' (cf. v. 12). Additional strength to the comparison with Matthew is evident in that the event is recorded as occurring *within* the temple; v. 2 notes that Yahweh instructed Jeremiah to 'Stand in the gate of the Lord's house and proclaim there this word.' Matthew adds emphasis to the quotation by redacting Mark's close following of the Jeremian question formula, οὐ γέγραπται ὅτι ('is it not written?'), and substitutes the more definitive γέγραπται ('it is written'). As such, Jesus' action in the temple should be understood primarily in regard to the temple's future destruction.[85] Nonetheless, Davies and Allison suggest that the 'symbolic destruction' and the 'cleansing' views of the temple incident are not necessarily antithetical: 'It is wrong to oppose the two interpretations … protestation against abuses and symbolic expressions of judgement belonged together.'[86] This view is reiterated by Allison in the following: 'Although current scholarship, following Sanders' statement of the problem, has tended to suppose that we should choose between two competing theories … these two theories are scarcely at odds. Protests against abuses and symbolic expression of judgement could readily have gone together.'[87] Thus, while both are possible, the Matthean text emphasizes the symbolic act of destruction as more prominent due to the factors discussed above.

---

82   Gundry, *Matthew*, p. 412. For detailed discussion regarding textual comparisons see R. H. Gundry, *The Use of the Old Testament in St. Matthew's Gospel with Special Reference to the Messianic Hope* (Leiden: Brill, 1967), p. 19.

83   Sanders, *Jesus and Judaism*, p. 75.

84   Hooker, *Prophet*, p. 45.

85   Regarding the λῃστῶν, a concept connoting more violent force than merely a thief, it is significant to note that in Mt. 26.47, representatives of the chief priests and elders arrive to arrest Jesus μετὰ μαχαιρῶν καὶ ξύλων ('with swords and clubs').

86   Davies and Allison, *Matthew 3*, p. 136.

87   Allison, *Jesus*, p. 98.

5.3.b.ii. The fig tree incident
Although Matthew extracts the Markan story of the temple incident from being interwoven with the fig tree story (cf. Mk 11.12-14, 20-24), he does place them in close proximity, and reinforces negative association with the three parables of judgement (21.28–22.10). Far from being an outburst of anger by a hungry traveller,[88] the story of the fig tree in Mt. 21.18-22 is a further enactment of the coming judgement on Israel.[89] In reference to (1) entry into Jerusalem, (2) the temple event, and (3) the fig tree story, Davies and Allison state that, 'for the third time in three paragraphs Jesus the prophet performs a symbolic act'.[90]

The 'withering' of trees is a common metaphor for judgement in the Hebrew Bible. Jeremiah 27.27 [LXX] describes the coming of Yahweh's judgement as, 'Dry up all her fruits (καρπούς), and let them go down to the slaughter. Woe to them! for their day is come, and the time of their retribution.'[91] Similarly, Isa. 34.4 talks of withered leaf and fruit alike: 'All their host shall wither, like a leaf withering on a vine, and fruit withering on a fig tree.' Among other potential candidates,[92] two passages from the Hebrew Bible provide particular illumination. Jeremiah 8.13 states, 'When I wanted to gather them, says the Lord, there are no grapes on the vine, nor figs (σῦκα/ הַתְּאֵנִים) on the fig tree; even the leaves are withered (τὰ φύλλα κατερρύηκεν/ וְהֶעָלֶה נָבֵל). It combines the elements of (1) the temple (the location of utterance); (2) figs; (3) withered leaves; and (4) negative judgement, all in the context of a divine oracle concerning Judah and Jerusalem. According to B.Mig 31b, this Jeremian passage was read as the haftarah for the ninth of Av fast-day, i.e. the day of mourning which, according to Talmudic tradition, was when the first temple was destroyed.[93] Similar is Hos. 9.10-16 which is part of the prophet's declaration of the punishments of abandoning Yahweh for Baal, wherein Israel is depicted as a fruit tree (v. 10), and her judgement is symbolized as withering (v. 16).

---

88   See McNeile, *Matthew*, p. 302, who states, 'Both physically by his hunger, and mentally by his disappointed expectation … the Lord's real humanity is indicated.' McNeile, *Matthew*, p. 303 later notes that Jesus was not 'venting upon the tree his disappointment at finding no fruit'.

89   Telford, *Barren*.

90   Davies and Allison, *Matthew 3*, p. 148. Hooker, *Prophet*, p. 44, states that 'the story is an example of a prophetic drama'.

91   Cf. Isa. 40.24; Hos. 9.16; Job 18.16.

92   Isa. 28.3-4; Mic. 7.1; Joel 1.7, 12; Isa. 5.1-7, where Israel is symbolized as a fruit tree. The comparison is made on the basis of the fruitlessness of the produce; as such the vine/fig differentiation poses no real problem. In the Isaian parable, Israel continually yields only bad fruit (Isa. 5.4), and the consequences are devastating; vv. 5–6 state, 'And now I will tell you what I will do to my vineyard. I will remove its hedge, and it shall be devoured; I will break down its wall, and it shall be trampled down. I will make it a waste; it shall not be pruned or hoed, and it shall be overgrown with briers and thorns; I will also command the clouds that they rain no rain upon it.' For further discussion see Telford, *Barren*, pp. 142–45.

93   For further discussion of Jeremiah 7–10 see the analysis in chapter 4.

Matthew introduces the story concerning Jesus by noting the time of day, πρωί ('in the morning'), which is an appropriate literary foil for Jesus' expected satisfaction of hunger, 'he was hungry, and seeing a fig tree by the side of the road ...' (vv. 18b-19a). Interestingly, Matthew singles out 'υκῆν μίαν (one fig tree, cf. Mk 11.13, συκῆν 'a fig tree'), and Gundry suggests that it is 'as representative of Jerusalem, or the Jewish leaders there'.[94] Upon approaching the fig tree, Matthew notes that Jesus 'found nothing at all on it but leaves' (v. 19). R. K. Harrison notes the oddity of this by suggesting, 'When the young leaves are appearing in spring every fertile fig will have some *taksh* [undeveloped fruit] ... When the leaves are fully developed the fruit ought to be mature also.'[95] Morris notes that 'the tree gave every outward sign of bearing fruit but in fact bore none'.[96] Matthew omits Mk 11.13b, ὁ γὰρ καιρὸς οὐκ ἦν σύκων ('for it was not the season for figs'), in an attempt to intensify the polemic and not allow any excuse for the lack of produce. In so doing he highlights the guilt of those to whom the parable is directed, namely the religious authorities. It is in this regard that Hooker makes the connection between Israel's former failure and their current state; she concludes 'the drama symbolizes Israel's failure to respond to her Messiah and the inevitable destruction to which that failure will lead'.[97] Similarly, F. W. Beare concludes that 'the story in its setting ... is surely taken by the evangelists as a sign of the coming destruction of Israel'.[98]

5.3.b.iii. Preliminary conclusion

This section has attempted to demonstrate that Matthew did in fact utilize the concept of 'prophet' in a theologically important and sophisticated manner.[99] In so doing Matthew employed (1) the specific terminology in Jesus' speech or that of his interlocutors (16.13-16; 21.11,

---

94   R. H. Gundry, *Matthew: A Commentary on His Handbook for a Mixed Church under Persecution* (Grand Rapids: Eerdmans, 1994), p. 416. See also Luz, *Matthew 21–28*, pp. 21–22, who states that there is general agreement that the incident 'was a story not about a fig tree, but about Israel'.

95   R. K. Harrison, 'Fig Tree', in *International Standard Bible Encyclopedia*, ed. G. W. Bromiley (4 vols; Grand Rapids: Eerdmans, 1994), pp. 2.301–302 (302).

96   L. Morris, *The Gospel according to Matthew* (Grand Rapids: Eerdmans, 1992), p. 530.

97   Hooker, *Prophet*, p. 44. The following saying in Mt. 21.21 no way detracts from this sentiment. Wright, *Jesus*, pp. 334–35 suggested that the idea is reinforced by the saying of the mountain being cast into the sea: 'The evident proverbial nature of the saying should not disguise the fact that someone speaking of "this mountain" ... in the context of a dramatic action of judgement in the Temple, would inevitably be heard to refer to Mount Zion.' See a similar approach in Telford, *Barren*, pp. 95–119 on the Markan parallel.

98   Beare, *Matthew*, p. 419.

99   *Pace* Witherington, *Seer*, p. 339, who argues 'In Matthew Jesus is Emmanuel, Wisdom, the Davidic Messiah, God's Son, the Son of Man, but there is hardly a mention of Jesus as a prophet. "Prophet" does not seem to have been seen by this evangelist as either a christological or an eschatological term.'

23-27, 46; two of which are uniquely Matthean), and (2) prophetic symbolic action of the Old Testament (Hosea, Jeremiah, and Ezekiel) in shaping the narratives of the temple incident and the fig tree, both of which were seen to have strong overtones of prophetic denunciation. As such Matthew draws on well-known, standard Old Testament images for the purpose of communicating Jesus' message of coming destruction on unfaithful Israel.

5.4. Gentiles in Matthew and the Abomination of Desolation

The picture sketched thus far is confirmed by the broader motif of Gentiles and Israel in Matthew's larger schema. Matthew's apparent Gentile bias was notably discussed by K. Clark in his 1947 article,[100] in which he focused on this motif for implications for the identity of the author.[101] Clark concluded on the basis of 8.12; 12.21; and 21.28 that one of Matthew's leading themes was 'the definite and final rejection of Israel by her God'.[102] Analysis of these passages, in conjunction with 14.13-21 and 15.22-28, suggests that this is an accurate portrayal of Matthew's future horizon, and supports our discussion on how the βδέλυγμα τῆς ἐρημώσεως is to be understood.

5.4.a. The centurion's paralysed servant (Mt. 8.5-13)

In most discussion of the unique Matthean phrase in Mt. 8.11, λέγω δὲ ὑμῖν ὅτι πολλοὶ ἀπὸ ἀνατολῶν καὶ δυσμῶν ('and I say to you "many will come from east and west"'), commentators assume all too quickly, perhaps on the basis of the mention of Abraham's name (cf. Gen. 12.1-3, 'so that you will be a blessing'), that the phrase refers to Gentiles without appreciating its original context in earlier Jewish literature. Psalm 107 introduces the fifth book of the Psalter with a thanksgiving hymn for Yahweh's deliverance from the enemy (v. 2). This is envisioned in the diaspora communities' return from exile 'from the east and from the west, from the north and from the south' (v. 3, cf. the later *Mid.Ps.* 107.2-3). Similarly, in Isaiah's redemptive vision of Israel's return from exile Yahweh states, 'Do not fear, for I am with you; I will bring your offspring from the east, and from the west I will gather you' (Isa. 43.5), and in this way also envisions the return from exile in 'east/west' language. Furthermore, after Zechariah's eight night visions, Yahweh himself promises 'I will save my people from the east country and from the west country; and I will bring them to live in Jerusalem. They shall be my people and I will be their God, in faithfulness and in righteousness' (Zech. 8.7-8). To this may be added

---

100 Clark, 'Gentile', pp. 165–72.
101 Clark, 'Gentile', p. 165.
102 Clark, 'Gentile', p. 165.

the similar theme from Baruch: 'Look, your children are coming, whom you sent away; they are coming, gathered from east and west, at the word of the Holy One, rejoicing in the glory of God' (Bar. 4.37) and 'Arise, O Jerusalem, stand upon the height; look toward the east, and see your children gathered from west and east at the word of the Holy One, rejoicing that God has remembered them' (Bar. 5.5). As these and other references in Jewish literature indicate,[103] the primary meaning in the crowds coming from ἀνατολῶν καὶ δυσμῶν ('east and west') refers to Israel's return from exile and not to the eschatological gathering of Gentiles grafted in as God's new people. This seems appropriate given that (1) the region of Assyria/Babylon was considered synonymous with 'the east',[104] and that (2) the region of Egypt was considered to be the antithesis of the 'east' and hence 'west'.[105] In this regard Hagner concludes that the original source of the image in Mt. 8.11-12 'was understood as the return of diaspora Jews to Israel'.[106] Allison takes this one step further by stating that there are no known Jewish documents before the first century that use the 'east/west' language in reference to the eschatological gathering of Gentiles, and hence concludes that the image is exclusively one of Jews returning to their homeland.[107]

However, in Matthew's retelling of Jesus' words and activities there is one significant twist. As described above, the reference to 'east/west' was a metaphor for *Jewish* exiles (not Gentiles) returning to celebrate Yahweh's final victory with their patriarchs Abraham, Isaac, and Jacob in a great messianic banquet,[108] a meaning which seems more apt to Luke's context in Lk. 13.23-30.[109] However in Mt. 8.5-13 it seems clearly to be a reference to the eschatological gathering of Gentiles. This perceived deviation in usage has caused Allison to follow McNeile[110] and conclude that Matthew

---

103 Deuteronomy 30.4 LXX; Isa. 27.13; Ezek. 37.9; Hos. 11.10-11; Zech. 10.10; *Pss Sol.* 11.2-4; *1 En.* 57.1; *Sib. Or.* 5.113; *Ant.* 11.131-33; 2 Macc. 1.27-28; 2.18; *Sir.* 36; 40.10; 1QM 2.1-3.

104 Isaiah 46.11; *Sib. Or.* 5.13; *Ass. Mos.* 3.1, 13-14.

105 First Kings 4.30; *Sib. Or.* 5.112-13. References from D. Allison, 'Who will come from East and West? Observations on Matt. 8.11-12 = Luke 13.28-29', *IBS* 11 (1989), pp. 158-70 (162).

106 Hagner, *Matthew 1–13*, p. 205.

107 Allison, 'East and West', p. 162. However, although Isa. 26.5 does not explicitly refer to Gentile-exiles coming from east and west, it does cast some doubt on Allison's categorical ruling out of any reference to Gentiles' participation in the eschatological era.

108 See Isa. 25.6; *Exod. Rab.* 25, 10; *b. Pesah* 119b. Also see Mt. 22.1-14; 25.10; Rev. 19.9; Lk. 14.15-16.

109 The context warns of the consequences of not entering the house before the master shuts the door.

110 McNeile, *Matthew*, p. 105 says 'the original context of these words is doubtful. Mt., in placing them here, understands them to refer to the admission of Gentiles into the Kingdom; the centurions' faith is interpreted as a "faith unto salvation." Lk places them, more suitably, after the passage which is parallel with Mt. vii 21f., in a context which contains no mention of Gentiles.'

'unfortunately placed the logion [Mt. 8.11-12] in the middle of a pericope which contained a Jew/Gentile contrast'.[111] However, within the prophetic tradition, there is some evidence that casts significant doubt on Allison's categorical ruling out of an eschatological return of the Gentiles. Isaiah 2.2-3 states, 'In days to come the mountain of the Lord's house shall be established ... all the nations shall stream to it. Many peoples shall come and say, "Come, let us go up to the mountain of the Lord, to the house of the God of Jacob; that he may teach us his ways and that we may walk in his paths ... ."' Furthermore, although in less explicit terms, Malachi's rebuke of faithless priests in his second oracle (1.6–2.9) envisions a connection between the 'east and west' motif and the Gentiles. Malachi 1.11 states 'from the rising of the sun [east] to its setting [west] my name is great among the nations, and in every place incense is offered to my name, and a pure offering; for my name is great among the nations, says the Lord of hosts.' The image of the sun's east–west movement indicates the totality of place in which the 'literary figure of distribution specifies the territorial extent of the nations paying homage to Yahweh'.[112] This also indicates that Malachi affirms that legitimate ritual outside Israel can occur; in this sense Peterson concludes that 'whether or not appropriate ritual occurs in Jerusalem, Yahweh's name will be appropriately venerated in other venues'.[113] Significantly, J. Baldwin,[114] P. A. Verhoef,[115] and M. Rehm[116] find precedent for understanding v. 11 not only in the context of the current series of events portrayed by Malachi but also in the context of the eschatological age.

Based on this understanding, it seems most plausible to understand Mt. 8.11-12 not as a Matthean theological embellishment that has misinterpreted 'Q', but rather as a legitimate appropriation (cf. Isaiah 2; Malachi 1) of an exilic/Exodus image which envisions the oppressed (including both tribes and nations) being led out of exile.[117] In this sense, Matthew has inverted the image of return from exile primarily to refer to Gentiles, indeed the sons of the kingdom have been 'thrown into the outer darkness, where there will be weeping and gnashing of teeth',[118] which in itself involves an element of ironic reversal.

---

111 Allison, 'East and West', p. 167.

112 A. E. Hill, *Malachi: A New Translation with Introduction and Commentary* (New York: Doubleday, 1988), p. 186.

113 D. L. Petersen, *Zechariah 9–14 and Malachi* (Kentucky: John Knox Press), p. 184.

114 J. Baldwin, 'Mal 1:11 and the Worship of the Nations in the Old Testament', *TynBul* 23 (1972), pp. 117–24.

115 P. A. Verhoef, *The Books of Haggai and Malachi* (Grand Rapids: Eerdmans, 1987), pp. 222–32.

116 M. Rehm, 'Das Opfer der Volker nach Mal 1:11', in *Lex Tua Veritas: Festschrift fur Hubert Junker*, ed. H. Gross and F. Mussner (Stuttgart: Trier Publishers), pp. 144–235 (195–96).

117 See Luz, *Matthew 21–28*, p.11.

118 Matthew 8.12; cf. 24.51; 22.13; 25.10, 30.

5.4.b. The Canaanite Woman and the Loaves (Mt. 14.13-21; 15.22-28, 29-39

That there is some justification for the association of chs 8.5-13 and 15.22-28 is evident in Bultmann's (nonetheless overstated) suggestion that the 'two stories are variants' of a related predecessor.[119] As Davies and Allison have rightly noted, 'the differences make that nearly inconceivable'.[120] Nonetheless, they find the thematic and linguistic parallels between the two pericopes 'truly striking'.[121] (1) In both stories Jesus encounters a despised Gentile (military officer, Canaanite woman); (2) chs 8 and 15 are the only two times in Matthew where Jesus clearly gives aid to a Gentile; (3) in both accounts the Gentile approaches Jesus and asks for healing on behalf of their child (ὁ παῖς μου in 8.6; and ἡ θυγάτηρ μου in 15.22); (4) although this is not unique to these accounts, Jesus is addressed as κύριε (8.6; 15.22); (5) there is significant emphasis on the discussion preceding the miracle which also includes a general statement about Israel (8.10; 15.24 cf. v. 28); (6) before acting, Jesus is somewhat hesitant in both instances; and (7) both healings occur at a distance. Davies and Allison suggest that these similarities can be accounted for by the possibility of the stories being associated in the oral tradition or by virtue of their similar genre, that is, 'the same *Gattung* or *Untergattung*'.[122] We suggest, however, that Matthew has associated these stories to advance the theological trajectory, set out in 8.5-13, regarding the role and function of Gentiles subsequent to Jesus' ministry within Israel. That is, Israel's lack of receptivity has brought judgement on themselves and opened broader possibilities with τὰ ἔθνη. As such, Chrysostom *Hom. on Matthew* 52.1 suggested that this story concerns the place of Israel and the place of the Gentiles in the broader spectrum of salvation history.

What then can be said regarding the portrayal of Gentiles in the story of the Canaanite woman narrated in Mt. 15.22-28? One common conception amongst interpreters is that this pericope portrays Israel very positively, and in this regard Jesus' response to the Canaanite woman's request for help is consistently cited: 'I was sent only to the lost sheep of the house of Israel' (Mt. 15.24). Typical in this regard are Davies and Allison, who state that 'the primacy of the Jews and God's covenant with them are unequivocally upheld'.[123] Similarly, Brandon states that there is an 'obvious unpalatableness to [the] Gentile Christian'.[124] Furthermore, Davies and Allison argue that there is no obvious suggestion which indicates that 'God has rejected his people or introduced a new way of salvation'[125] at this point in the narrative.

---

119 Bultmann, *History*, p. 58.
120 Davies and Allison, *Matthew* 2, p. 558.
121 Davies and Allison, *Matthew* 2, p. 558.
122 Davies and Allison, *Matthew* 2, p. 558.
123 Davies and Allison, *Matthew* 2, p. 543. Also note p. 542, 'Mt. 15.21-8 is more Jewish than its [Markan] parallel ... [in that] it is more potentially offensive to non-Jews.'
124 Brandon cited in Davies and Allison, *Matthew* 2, p. 544.
125 Davies and Allison, *Matthew* 2, p. 543.

While one may be inclined to accept a tempered version of this statement, it remains clear that given (1) that the immediately preceding story involves serious disputations between Jesus and the 'Pharisees and the teachers of the law' (15.1), and (2) that 15.21 involves Jesus ἐξελθὼν ἐκεῖθεν ('leaving that place', cf. 24.1) and offering help to a Χαναναία, this story functions as a strong polemic against the Jewish leaders of 15.1-20.[126] In this regard F. Moloney concludes that 'in the face of a negative reception, Jesus has risen from his place in Israel and walked away'.[127]

Significant for our discussion is the comment made by Davies and Allison that '15.21-28 can only be rightly grasped when it is interpreted within its broader context'.[128] What becomes immediately apparent, upon taking this advice, is that the immediately following story (the feeding of the 4,000) is also about superfluous crumbs (ἄρτον and ψιχίων in 15.26-27; ἄρτος and κλασμάτων in 15.33-34, 37). As such, we suggest that the two stories are mutually interpretive in that the ambiguity regarding the status of Gentiles in Mt. 15.21-28 is elucidated in 15.29-39. If the Gentiles are permitted to eat only the leftover crumbs, 'Yes, Lord, yet even the dogs eat the crumbs that fall from their masters' table ...' (15.27), then the abundant amount of leftovers in the subsequent feeding story (15.37) has important implications. Although Donaldson[129] (agreeing with Davies and Allison) suggests that this pericope 'leaves the status of Gentiles hanging in the air',[130] our observation would suggest that D. Hill is more accurate in concluding that 15.21-28 would have aided 'Matthew's community' in their relations with the Gentiles because of the positive elements within.[131] This is highlighted by Cranfield's statement regarding the Markan parallel: 'she does not want to diminish Israel's privileges, but desires a superfluous crumb'.[132] However, rather than a leftover crumb, the subsequent pericope offers seven baskets full of bread.[133] This interpretation is also confirmed by the close proximity of the other Matthean feeding story, namely the feeding of the 5,000 in

126 See discussion of the fact that the region into which Jesus departed was Gentile territory in Gundry, *Matthew*, pp. 310–11. Donaldson, *Mountain*, p. 132 notes that this would naturally expose 'Israel's deeply-engrained fear of and revulsion towards Gentile ways'. Although Tyre was predominantly Gentile, there is also evidence of Jewish population. See discussion in M. Hooker, *The Gospel According to Mark* (Peabody: Hendrickson, 1991), p. 181: 'the population was as mixed as it was in Galilee'.

127 F. Moloney, *The Gospel of Mark* (Peabody: Hendrickson, 2002), p. 147 on the Markan parallel.

128 Davies and Allison, *Matthew 2*, p. 544.

129 Donaldson, *Mountain*, p. 134.

130 Davies and Allison, *Matthew 2*, p. 544.

131 Hill, *Matthew*, p. 253.

132 C. E. B. Cranfield, *The Gospel according to St. Mark* (Cambridge: Cambridge University Press, 1974), p. 249.

133 Although this 'literary sandwich' has been noted in the Markan parallel (see Moloney, *Mark*, pp. 146–47), the suggestion has yet to be integrated into discussions of Matthean structure and meaning.

14.13-21. This pericope and the narrative in ch. 15 are separated only by Jesus' walking on the water in 14.22-36, a miracle that many commentators have seen as metaphorically demonstrative of the disciples'/Israel's insufficient faith, especially so because of Matthew's unique addition of the 'sinking Peter' incident in 14.28-33.[134]

Although abundance and leftovers from miraculous provisions is a common motif in miracles of providence,[135] what is particularly striking in the broader association is the respective number of leftover baskets; twelve in the feeding of the 5,000 (14.20) and seven in the feeding of the 4,000 (15.37). The suggestion that the number of baskets in 14.20 simply refers to the practical result of having twelve in charge of the distribution and collection does not take into account the parallel story in 15.21-39, which is similarly organized but mentions only seven baskets. Q. Quesnell suggests that the 'probable significance of the number of baskets' is that 'twelve and seven … [are] representative respectively of Judaism and Gentility'.[136] In support of this is the association of the number *twelve* and Israel within Matthew's narrative in Mt. 19.28, which states 'Truly I tell you, at the renewal of all things, when the Son of Man is seated on the throne of his glory, you who have followed me will also sit on twelve thrones, judging the twelve tribes of Israel.' This association between *twelve* and Israel is again utilized in Matthew's account of Jesus' selection of twelve disciples[137] to carry on his work of healing and restoration[138] in 10.1-4.

The representative nature of the number *seven* for the Gentile world is less specific but nonetheless discernible from various usages in the LXX and New Testament. Commentators have been inclined to find support for this idea in Acts 6.1-6, where seven men are chosen to aid in the daily distribution of food to the Hellenists' widows. That οἱ ἑπτά ('the seven') corresponds to a definitive group is evident from Acts 21.8: 'The next day we left and came to Caesarea; and we went into the house of Philip the evangelist, one of the

---

134 Davies and Allison, *Matthew 2*, pp. 497–98, who state that 'This passage … is rich in both its christological implications and its instruction on discipleship.'

135 First Kings 17.16; 2 Kgs 4.6-7, 44; *b.Ta'an.* 24b.

136 Q. Quesnell, *The Mind of Mark: Interpretation and Method Through the Exegesis of Mark 6:52* (Rome: Pontifical Biblical Institute, 1969), p. 229 n.56.

137 The phrase Matthew uses in 10.1 (δώδεκα μαθητὰς) finds attestation in 11.1; 20.17 and 26.20. Elsewhere Matthew refers to 'the twelve' (Mt. 10.5; 26.14, 47 [cf. Mk 3.14; 4.10; 6.7; 9.35; 10.32; 11.11; 14.14, 17, 20, 43; Lk. 8.1; 9.1, 12; 18.31; 22.3, 47; Jn 6.67, 70-71; 20.24; Acts 6.2]), and also to the δώδεκα ἀποστόλων ('twelve apostles') (Mt. 10.2 par. Lk. 6.13).

138 Further evidence of this understanding of the number *twelve* is supported by W. Horbury, who has noted that in Numbers 1, 4, and 7, Moses is directed by Yahweh to choose twelve men to be his associates in the compilation of Israel's census (W. Horbury, 'The Twelve Phylarchs', *NTS* 32 [1982], pp. 503–27 (503)). In Philo's work *Fug. et Inv.* 73, he speaks of the Patriarchs as 'rulers of the nation twelve in number … customarily called φυλάρχους (Phylarchs)'. In *Ant.* 3.169, Josephus similarly refers to the Patriarchs as φυλάρχους.

seven, and stayed with him.' Greater specificity in this regard is seen in Deut. 7.1, where the ἔθνη are in parallel with the ἑπτά:

> When the Lord your God brings you into the land that you are about to enter and occupy, and he clears away many nations (ἔθνη μεγάλα) before you – the Hittites, the Girgashites, the Amorites, the Canaanites, the Perizzites, the Hivites, and the Jebusites, seven nations (ἑπτά ἔθνη) mightier and more numerous than you ...[139]

Indeed, there seems to be no better numeric representation for a Gentile referent in Matthew's narrative than the number seven, which is elsewhere consistently employed to express fullness, completion, and perfection.[140] Thus, rather than attempting to find nuances of vocabulary describing the receptacle of the fragments (σπυρίδας/κόφινος) and their possible respective sizes to account for the numerical difference in the feeding stories,[141] the key lies in the symbolic identification with Israel and the Gentiles. In this regard, it is unwarranted to claim that if Gentiles were the key in 15.21-28 then 'surely [the author] ... would have done a better job of making his intentions clearly known'.[142] It seems as though Matthew has indeed provided enough clues enabling the reader/listener to associate the stories of 'crumbs' and draw conclusions regarding the representation of Gentiles within the narrative.

The tension between 10.5-6 and our interpretation need not be overstated: 'These twelve Jesus sent out with the following instructions. "Go nowhere among the Gentiles, and enter no town of the Samaritans, but go rather to the lost sheep of the house of Israel ... ."'' Although it is true that many commentators have seen a tension between Mt. 28.16-20 and 10.5-6,[143] and there always exists the possibility that Matthew's comments are irreconcilable,[144]

---

139 Cf. Acts 13.19.

140 The seven-day week constitutes a complete cycle of time (Gen. 1.1–2.3; Exod. 20.10); the sprinkling the blood of a sacrifice seven times (Lev. 16.14, 19); the seven 'eyes of the Lord, which range through the whole earth' (Zech. 4.10); the seven steps in the temple seen in Ezekiel's vision (Ezek. 40.22, 26); Nebuchadnezzar increases the heat of his furnace sevenfold (Dan. 3.19); the light of the sun intensified sevenfold (Isa. 30.26); Israel risks sevenfold punishment (Lev. 26.18-21); silver purified seven times (Ps. 12.6).

141 Davies and Allison, *Matthew 2*, p. 573 suggest that 'perhaps the difference in numbers of baskets ... reflects the fact that σπυρίς ... was larger than κόφινος'. This has proven problematic in various attempts. It is unfortunate, however, that the different kinds of basket cannot be prominently identified with either Jewish or Gentile association. See further Quesnell, *Mind*, p. 230.

142 Davies and Allison, *Matthew 2*, p. 545. Davies and Allison nonetheless admit that 'it may even be that the bread should be considered a symbol of salvation' (p. 553).

143 F. Hahn, *Mission in the New Testament* (trans. F. Clark; London: SCM, 1965), p. 120.

144 On this issue Foster, *Community*, p. 219 n.3 states: 'This view should perhaps only be adopted either if an obvious contradiction can be demonstrated within the gospel, or if attempts to find a unified, or overarching, train of thought are seen to fail.'

the clue to this conundrum may lie in the motif of salvation history. That is, within the Matthean narrative itself, a new dispensation unfolds in which the nature of mission evolves.[145] D. C. Sim, however, has argued that Matthew's omission of the Markan return of the disciples (Mk 6.30) was motivated by a desire to hold the continuing legitimacy of the barring of mission εἰς ὁδὸν ἐθνῶν ... εἰς πόλιν Σαμαριτῶν.[146] P. Foster has responded by noting, however, that the return of the disciples would 'in no sense undo ... a restriction of an "Israel only" mission'.[147] Furthermore, there is no parallel to Mt. 10.5-6 in the Markan text, and as such it is questionable as to how Mk 6.30 would make the former claim. In this regard, J. P. Meier accurately notes that Matthew 'quite consciously orders an "economy" of salvation: to the Jews first and then to the Gentiles'.[148] Meier suggests that it is only 'after the death and resurrection ... [that] this "economical" limitation falls at Jesus' all powerful command (Mt. 28.16-20)'.[149]

The rationale for this salvation-history approach has typically been envisioned as having a (related) twofold purpose. First, H. Frankemölle has suggested that the phrase was included to demonstrate God's covenantal faithfulness.[150] Frankemölle notes this theme in the Hebrew Bible, particularly Deuteronomy, and demonstrates how it would have been of interest to Matthew. Second, and perhaps not unrelated, is the proposal by W. Trilling, who suggests that Matthew's dedication to Israel was undertaken predominantly for the purpose of portraying Israel as guilty, and precludes any excuse on their behalf.[151] This, in fact, coheres well with Frankemölle's proposal in that within the Deuteronomistic covenant God would remain faithful to his people (Deut. 4.31; 7.9; 32.4), but Israel had the ability to reject God and break the covenant relationship. This however, inevitably led to suffering the covenant curses of Deut. 28.15-68.

5.4.c. Preliminary conclusion

It seems relatively clear how the general portrayal of Gentiles in Matthew contributes to our discussion. In Matthew's theological horizon, proleptic judgement has come upon Israel for the rejection of their

145 On the importance of reading the wider Matthean narrative in this process see U. Luz, *The Theology of the Gospel of Matthew* (Cambridge: Cambridge University Press, 1995), p. 16. P. Foster has noted, 'after chap. 15 there is almost without exception a positive attitude displayed to bringing Gentiles into the community', Foster, *Community*, p. 220.

146 D. C. Sim, *The Gospel of Matthew and Christian Judaism: The History and Social Setting of the Matthean Community* (Edinburgh: T&T Clark, 1999), p. 158.

147 Foster, *Community*, p. 222.

148 J. P. Meier, *Law and History in Matthew's Gospel* (Rome: Biblical Institute, 1979), p. 27.

149 Meier, *Law*, p. 27.

150 Frankemölle, *Jahwe-Bund*, p. 123.

151 W. Trilling, *Hausordnung Gottes* (Düsseldorf: Patmos-Verlag, 1960), pp. 103–105.

messianic king; as such the concept of 'God's people' as 'national Israel' is radically redefined. Matthew argues that it is only those who accept Jesus' messianic claim who are to be accepted as the 'true Israel'.[152] It is for this reason that we find cause to disagree with Davies and Allison when they state that 'One should not, therefore, come away from Matthew with the notion that Israel's election no longer counts for anything. Notwithstanding the rejection of the Messiah, the Jews, in some mysterious way, remain divinely advantaged.'[153] At this point Davies and Allison seem to be more influenced by the Pauline tradition than the extant text of Matthew's Gospel. By their own admission 'there is, to use a Pauline phrase, neither Jew nor Greek, and yet there is a continued place for the Jewish people as such'.[154] Matthew hints at no such continued place, and in so presenting the role of Gentiles suggests a more radical shift. In this way Matthew weaves together a seamless prophetic denouncement of Israel for her stubbornness in refusing to accept the legitimacy of Jesus' words and deeds, and offers renewed hope to the Gentile world.[155]

5.5. Concluding Thoughts on the Son of Man in Matthew: A Varied Motif[156]

Although an exhaustive discussion of the 'Son of Man' in Matthew is beyond the purview of this work, it remains to provide some concluding thoughts on the role and function of ὁ υἱὸς τοῦ ἀνθρώπου employed elsewhere in Matthew's narrative and the extent to which Jesus as 'Son of Man' might be a homogeneous or varied concept. It was argued above that the coming of the 'Son of Man' in Matthew 24 was realized in the destruction of Jerusalem by the Roman army in 70 AD. Some may object that Matthew employs the phrase elsewhere with clear overtones of 'eschatological' finality, particularly in Mt. 13.41; 19.28-29; or 25.31.

Before we briefly discuss these more problematic texts, it is important to note that there is justification for understanding the 'Son of Man' as representative of the Roman army within Matthew's Gospel but *outside* ch. 24. There are two passages which operate in this fashion. First Mt. 10.23:

152 Cf. John the Baptist's words in Mt. 3.7-10.

153 Davies and Allison, *Matthew 2*, p. 558.

154 Davies and Allison, *Matthew 2*, p. 558.

155 Cf. Mt. 21.43, where it is explicitly stated that the Kingdom is finally taken from those who previously possessed it, 'Therefore I tell you, the kingdom of God will be taken away from you and given to a people that produce the fruits of the kingdom.' Clark states '... the assurance that the gentiles have replaced the Jews is the basic message and the gentile bias of Matthew', Clark, 'Gentile', p. 172.

156 For the following analysis I am grateful for the stimulating and critical personal discussions with R. E. Watts (Professor of New Testament, Regent College, Vancouver), whose reflections assisted in the formulation of this hypothesis.

'When they persecute you in one town, flee to the next; for truly I tell you, you will not have gone through all the towns of Israel before the Son of Man comes.' This saying occurs in the context of the mission of the disciples and reflects the historical reality of the first century rather than an eschatological future dispensation. This is evident in regard to the specific mention of 'going through the towns of Israel', which has clear connections with the injunction in Mt. 10.5b-6. As such, A. Feuillet has argued that this logion finds its fulfilment in the destruction of Jerusalem.[157] A second passage that reflects similar concerns regarding the 'Son of Man' is Mt. 16.27-28:

> For the Son of Man is to come with his angels in the glory of his Father, and then he will repay everyone for what has been done. Truly I tell you, there are some standing here who will not taste death before they see the Son of Man coming in his kingdom.

That this refers to 70 AD is evident through the reference to τινες των ὧδε ἑστώτων ('some standing here'), which would otherwise be inexplicable.[158] It is in this regard that J. J. Wettstein,[159] and H. Alford[160] connect the destruction of Jerusalem and the judgement on Israel. Furthermore, there is a tradition which attests to the role of the heavenly angels in the destruction of Jerusalem.[161] The second book of Baruch 7.1-8.2 states:

> And after these things I heard that angel saying to those angels who held the lamps. Destroy, therefore, and overthrow the wall [of Jerusalem] to its foundations ... Now the angels did as he had commanded them, and when they had broken up the corners of the walls, a voice was heard from the interior of the temple, after the wall had fallen, saying. 'Enter, you enemies, and come, you adversaries; For he who kept the house has forsaken it.'

What then can be said of those passages in Matthew which do seem to refer to a future-orientated 'eschatological' 'Son of Man'?[162] We here refer to 13.41: 'The Son of Man will send his angels, and they will collect out of his kingdom all causes of sin and all evildoers'; and 19.28-29:

---

157 Feuillet, 'Le discours', pp. 481–502.

158 We find the various proposals to reconcile this phrase with (1) the transfiguration (Clement of Alexandria *Exc. Thdot.* 4.3; Origen *Comm on Mt.* 12.31); (2) the resurrection (Meier, *Matthew*, p. 188); (3) Pentecost (T. F. Glasson, *The Second Advent* [London: Epworth, 1963], p. 112); or (4) the spiritualization of death (Cranfield, *Gospel*, p. 286) as unconvincing.

159 Wettstein, *Novum*, p. 231.

160 Alford, *Greek*, p. 177.

161 See Hoppe, *City*, p. 164.

162 There are also motifs of vindication (26.64) and suffering (12.40; 17.9, 12, 22; 20.18, 28; 26.2, 24, 45) related to the 'Son of Man' phrase.

Truly I tell you, at the renewal of all things, when the Son of Man is seated on the throne of his glory, you who have followed me will also sit on twelve thrones, judging the twelve tribes of Israel. And everyone who has left houses or brothers or sisters or father or mother or children or fields, for my name's sake, will receive a hundredfold, and will inherit eternal life.

Of even more apparent difficulty for our interpretation is 25.31: 'When the Son of Man comes in his glory, and all the angels with him, then he will sit on the throne of his glory ... .' This latter reference is particularly problematic because of (1) its proximity to ch. 24; (2) the specific mention of the 'coming' of the 'Son of Man'; and (3) the finality implicit in the accompanying parable of sheep and goats.

The clue to understanding the role of the 'Son of Man' in 25.31 (and related passages) is within the context of Matthew's broader hermeneutical horizon of *Heilgeschichte* (salvation history). J. Meier defines this concept as the

schematic understanding of God's dealings with men that emphasizes continuity – yet difference. In so far as the theologian, reflecting on saving events, sees the one and the same God acting faithfully and consistently within the flow of time, he perceives continuity. ... In so far as the theologian sees the different ways in which God acts at different times and the different ways in which man responds, he perceives the lines of demarcation which delimit the distinct periods of this history. ... Difference within continuity, the various stages within the one divine economy. this is the basic insight on which any outline or pattern of salvation history is built.[163]

R. Walker[164] is generally credited with underscoring the importance of Matthew's *Heilgeschichte*.[165] In his main work, Walker argued that Matthew was to be envisioned in three periods of sacred history. Walker argues, on the basis of the Genealogy (Mt. 1.1-18), that the first period of history ran from Abraham until the time of the Messiah. The second phase was the Messianic age which fell into two distinct categories: (a) the proclamation of the Gospel to Israel (cf. Mt. 10.5b-6; 15.24) until (b) the destruction of the Jerusalem temple. The third and final period of history is characterized by mission to the Gentiles (28.16-20). As such, Walker presents a 'symbolic presentation of salvation history ... [in which] the hostility between Jesus and the Jewish leaders is not reflective of a contemporary polemic between Matthew and Pharisaic Judaism but plays out the first stage of messianic salvation history'.[166]

163 Meier, *Law*, p. 30.

164 R. Walker, *Die Heilsgeschichte im ersten Evangelium* (Göttingen: Vandenhoeck & Ruprecht, 1967).

165 J. P. Meier, 'Salvation-History in Matthew: In Search of a Stating Point', *CBQ* 37 (1975), pp. 203–15 (203).

166 D. Senior, *What Are They Saying about Matthew?* (New York: Paulist Press,

We find Walker's analysis convincing, bar one element which needs modification. Walker suggests that a mission to Israel is operative up until 70 AD, at which point mission to Israel ceases. He argues that not only does mission exclusively turn to the Gentile world, but that the Gentile mission *commences* with the events of 70 AD. Although acknowledging that Mt. 28.18-20 poses a particular problem for this hypothesis, Walker suggests Matthew was not concerned to align these concluding verses with the trajectory of his narrative thus far. This is a dubious claim at best, since 28.18-20 reflects significant Matthean redaction.[167]

A reasonable resolution to these different sets of problems comes from a particular understanding of the parable of sheep and goats (Mt. 25.31-46). We suggest that πάντα τὰ ἔθνη in 25.31 refer specifically to Gentiles.[168] Not only is this the most fundamental meaning of ἔθνος, but the phrase πάντα τὰ ἔθνη commonly refers to Gentiles in the LXX.[169] Furthermore, the key to understanding the parable are the words in 25.40: 'Truly I tell you, just as you did it to one of the least of these who are members of my family (ἐφ᾽ ὅσον ἐποιήσατε ἑνὶ τούτων τῶν ἀδελφῶν μου τῶν ἐλαχίστων), you did it to me.' As several commentators have noted in light of 10.40-41, τῶν ἀδελφῶν μου most plausibly refers to missionaries and their reception.[170] The basis of their rejection or reception is connected to the manner in which the message they proclaim is appropriated. Furthermore, it is a common characteristic of Matthew to refer to fellow Christians with the non-biological use of ἀδελφός (Mt. 12.48-50; 28.10). The interpretation of the parable then, is related not to an abstracted moral principle of aiding the hungry, thirsty, stranger, naked, sick, or prisoner in some kind of generalized Christian charity, but rather to the way in which people receive those who proclaim the message of Jesus. It is in this regard that Luz concludes: 'the brothers of Jesus... can only be Christian missionaries ... who are traveling without means of support and are thus dependent on the love and hospitality of others'.[171] That is, for Matthew, 'the determining factor for the fate of the *ethne* (nations or Gentiles) in the Last Judgement will be their behaviour

---

1983), p. 30. G. Strecker, *Der Weg der Gerechtigkeit, Untersuchung zur Theologie des Matthäus* (Göttingen: Vandenhoeck & Ruprecht, 1971), also has a threefold division of salvation history, but prefers to see the second phase ending with the death/resurrection of Jesus rather than the destruction of the Temple in 70 AD. Meier, 'Salvation', p. 203 specifically emphasizes the resurrection as the turning point. See also Kingsbury, *Structure*, p. 31, who finds precedent for only a twofold division of salvation history, namely pre and post the life of Jesus.

167 Davies and Allison, *Matthew 3*, pp. 677-78.

168 This is not to deny that 28.16-20 cannot have a universal meaning. On the contrary, the context would seem to imply a universalistic meaning.

169 Genesis 18.18; 22.18; 26.4; Exod. 23.27; 33.16; Deut. 7.6-7.

170 Zahn, *Matthäus*, p. 332; Gundry, *Matthew*, p. 567; Luz, *Theology*, pp. 129–32; G. N. Stanton, 'Once More: Matthew 25:31-46', in *A Gospel for a New People*, ed. G. N. Stanton (Edinburgh: T&T Clark, 1992), pp. 207–31.

171 Luz, *Theology*, pp. 129–30.

toward the Christian missionaries'.[172] Indeed, this was precisely the same scenario that was portrayed for the mission to Israel (Mt. 10.14-15; 23.34-36). The issue is not moral behaviour, but the corollary that welcoming a person is indicative of accepting their message, in this case, the proclamation of the Kingdom of God.

In relating these findings to our discussion concerning the coming of the Son of Man in chs 24 and 25, we propose that Matthew conceives of a two-stage process. That is, a 'Jewish' and 'Gentile' coming of the Son of Man, so that both Jesus' parousia and the 'end of the age' are a dual two-stage process. The first being Jesus' coming as (1a) Messiah to Israel, then returning as (1b) Son of Man in Judgement on Jerusalem, and second, (2a) the proclamation of the message of Jesus (cf. Matthew 25) and (2b) final judgement. This can be diagrammatically portrayed as shown in Fig. 5.1:

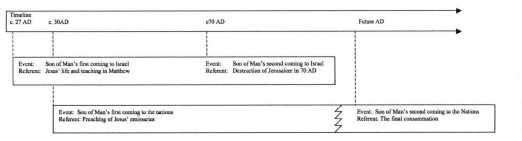

Fig. 5.1. Two-stage coming of the 'Son of Man'.

In this way, Israel and her temple function as a microcosm for the cosmos. Indications of this are evident through the 'Palace-Temple' architectural descriptions of creation.[173] It is described as having 'foundations',[174] 'pillars',[175] 'windows',[176] 'chambers and beams',[177] and 'heaven as a canopy/roof'.[178] The identification is explicitly made in Isa. 66.1 in connection with

172 Luz, *Theology*, p. 130.

173 See further R. E. Watts, 'On the Edge of the Millennium: Making Sense of Genesis 1', in *Living in the Lamblight*, ed. H. Boersma (Vancouver: Regent College Publishing, 2001), pp. 129–52 (147).

174 Psalm 18.15; 82.5; 102.25; 104.5; Prov. 8.29; Isa. 48.13; 51.13; 2 Sam. 22.8, 16; Zech. 12.1.

175 First Samuel 2.8; Job 9.6; 26.11; Ps. 75.3.

176 Genesis 7.11; 8.2; Isa. 24.18; Mal. 3.10; 2 Kgs 7.2.

177 Psalm 104.2-3; Amos 9.6.

178 Isaiah 40.12, 22; 44.24; 45.12; 48.13; 51.13; Jer. 10.12; 31.37; 51.15; Zech. 12.1; Job 9.8; Ps. 102.25.

the earthly temple.[179] That this idea was prominent in the first century is evidenced by Josephus, *War* 5.212–14.

> But before these doors there was a veil of equal largeness with the doors. It was a Babylonian curtain, embroidered with blue, and fine linen, and scarlet, and purple, and of a contexture that was truly wonderful. Nor was this mixture of colors without its mystical interpretation, but was a kind of *image of the universe* (ὥσπερ εἰκόνα τῶν ὅλων); for by the scarlet there seemed to be enigmatically signified fire, by the fine flax the earth, by the blue the air, and by the purple the sea; two of them having their colors the foundation of this resemblance; but the fine flax and the purple have their own origin for that foundation, the earth producing the one, and the sea the other. This curtain had also embroidered upon it all that was mystical in the heavens, excepting that of the [twelve] signs, representing living creatures.

As such, J. Davila has noted that 'the Jerusalem Temple ... [was] a microcosm of the universe'.[180] Similarly D. D. Kupp states that 'the Jerusalem Temple explained YHWH's active presence in his created order and functioned as a spiritual and symbolic microcosm or the macrocosm; containing within itself the tension of the earthly and the heavenly, the imminent and the transcendent'.[181] In the light of this, it is understandable that what happens to the earthly temple has a cosmic corollary,[182] in this case a final consummation.

In conclusion then, the phrase ὁ υἱὸς τοῦ ἀνθρώπου occurs thirty times in Matthew,[183] and in all instances is found on the lips of Jesus. As has frequently been pointed out by commentators, the phrase has a variety of uses including references to (1) suffering and crucifixion; (2) vindication; or even (3) used in place of a pronoun. We suggest therefore that the way in which the 'Son of Man' represents the Roman army, primarily in ch. 24, but also attested in 10.23 and 16.27-28, is one further legitimate implementation of a varied and highly metaphoric concept.

179 For further discussion see C. Fletcher-Louis, 'The Temple Cosmology of P and Theological Anthropology in the Wisdom of Jesus ben Sira', in *Of Scribes and Sages: Studies in Early Jewish Interpretation and Transmission of Scripture*, ed. C. A. Evans (Sheffield: Sheffield Academic Press, 2002), pp. 1–51.

180 Davila, *Provenance*, p. 17.

181 D. D. Kupp, *Matthew's Emmanuel: Divine Presence and God's People in the First Gospel* (Cambridge: Cambridge University Press, 1996), p. 133.

182 The function of a deity's temple as microcosmic was common in ANE sources. See S. Paas, *Creation and Judgement: Creation Texts in Some Eighth Century Prophets* (Leiden: Brill, 2003), p. 128.

183 Matthew 8.20; 9.6; 10.23; 11.19; 12.8, 32, 40; 13.37, 41; 16.13, 27-28; 17.9, 12, 22; 19.28; 20.18, 28; 24.27, 30, 37, 39, 44; 25.31; 26.2, 24, 45, 64.

5.6. Summary and Conclusion

We began our discussion by surveying modern scholarship on the βδέλυγμα τῆς ἐρημώσεως (chapter 1). Among multiple hypotheses, we found that because of the association of the phrase with Antiochus Epiphanes in the Daniel narrative, commentators had almost exclusively argued for a 'pagan' (*contra* Jewish) referent in relation to Mt. 24.15 (and synoptic parallels). However, on the basis of Josephus and several modern commentators,[184] we found precedent to pursue the question of interpretation in regard to an internal Jewish polemic (vis-à-vis Hebrew Bible prophetic literature) rather than an external pagan referent.

Chapter 2 then investigated Matthew as a deliberately structured document intended to recall certain aspects of the Deuteronomistic framework, namely the blessings and curses of the covenant in Deut. 27-30. Furthermore, it was seen that Matthew's presentation of Jesus' lament over Jerusalem (23.39) sought to emphasize Israel's culpability in rejecting her Messianic King, which in turn provided the framework for understanding ch. 24, namely the destruction of Jerusalem through the advent of the Son of Man. The idea that Jerusalem's destruction was engendered by Israel's infidelity was seen to be a common motif in post-70-AD pseudepigraphical material.

Our analysis in chapter 3 then turned to a detailed discussion of the language and meaning of Matthew 24, wherein it was argued that, given the introductory marker 'As Jesus came out of the temple' and the questions relating to the temple's buildings, there is no reason to suppose that the author switches from a 'historical' to an 'end time eschatology' at any point in ch. 24. Even such theologically loaded terms as παρουσία (vv. 3, 27, 37, 39), which have traditionally been interpreted in reference to Jesus' physical return, are more suitably understood with regard to their royal and military motifs. Furthermore, far from the false-prophets (24.4-5, 11, 24) indicating any interest in anti-Christ figures (cf. Thessalonians), substantial parallel was substantiated from Josephus' 'sign-prophets'. Of particular significance in our findings was the attestation of at least one other Matthean contemporary author who describes the military action of the Roman army as 'desert making' (Tacitus *Agr.* 30.3b-6). A similar association was also seen in representing the Roman troops as the ἀετοί of 24.28. The so-called 'apocalyptic' language of sun, moon, and falling stars was seen to have background in the prophetic literature in reference to descriptions of military invasions. In this sense, the parousia of the Son of Man was seen to refer to the city's destruction through Roman intervention.

Chapter 4 then demonstrated that this understanding of the 'Son of Man' is consistent with Jewish hopes of redemption, specifically in regard to the Danielic Son of Man who comes to destroy Israel's enemies. This theme also

---

184 Pfleiderer, 'Komposition'; Bevan, *Commentary*; and Balabanski, *Eschatology*.

found attestation in pre-first-century Jewish literature, namely 1 *Enoch* and 4 *Ezra*. Important in this broader discussion were our findings that (1) the terms βδέλυγμα/שִׁקּוּצִים ('abomination') and ἐρήμωσις/מְשֹׁמֵם ('desolation') are readily attested in the prophetic literature and used in description (i.e. abomination) and consequence (i.e. desolation) of Israel's covenantal infidelity; (2) the prophetic literature exhibits a pervasive and thoroughgoing influence on the book of Daniel; and (3) these two issues potentially provided Matthew with the theological motivation ironically to employ the Danielic material in description of the destruction of Jerusalem in Matthew 24. The ironic element in the Matthean narrative is that Israel herself has become her own enemy and as such stands under the curses of the covenant and subsequent destruction.

Chapter 5 then sought to bring an appropriate conclusion to our discussion by noting (1) the possible rationale for the typological and metaphorical association in Matthew's Gospel being a combination of Plato's pedagogical maxim, Ludwig Josef Wittgenstein's philosophy of human epistemology, and Ernst Troeltsch's understanding of event narration; (2) the Matthean Jesus' representation in similar manner to Hebrew Bible prophets; (3) the role and function of Gentiles in the narrative; and (4) the multifaceted use of the 'Son of Man' phrase in Matthew, including those elements we saw operative in ch. 24.

Thus we may conclude that, within the Matthean narrative, the βδέλυγμα ('abomination') refers to Israel's covenantal infidelity, particularly her rejection of Jesus as Messianic King, and the ἐρήμωσις ('desolation') is the natural consequence of her disobedience, in this case Yahweh's punishment of Jerusalem through Roman intervention.

Bibliography

Abramowski, L., 'Die Entstehung der dreigliedrigen Taufformel – ein Versuch', *ZTK* 81 (1984), pp. 417–46.

Aland, K., *Synopsis Quattuor Evangeliorum* (10th edn; Stuttgart: Biblia-Druck, 1970).

Albright, W. F. and C. S. Mann, *Matthew* (New York: Doubleday, 1971).

Alford, H., *The Greek New Testament, Volume 1: The Four Gospels* (Cambridge: Deighton Bell, 1968).

Allen, L. C., *Ezekiel 1–19* (Dallas: Word Books, 1994).

Allen, W. C., *A Critical and Exegetical Commentary on the Gospel according to St. Matthew* (Edinburgh: T&T Clark, 1912).

Allison, D. C, 'Who will come from East and West? Observations on Matt. 8.11-12 = Luke 13.28-29', *IBS* 11 (1989), pp. 158–70.

——, *The New Moses: A Matthean Typology* (Minneapolis: Fortress Press, 1993).

——, *Jesus of Nazareth: Millenarian Prophet* (Minneapolis: Fortress Press, 1998).

Alter, R., *The Pleasures of Reading in an Ideological Age* (New York: Simon and Schuster, 1989).

Amerding, C. E., *Obadiah* (Grand Rapids: Zondervan, 1985).

Andersen, F. and D. N. Freedman, *Micah: A New Translation with Introduction and Commentary* (London: Doubleday, 2000).

Archer, G., *Jerome's Commentary on Daniel* (Grand Rapids: Baker, 1958).

Arnold, B. T. and J. H. Choi, *A Guide to Biblical Hebrew Syntax* (Cambridge: Cambridge University Press, 2003).

Ashley, J. R., *The Macedonian Empire* (North Carolina: McFarland and Company, 2004).

Atkinson, J. E., 'Q. Curtius Rufus' "Historiae Alexandri Magni"', *ANRW* II.34.4 (1997), pp. 3447–83.

Augsburger, M. S., *Mastering the New Testament: Matthew* (USA: Word, 1982).

Aulén, G., *Jesus in Contemporary Historical Research* (Philadelphia: Fortress, 1976).

Aus, R. D., *Caught in the Act, Walking on Sea and the Release of Barabbas Revisited* (Atlanta: Scholars Press, 2007).

Bacon, B. W., *Studies in Matthew* (London: Henry Holt, 1930).

Balabanski, V., *Eschatology in the Making* (Cambridge: Cambridge University Press, 1997).

——, 'Mission in Matthew Against the Horizon of Matthew 24' (Unpublished Seminar Paper at the Society of Biblical Literature Annual Meeting, Philadelphia, November 2005), pp. 1–16.

Baldwin, J., 'Mal 1:11 and the Worship of the Nations in the Old Testament', *TynBul* 23 (1972), pp. 117–24.

Barclay, W., *Matthew* (2 vols; Daily Study Bible; Edinburgh: St Andrew's, 1958).

Barnett, P. W., 'The Jewish Sign Prophets: A.D. 40–70', *NTS* 27 (1981), pp. 679–97.

Baron, S., *A Social and Religious History of the Jews* (New York: Columbia University Press, 1952).

Barr, J., *The Semantics of Biblical Language* (Oxford: Oxford University Press, 1961).

Barrett, C. K., *Jesus and the Gospel Tradition* (London: SPCK, 1967).

Barton, J., *Oracles of God: Perceptions of Ancient Prophecy in Israel After the Exile* (Oxford: Oxford University Press, 1986).

Bauckham, R., 'The Eschatological Earthquake in the Apocalypse of John', *NovT* 19 (1977), p. 224–33.

——, 'The Relevance of Extracanonical Jewish Texts to New Testament Study', in *Hearing the New Testament*, ed. J. B. Green (Grand Rapids: Eerdmans, 1995), pp. 90–108.

——, *The Gospels for All Christians* (Grand Rapids: Eerdmans, 1998).

Bauer, D. R. and M. A. Powell, *Treasures New and Old* (Atlanta: Scholars Press, 1996).

Bauman, R. A., *Human Rights in Ancient Rome* (London: Routledge, 1999).

Baumgartner, W., *Jeremiah's Poems of Lament* (Sheffield: Almond Press, 1988).

Baur, F. C., *Kritische Untersuchungen über die kanonischen Evangelien* (Tübingen, 1847).

Baynham, E., *Alexander the Great: The Unique History of Quintus Curtius* (Ann Arbor: University of Michigan Press, 1998).

Beale, G. K., *The Use of Daniel in Jewish Apocalyptic Literature and in the Revelation of St. John* (Lanham: University Press of America, 1984).

Beare, F. W., *The Gospel according to Matthew* (Oxford: Blackwell, 1981).

Beasley-Murray, G. R., *A Commentary on Mark 13* (London: Macmillan, 1957).

——, *Matthew* (London: Scripture Union, 1984).

Beilner, W., *Christus und die Pharisäer: Exegetische Untersuchung über Grund und Verlauf der Auseinandersetzungen* (Vienna: Herder, 1959).

Bengel, J. A., *New Testament Commentary* (repr.; Grand Rapids: Kregel, 1742).

Benoit, P., *L'Evangile selon Matthieu* (Paris: Cerf, 1961).

Berlin, A., 'Qumran Laments and the Study of Lament Literature', in *Liturgical Perspectives: Prayer and Poetry in Light of the Dead Sea Scrolls*, ed. E. G. Chazon (Leiden: Brill, 2003), pp. 1–18.

Berridge, J. M., *Prophet, People, and the Word of Yahweh* (Zürich: EVZ-Verlag, 1970).

Berthodt, L., *Daniel aus dem Hebräisch-Aramäischen neu übersetzt und erklärt mit einer vollständigen Einerleitung und einigen historischen und kritschen* (Erlangen: Palm, 1808).

Bevan, A. A., *A Short Commentary on the Book of Daniel* (Cambridge: Cambridge University Press, 1892).

———, *The House of Seleucus* (New York: Barnes and Noble, 1902).

Bickerman, E., *Der Gott der Makkabaâer* (Berlin: Schocken, 1937).

Black, D. A., 'The Text of John 3:13', *GTJ* 6 (1985), pp. 49–66.

Blair, E. P., *Jesus in the Gospel of Matthew* (Nashville: Abingdon, 1960).

Blake, R. P., 'The Georgian Version of Fourth Esdras from the Jerusalem Manuscript', *HTR* 19 (1926), pp. 299–375.

Blass, F. and A. Debrunner, *A Greek Grammar of the New Testament and Other Early Christian Literature* (trans. R. W. Funk; Cambridge: Cambridge University Press, 1961).

Blenkinsopp, J., *Prophecy and Canon: A Contribution to the Study of Jewish Origins* (Notre Dame: University Press, 1977).

———, *Ezekiel* (Louisville: John Knox Press, 1990).

———, *Isaiah 1–39* (London: Doubleday, 2000).

Bloch, R., 'Écriture et Tradition dans le Judaïsme', *CahSion* 8 (1954), pp. 9–34.

Block, D. I., *The Book of Ezekiel: Chapter 1–24* (Grand Rapids: Eerdmans, 1997).

Blomberg, C., *Matthew* (Nashville: Broadman, 1992).

Bogaert, P. M., *L' Apocalypse de Baruch* (2 vols; Paris: Editions du Cerf, 1969), pp. 1.294–95.

Bonnard, P., *L'Evangile selon Saint Matthieu* (Neuchâtel: Delachaux & Niestlé, 1972).

Bornkamm, G., 'End-Expectation and Church in Matthew', in *Tradition and Interpretation in Matthew*, ed. G. Bornkamm, G. Barth, and H. J. Held (London: SCM Press, 1967), pp. 15–51.

Bosworth, A. B., 'History and Rhetoric in Curtius Rufus', *ChP* 78 (1983), pp. 150–61.

Bowker, J., 'The Son of Man', *JTS* 28 (1977), pp. 19–48.

Brandon, S. G. F., *Jesus and the Zealots: A Study of the Political Factor in Primitive Christianity* (New York: Scribner's, 1967).

Branscomb, B. H., *The Gospel of Mark* (London, 1937).

Bright, J., *Jeremiah* (New York: Doubleday, 1965).

Brin, H. B., *A Catalogue of Judaea Capta Coinage* (Minneapolis: Emmett Publishing, 1986).

Brooks, E., *The Germany and Agricola of Tacitus* (Whitefish, MT: Kessinger Publishing, 2004).

Brooks, S. H., *Matthew's Community: The Evidence of his Special Sayings Material* (Sheffield: JSOT Press, 1987).

Brown, J. P., 'The Form of "Q" Known to Matthew', *NTS* 8 (1962), pp. 27–42.

Brown, R. E., *An Introduction to the New Testament* (New York: Doubleday, 1997).

Brown, S., 'The Matthean Apocalypse', *JSNT* 4 (1979), pp. 2–27.

Bruner, F. D., *Matthew* (vol. 2; Grand Rapids; Eerdmans, 1990).

Bultmann, R., 'History and Eschatology in the New Testament', *NTS* 1 (1954–55), pp. 5–16.

———, *Jesus Christ and Mythology* (London: SCM Press, 1960).

———, *The History of the Synoptic Tradition* (trans. J. Marsh; Oxford: Blackwell, 1963).

Burnett, A., M. Amandry, and P. P. Ripollès, *Roman Provincial Coinage, Vol. 1, From the Death of Caesar to the Death of Vitellius (44 BC–AD 69)* (London: British Museum Press, 1992).

———, *Roman Provincial Coinage, Vol. 2, From Vespasian to Domitian (AD 69–96)* (London: British Museum Press, 1999).

Burnett, F. W., *The Testament of Jesus Sophia: A Redaction-Critical Study of the Eschatological Discourse in Matthew* (Washington DC: University Press of America, 1979).

Caird, G. B., *Jesus and the Jewish Nation* (London: The Athlone Press, 1965).

———, *The Language and Imagery of the Bible* (London: Duckworth, 1980).

Cantinat, J., *Les Épîtres de Saint Jacques et de Saint Jude* (Paris: Gabalda, 1973).

Caragounis, C., *The Son of Man* (Tübingen: Mohr, 1986).

Carley, K. W., *The Book of the Prophet Ezekiel* (Cambridge: Cambridge University Press, 1974).

Carson, D. A., *The Sermon on the Mount* (Grand Rapids, MI: Eerdmans, 1978).

———, *The Gospel according to John* (Leicester: IVP, 1991).

Carter, W., *Matthew and the Margins* (Sheffield: Sheffield Academic Press, 2000).

———, 'Are There Imperial Texts in the Class? Intertextual Eagles and Matthean Eschatology as "Lights Out" Time for Imperial Rome (Matthew 24:27-31)', *JBL* 122 (2003), pp. 467–87.

Casey, M., 'The Use of the Terms "Son of Man" in the *Similitudes* of Enoch', *JSJ* 7 (1976), pp. 11–29.

——, *Son of Man: The Interpretation and Influence of Dan 7* (London: SPCK, 1979).

Catchpole, D., 'Review of *Midrash and Lection in Matthew*, by M. D. Goulder', *EvQ* 47 (1975), pp. 239–40.

Charette, B., *The Theme of Recompense in Matthew's Gospel* (Sheffield: Sheffield Academic Press, 1992).

Charlesworth, J. H., *The Pseudepigrapha and Modern Research* (Missoula: Scholars Press, 1981).

Childs, B., *Isaiah* (London: Westminster John Knox Press, 2001).

Chilton, B., *The Isaiah Targum* (New York: Glazier, 1987).

Clark, K., 'The Gentile Bias in Matthew', *JBL* 66 (1947), pp. 165–72.

Clements, R. E., *Isaiah 1–39* (Grand Rapids: Eerdmans, 1980).

Cohen, M. E., *The Canonical Lamentations of Ancient Mesopotamia* (Potomac: CDL Press, 1988).

Collins, A. Y., 'Introduction: Early Christian Apocalypticism', *Semeia* 36 (1986), pp. 1–174.

——, 'The Influence of Daniel on the New Testament', in *Daniel*, ed. J. J. Collins (Minneapolis: Augsburg Press, 1993), pp. 90–123.

——, 'Apocalypticism and New Testament Theology', *New England Region of the Society of Biblical Literature* (Newton, MA, 22 April 2005), pp. 1–26.

Collins, J. J., *Daniel with an Introduction to Apocalyptic Literature* (Grand Rapids: Eerdmans, 1984).

——, *The Apocalyptic Imagination* (New York: Crossroad, 1987).

——, *Daniel* (Minneapolis: Augsburg Press, 1993).

——, *The Scepter and the Star* (New York: Doubleday, 1995).

——, 'Stirring up the Great Sea: The Religio-Historic Background in Daniel 7', in *Seers, Sybils and Sages in Hellenistic-Roman Judaism*, ed. J. J. Collins (Leiden: Brill, 1997), pp. 139–56.

Colpe, C., 'ὁ υἱὸς τοῦ ἀνθρώπου', in *Theological Dictionary of the New Testament*, ed. G. Friedrich (trans. G. W. Bromiley; 10 vols; Grand Rapids: Eerdmans, 1970), pp. 8.403–81.

Combrink, H. J. B., 'The Structure of the Gospel of Matthew as Narrative', *TynB* 34 (1983), pp. 61–90.

Cook, M. J., *Mark's Treatment of the Jewish Leaders* (Leiden: Brill, 1997)

Cousland, J. R. C., *The Crowds in the Gospel of Matthew* (Leiden: Brill, 2002).

Coward, R. and J. Ellis, *Language and Materialism: Developments in Semiology and the Theory of the Subject* (London: Routledge, 1977).

Cowley, A. E., *Gesenius' Hebrew Grammar as Edited and Enlarged by E. Kautzsch* (28th edn; Oxford: Clarendon, 1970).

Cox, G. E. P., *The Gospel according to Matthew* (London: SCM Press, 1952).

236   *Bibliography*

Craigie, P. C., *Jeremiah 1–25* (Dallas: Word Books, 1991).
Cranfield, C. E. B.,*The Gospel according to St. Mark* (Cambridge: Cambridge University Press, 1974).
——, *The Epistle to the Romans* (Edinburgh: T&T Clark, 1975).
Cross, F. M., *The Ancient Library at Qumran* (Sheffield: Sheffield Academic Press, 1958).
——, *Canaanite Myth and Hebrew Epic* (Cambridge: Harvard University Press, 1973).
Crossan, J. D., *The Birth of Christianity: Discovering What Happened in the Years Immediately after the Execution of Jesus* (San Francisco: Harper San Francisco, 1998).
Culler, J., *The Pursuit of Signs: Semiotics, Literature, Deconstruction* (London: Routledge, 1981).
Cunliffe-Jones, H., *The Book of Jeremiah* (Naperville: Northumberland Press, 1960).
D'Agostino, V., *Cornelii Taciti: De Vita et Moribus Iulii Agricolae Liber* (Florence: Biblioteca Della Rivista, 1962).
Darwell-Smith, R. H., *Emperors and Architecture: A Study of Flavian Rome* (Brussels: Latomus, 1996).
Daube, D., *The New Testament and Rabbinic Judaism* (London: The Athlone Press, 1956).
Davids, P. H., *The Epistle of James: A Commentary on the Greek Text* (Exeter: The Paternoster Press, 1982).
Davies, W. D., *The Setting of the Sermon on the Mount* (Cambridge: Cambridge University Press, 1964).
Davies, W. D. and D. C. Allison, *The Gospel According to Matthew* (Vol. 1; Edinburgh: T&T Clark, 1988).
——, *The Gospel according to Matthew* (vol. 2; Edinburgh: T&T Clark, 1991).
——, *The Gospel according to Matthew* (vol. 3; Edinburgh: T&T Clark, 1997).
——, *Matthew: A Shorter Commentary* (London: T&T Clark International, 2004).
Davila, J., *The Provenance of the Pseudepigrapha* (Leiden: Brill, 2005).
Day, J., 'Da'at "humiliation" in Isa. liii 3 in the light of Isa. liii and Dan. xii 4 and the Oldest Known Interpretation of the Suffering Servant', *VT* 30 (1980), pp. 97–103.
——, *God's Conflict with the Dragon and the Sea* (Cambridge: Cambridge University Press, 1985).
——, 'The Dependence of Isa. 26:13–27:11 on Hos. 13:4–14:10 and Its Relevance to Some Theories of the Redaction of the "Isaiah Apocalypse"', in *Writing and Reading the Scroll of Isaiah*, ed. C. C. Broyles and C. A. Evans (Leiden: Brill, 1997), pp. 357–69.
Deissmann, A., *Light From the Ancient East* (Edinburgh: Kessinger Publishing, 1927).

Delitzsch, F., 'Daniel', *Realencyklopädie für protestantische Theologie und Kirche* 3 (1855), pp. 271–87.

Delobel, J., 'Textual Criticism and Exegesis: Siamese Twins?', in *New Testament Textual Criticism, Exegesis and Church History*, ed. B. Aland and J. Delobel (The Hague: Pharos, 1994), pp. 98–117.

Dequeker, L., 'The Saints of the Most High in Qumran and Daniel', *OTS* 18 (1973), pp. 108–87.

Dibelius, M., *James* (Philadelphia: Fortress Press, 1976).

Dines, J., 'Greek Daniel's Debt to Isaiah – But Which Isaiah?' (unpublished paper presented at the Summer Meeting of the Society for Old Testament Study, University College, Durham, July 2006), pp. 1–13.

Dodd, C. H., *The Parables of the Kingdom* (London: James Nisbet, 1936).

Dodewaard, J. van, 'De gruwel der verwoesting (Mt. 24:15 = Mk 13:14)', *St. Cath* 20 (1944), pp. 125–35.

Donahue, J. R., *Are You the Christ?: The Trial Narrative in the Gospel of Mark* (Atlanta: Society of Biblical Literature, 1972).

Donaldson, T. L., *Jesus on the Mountain: A Study in Matthean Typology* (Sheffield: Academic Press, 1985).

Draper, J., 'The Development of "the Sign of the Son of Man" in the Jesus Tradition', *NTS* 39 (1993), pp. 1–21.

Dudley, D. R., *The World of Tacitus* (London: Secker & Warburg, 1968).

Duff, P. B., 'The March of the Divine Warrior and the Advent of the Greco-Roman King: Mark's Account of Jesus' Entry into Jerusalem', *JBL* 111 (1992), pp. 55–71.

Dumbrell, W. J., 'The Purpose of the Book of Isaiah', *TynBul* 36 (1985), pp. 111–28.

Dupont, J., *Les trois apocalypses synoptiques: Marc 13; Matthieu 24–25; Luc 21* (Paris: Cerf, 1985), pp. 467–68.

Dyer, K. D., *The Prophecy on the Mount: Mark 13 and the Gathering of the New Community* (Bern: Peter Lang, 1998).

——,'"But Concerning that Day ..." (Mark 13:32). "Prophetic" and "Apocalyptic" Eschatology in Mark 13', in *Society of Biblical Literature 1999 Seminar Papers* (Atlanta: Society of Biblical Literature, 1999), pp. 104–22.

Eaton, J. H., *Obadiah, Nahum, Habakkuk and Zephaniah* (London: SCM Press, 1961).

Edersheim, A., *The Life and Times of Jesus the Messiah* (2 vols; Grand Rapids: Eerdmans, 1936).

Ehrhardt, A. A. T., 'Greek Proverbs in the Gospel', *HTR* 46 (1953), pp. 68–72.

Eissfeldt, O., *Baal Zaphon, Zeus Kasios und der Durchzug der Israeliten durchs Meer* (Halle: Niemeyer, 1932).

Elliott, K. and I. Moir, *Manuscripts and the Text of the New Testament* (New York: Continuum, 1995).

Ellis, P. F., *Matthew: His Mind and His Message* (Collegeville: Liturgical Press, 1974).

Ellison, H. L., 'Lamentations', in *The Expositors Bible Commentary* Vol. 6, ed. F. E. Gaebelein (Grand Rapids: Zondervan, 1986), pp. 693–733.

Emerton, J. A., 'The Historical Background of Isaiah 1:4-9', in *Avraham Malamat Volume*, ed. S. Ahituv and B. A. Levine (Jerusalem: Israel Exploration Society), pp. 34–40.

Evans, C. A., 'Jesus' Action in the Temple: Cleansing or Portent of Destruction?' *CBQ* 51 (1989), pp. 237–70.

———, *Noncanonical Writings and New Testament Interpretation* (Peabody: Hendrickson, 1992).

Evans, C. S., *Mark 8:27–16:20* (Nashville: Nelson, 2001).

Falk, Z. W., *Introduction to Jewish Law of the Second Commonwealth* (vol. 1; Brill: Leiden, 1972).

Fassberg, S. E., 'The Movement from *Qal* to *Pi'el* in Hebrew and the Disappearance of the *Qal* Internal Passive', *Hebrew Studies* 42 (2001), pp. 243–55.

Fears, J. R., 'The Theology of Victory at Rome: Approaches and Problems', *ANRW* 2.17.2 (1981), pp. 736–826.

Fenton, F. C. *The Gospel of St. Matthew* (Philadelphia: Westminster, 1977).

Fenton, J. C., 'Inclusio and Chiasmus in "Matthew"', *Studia Evangelica* 1 (1959), pp. 174–79.

Ferguson, E., *Backgrounds of Early Christianity* (Grand Rapids: Eerdmans, 1987).

Feuillet, A., 'Le discours de Jésus sur la ruine du temple d'après Marc XIII et Luc XXI, 5–36', *RB* 55 (1948), pp. 481–502.

———, 'Le sens du mot Parusie dans l'évangile de Matthieu', in *The Background of the New Testament and Its Eschatology*, ed. D. Daube and W. D. Davies (Cambridge: Cambridge University Press, 1956), pp. 261–80.

Filson, F. V., *A Commentary on the Gospel According to Matthew* (London: Adam and Charles Black, 1960).

Fishbane, M., *Biblical Interpretation in Ancient Israel* (Oxford: Clarendon Press, 1985).

Fitzmeyer, J., *The Gospel according to Luke X–XXIV* (New York: Doubleday, 1985).

Fletcher-Louis, C., 'The Temple Cosmology of P and Theological Anthropology in the Wisdom of Jesus ben Sira', in *Of Scribes and Sages: Studies in Early Jewish Interpretation and Transmission of Scripture*, ed. C. A. Evans (Sheffield: Sheffield Academic Press, 2002), pp.1–51

Foerster, W., 'βδελύσσομαι ...', in *TDNT*, ed. G. Kittel and G. Friedrich (Grand Rapids: Eerdmans, 1964), pp. 1.598–600.

Fohrer, G., 'Die Gattung der Berichte über sumbolische Handlungen der Propheten', *ZAW* 64 (1952), pp. 101–20.

Ford, D., *The Abomination of Desolation in Biblical Eschatology* (New York: University Press of America, 1979).

Foster, P., *Community, Law and Mission in Matthew's Gospel* (Tübingen: Mohr Siebeck, 2004).

France, R. T., 'Jewish Historigraphy, Midrash and the Gospels', in *Gospel Perspectives III: Studies in Midrash and Historiography*, ed. R. T. France and D. Wenham (Sheffield: JSOT, 1983), pp. 99–127.

——, *Matthew* (Grand Rapids: Eerdmans, 1985).

Frankemölle, H., *Jahwe-Bund und Kirche Christi* (Münster: Aschendorff, 1984).

Fuller, R. H., 'Matthew', in *Harper's Bible Commentary*, ed. J. L. Mays (San Francisco: Harper & Row, 1988), pp. 951–82.

Gaecher, P., *Das Matthäus Evangelium* (Innsbruck: Tyrolia-Verlag, 1963).

Gaide, C., *Le Livre de Daniel* (Paris: Mame, 1969).

Garland, D. E., *The Intention of Matthew 23* (Leiden: Brill, 1979).

Gaston, L., 'The Messiah of Israel as the Teacher of Gentiles', *Int.* 29 (1970), pp. 24–40.

Gaston, L., *No Stone on Another* (Leiden: Brill, 1970).

Gebhardt, C., *Theologisch-Politischer Traktat* (Hamburg: Meiner, 1955).

Geiger, A., *Ursprung und Übersetzungen der Bibel* (Breslau, 1875).

Gerhardsson, B., *Memory and Manuscript* (Uppsala: Copenhagen, 1961).

Gese, H., 'Die Bedeutung der Krise unter Antiochus IV. Epiphanes für die Apokalyptik des Danielbuches', *ZTK* 80 (1983), pp. 373–88.

Gfrörer, A. F., *Kritische Geschichte des Urchristenthums* (Stuttgart, 1838).

Gibbs, G. A., *Let the Reader Understand: The Eschatological Discourse in Matthew's Gospel* (unpublished PhD dissertation; Union Theological Seminary, 1995).

Glasson, T. F., *The Second Advent* (London: Epworth, 1963).

——, 'Schweitzer's Influence – Blessing or Bane?', *JTS* 28 (1977), pp. 289–302.

Gnilka, J., *Matthäusevangelium* (2 vols; Freiburg: Herder, 1988).

Goldberg, A. A., *Untersuchungen über die Vorstellung von der Schekinah* (Berlin: de Gruyter, 1969).

Goldin, J., 'The Three Pillars of Simeon the Righteous', *PAAJR* 27 (1957), pp. 43–58.

Goldingay, J. E., *Daniel* (Dallas: Word Books, 1988).

Goldstein, J. A., *I Maccabees* (New York: Doubleday, 1976).

Goodwin, W. W., *A Greek Grammar* (London: Macmillan, 1916).

Gordon, R. P., *1 & 2 Samuel: A Commentary* (Exeter: Paternoster Press, 1986).

Goulder, M. D., *Midrash and Lection in Matthew* (London: SPCK, 1974).

———, *Luke* (Sheffield: Sheffield Press, 1989).

Graetz, H., *Kohelet oder des Somonische Prediger* (Leipzig, 1871).

Grant, F. C., *Ancient Judaism and The New Testament* (London: Oliver and Boyd, 1960).

Gray, R., *Prophetic Figures in Late Second Temple Jewish Palestine: The Evidence from Josephus* (Oxford: Oxford University Press, 1993).

Green, H. B., *The Gospel according to Matthew* (London: Oxford University Press, 1975).

Greenberg, M., *Ezekiel 1–20* (New York: Doubleday, 1983).

Grundmann, W., *Das Evangelium nach Matthäus* (Berlin: Evangelische Verlagsanstalt, 1975).

Gundry, R. H., *The Use of the Old Testament in St. Matthew's Gospel with Special Reference to the Messianic Hope* (Leiden: Brill, 1967).

———, *Matthew: A Commentary on His Literary and Theological Art* (Grand Rapids: Eerdmans, 1982).

Gunkel, H., *Schöpfung und Chaos in Urzeit und Endzeit: Eine religionsgeschichtliche Untersuchung über Gen 1 und Ap Joh 12* (Göttingen: Vandenhoeck & Ruprecht, 1895).

———, *Matthew: A Commentary on His Handbook for a Mixed Church under Persecution* (Grand Rapids: Eerdmans, 1994).

Haenchen, E., 'Matthäus 23', *ZTK* 48 (1951), pp. 38–63.

———, *Der Weg Jesu: Eine Erklärung des Markus-Evangeliums und der kanonischen Parallelen* (Berlin: Walter de Gruyter, 1968).

Hagner, D.A., *Matthew 1–13* (Dallas: Word, 1993).

———, *Matthew 14–28* (Dallas: Word, 1995).

Hahn, F., *Mission in the New Testament* (trans. F.Clark; London: SCM, 1965).

———, *The Titles of Jesus in Christology: Their History in Early Christianity* (trans. H. Knight and G. Ogg; New York: World, 1969).

Hahn, S. and C. Mitch, *The Gospel of Mark* (San Francisco: Ignatius Press, 2001).

Hall, R. G., *Revealed Histories* (Sheffield: Academic Press, 1991).

———, 'The "Christian Interpolation" in the Apocalypse of Abraham', *JBL* 107 (1998), pp. 107–109.

Harden, D., *The Phoenicians* (London: Penguin Books, 1963).

Hare, D. R. A., *The Theme of Jewish Persecutions of Christians in the Gospel according to St. Matthew* (Cambridge: Cambridge University Press, 1982).

Harrington, D. J., 'The Original Language of Pseudo-Philo's *Liber Antiquitatum Biblicarum*', *HTR* 63 (1970), pp. 503–14.

——, 'The Biblical Text of Pseudo-Philo's *Liber Antiquitatum Biblicarum*', *CBQ* 33 (1971), pp. 1–17.

——, *The Hebrew Fragments of Pseudo-Philo's Liber Antiquitatum Biblicarum Preserved in the Chronicles of Jerahmeel* (Cambridge: Harvard University Press, 1974).

——, *The Gospel of Matthew* (Collegeville: Liturgical Press, 1991).

——, *Invitation to the Apocrypha* (Grand Rapids: Eerdmans, 1999), pp. 189–90.

Harrison, R. K., *Jeremiah and Lamentations* (Leicester: IVP, 1973).

——, 'Fig Tree', in *International Standard Bible Encyclopedia*, ed. G. W. Bromiley (4 vols; Grand Rapids: Eerdmans, 1994), pp. 2.301–302.

Hartman, L., *Prophecy Interpreted: The Formation of Some Jewish Apocalyptic Texts and of the Eschatological Discourse Mark 13 par* (Lund: Gleerup, 1966).

Hartman, L. F. and A. A. DiLella, *The Book of Daniel* (New York: Doubleday, 1978).

Harvey, A. E., *Jesus and the Constraints of History* (London: Duckworth, 1982).

Harvey, A. H., 'Review of *Midrash and Lection in Matthew*, by M.D. Goulder' *JTS* 27 (1975), pp. 188–195.

Hawkins, J. C., *Horae Synopticae: Contributions to the Study of the Synoptic Problem* (Oxford: Clarendon Press, 1899).

Hayes, J., *Old Testament Form Criticism* (San Antonio: Trinity University Press, 1974).

Hayes, J. and S. Irvine, *Isaiah the Eighth-Century Prophet: His Times and His Preaching* (Nashville: Abingdon, 1987).

Haynes, I., 'Religion in the Roman Army: Unifying Aspects and Regional Trends', in *Römische Reichsreligion und Provinzialreligion*, ed. H. Cancik and J. Rüpke (Tübingen: Mohr Siebeck, 1997).

Hays, R., *Echoes of Scripture in the Letters of Paul* (New Haven: Yale University Press, 1989).

Head, P., 'Some Recently Published NT Papyri from Oxyrhynchus: An Overview and Preliminary Assessment', *TynBul* 51 (2000), pp. 1–16.

Heal, J., 'Wittgenstein, Ludwig Josef Johann', in *The Shorter Routledge Encyclopedia of Philosophy*, ed. E. Craig (London: Routledge), pp. 1057–71.

Heaton, E. W., *The Book of Daniel* (London: SCM Press, 1956).

Hendriksen, W., *The Gospel of Matthew* (Edinburgh: The Banner of Truth Trust, 1973).

Hengel, M., *Studies in the Gospel of Mark* (London: SCM Press, 1985).

Herbert, A. S., *Isaiah: Chapters 1–39* (Cambridge: Cambridge University Press, 1973).

Hertzberg, H. W., *I & II Samuel: A Commentary* (London: SCM Press, 1960).

Hiers, R. H., *The Kingdom of God in the Synoptic Tradition* (Gainsville: University of Florida Press, 1970).

——, *The Historical Jesus and the Kingdom of God* (Gainsville: University of Florida Press, 1973).

Higgins, A. J. B., 'The Sign of the Son of Man (Matt. XXIV.30)', *NTS* 9 (1962–63), pp. 380–82.

——, *The Son of Man in the Teaching of Jesus* (Cambridge: Cambridge University Press, 1980).

Hill, A. and J. H. Walton, *A Survey of the Old Testament* (Grand Rapids: Zondervan, 1991).

Hill, A. E., *Malachi: A New Translation with Introduction and Commentary* (New York: Doubleday, 1988).

Hill, D., *The Gospel of Matthew* (London: Marshall, Morgan & Scott, 1972).

——, *New Testament Prophecy* (London: Marshall, Morgan & Scott, 1979).

Hindley, J. C., 'Towards a Date for the Similitudes of Enoch. An Historical Approach', *NTS* 14 (1967–68), pp. 551–65.

Hoffmann, P., *Studien zur Theologie der Logienquelle* (Münster: Verlag Aschendorff, 1972).

Holladay, W. L., *Jeremiah 1: Commentary on the Book of Jeremiah Chapters 1–25* (Philadelphia: Fortress Press, 1986).

Hölscher, G., 'Die Entstehung des Buches Daniel', *Theologische Studien und Kritiken* 92 (1919), pp. 114–38.

Hooker, M., *The Gospel according to Mark* (Peabody: Hendrickson, 1991).

——, *The Signs of a Prophet* (London: SCM Press, 1997).

Hoppe, L. J., *Holy City: Jerusalem in the Theology of the Old Testament* (Collegeville: Liturgical Press, 2000).

Horbury, W., 'The Messianic Associations of "The Son of Man"', *JTS* 36 (1985), pp. 34–55.

Horgan, M. P., 'A Lament Over Jerusalem (4Q179)', *JSS* 18.2 (1973), pp. 222–34.

Horsley R. A., *Jesus and the Spiral of Violenc : Popular Jewish Resistance in Roman Palestine* (Minneapolis: Fortress Press, 1993).

Horsley R. A. and J. S. Hanson, *Bandits, Prophets, and Messiahs: Popular Movements in the Time of Jesus* (San Francisco: Harper and Row, 1998).

Huck, A. and H. Greeven, *Synopses der drei ersten Evangelien* (Mohr: Tübingen, 1981).

Huffmon, H. B., 'The Covenant Lawsuit', *JBL* 78 (1959), pp. 285–95.

Hummel, R., *Die Auseinandersetzung zwishcen Kirche und Judentum im Matthäus-evangelium* (Munich: Chr. Kaiser Verlag, 1966).

Hutton, M., *Tacitus* (vol. 1; Cambridge, MA: Harvard University Press, 1970).

Instone-Brewer, D., *Traditions of the Rabbis from the Era of the New Testament: Volume 1: Prayer and Agriculture* (Grand Rapids: Eerdmans, 2004).

Isaac, E., '1 (Ethiopic Apocalypse of) Enoch', in *The Old Testament Pseudepigrapha*, ed. J. H. Charlesworth (2 vols; London: Darton, Longman & Todd, 1983), pp. 1.5–89.

Jacobson, H., *A Commentary on Pseudo-Philo's Liber Antiquitatum Biblicarum* (2 vols; Leiden: Brill, 1996).

Jenni, E., *Das hebräische Pi'el: Syntaktisch-semasiologische Untersuchung einer Verbalform im Alten Testaments* (Basel: Helbing und Lichtenhahn, 1968).

Jensen, J., *The Use of Torah by Isaiah. His Debate with the Wisdom Tradition* (Washington, DC: Catholic Biblical Association, 1973).

Jeremias, J., 'Μωυσῆς', in *Theological Dictionary of the New Testament*, ed. G. Friedrich (trans. G. W. Bromiley; 10 vols; Grand Rapids: Eerdmans, 1967), pp. 4.848–73.

———, *New Testament Theology* (London: SCM Press, 1971).

———, *The Parables of Jesus* (London: SCM Press, 1972).

Johnson, L. T., 'The New Testament's Anti-Jewish Slander and the Conventions of Ancient Polemic', *JBL* 108 (1989), pp. 419–41.

———, *The Gospel of Luke* (Collegeville: Liturgical Press, 1992).

Jones, D. R., *Jeremiah* (Grand Rapids: Eerdmans, 1992).

Joosten, J., 'The Functions of the Semitic D Stem: Biblical Hebrew Materials for a Comparative-Historical Approach', *Or.* 67 (1998), pp. 202–30.

Joüon, P. and T. Muraoka, *A Grammar of Biblical Hebrew* (2 vols; Rome: Biblical Institute Press, 1993).

Kaiser, O., *Isaiah 13–39: A Commentary* (London: SCM Press, 1973).

Kaiser, W., *Preaching and Teaching From the Old Testament* (Grand Rapids: Baker Academic, 2003).

Kaufman, S. A., 'Semitics: Directions and Re-Directions', in *The Study of the Ancient Near East in the Twenty-First Century*, ed. J. S. Cooper and G. M. Schwarz (Winona Lake: Eisenbrauns), pp. 273–82.

Keener, C. S., *Matthew* (Illinois: IVP, 1997).

———, *A Commentary on the Gospel of Matthew* (Grand Rapids: Eerdmans, 1999).

Keim, K. T., *Geschichte Jesu von Nazara* (Zurich, 1872).

Kik, J. M., *Matthew Twenty-Four* (Pennsylvania: Bible Truth, 1948).

Kilpatrick, G. D., *The Origins of the Gospel according to Saint Matthew* (Oxford: Clarendon Press, 1946).

Kimelman, R., '*Birkat Ha-Minim* and the Lack of Evidence for an Anti-Christian Jewish Prayer in Late Antiquity', in *Jewish and*

Christian Self Definition, ed. E. P. Sanders, A. J. Baumgarten, and A. Mendelson (Philadelphia: Fortress Press, 1989), pp. 226–44.

Kingsbury, J. D., *Matthew: Structure, Christology, Kingdom* (Philadelphia: Fortress, 1975).

———, *Matthew as Story* (Philadelphia: Fortress, 1986).

Kisch, G., *Pseudo-Philo's Liber Antiquitatum Biblicarum* (Notre Dame, IN: University of Notre Dame, 1949).

Kittel, G., 'ἄγγελος, ἀρχάγγελος, ἰσάγγελος', in *Theological Dictionary of the New Testament*, ed. G. Friedrich (trans. G. W. Bromiley; 10 vols; Grand Rapids: Eerdmans, 1967), pp. 1.74–87.

Klijn, A. F. J., '2 (Syrian Apocalypse of) Baruch', in *The Old Testament Pseudepigrapha*, ed. J. H. Charlesworth (2 vols; London: Darton, Longman & Todd, 1983), pp. 1.615–52.

Kloppenborg, J. S., 'City and Wasteland: Narrative World and the Beginning of the Sayings Gospel (Q)', in *How Gospels Begin*, ed. D. E. Smith (Atlanta: Scholars Press, 1990), pp. 145–60.

———, *Excavating Q: The History and Setting of the Sayings Gospel* (Minneapolis: Fortress, 2000).

———, 'Evocatio Deorum and the Date of Mark', *JBL* 124 (2005), pp. 419–50.

Klosterman, E., *Das Matthäusevangelium* (Tübingen: Paul Siebeck, 1927).

———, *Das Markusevangelium* (Tübingen: Paul Siebeck, 1950).

Knight, G. A. F., *Hosea: Introduction and Commentary* (London: SCM Press, 1960).

Koch, K., *Das Buch Daniel* (Darmstadt: Wissenschaftliche Buchgesellschaft, 1986).

Körtner, U. H., *Papias von Hierapolis* (Göttingen, 1983).

Kreitzer, L. J., *Striking New Images: Roman Imperial Coinage and the New Testament World* (Sheffield: Sheffield Academic Press, 1996).

———, 'The Horror! The Whore! The Abomination of Desolation and Conrad's Heart of Darkness', in *Apocalyptic in History and Tradition*, ed. C. Rowland and J. Barton (Sheffield: Sheffield Academic Press, 2002), pp. 284–318.

Kristeva, J., *Desire in Language: A Semiotic Approach to Literature and Art* (New York: Columbia University Press, 1980).

Kulik, A., *Retroverting Slavonic Pseudepigrapha: Toward the Original of the Apocalypse of Abraham* (Atlanta: Society of Biblical Literature, 2004).

Kümmel, W. G., *Promise and Fulfillment* (London: SCM Press, 1957).

Kupp, D. D., *Matthew's Emmanuel:Divine Presence and God's People in the First Gospel* (Cambridge: Cambridge University Press, 1996).

Kvanvig, H. S., *Roots of Apocalyptic: The Mesopotamian Background of the Enoch Figure and of the Son of Man* (Neukirchen-Vluyn: Neukirchener Verlag, 1988).

Kwaak, H. van der, 'Die Klage über Jerusalem', *NovT* 8 (1966), pp. 156–70.

Lachs, S. T., *A Rabbinic Commentary on the New Testament* (Hoboken: Ktav Publishing House, 1987).

Lambdin, T., *An Introduction to Biblical Hebrew* (London: Prentice Hall, 1971).

Lane, E. N. 'Sabazius and the Jews in Valerius Maximus: A Re-examination', *JRS* 69 (1979), pp. 35–38.

Lang, B., *Monotheism and the Prophetic Minority* (Sheffield: Almond, 1983).

Lauterbach, J., 'Midrash and Mishnah. A Study in the Early History of the Halakah', *JQR* 5 (1915), pp. 503–27.

Laws, S., *A Commentary on the Epistle of James* (London: SCM Press, 1980).

Leiman, S. Z., *The Canonization of the Hebrew Scriptures* (Hamden: Archon Books, 1976).

Lenglet, A., 'La Structure littéraire de Daniel 2–7', *Bib* 53 (1972), pp. 169–90.

Lewis, J. P., 'What Do We Mean by Jabneh?', *JBR* 32 (1964), pp. 125–32.

———, 'Jamnia (Jabneh), Council of', in *Anchor Bible Dictionary*, ed. D. N. Freedman (vol. 3; New York: Doubleday, 1992), pp. 634–37.

Lewis, N. and M. Reinhold, *Roman Civilization* II (New York: Columbia University Press, 1990).

Licht, J., 'Abraham: Apocalypse of', *EJ* 2 (1972), pp. 126–27.

Liddell, H. G. and R. Scott, *Greek–English Lexicon* (9th edn; Oxford: Clarendon Press, 1996).

Lierman, J., *The New Testament Moses: Christian Perceptions of Moses and Israel in the Setting of Jewish Religion* (Tübingen: Mohr Siebeck, 2002).

Lightfoot, J., *A Commentary on the New Testament from the Talmud and Hebraica* (Oxford: Oxford University Press, 1859).

Lim, T. H., 'Deuteronomy in the Judaism of the Second Temple Period', in *Deuteronomy in the New Testament*, ed. S. Moyise and J. J. Menken (New York: T&T Clark, 2007), pp. 6–26.

Llewelyn, S., *New Documents Illustrating Early Christianity, Volume 7. A Review of the Greek Inscriptions and Papyri published in 1982–83* (Macquarie: The Ancient History Documentary Research Centre, 1994).

Lohmeyer, E., *Das Evangelium des Markus* (Göttingen: Vandenhoeck & Ruprecht, 1967).

Lohr, C. H., 'Oral Techniques in the Gospel of Matthew', *CBQ* 23 (1961), pp. 403–35.

Loisy, A., *Les Évangiles synoptiques* (2 vols; Paris: Cerf, 1907–1908).

Lüdemann, G., *Jesus After 2000 Years: What He Really Said and Did* (New York: Prometheus Books, 2001).

Lührmann, D., *Das Markusevangelium* (Tübingen: Mohr, 1987).

Lundbom, J. R., *Jeremiah 1–20* (New York: Doubleday, 1999).

——, *Jeremiah 37–52* (New York: Doubleday, 2004).

Lundstrom, G., *The Kingdom of God in the Teaching of Jesus* (Richmond: John Knox Press, 1963).

Lust, J., 'Cult and Sacrifice in Daniel. The Tamid and the Abomination of Desolation', in *Ritual and Sacrifice in the Ancient Near East: Proceedings of the International Conference organized by the Katholieke Universiteit Leuven from the 17th to the 20th of April 1991*, ed. J. Quaegebeur (Leuven: Uitgeverij Peeters en Departement Orientalistiek, 1993), pp. 283–99.

Luz, U., *Matthew 1–7: A Commentary* (trans. W. C. Linss; Edinburgh: T&T Clark, 1989).

——, *The Theology of the Gospel of Matthew* (Cambridge: Cambridge University Press, 1995).

——, *Das Evangelium nach Matthäus 3 Teilband Mt. 18–25* (Düsseldorf: Benziger Verlag, 1997).

——, *Matthew 8–20: A Commentary* (trans. J. E. Crouch; Minneapolis: Fortress Press, 2001).

——, *Matthew 21–28: A Commentary* (trans. J. E. Crouch; Minneapolis: Fortress Press, 2005).

McBride, S. D., 'Polity of the Covenant People: The Book of Deuteronomy', *Int* 41 (1987), pp. 229–44.

MacDonald, J., *The Theology of the Samaritans* (Philadelphia: Westminster Press, 1964).

McDonald, J. I. H., *The Resurrection: Narrative and Belief* (London: SPCK, 1989).

McKane, W., *Proverbs* (London: SCM Press, 1970).

McKeating, H., *The Books of Amos, Hosea and Micah* (Cambridge: Cambridge University Press, 1971).

McNamara, M., *Intertestamental Literature* (Wilmington: Michael Glazier, 1983).

McNeile, A. H., *The Gospel according to Matthew* (London: Macmillan, 1915).

Malcolm, N., 'Wittgenstein, Ludwig Josef Johann', in *The Encyclopedia of Philosophy*, ed. P. Edwards (8 vols; London: Macmillan, 1967), pp. 8.327–40.

Manson, T. W., *The Sayings of Jesus* (London: SCM Press, 1957).

——, 'The Son of Man in Daniel, Enoch and the Gospels', in *Studies in the Gospels and Epistles*, ed. M. Black (Manchester: Manchester University Press, 1962), pp. 123–45.

Marchant, E. C., *Commentary on Thucydides Book 3* (London: Macmillan, 1909).

Marcus, J., 'The Gates of Hades and the Keys of the Kingdom (Matt. 16:18-19)', *CBQ* 50 (1988), pp. 453–54.

———, 'The Jewish War and the *Sitz im Leben* of Mark', *JBL* 111 (1992), pp. 441–62.

Marks, R. G., *Image of Bar Kokhba* (Philadelphia: Pennsylvania State Press, 2004).

Marshall, C. D., *Beyond Retribution* (Grand Rapids: Eerdmans, 2001).

Marshall, I. H., *The Gospel of Luke* (Grand Rapids: Eerdmans, 1978).

Marxen, W., *Mark the Evangelist* (New York: Abingdon Press, 1969).

Mattingly, H., *Coins of the Roman Empire in the British Museum Vol. 3* (London: Trustees of the British Museum, 1936).

Mattingly, H. and E. A. Sydenham, *Roman Imperial Coinage: Volume 1 Nerva to Hadrian* (London: Spink and Son, 1972).

———, *A Catalogue of The Roman Coins in the British Museum: Volume II Vespasian to Domitian* (London: British Museum Publications Limited, 1976).

Mays, J. L., *Hosea: A Commentary* (London: SCM Press, 1969).

Meeks, W. A., *The Prophet-King: Moses Traditions and Johannine Christology* (Leiden: Brill, 1967).

Meier, J. P., 'Salvation-History in Matthew: In Search of a Stating Point', *CBQ* 37 (1975), pp. 203–15.

———, *Law and History in Matthew's Gospel* (Rome: Biblical Institute, 1976).

———, *Law and History in Matthew's Gospel* (Rome: Biblical Institute, 1979).

———, *The Vision of Matthew: Christ, Church and Morality in the First Gospel* (New York: Paulist Press, 1979).

———, *Matthew* (Dublin: Veritas Publications, 1980).

———, *A Marginal Jew: Rethinking the Historical Jesus: Mentor, Message, and Miracles* (New York: Doubleday, 1994).

Mendenhall, G. E., 'Ancient Oriental and Biblical Law', *BA* 17.2 (1952), pp. 26–46.

Menken, M. J. J., *Matthew's Bible* (Leuven: Peeters, 2004).

———, 'Deuteronomy in Matthew's Gospel', in *Deuteronomy in the New Testament*, ed. S. Moyise and J. J. Menken (New York: T&T Clark, 2007), pp. 42–62.

Merx, A., *Die vier kanonischen Evangelien nach ihrem ältesten bekannten Texte: Das Evangelium Matthaeus* (Berlin: Georg Reimer, 1902).

Metcalfe, J., *Matthew* (Buckinghamshire: John Metcalfe Publishing Trust, 1995).

Metzger, B., *An Introduction to the Apocrypha* (Oxford: Oxford University Press, 1957).

——, 'The "Lost" Sections of II Esdras (IV Ezra)', *JBL* 76 (1957), pp. 153–56.

——, *The Text of the New Testament* (Oxford: Oxford University Press, 1968).

——, 'Literary Forgeries and Canonical Pseudepigrapha', *JBL* 91 (1972), pp. 3–24.

——, 'The Fourth Book of Ezra', in *The Old Testament Pseudepigrapha*, ed. J. H. Charlesworth (2 vols; London: Darton, Longman & Todd, 1983), pp. 1.516–613.

——, *A Textual Commentary on the Greek New Testament* (Stuttgart: Deutsche Bibelgesellschaft, 1994).

Meyer, H. A. W., *Critical and Exegetical Handbook to The Gospel of Matthew* (2 vols; Edinburgh: T&T Clark, 1879).

Meyers, C., *Binding the Strong Man* (New York: Orbis, 1988).

Milik, J. T., 'Problème de la Littérature Hénochique à la Lumière des Fragments Araméens de Qumran', *HTR* 64 (1971), pp. 333–78.

——, *The Books of Enoch: Aramaic Fragments at Qumran Cave 4* (Oxford: Clarendon Press, 1976).

Min, K. S., *Die fruheste Uberlieferung des Matthausevangeliums* (Münster: Walter de Gruyter, 2004).

Mitton, C. L., 'Review of *Midrash and Lection in Matthew*, by M. D. Goulder', *ExpTim* 86 (1975), pp. 97–99.

Montgomery, J. A., *A Cricitcal and Exegetical Commentary on the Book of Daniel* (Edinburgh: Clark, 1927).

Moore, S. D., *Literary Criticism and the Gospels* (New Haven: Yale, 1989).

Morris, L., *The Gospel according to Matthew* (Grand Rapids: Eerdmans, 1992).

Mosca, P. G., 'Ugarit and Daniel 7: A Missing Link', *Bib* 67 (1986), pp. 496–517.

Moscati, S., *The World of the Phoenicians* (London: Phoenix, 1970).

Moule, C. F. D., *An Idiom Book of New Testament Greek* (Cambridge: University Press, 1959).

Moulton, J. H. and W. F. Howard, *A Grammar of New Testament Greek: Accidence and Word Formation* (Edinburgh: Clark, 1929).

Moulton, J. H., W. F. Howard, and N. Turner, *A Grammar of New Testament Greek* (4 vols; Edinburgh: Clark, 1906–76).

Mounce, R. H., *Matthew* (San Francisco: Harper and Row, 1985).

Mowinckel, S., *He That Cometh* (trans. G. W. Anderson; Oxford: Oxford University Press, 1956).

Mueller, J. R., 'The Apocalypse of Abraham and the Destruction of the Second Jewish Temple', in *SBL Seminar Papers* (1982), pp. 341–49.

Murphy, F. J., 'Second Temple Judaism', in *The Blackwell Reader in Judaism*, ed. J. Neusner and A. J. Avery-Peck (Oxford: Blackwell Publishing, 2000), pp. 42–59.

Murphy, R. E., *The Wisdom Literature* (Grand Rapids: Eerdmans, 1981).

——, *Proverbs* (Nashville: Thomas Nelson Publishers, 1998).

Myllykoski, M., 'The Social History of Q and the Jewish War', in *Symbols and Strata: Essays on the Sayings Gospel Q*, ed. R. Uro (Göttingen: Vandenhoeck & Ruprecht, 1996), pp. 143–99.

Nestle, E., 'Zu Daniel', *ZAW* 4 (1884), pp. 247–50.

Nestle, E., K. Aland, and B. Aland, *Novum Testamentum Graece* (27th edn; Stuttgart: Deutsche Bibelgesellschaft, 1991).

Neusner, J., 'The Use of the Later Rabbinic Evidence for the Study of First-Century Pharisaism', in *Approaches to Ancient Judaism: Theory and Practice*, ed. W. S. Green (Brown Judaic Studies 1; Missoula: Scholars Press, 1978), pp. 215–25.

New, D. S., *Old Testament Quotations in the Synoptic Gospels, and the Two Documentary Hypothesis* (Atlanta: Scholars Press, 1993).

Newport, K. G. C., *The Sources and Sitz im Leben of Matthew 23* (Sheffield: Sheffield Academic Press, 1995).

Nickelsburg, G. W. E., *Jewish Literature between the Bible and the Mishnah. A Historical and Literary Introduction* (Minneapolis: Fortress Press, 1981).

——, 'Son of Man', in *Anchor Bible Dictionary*, ed. D. N. Freedman (New York: Doubleday, 1992), pp. 4.137–150.

Nicole, W., *The Sêmeia in the Fourth Gospel* (Leiden: Brill, 1972).

Nineham, D. E., *The Gospel of St. Mark* (London: Penguin Books, 1963).

Nolland, J., *Luke 1:1–9:20* (Dallas: Word Books, 1989).

——, *The Gospel of Matthew* (Grand Rapids: Eerdmans, 2005).

Noth, M., 'Noah, Daniel und Hiob in Ez 14', *VT* 1 (1951), pp. 251–60.

Nuesner, J., *A History of the Mishnaic Law of Purities* (Leiden: Brill, 1977).

Oepke, A., 'Παρουσία, Πάρειμί, in *Theological Dictionary of the New Testament*, ed. G. Friedrich (trans. G. W. Bromiley; 10 vols; Grand Rapids: Eerdmans, 1970), pp. 5.858–71.

Ogilvie, R. M. and I. Richmond, *Cornelii Taciti: De Vita Agricolae* (Oxford: Clarendon Press, 1967).

Oster, R., 'Numismatic Windows into the Social World of Early Christianity: A Methodological Inquiry', *JBL* 101 (1982), pp. 195–223.

Overman, A., 'The First Revolt and the Flavian Politics', in *The First Jewish Revolt Against Rome*, ed. A. Berlin and A. Overman (London: Routledge, 2002), pp. 213–20.

Owen, O. T., 'One Hundred and Fifty Three Fishes', *ExpTim* 100 (1988), pp. 52–54.

Paas, S., *Creation and Judgement: Creation Texts in Some Eighth Century Prophets* (Leiden: Brill, 2003).

Parsons, P., 'Matthew xxiii 30–4; 35–9', in *The Oxyrhynchus Papyri Vol.* XXXIV, ed. L. Ingrams et al. (London: Egypt Exploration Society, 1968), pp. 1–4.

Patte, D., *The Gospel according to Matthew* (Philadelphia: Fortress Press, 1987).

Perrin, N., 'The Son of Man in Ancient Judaism and Primitive Christianity: A Suggestion', *BR* 11 (1963), pp. 17–28.

——, *The Kingdom of God in the Teaching of Jesus* (London: SCM Press, 1963).

Perrot, C. and P.-M. Bogaert, *Pseudo-Philon: Les Antiquités Bibliques* (Paris, 1976).

Pesch, R., *Das Markusevangelium* (2 vols; Herder: Freiburg im Breisgau, 1976).

Peters, F. E., *The Harvest of Hellenism: A History of the Near East From Alexander to the Triumph of Christianity* (New York: Simon and Schuster, 1970).

Petersen, D. L., *Zechariah 9–14 and Malachi* (Kentucky: John Knox Press).

Pfleiderer, O., 'Über die Komposition der eschatologischen Rede, Mt. 24:4ff.' *Jahrbücher für deutsche Theologie* 13 (1868) pp. 134–49.

Philonenko, M., 'Le Poimandrès et la liturgie juive', in *Les syncrétismes dans les religions de L'antiquité*, ed. F. Dunand et al. (Leiden: Brill, 1975), pp. 204–11.

Plummer, A., *An Exegetical Commentary on the Gospel according to St. Matthew* (London, 1910).

Porteous, N. W., 'The Present State of Old Testament Theology', *ET* (1963), pp. 70–74.

Porter, J. T., *Moses and Monarchy: A Study in the Biblical Tradition of Moses* (Oxford: Basil Blackwell, 1963).

Porter, S. E. *Idioms of the Greek New Testament* (Sheffield: Sheffield Academic Press, 1992).

——, 'The Use of the Old Testament in the New Testament: A Brief Comment on Method and Terminology', in *Early Christian Interpretation of the Scriptures of Israel: Investigations and Proposals*, ed. C. A. Evans and J. A. Sanders (Sheffield: Sheffield Academic Press, 1997), pp. 79–96.

——, *The Criteria for Authenticity in Historical-Jesus Research* (Sheffield: Sheffield Academic Press, 2000).

Powell, M. A., 'Do and Keep What Moses Says (Matthew 23:2-7)', *JBL* 114 (1995), pp. 419–35.

Pritchard, J. B., *The Ancient Near East in Pictures* (Princeton: Princeton University Press, 1954).

Pryke, J., 'Eschatology in the Dead Sea Scrolls', in *The Scrolls and Christianity: Historical and Theological Significance*, ed. M. Black (London: SPCK), pp. 45–57.

Quesnell, Q., *The Mind of Mark: Interpretation and Method Through the Exegesis of Mark 6:52* (Rome: Pontifical Biblical Institute, 1969).

Raabe, P. R., *Obadiah* (London: Doubleday, 1996).

Racine, J. F., *The Text of Matthew in the Writings of Basil of Caesarea* (Atlanta: Society of Biblical Literature, 2004).

Rehm, M., 'Das Opfer der Volker nach Mal 1:11', in *Lex Tua Veritas: Festschrift fur Hubert Junker*, ed. H. Gross and F. Mussner (Stuttgart: Trier Publishers), pp. 144–235.

Reicke, B., 'Synoptic Prophecies on the Destruction of Jerusalem', in *Studies in New Testament and Early Christian Literature*, ed. D. E. Aune (Leiden: Brill, 1972).

Reimarus, H. S., *Fragments* (trans. R. S. Fraser; Philadelphia: Fortress Press, 1970).

Repschinski, B., *The Controversy Stories in the Gospel of Matthew* (Göttingen: Vandenhoeck & Ruprecht, 2000).

Richardson, P., *Herod: King of the Jews and Friend of the Romans* (Columbia: University of South Carolina Press, 1996).

Rigaux, B., '"βδέλυγμα τῆς ἐρημώσεως" Mk 13:14; Mt. 24:15', *Biblica* 40 (1959), pp. 675–83.

Robinson, H. W., 'Prophetic Symbolism', in *Old Testament Essays*, ed. D. C. Simpson (London: C. Griffin), pp. 1–17.

Robinson, J. A. T., *Jesus and His Coming* (London: SCM Press, 1957).

Rogerson, J. W., 'The Hebrew Concept of Corporate Personality – A Re-Examination', *JTS* 21 (1970), pp. 1–16.

Rosenthal, L. A., 'Die Josephgeschichte, mit der Büchen Ester und Daniel verglichen', *ZAW* 15 (1895), pp. 278–84.

Rost, L., *Judaism Outside the Hebrew Canon* (Nashville: Abingdon, 1976).

Rowland, C., *The Open Heaven: A Study of Apocalyptic in Judaism and Early Christianity* (New York: Crossroad, 1982).

Rowley, H. H., *The Relevance of Apocalyptic* (London: Lutterworth Press, 1947).

——, *Darius the Mede and the Four World Empires in the Book of Daniel* (Cardiff: University of Wales Press, 1964).

Rubinkiewicz, R., 'Apokalipsa Abraham', *Ruch Biblijny i Liturgiczny* 27 (1974), pp. 230–37.

——, 'La Vision de l'histoire dans l'Apocalypse d'Abraham', *ANRW* 2.19.1 (1979), pp. 137–51.

——, 'Apocalypse of Abraham', in *The Old Testament Pseudepigrapha*, ed. J. H. Charlesworth (London: Darton, Longman & Todd, 1983), pp. 1.681–705.

——, 'Les sémitismes dans l'Apocalypse d'Abraham', *Folia Orientalia* 21 (1989), pp. 141–48.

——, 'Abraham, Apocalypse of', in *Anchor Bible Dictionary*, ed. D. N. Freedman (vol. 1; New York: Doubleday, 1992), pp. 41–43.

Russell, D. S., *The Method and Message of Jewish Apocalyptic* (London: SCM Press, 1964).

Rutz, W., 'Zur Erzählungskunst des Q. Curtius Rufus', *Hermes* 93 (1965), pp. 370–82.

Ryle, J. C., *Matthew* (Illinois: Crossway Books, 1993).

Sabourin, L., 'l discorso sulla parousia e le parabole della vigilanza (Matteo 24–25)', *BeO* 20 (1978), pp. 193–212.

Sahlin, H., 'Antiochus IV Epiphanes und Judas Mackabäus', *StTh* 23 (1969), pp. 41–68.

Sanders, E. P., 'The Testament of Abraham', in *Outside the Old Testament*, ed. M. De Jonge (Cambridge: Cambridge University Press, 1985), pp. 56–70.

——, *Jesus and Judaism* (London: SCM Press, 1985).

——, *Judaism: Practice and Belief, 63BCE–66 CE* (London: SCM Press, 1992).

Sandmel, S., 'Parallelomania', *JBL* 81 (1962), pp. 1–13.

Schaberg, J., *The Father, the Son and the Holy Spirit* (Chico: Scholars, 1982).

Schlatter, A., *Der Evangelist Matthäus* (Stuttgart: Calwer Verlag, 1963).

Schmid, H., 'Daniel der Menschensohn', *Judaica* 27 (1971), pp. 192–221.

Schmidt, J. M., *Die jüdische Apokalyptik* (Neukirchen-Vluyn: Neukirchener Verlag des Erziehungsvereins, 1969).

Schniewind, J., *Das Evangelium nach Markus* (Göttingen: Vandenhoeck & Ruprecht, 1952).

Schweitzer, A., *The Quest for the Historical Jesus: A Critical Study of Its Progress from Reimarus to Wrede* (trans. W. Montgomery; London: A&C Black, 1910).

——, *The Mystery of the Kingdom of God: The Secret of Jesus' Messiahship and Passion* (trans. W. Lowrie; New York: Schoken, 1925).

——, *The Kingdom of God and Primitive Christianity* (trans. L. A. Garrard; London: A&C Black, 1967).

Schweizer, E., *The Good News according to Matthew* (trans. D. E. Green; London: SPCK, 1975).

Scott, K., *The Imperial Cult under the Flavians* (Stuttgart: Kohlhammer, 1936).

Seeligmann, I. L., *The Septuagint Version of Isaiah: A Discussion of Its Problems* (Leiden: Brill, 1948).

Segal, A., *Two Powers in Heaven: Early Rabbinic Reports about Christianity and Gnosticism* (Leiden: Brill, 1977).

Sellin, E., *Einleitung in das Alte Testament* (Leipzig: Quelle & Meyer, 1910), pp. 233–34.

Senior, D., *What Are They Saying about Matthew?* (New York: Paulist Press, 1983).

———, 'Between Two Worlds: Gentile and Jewish Christians in Matthew's Gospel', *CBQ* 61 (1999), pp. 1–23.

Seow, C. L., *A Grammar for Biblical Hebrew* (Nashville: Abingdon Press, 1995).

Sherwood, J., 'The Only Sure Word', *MSJ* 7 (1996), pp. 53–74.

Siegman, E. F., 'The Stone Hewn from the Mountain (Daniel 2)', *CBQ* 18 (1956), pp. 364–79.

Sim, D. C., *Apocalyptic Eschatology in the Gospel of Matthew* (Cambridge: Cambridge University Press, 1996).

———, *The Gospel of Matthew and Christian Judaism: The History and Social Setting of the Matthean Community* (Edinburgh: T&T Clark, 1999).

Singer, I. and C. Adler, *The Jewish Encyclopedia: A Descriptive Record of the History, Religion, Literature, and Customs of the Jewish People from the Earliest Times to the Present Day* (12 vols; New York: Funk and Wagnalls, 1925).

Smallwood, E. M., *The Jews Under Roman Rule: From Pompey to Diocletian* (Leiden: Brill, 1981).

Soderlund, S., *The Greek Text of Jeremiah* (Sheffield: JSOT Press, 1985).

Sowers, S., 'The Circumstances and Recollection of the Pella Flight', *Theologische Zeitschrift* 26 (1970), pp. 305–20.

Stacey, W. D., *Prophetic Drama in the Old Testament* (London: Epworth Press, 1990).

Stalker, D. M. G., *Ezekiel* (London: SCM Press, 1968).

Stanton, G. N., 'Matthew as Creative Interpreter of the Sayings of Jesus', in *Das Evangelium und die Evangelien*, ed. P. Stuhlmacher (Tübingen: Mohr, 1983), pp. 273–87.

———, '"Pray that your Flight May Not Be in Winter or on a Sabbath" (Matthew 24.20)', *JSNT* 37 (1989), pp. 17–30.

———, '5 Ezra and Matthean Christianity in the Second Century', in *A Gospel for a New People*, ed. G. N. Stanton (Edinburgh: T&T Clark, 1992), pp. 256–77.

———, 'Once More: Matthew 25:31–46', in *A Gospel for a New People*, ed. G. N. Stanton (Edinburgh: T&T Clark, 1992), pp. 207–31.

Steck, O. H., *Israel und das gewaltsame Geschick der Propheten* (Neukirchen: Neukirchener Verlag, 1967).

———, 'Weltgeschehen und Gottesvolk im Buche Daniel', in *Kirche*, ed. D. Lührmann and G. Strecker (Tübingen: Mohr, 1980), pp. 53–78.

Steinman, J., *Daniel: Text français, introduction et commentaries* (Bruges: Desclée de Brouwer, 1961).

Stendahl, K., *The School of St. Matthew and Its Use of the Old Testament* (Philadelphia: Fortress, 1968).

Steuernagel, V. R., *Der Rahmen des Deuteronomy* (Gesetzes, 1894).

Stone, M., 'Apocalyptic Literature', in *Jewish Writings of the Second Temple Period*, ed. M. Stone (Assen: Van Gorcum, 1984), pp. 383–441.

———, 'Fourth Ezra', in *Harper's Bible Commentary*, ed. J. L. Mays (San Francisco: Harper and Row, 1988), pp. 776–77.

———, *Fourth Ezra* (Minneapolis: Fortress Press, 1990).

———, 'Esdras, Second Book of', in *Anchor Bible Dictionary*, ed. D. N. Freedman (vol. 2; New York: Doubleday, 1992), pp. 634–37.

Strack, H. L. and P. Billerbeck, *Kommentar zum New Testament* (6 vols; Munich: Beck, 1926–28).

Strack, H. L. and G. Stemberger, *Introduction to Talmud and Midrash* (trans. Markus Bockmuehl; Minneapolis: Fortress, 1996).

Strecker, G., *Der Weg der Gerechtigkeit, Untersuchung zur Theologiedes Matthäus* (Göttingen: Vandenhoeck & Ruprecht, 1971).

Streeter, B. H., *The Four Gospels* (London: Macmillan, 1925).

Stuart, D., *Hosea-Jonah* (Waco: Word, 1987).

Swete, H. B., *The Gospel according to St. Mark* (London: Macmillan, 1902).

Syme, R., 'The *Argonautica* of Valerius Flaccus', *CQ* 23 (1929), pp. 135–36.

———, *Tacitus* (Vol. 2; Oxford: Oxford University Press, 1958).

Tarn, W. W., 'Alexander: The Conquest of Persia', in *Cambridge Ancient History*, ed. D. M. Lewis (6 vols; Cambridge: Cambridge University Press, 1927), pp. 6.352–86.

Tasker, R. V. G., *The Gospel according to St. Matthew* (London: Tyndale Press, 1961).

Taylor, N. H., 'Palestinian Christianity and the Caligula Crisis. Part 1. Social and Historical Reconstruction', *JSNT* 61 (1996), pp. 101–24.

———, 'Part II. The Markan Eschatological Discourse', *JSNT* 62 (1999), pp. 13–41.

Taylor, V., 'The Apocalyptic Discourse of Mark XIII', *ExpTim* 60 (1949), pp. 94–98.

———, *The Gospel According to St. Mark* (London: Macmillan, 1952).

Tcherikover, V., *Hellenistic Civilization and the Jews* (New York: Athenaeum, 1959).

Teeple, H. M., *The Mosaic Eschatological Prophet* (Philadelphia: SBL, 1957).

Telford, W., *The Barren Temple and the Withered Tree* (Sheffield: JSOT Press, 1980).

Thomas, D. J., 'Matthew xxiii 30–34; 35–39', in *The Oxyrhynchus Papyri Vol. LXIV*, ed. E. W. Handley et al. (London: Egypt Exploration Society, 1997), pp. 10–12.

Thomson, A. L., *Responsibility for Evil in the Theodicy of IV Ezra* (Montana: University of Montana Printing Department, 1997).

Thomson, J. A., *The Book of Jeremiah* (Grand Rapids: Eerdmans, 1980).

Tigay, J. H., *The Evolution of the Gilgamesh Epic* (Philadelphia: University of Pennsylvania Press, 1982).

Tilborg, S. van, *The Jewish Leaders in Matthew* (Leiden: Brill, 1972).

Torrey, C. C., *Documents of the Primitive Church* (London: Harper and Brothers, 1941).

Trilling, W., *Hausordnung Gottes* (Düsseldorf: Patmos-Verlag, 1960).

———, *Das Wahre Israel* (Munich: Kösel-Verlag, 1964).

Troxel, R. L., 'Matt 27.51-54 Reconsidered: Its Role in the Passion Narrative, Meaning and Origin', *NTS* 48 (2002), pp. 30–47.

Tsevat, M., 'Ishbosheth and Congeners: The Names and Their Study', *HUCA* 46 (1975), pp. 71–87.

Tuckett, C., 'The Minor Agreements and Textual Criticism', in *Minor Agreements*, ed. G. Strecker (Göttingen: Vandenhoeck & Ruprecht, 1993), pp. 119–42.

Tuckett, C. M., *Q and the History of Early Christianity* (Peabody: Hendrickson, 1996).

———, 'Luke', in *The Synoptic Gospels*, ed. J. Riches et al. (Sheffield: Sheffield Academic Press, 2001), pp. 252–342.

Turner, N., *A Grammar of New Testament Greek: IV Style* (Edinburgh: T&T Clark, 1976).

Verhoef, P. A., *The Books of Haggai and Malachi* (Grand Rapids: Eerdmans, 1987).

Vermes, G., *Scripture and Tradition in Judaism: Haggadic Studies* (Leiden: Brill, 1961).

———, 'The Use of *bar nash/bar nasha* in Jewish Aramaic', in *An Aramaic Approach to the Gospels and Acts*, ed. M. Black (Oxford: Clarendon Press, 1967), pp. 310–28.

———, 'The "Son of Man" Debate', *JSNT* 1 (1978), pp. 19–32.

Verseput, D. J., 'Jesus' Pilgrimage to Jerusalem and Encounter in the Temple: A Geographical Motif in Matthew's Gospel', *NovT* 36 (1994), pp. 105–21.

Volz, P., *Die Eschatologie der jüdischen Gemeinde im neutestament-lichen Zeitalter* (Tübingen: Mohr, 1934), pp. 344–50.

Waetjen, H. C., *The Origin and Destiny of Humanness: An Interpretation of the Gospel according to St. Matthew* (Simi Valley, CA: Crystal Press, 1976).

Walker, R., *Die Heilsgeschichte im ersten Evangelium* (Göttingen: Vandenhoeck & Ruprecht, 1967).

Wallace, D. B., 'The Semantic Range of the Article-Noun-Kai-Noun Plural Construction in the NT', *GTS* 4 (1983), pp. 59–84.

———, *Greek Grammar Beyond the Basics* (Grand Rapids: Zondervan, 1996).

Waltke, B. and M. O'Connor, *An Introduction to Biblical Hebrew Syntax* (Winona Lake: Eisenbrauns, 1990).

Walvoord, J. F., 'Christ's Olivet Discourse on the Time of the End: Prophecies Fulfilled in the Present Age', *BSac* 128 (1971), pp. 206–14.

Watts, J. D. W., *Isaiah 1–33* (Waco: Word, 1985).

Watts, R. E., *Isaiah's New Exodus in Mark* (Grand Rapids: Baker, 1997).

———, 'On the Edge of the Millennium: Making Sense of Genesis 1', in *Living in the Lamblight*, ed. H. Boersma (Vancouver: Regent College Publishing, 2001), pp. 129–52.

Weiffenbach, H. W., *Der Wiederkunftsgedanke Jesu* (Leipzig: Druck und Verlag von Breitkopf und Härtel, 1873).

Weinbrot, H. D., 'Politics, Taste, and National Identity: Some Uses of Tacitism in Eighteenth-Century Britain', in *Tacitus and the Tacitean Tradition*, ed. T. J. Luce and A. J. Woodman (Princeton: Princeton University Press, 1993), pp. 168–84.

Weiss, J., *Das älteste Evangelium: ein Beitrag zum Verstädnis des Markus-Evangeliums und der ältesten evangelischen Uberlieferung* (Göttingen: Vandenhoeck & Ruprecht, 1903).

Weizsäcker, C. H., *Untersuchungen über die evangelische Geschichte* (Gotha, 1864).

Wellhausen, J., *Das Evangelium Marci* (Berlin, 1909).

Wenham, D., *Rediscovery of Jesus' Eschatological Discourse* (Sheffield: JSOT Press, 1985).

———, *The Parables of Jesus* (London: Hodder & Stoughton, 1989).

Wenham, J. W., *The Elements of New Testament Greek* (Cambridge: Cambridge University Press, 1965).

Wettstein, J. J., *Novum Testamentum Graecum* (vol. 1; Graz: Akademische Druck und Verlagsanstalt, 1962).

White, R. F., 'Reexamining the Evidence for Recapitulation in Rev 20.1-10', *WTJ* 51.2 (1989), pp. 319–44.

Wildberger, H., *Isaiah 1–12* (Minneapolis: Fortress Press, 1991).

———, *Isaiah 13–27* (Minneapolis: Fortress Press, 1997).

Wilken, U., *Alexander the Great* (New York: Dial Press, 1932).

Williamson, H. G. M., 'Relocating Isaiah 1:2-9', in *Writing and Reading the Scroll of Isaiah*, ed. C. C. Broyles and C. A. Evans (Leiden: Brill), pp. 263–77.

Wilson, A. I., *When Will These Things Happen? A Study of Jesus as Judge in Matthew 21–25* (Nottingham: Paternoster Press, 2004).

Winer, G. B., *A Treatise on the Grammar of NT Greek* (trans. W. F. Moulton; Edinburgh: T&T Clark, 1882).

Wise, M. O., M. G. Abegg Jr and E. M. Cook, *The Dead Sea Scrolls: A New English Translation* (New York: Harper Collins, 1996).

Witherington, B., *Jesus the Seer* (Peabody: Hendrickson, 1999).

Wolff, H. W., *Hosea* (Philadelphia: Fortress, 1974).

Wolthuis, T. R., *Experiencing the Kingdom: Reading the Gospel of Matthew* (unpublished PhD dissertation; Duke University, 1987).

Wright, N. T., *The New Testament and the People of God* (London: SPCK, 1993).

———, *Jesus and the Victory of God* (Minneapolis: Fortress Press, 1996).

———, *The Resurrection of the Son of God* (Minneapolis: Fortress Press, 2003).

Zahn, T., *Das Evangelium des Matthäus* (Leipzig: Deichert, 1903).

Zerwick, M., *Biblical Greek* (Rome: Pontifical Institute, 1963).

Zetterholm, M., *The Formation of Christianity in Antioch* (London: Routledge, 2003).

Zimmerli, W., *Ezekiel 1* (Philadelphia: Fortress Press, 1979).

INDEX OF AUTHORS